Bouillabaisse

A Novel

Stacey Sauter

THORNTON CREEK PRESS, LLC

Full CIP data for this book is available from the Library of Congress.

ISBN (Softcover): 978-1-7323574-0-2
ISBN (Ebook): 978-1-7323574-1-9

Cover Art: Jacket Design by Stacey Sauter; Cover Photo by Eric Hartley; Graphic Design by Bridget Manifold; Author Photo by Clay Blackmore.

This book is dedicated in honor of Patrick and Elena Kilner,
whose genuine selflessness astounds me.
And to the memory of their beloved son, John Paul Kilner,
December 6, 2011 - February 20, 2013.

And in honor of one formidable, loving, creative and sparkling sprite:
Sabrina Remy.
You and your parents, John and Christine Remy, are also my kind of
heroes.

This book is also a tribute to all people who lovingly
open their homes to abandoned, neglected and abused
children, particularly my sister Pam who brought calm,
light and love to one very special young man.

Finally, thank you to my enduring source
of inspiration – my daughter –
who made one Mother's Day particularly poignant by
sharing with me the following quote:

"My mother was my first country, the first place I ever lived."

—— Nayyirah Waheed

Vanessa, I never knew I possessed such strength and
seeming invincibility until I first held you.
I never knew how truly fallible I was until I became your mother.
And I never knew how incredibly transformative and emboldening a
child's love could be until you chose to live with me.

—— Mom

"If you bungle raising your children, I don't think whatever else you do matters very much."

— Jacqueline Kennedy Onassis

Prologue

Her feet were so swollen and tender she could barely walk. For that matter, Caitlin O'Brien's whole body was bloated and aching. This final stretch of her fifth pregnancy was taking a toll on her worse than her four previous ones combined – a condition aggravated by the sweltering summer heat, no air conditioning, and now premature labor. She moaned loudly as another contraction seized, its intensity longer and stronger than the last. Her due date wasn't for another two weeks, which troubled her far less than the child's welfare afterwards. They were broke and barely keeping afloat with the shared earnings of their two teenaged sons from cutting grass and doing odd jobs.

As the contraction waned she pushed herself out of bed and shuffled towards the bathroom. That's when the phone rang again and again. It stopped. And then started again.

Where is he? she wondered as to why her husband, Francis, hadn't answered it. Truthfully she hoped he'd left the house and that it was her sister checking in on her. Or, perhaps, that one of her kids was calling. Particularly after their incredibly harsh morning; all of which replayed in her mind as she dragged herself to the phone.

"Pass the cereal," Francis had said to Paul during breakfast. Paul quietly did as asked, then seconds later suffered an uppercut to his jaw so hard that his chair tipped backwards, his head taking another blow when hitting the linoleum floor.

"Wanna know where cold shoulders come from?" Francis hissed while suddenly jumping up. After forcibly yanking Paul off the floor, he then jammed their fourteen-year-old son's head into the refrigerator's nearly-empty freezer compartment.

ix

"Is that cold enough for you?" he asked while rubbing Paul's face against an encrusted layer of frost, then turned him around to face the family. With his brown, terrified eyes filled with tears, his forehead red with ice-burn, and blood trickling from his mouth, Paul looked directly at her as if pleading for mercy. She, too, was frozen in terror.

"The next time I ask you to do something, you better show me some respect by answering, 'Yes, sir.' Do you understand?"

Yes, Paul silently nodded. He was in obvious pain.

"I didn't hear you," shouted Francis, promptly shoving Paul's head back inside the freezer. "Do you understand?"

"Yes, sir," Paul's muffled response was finally heard.

At last releasing his grip, Francis turned and calmly faced the family again. His six-foot frame was forbidding enough. But compounding that was an excessively dark mood and a filthy, unhinged appearance. He'd not showered nor shaved in days, his black hair looked electrified, and he'd been wearing the same clothes for nearly a week. Today, not even his counterfeit nourishment of orange juice and vodka worked to soften his raw edge.

"Everyone hear that?" he asked, then guffawed at the barely audible chorus of "'yessirs.'" Even she nodded her head in unison, holding her breath as Paul slowly began to leave the kitchen.

Francis caught him out of the corner of his eye. "Where do you think you're going?" he bellowed while shoving Paul to the floor, at which point seventeen-year-old Frankie boldly left the table and bravely wedged himself between the two. Just shy of his father's height, and only a whisper away from his face, Frankie's eyes fiercely threatened the man: don't make another move, or else.

"Get the hell out of here. That goes for all of you," Francis growled while slightly backing away. Swiftly helping Paul off the floor, Frankie wrapped an assuring arm around the shoulder of his now sobbing, younger brother and quickly escorted him outside. Raymond and Patty immediately scrambled leaving their mother and bowls of half-eaten cereal behind. Even their dog darted. Glowering at her, Francis freshened his drink and retreated to the living room. She knew better than to speak. Instead, with a heavy heart she gathered a few provisions and headed back to bed; her anguish tempered only by knowing that Frankie would tend to his siblings and, in particular, to Paul.

By nature Francis was disagreeable. Still, it was difficult to say what was driving his excessively hellish temper lately. He usually spent a portion of his days doing odd jobs himself, then the rest of it at local saloons or the nearby race track. For the past month, however, he'd barely left the house, thus making everyone's life exceedingly miserable. Why she didn't leave last year as planned was beyond her. Instead, she let him sweet talk her into staying; a conversation that turned into another pregnancy; a pregnancy that turned into more reason to despise her — as if it was all her fault.

Where is he? she wondered once more as the phone stopped and started ringing yet again. Hoping he'd passed out early, she reached the bedside table and picked it up at the same time he did.

"So, O'Brien, you think you can hide from me?" stated an angry male caller.

Frightened, she didn't respond. The caller persisted.

"Don't pretend like you're not there."

"You'll get your money," Francis finally spoke from the living room phone. His tone was dark and unapologetic.

"Really? When?"

More silence. She trembled.

"WHEN?"

"This week."

"Am I the only one who remembers that's what you said *last* week and the week *before* that?"

"I'm still working it out."

The caller's gruff voice deceptively softened. "You know what, O'Brien? I understand things are a bit tough. And that your pretty little wife is about to have another baby, right?"

"Yeah. Any day. What of it?"

"Well, I'm a family man too, you know. So I'm gonna give you a little break here, okay? Another month to pay up. That work for you?"

She knew by her husband's tone of voice that he believed he'd won the upper hand. "Sure, man. One month works," he replied as if the choice were truly his to make.

"Good. Because if it don't, and you can mark the date on your calendar," the caller's voice turned ominous, "I will have your nuts cut off and that pretty little wife of yours won't be having any more children. In fact, don't be surprised if one of your kids goes missing, too. You hear? One month. Paid in full. Otherwise your manhood goes down the toilet and your kids are fair game. Oh, and you still owe me the money. Got it?"

Utterly terrified, she sank to the bed. It wasn't the first time Francis had run afoul of a loan shark. She'd known of previous threats to him, but never their children. There was no telling who the man was or how much money was at stake. Still, she knew better than to get involved. As gently as possible she tried replacing the receiver when another harsh contraction clutched. Her hands now unsteady, the receiver slipped and the switch hook loudly clicked.

Within seconds she heard his footsteps on the stairs — two at a time. Thrusting open their bedroom door and slamming it against the wall, he abruptly stopped and stared at her — his cold, deranged eyes daring her to move. It was hard to say if her water just broke or she was merely pissing herself — something she'd done before in reaction to his brutality. Instinctively, Caitlin sunk deeper into the bed and covered her belly.

"Since when," he asked calmly moving her way, "did I give you permission to listen in on my phone conversations?"

"I didn't mean to," she softly stammered. "Honestly, it was an accident."

"An accident?" he mocked her while swiftly clutching a fistful of her long, black hair as he yanked her off the bed. "An accident?" he held fast. "You wanna know what an accident is?"

She gulped and tried to shake her head no, but couldn't as he pressed his tightly balled fist hard against her skull. "I thought it might be one of the kids," she struggled to say. "Have you seen them?"

"I don't give a shit about those kids," he tugged again, leaning into her face. He reeked of rot gut and body odor.

"I'm sorry, okay?" she wept. "I didn't know the call was for you. I promise it will never happen again."

"Oh, you can be sure of that," he said, at last letting go.

Momentary relief set in. But before she could sink back on to the bed he shoved her to the floor and fiercely kicked her in the rear end. Gasping in pain, she impulsively turned on her side and balled up. The baby was now kicking her, too. She wanted to scream, but puked instead. Her face now smothered with vomit, she began to whimper. He kicked her again.

"Francis, please," she begged through halting sobs. "For the love of God. Please don't hurt me or this baby." He responded by gently kneeling beside her, the acrid smell of her vomit filling the tense void. She knew his manic nature and that in an instant his actions could sway towards either heaven or hell. It was during such teetering interludes she typically began the appeasement. *You are such a good husband and father. We couldn't make it without you. We love you, we...*

"I'm sorry. Do you need help?" he asked with contrived tenderness, his face close to hers. The stench of his putrid breath made her retch again. "That's what I thought. Poor girl. So sick to her stomach. And about to have another baby. Let me help you up." For the briefest of moments she wanted to believe he was sincere. That is until he began dragging her out to the hallway. At best her petite stature was no match for his size and strength. Now hugely pregnant and already weakened with pain, she saw no chance of breaking free.

"I want you to know," he said with calm indifference while standing her up at the top of the stairs, "the true meaning of an accident."

Pure panic paralyzed her only weapon. She could not speak. She could not scream. She looked down into the abyss, the final stair surely being her first step into the hereafter. In the split second before he shoved her, and with whatever strength she could muster, she grabbed ahold of the banister.

"Oh, no you don't!" he said, swiftly passing in front of her and then grabbing a foot pulled her down fast. She desperately tried kicking him with her other foot, which soon he gripped and with insane ferocity dragged her downward, her head thudding unmercifully against several hardwood stairs.

Stars and lights seemed to flash all around her. And then – for how long she did not know – darkness. At first only a hazy awareness arose.

As bombs of pain exploded in her head and contractions wracked her body, she perceived familiar surroundings. Through her dim consciousness she heard a baseball game on the living room TV, but didn't sense anyone near. If Francis weren't at home, he could tell everyone his wife had accidentally fallen down the stairs. No doubt he was hoping she and the baby were dead. Which is when she felt the faintest flicker of hope. The baby moved.

"In fact, don't be surprised if one of your kids goes missing, too. You hear?"

A primal instinct flared, and in spite of excruciating pain Caitlin managed an inching crawl toward the living room phone. Picking it up she feebly dialed. It rang three times. Then "Hello."

"Mary Claire," she barely whispered upon hearing her sister's voice. "Please - come - help - me."

Chapter 1

*N*o fire alarm is as shrill as a hungry infant's cry. Especially that of a newborn who has finally pressurized his lungs. Even worse, one that has been wrenched away from its newly deceased mother. This I know because such a helpless soul unexpectedly introduced himself to me early one Sunday morning when I happened to be hung over and when he was hungry as hell.

Just a few hours earlier I'd been celebrating the end of the school year at a rowdy keg party with dozens of friends. In my possession was a fake ID, a legitimate learner's permit, plus $734 in my savings account which I would transform into a car as soon as I turned sixteen. Best of all, my long-time secret crush, John Aloysius-you're-incredibly-delicious-O'Neill, finally seemed to take notice. Life on June 11th, 1967 was good. At least for me.

But not so for a five-pound, six-ounce creature who had slid into the world just as his mother had slid out. I was fast asleep when his angry wail broke the sound barrier. With five kids in my family a crying baby was not an unfamiliar sound, just a distant one as my youngest brother was now seven. *Timmy must be having a bad dream*, I drunkenly reasoned. Folding my pillow over my head I nestled in knowing that my mother would swiftly take control. Shortly the crying stopped.

But, as I soon discovered, the silence was equal only to the amount of time needed to suck in more oxygen for another nuclear outburst. It was then that I sat bolt upright in bed, quickly realizing that my sock drawer was screaming mad. Miniature reel-to-reel tape recorders were all the rage, so I assumed this was a prank one of my sick friends was playing on me. Or perhaps my twelve-year-old brother, Joey, who loved practical jokes – mostly those he played on me. Any hint of snickering on the other side of the door, however, was most definitely drowned out by the incessant wailing. Rolling out of bed, I stepped unsteadily on a stack of my favorite teen and gossip magazines which slid out beneath my feet.

"Ow! Thanks a lot!" I berated the Monkees, *Tiger Beat's* obliviously happy cover boys as I fell fast to the hardwood floor and on to my knees. The bawling escalated. And so, a bit painfully, I crept closer to the bottom drawer that was open and slightly tilted toward the floor. Now it was I needing to catch my breath, as peering downward I discovered nestled in a bed of my old gym socks and ratty sweatshirts a very real and red-faced, dark-haired baby. I quickly scanned my lilac-colored room with matching white-framed twin beds to see if anyone was spying on me. Apparently not.

"Shh, shh!!" I commanded, which only seemed to aggravate him. Angrily writhing free of a skimpy blanket, he now revealed his puny body loosely clothed in a diaper and rubber pants, a teeny-tiny T-shirt, and a large, bloodied Band-Aid over the site of his recently detached umbilical cord. I peeked inside his diaper to confirm, and for no particular reason, that it was a boy. And one who'd clearly pissed himself.

Had I had any idea at that moment that he was there with me because my Aunt Cate had just died, I might have instantly swaddled him and cried my heart out, too. Instead, after raising myself off the floor, I promptly opened my bedroom door and began screaming at the top of *my* lungs.

"Ma! Dad! Hello! Will someone please tell me what is going on here? Why is there a crying baby in *my* sock drawer?"

It was odd in a house usually teeming with people that no one answered. As his crying intensified, I marched down the hall, banged on their door then brazenly opened it. Strangely, the bed was made and they weren't there.

"All right. The joke is over. Come get that baby out of my room," I announced after flinging open my brothers' bedroom door. Joey didn't budge. Instead, he remained fast asleep in his lower bunk as his best friend, Marty, snored loudly from above. Since our older brother, Tommy, was working at the beach, Timmy slept soundly in his bed. In spite of my dramatic entrance and the persistent howling down the hall, not a one of them stirred.

Charging back to my room I discovered salvation, though no answers, in a note I'd missed on my bedside table atop two clean diapers. It was from my mother — as nonchalant as if she were reminding me to feed the dog: *Gail, there's a bottle in the fridge.*

I went to the kitchen and quickly retreated to my room with said bottle for the little monster and a cream soda for me. Finally picking him up, I jammed the nipple in his mouth. Apparently he was famished. Within a few minutes he'd greedily sucked the entire contents of the small bottle, then cried out for more.

"Who are you?" I asked, now holding him against my shoulder while patting him gently on the back. Burping worked with infants I'd babysat, but generally they were a bit older and easier to soothe. He was having none of it.

"Oh, yeah, your diaper," I realized. Setting him down on my bed I went about the task of changing him, dropping the spent nappy on the four smiling faces of the Monkees. But his crying persisted. Nothing contented him.

Many years earlier my Irish Aunt Cate had knit for me the beautiful afghan blanket on my bed as an heirloom gift for my First Holy Communion. I loved its Celtic pattern and warm weight. Wrapping the baby up in its soft wool, I cranked up the window air conditioning unit, then embraced and rocked him anew while pacing my room. Shortly he simmered down and dozed off. So too did I. Climbing back into bed, I tucked him in beside me, wrapped Cate's heartfelt handiwork around us, and before long I was sleeping off the effects of my hangover.

This time it was my mother's shriek that awakened me.

"Jesus, Mary, and Joseph, Gail Marie," she screamed while tearing apart the contents of my sock drawer. "Where is the baby?"

Her Irish-accented words fused together like currents in the River Shannon. Regardless of her sing-song lilt, whenever she mentioned my name in the same sentence of those holy three it was not to sing my praises.

"I'm never drinking again," I muttered, opening a single eye to see that the full day had dawned and that I was clearly not dreaming.

3

"WHERE IS THE BABY?" she frantically screamed.

"What baby?" I drowsily inquired.

"What do you mean, 'what baby?' The one I left in your drawer!"

What drawer? I was going to ask when reality struck. Sitting bolt upright yet again, I glanced at the bureau, then downward at the tangled afghan on my bed.

"OH MY GOD! THE BABY!! WHERE IS THE BABY?" I screamed at her while desperately unraveling the blanket, immediately drawing a grateful hand to my chest upon discovering him pink and peaceably sleeping beneath it. As my older sister, Mary Joyce, was also working at the beach, my mother plunked down on MJ's empty bed and let out an exhaustive sigh while compulsively fluffing a pillow.

"Just whose baby is this?" I asked, blind to the emotional depth charge about to explode.

"Cate's."

"Good golly, she has *another* son."

"No. We do," she mechanically replied.

"I don't get it."

"Cate's dead."

Unconsciously recoiling from my newborn cousin as if he were contaminated by darkness, my voice pitched high. "Dead? How?"

My mother's fragile facade suddenly cracked, and in between heartwrenching sobs and uncharacteristic expletives she haltingly explained the tragic events. "She died during labor last night. And Francis, that God-forgive-me," she paused while rolling her eyes heavenward and crossing herself, "rat-bastard-good-for-nothing-drunk-son-of-a-bitch, has rejected him. Just gave him up!"

At thirty-eight, Cate — my mother's only sibling — had left behind four other children aged eight to seventeen. I knew from eavesdropping on a phone conversation between my mother and her younger sister that Cate's last pregnancy had come as a shock. My aunt hated her husband, an abusive drunk who was more skilled at holding a mugful of beer than a reliable job.

4

"Why would he give his own son away?" I asked, suddenly choking on my own tears.

"Says he can't feed another mouth," she answered defiantly. "I caught him just as he was about to sign the baby over to one of the Daughters of Charity. Sister said she had just the perfect family for him, too. Over *my* dead body I thought to say, but instead minded my manners.

"'That's nice of you Sister, and thank you,' I said. 'But he already has the perfect family.' Then when no one was looking I snatched him away, marched up the street and left him here for you to look after," she said, her voice rising a triumphant notch. "I knew I could count on you."

I sat in stunned silence, looking first at my mother and then back at the baby, quickly realizing four things. To start, Aunt Cate must have died at the small, community hospital two blocks away. Secondly, that it must have been a horrible death. Third, that my mother had essentially kidnaped her nephew which, apparently, no one seemed to mind. And finally, that she was making no attempt to take him away from me.

"Why didn't you wake me up first?"

"I did," she said emphatically. "I shook your shoulder and told you I was leaving your new cousin in your sock drawer because your father and I had some other serious business that needed tending. You agreed to watch him."

I'm never drinking again. "I did?"

"You said 'okay.' He was sleeping, too, so I left you two alone. By the way, what time did you get in last night?"

"Late," I said, wiping away tears. "But Ma, what about Cate? What happened?"

"How late?"

This conversation was like sitting in a darkened room while someone randomly turned the light switch off and on. One second she was crying and needed mothering. The next moment she was a concerned mother.

"I don't know. Twelve-thirty. Ish."

She grimaced. "Didn't we agree on a midnight curfew?"

This was beyond absurd. And had I been any more observant I would have realized the insanity it foretold. I thought of pinching the baby awake so that his crying would distract her from this inane questioning.

"For Pete's sake, Ma. Right now that hardly matters," I said, my voice now trembling with grief. "Poor Cate. What happened?"

"I don't know. I don't know," she broke down, now holding her face in her hands. It did little to mute her wails.

"She was already in labor, then took a terrible spill," she finally looked up, her face and hands glistening wet. "Fell *ALL* the way down the stairs. The doctor said there was probably a blood clot somewhere."

"I don't understand. Why would Uncle Francis just give him up?" I cried while wiping my eyes and then blowing my nose into his remaining clean diaper. Producing a spent tissue from her dress pocket she dabbed her eyes while falling strangely quiet. She rarely wore make-up, save a dash of lipstick for special occasions. I noticed remnants of color on her lips, meaning she'd tried looking her best when she told my cousins they were now motherless.

The baby stirred. Now that he was no longer red-faced and screaming I could actually study him. He was beautiful. Hopefully looking more like Cate than his "God-forgive-me-rat-bastard-good-for-nothing-drunk-son-of-a-bitch father." Suddenly the gravity of the whole situation hit me and *I* began sobbing. Instead of offering answers or comfort, my mother's detached response was to reach inside another front pocket of her lime-green shift for her cigarette case. She lit one up and inhaled deeply.

"Want one?" she surprisingly asked, smoke clinging to her raspy words.

"What, are you crazy? I don't smoke."

She lit up a second cigarette, and while handing it over opened the top drawer of my bedside table revealing an ashtray full of spent butts. "G'head," she dared me.

I took the bait as well as a long, nervous drag while wondering which one of us was the bigger snoop.

"Thank God Mary Joyce doesn't smoke."

"Don't kid yourself."

"Where did I go wrong?"

It was an awkward moment of adult-like bonding. Even though I hated her menthol brand and had long stopped stealing them, I had always looked forward to the day when I could openly smoke in the house, presumably when I turned sixteen and could legally buy cigarettes. Wanting to impress her, I took an exaggerated drag off mine, then blew two perfect smoke rings in her direction – one inside the other.

"Well, that'll getcha' nowhere in life," she said sarcastically while smoothing MJ's pillow again. She might have been momentarily pacified, but not the baby who began whimpering anew. With my cigarette dangling from one corner of my mouth, I picked him up and tried handing him over. She stood up, but didn't take him.

"I'll go fetch another bottle," she replied and disappeared.

His whimper soon morphed into a fierce howl. Nervously stubbing out my cigarette, I tried soothing him by putting my finger in his mouth. He viciously sucked at it, but with no return on his investment began screeching. It seemed an eternity before she returned – this time handing me a warmed-up bottle twice the size as the last.

"Don't forget to burp him," she said, heading for the door again.

"What? Wait a minute!" I responded with genuine shock. "You're passing him off as if he's *my* responsibility."

"For the moment," she replied deeply exasperated, "he is."

Which is how, at the age of fifteen, I became a mother.

Chapter 2

My hometown, Laurel, Maryland, sits on the banks of the Patuxent River about halfway between Baltimore and Washington, D.C. Once a thriving mill town, our now dog-eared, light-blue collar community was left to fend for itself after the mill operations closed. Somehow it survived. And though the world around us was transforming at a frenetic pace during this so-called "Summer of Love," Laurel remained a seemingly impervious cocoon.

Our predominantly Irish Catholic neighborhood is anchored by the beautiful and ancient St. Mary of the Mills Church and the nearby Pallottine Convent. One can barely turn a corner without running into a parish priest or nun. And if that wasn't enough to scare the devil out of anyone, Mrs. Sweeney certainly would. The big-mouthed and persnickety watchdog seemed to know everything we did – or were even thinking of doing – followed by a casual report to Monsignor Wilson. I discovered this during one confession when I failed to mention that I'd recently stolen some candy from the local ice cream parlor.

"Is there anything else you'd like to confess?" He persisted. I knew that dark, faceless voice behind the partition. It was monsignor.

"No," I stated, truly believing my conscience was clear.

"Hmmm. Nothing else for which you'd like to seek forgiveness? Remember, thou shalt not steal. Even for something as trivial perhaps as...," he paused, his truncated comment now loitering in my mind as if I'd robbed a bank. I held my breath. "...candy," he finally concluded.

It struck me. "From Guvelli's?"

"Maybe."

"Oh, yeah. I did steal some licorice," I said incredulously. "But I'd run out of money and really, I swear I just forgot to pay them back. I'll do it today. I promise."

"I'm curious, is this your habit to steal first and make restitution later?"

"It was only licorice and just that one time," I said emphatically, then paused, now feeling curious as to how he knew and, more to the point, how he knew it was me he was talking to. "Forgive me, Father," I added. "But how did you know?"

"God works in mysterious ways."

It was no mystery that Mrs. Sweeney – God's fat, gossipy handmaiden and also monsignor's volunteer secretary – just happened to be in Guvelli's the day I was short on both dollars and sense.

Anyway, the scene of that crime was on Main Street, a very self-contained business district and the site of many family-owned and operated stores. Within blocks of my house we could get hand-made ice cream, a gallon of milk, warmly baked bread, a prescription filled, a newly cut slab of beef, or even a freshly killed chicken. There was also a hardware center with enough supplies to build a house, plus stores with appliances and furniture – both new and used. For the love struck, engagement rings and wedding dresses – both new and used – could be purchased. If the engagement didn't work out one could pawn the ring or dress at Things Gone Buy, then drown one's sorrows with a bottle of liquor from the local package store. If the wedding happened, there were five churches, a synagogue and, of course, the booze to celebrate.

We could attend a movie or a play, swim in the community pool or the river, plus take our parents' pick of parochial or public schools. And, if need be, one could get a broken bone set or even deliver a baby at Warren's Hospital – a fifteen-bed facility just down the street from my house where, most conveniently, all five children in my family were born.

For the serious drinkers – including Father Ryan – Main Street offered bookend bars: Oliver's and the Laurel Tavern. And for the gamblers (again, Father Ryan) we were a short walk to Laurel's horse racing track. No one had far to travel after dying, either, as our neighborhood boasted a funeral home and two cemeteries; one was for Catholics, the other for every one else.

As I discovered via Mrs. Sweeney, Laurel was just large enough that we thought no one knew our business, and just small enough that everybody did. I knew the occupants and embarrassing secrets of nearly every house in my neighborhood, at least those bursting with chatty children. And any house with fewer than four kids generally meant one thing: Protestants. Not that we didn't like them. But there were clear tribal differences. Fewer children usually meant more money and bigger houses – or at least finer furniture and often better food. So when I didn't like what my own mother was cooking, I often sauntered over to a Methodist or Episcopalian household in search of a place at their dinner table. I avoided the Baptists. And not because their food was bad, just that they were really preachy and feared depths of hell far more viscerally than us Catholics.

The most exotic fare could be found at the Millstein's house where Sarah and Marty's warm-hearted, Jewish mother often served up generous portions of rice wrapped in grape leaves and heavy matzoh balls in hearty chicken soup. The fact that the Millsteins owned the local bakery also helped my family's budget as Mrs. Millstein often sent us kids home with a gift of freshly baked bread or, occasionally, a box of my personal favorites – bear claws.

We lived in the 400 block of Montgomery Avenue in a white clapboard, Victorian-era house with ten-foot ceilings and hardwood floors. During the height of the mill operations it was owned and occupied by a wealthy merchant and his fancy family. Its expansive front porch, gingerbread trim, cornflower-blue shutters, and white-picket fence entwined with wild honeysuckle and a flourishing rose vine, all radiated genteel prosperity. The facade, however, completely belied its present-day interior, which was a bloody eyesore.

Inside, the house had dingy paint, peeling wallpaper, and hardwood flooring worse than that found in Oliver's Tavern. We had no central air conditioning, steam-radiated heat, and fireplaces in the living room, dining room and four bedrooms. Fortunately all but the living room fireplace had been sealed shut, only because our phone-booth sized closets meant that we lived with junk piles everywhere, including the inside of the unused fireboxes. In fact, some of the biggest fights among my siblings involved touching one another's piles. Or in the case of my brother Joey, "torching" one of mine. Following a petty argument with me he lit fire to the junk piled in my bedroom's fireplace, which caused choking smoke to fill the house and, gratefully, for my father to ground him for a week. He left my stuff alone after that, devising other ways to torture me.

The painfully small closets were a manageable deficiency at the time of purchase. Four children later, however, it was like living in a Salvation Army storehouse. The situation was worsened by the arrival of our youngest sibling, Timmy. My parents put him in the same room as his older brothers, reserving the fourth bedroom as a sewing room (truthfully, a junk room) and sick bay for any of us with fevers over one-hundred and stomachs incapable of quiet resolve.

Most frustrating was the one full bathroom, the other "bathroom" being just a toilet next to the washer and dryer in our damp cellar. Which is why "I need to do some laundry" was often code for taking a crap, prompting wisecracks such as 'Ya' got one load or two?' and 'Don't forget to separate the darks.' Or, as Joey once asked of our late Grandma Kenealy during a holiday visit, "dark or light load?" She scowled and whacked him on the side of his head with a newspaper before retreating to the basement for at least a half-an-hour. "Dark load," Joey later concluded for anyone that cared to listen.

What I loved best was our proximity to the Patuxent – Maryland's longest river – where I spent countless hours swimming or investigating its treasures with my friends. There was a swimming hole not far from the nearby Rocky Gorge dam with a rope swing that seemed to fly from the brink of the sun to the cusp of the moon while propelling an endless line of daredevils in seemingly death-defying aerial stunts. Long summer days were often consumed lazily rafting in the Patuxent, followed by regular trips to Main Street for sodas and candy.

The yards in our community were large, level and home to some towering trees that wove their broad branches into a lush summer canopy. And in spite of persistent neglect, our half-acre lot always flourished with flowering plants and bushes. This included the creeping rose and honeysuckle vines that miraculously kept our old picket fence from falling over.

We were just blocks away from St. Vincent Pallotti High School, a popular co-ed Catholic prep school that I attended with my older siblings. By contrast to Aunt Cate's family who lived a more impoverished life on the other side of the nearby tracks, our family existence was generally happy and predictable. My carefree life was leading me – I truly believed – to one day becoming Mrs. John Aloysius O'Neill.

Which brings me back to the baby. I'd been up all night trying to soothe him and eventually we'd both passed out on the living room sofa. At about twelve noon on his third day in our house my mother startled me awake.

"What do you want to name him?"

I slowly opened one eye. For different reasons she'd barely slept herself and looked spent. For the third straight day she was in the same lime-green shift, a garment she'd made herself. It was severely wrinkled and her hair shot out in five directions. Plus, her nail polish was uncharacteristically chipped.

Her appearance rarely changed. She was trim. And except for the time she'd foolishly tried looking like Jackie Kennedy by dying her hair black and flipping it up at the ends, she'd worn her hair in the same, boring beehive style since I could remember – the only difference being the color of dye she used. Last summer it was like peanut butter. This year it was like Heinz 57 Sauce, which truly flattered her cat-green eyes. She was only forty-two-years old. And I suppose to the casual observer she might be attractive for a middle-aged woman. But since I believed all women over forty aged in dog years, then to me she was already long in the tooth. The events of the past few days alone could have aged her another seven years.

"I need to fill out his birth certificate. What do you want to name him?" she repeated, her face drawn and her voice deep with fatigue. She'd been simultaneously working on funeral arrangements and an official adoption of the baby while caring for my pathetic cousins.

"Why are you asking *me*?"

"Because..." she started.

I cut her off. "Because he's all *mine?*" I groaned while sitting up.

"Don't you take that tone with me, lassie."

I brazenly reached over to the coffee table for her cigarettes and lit one up, daring her with my eyes to deny me this privilege. She angrily stared me down.

"You'd better not let your father catch you doing that. And I'd prefer you not let the other children see you, either. There are consequences, you know. Now, give me a name so I can complete his birth certificate."

I glowered while silently inhaling, realizing that my only compensation for taking care of this demon-seeded child was to openly smoke in front of her.

She sighed. "Please, help me. I'm too exhausted to think of one myself."

"Lucifer," I blurted before blowing an irreverent smoke ring her way. She gasped.

"For the love of God, Gail Marie. Be serious. We're doing this for your Aunt Cate," she said trotting out that already threadbare phrase. "This baby came into our lives for a reason," she added.

Yes. To remind me never to have sex. The thought of which immediately brought to mind my crush, John Aloysius-you're-incredibly-delicious-O'Neill. An ace student and star athlete now entering his senior year at Pallotti, he was someone I'd long ogled. But given my lack of assertiveness among his female admirers, he'd paid no romantic attention to me. That is until four nights ago at the keg party when he talked to me – just me – for about ten minutes. Mostly it was about Tommy, his best friend on the football team.

"I never noticed these before," he said at one point, playfully dipping a finger into one of my dimples. "They're cute, kinda like you," he smiled, his own dimples on full display. I loved that we had them in common, and at that precise moment I would have done anything to be the cute, dimpled mother of all his cute, dimpled babies. Presently, however, I'd just as soon march up the street and join the Pallottine Sisters if it meant sparing myself the hardship of caring for even this unnamed ogre.

"Ask Dad or the boys," I finally said. "I'm sure they can come up with something good."

"Your father's at work and the boys are at the pool."

Of course my responsibility-free, younger brothers were at the pool. And while my father had spent the first two days helping my mother cope with this unfolding tragedy, he couldn't afford to miss another day of work at his electrical company. His morning, however, was started by a big argument with my mother.

"Mary Joyce is going away to college and Tommy isn't far behind," her imploring voice carried through their bedroom wall as she laid out her plan to him. "Patty and the baby can sleep in the girls' room. And I'll clean out the sewing room so Cate's boys can share that space. I know it will be tight, but..."

"But nothing. Don't forget that MJ will be coming home on college breaks. That means ten children and two adults in this house with only one full bathroom. Those kids have a father. Let him be a man and rise to the occasion for a change."

"For crying out loud, Joe, you know he's incapable. Please, I'm doing this for my sister. She would have done it for me. For us."

There was a pause, during which time I imagined my father packing his wallet into a rear pocket of his khaki pants. At age forty-five he had sprouted a slight paunch and some gray strays in his black hair. Still, just shy of six-feet tall, he was a good-looking guy with warm, blue, wide-set eyes and straight teeth inside a lantern-sized jaw. Not long ago my mother told me that even after twenty years of marriage he still made her heart skip a beat.

"I'm not talking about this anymore, Mary Claire. Right now I think it's more than enough that I've agreed to keep the baby. I'm going to work."

In the silent wake of his departure, I headed downstairs to fix the baby a bottle before plopping down on the sofa with him where the two of us eventually fell asleep. Until my mother awakened me, that is.

"I would imagine you and your friends have dreamt up countless baby names," she impatiently prodded me. "This should be easy for you."

"Okay," I finally blurted. "John. John Aloysius."

She faintly smiled. "John Aloysius. After the saints?"

"Yes," I diabolically grinned back, stubbing out my cigarette.

"Well then, that it is. John Aloysius."

I immediately realized my folly. John Aloysius O'Neill might think of me as some star-struck stalker if he ever discovered the truth.

"No, no. Not John Aloysius," I urgently stood up to make my case, prompting the baby to stir and whimper. I picked him up and bounced him lightly in my arms. "I think we should name him, uhm…" I stammered while looking down as if hoping he'd suddenly introduce himself.

"I like John Aloysius," she said, a hint of cheerfulness cutting through her despair.

I looked up at her. "Brendan. Brendan James. That's a strong Irish name. It goes with his dark hair."

"Aloysius," my mother said, her accent making it sound like some Gregorian chant, "is the patron saint of Jesuit novices. Perhaps this young man will become the priest in the family. God only knows we could use one."

"Really, Ma, I like Brendan James *sooo* much better. Or how about James Brendan? That's a great combination. Hey, Jimmy B.," I said waving an arm like an imaginary friend.

Folding her arms across her chest, she thought about it while studying the baby's face.

"Nah, there's strength in John Aloysius. He deserves that and I like it."

"What about Connor? There are no Connors in the family."

"Connor is a lovely name. I've always liked that, too."

"Done. Connor Aloysius."

I felt a sliver of relief as she contemplated it. "Nope. I like John Aloysius best."

"Why did you even bother to ask if you weren't going to listen to me?" I snapped.

"I did listen to you. You suggested John Aloysius."

I was doomed. "Well then, I'm telling everyone that it's your pick and not mine."

"What does it matter?" she asked, when the phone rang. Without another word she retreated to the kitchen. "Hold on," I heard her say before hollering, "It's for you."

Shortly I was grabbing what I considered my only lifeline to sanity.

"I'm having a slumber party tonight," my best friend, Nadette, chirped. "Can you join us?"

"I don't know," I muttered, struggling to hold the phone to my ear while cradling – *aarrgghh!* – John Aloysius in my arms. "Things are still pretty rough around here."

"I figured you might need a break."

"Just a second," I said to her, then loudly hollered, "Ma, I'm sleeping over at Nadette's tonight. She's having a slumber party."

"No."

"Why not?"

"Because you are needed here."

"Don't I deserve a break?" I pushed my luck.

"No."

"What about Joey?"

"No," she emphatically stated.

I let loose. "You can't do this to me! I feel like I'm grounded and for no good reason. I'm going to Nadette's, dammit."

"WHISHT!" my mother darkly commanded.

"Oooh, boy," were the last words I heard Nadette speak before my mother hung up the phone. She knew the moment my mother started speaking in Irish Gaelic that I was typically doomed, especially as the translation was to be quiet – or more emphatically to shut the hell up.

"Why are you doing this to me?" I blurted, breaking into tears.

"Because we are a family and we take care of one another – do you understand? And right now I need you to help me with this baby so I can finish arranging a funeral."

"Isn't that Uncle Francis's job?" I snapped back.

Truthfully, I knew from her argument with my father that Uncle Francis was more absorbed with calling relatives around the country – even in the old country – to see who was willing to take his four other children. It seemed there were possible takers for everyone but Patty, who was mentally disabled. And pretending to possess some modicum of compassion, Uncle Francis insisted that Patty was a package deal who came with at least one of her siblings. This demoralizing turn of events was torturing my mother.

"Ma, it's just one night."

"Take John with you."

"What?" I responded harshly at such an absurdity.

"I trust you. You'll take good care of him."

"That's insane. No one will get any sleep."

"It's a slumber party. No one gets any sleep, anyway."

Which wasn't true. Because later that evening as the other girls giddily tended to his every need, I got what would be my last good night's sleep for months.

Chapter 3

Exactly one month and at least three-hundred diapers after Cate's death; sorely sleep-deprived and fiercely cranky, I was looking for any opportunity possible to abdicate myself from this responsibility. There were no takers.

My older siblings came home only briefly for Aunt Cate's funeral, both returning to their fun jobs and good wages at the beach with my parents' blessings. My younger brothers were virtually no help at all. My father was working extra long hours. And my mother was a wreck. Now dividing her time between us and the cousins, she'd not only subjected herself to the oversight of two households, but also to Uncle Francis's tyranny. He'd always shown at least some restraint around her. But before long he began belittling her in every conceivable way. I learned about this when my mother confronted my father once more about getting the kids away from that "rat-bastard-good-for-nothing-drunk-son-of-a-bitch."

"He says I'm just like Cate, only worse, and that I can't cook or clean worth a damn. I hate that man, Joe. He's downright evil. I'm begging you, please, can't the kids come and live with us? Even if it's just for a while. I need a break from him. They need a break from him. We're all walking on eggshells."

This time her plea was met with thick silence. I knew my father's conscience was deeper than his pockets. It was a question of which one turned inside-out first.

"They may just end up in foster care," he finally and remorsefully replied, then left.

Shortly, I heard my mother break-down. She was not simply crying, either. Painful, soul-searing sobs emanated from her room. Carrying the fussy baby, I knocked on her door. She didn't respond, so I let myself in, shocked to see her curled up in a fetal position on the floor. She was clearly unraveling.

"Ma, what's going on? Are you okay?" I asked hoping she was not coming completely unglued.

Seeing me she straightened up – and I mean literally. Still on the floor in her pink, sleeveless, cotton nightdress, she extended her skinny legs outward as if to demonstrate that she was fine. She nodded yes, then seconds later cracked.

"Oh, for the love of God," she lamented. "I tried, but not hard enough. Had I gotten her out of there last year our beautiful Cate would still be here. I hate him. I absolutely hate him. It's all my fault. She'd have never died if I'd stood firm against that…that…"

"I know, rat-bastard-good-for-nothing-drunk-son-of-a-bitch."

"Watch your mouth," she harshly reprimanded.

I stepped back, wondering if we needed an exorcism.

"I just want my Cate back. It's all my fault. And now those poor children without their mother and stuck with that rat bastard for a father."

Suddenly, the baby started wailing.

"Haven't you fed him?" she snapped at me.

The urge to deposit him on her stomach and run away was strong. "Yes, which is more than you've done lately," I shot back instead.

Still lying flat, her voice grew absurdly adolescent. "Oh, I see. And somehow taking care of two houses and two families just isn't enough? And somehow burying my only living sibling, who could have lived a better life with anybody but that rat bastard, just isn't enough?"

With that, she climbed off the floor and opened the top drawer of her bedside table and removed a flask. Unscrewing the cap, she took three hearty belts then lit up a cigarette.

"What are you doing?" I asked with utter disbelief as I'd never been witness to this type of behavior from her.

She didn't answer.

"Ma, it's 7:30 a.m."

"So."

"So, you're drinking."

"I'm just calming my nerves."

"Really? Because if I did that you'd call it drinking."

Her look darkened. "What do you want from me?" she snarled.

I stood motionless while holding the angst-filled baby. "My life back."

"Stop being so selfish," she said, then began sobbing anew.

Quietly turning, I left the room, closed the door and sank into a heap on the floor – all three of us now crying; and worse, each of us to some-one who didn't seem to care.

Chapter 4

The following morning started on a radically different note, at least where my mother was concerned. It came after another hellish night for me. The baby wouldn't stop crying. Plus he kept coughing and spitting up. I tried everything to soothe him, but nothing helped. At one point my father, who wasn't getting much sleep himself, stuck his head in my bedroom door. In one glance his look changed from stark frustration to utter defeat. I was crying, too.

He knew little about caring for newborns. So he did the best he could in that moment by hugging me. His warm embrace conveyed empathy, but no solutions. Shortly, he was dressed and headed to work.

I suppose it was sheer exhaustion that caused John to eventually fall asleep. I dozed off myself, only to be awakened by my mother.

"Good morning," she chirped

"For you, maybe," I muttered.

Ignoring my insolence, she began raising my bedroom blind. I jumped at the first ray of light.

"STOP!" I whispered like a tortured vampire. "YOU'LL WAKE THE BABY!"

"Ohhh," she cooed, closing the blind. "I wouldn't want to do that." She sat contentedly on Mary Joyce's bed. "Nadette called," she said, picking up her coffee mug. She still looked awful. Only the edge was off. Clearly there was more than cream and sugar in that coffee.

"She's having an impromptu party tonight. I told her you could go. You need to be at her house by 7:00 p.m. The dress code is 'cute.'"

"I'm not going," I uttered with pure exhaustion.

"Why not?" she sounded incredulous.

"What do you mean, 'why not?' You've been telling me for a month that I can't go anywhere – at least not without the baby. Do you really think I want to go to a party with this monster? Are you even aware that he cried ALL night long? Again. Something is wrong with him."

"Really?" she seemed truly surprised. Clearly she'd slept through it all. "What do you think it is?"

"You're asking me?" I shot back. "What do I KNOW about taking care of a baby?"

"I did ask you. And you seem to know a fair amount and are doing a darned good job of it."

"Did it ever occur to you that I don't want to do 'a darned good job of it?' I hate this. I hate him. I hate you. I hate everything right now."

"You'll be sorry you said that," she shot back.

"No I will not."

"I'm giving you an opportunity to go out with your friends tonight – without him. I'm just as happy to keep you home, too, you know."

"Why? As punishment? I'm already being punished. And for something I didn't do. Is it my fault that Uncle Francis is incapable of caring for his own children?"

Surprisingly, she said nothing. Instead, she took a long sip of her coffee. "I hate everything right now, too," she finally spoke.

It was startling to hear my mother sound so honest about her despair. I'd never known her as anything but loving, competent, caring and – aside from the occasional cocktail – sober. It felt pointless to argue with her anymore because it wasn't *her* I was arguing with. We were both in a world of hurt and living through it one moment at a time – or in her case, one sip at a time. The notion of getting out with friends prevailed. I softened up.

"I wonder why Nadette didn't mention this party before today," I whispered.

"I don't know."

My spirits suddenly rose. Nadette and MJ were the only ones who knew about my secret crush. Perhaps Nadette had run into John O'Neill and invited him to a party she'd spontaneously decided to throw to get the two of us together. I enthusiastically sat up. "You know what, Ma? I really could use a night out. Can I sleep over, too?"

"Nadette didn't say anything about that."

"She won't care."

"Don't push your luck."

"With her?"

She took a long sip of her coffee, then stood up. "I need you home by midnight."

Nice try.

Chapter 5

*S*hortly, I called Nadette. No one answered. Hoping she was at the community pool, I decided to head up there. Thankfully, John was a bit more mellow and I assumed his lethargy to be exhaustion from crying all night. Because my mother had gone to my cousins' house for a couple of hours, I figured it was a good time to escape. Besides, I wanted to work on my tan in hopes that John O'Neill would show up at Nadette's.

So I put on my bikini, wrapped the baby inside a beach towel, stuffed him, a bottle and a diaper into the front basket on my bike and pedaled my way to the pool. Nadette wasn't there. However, Joey, Timmy and Marty were present and already at work churning up trouble – Joey's specialty. Joey – a rascally, adventuresome and sometimes charming rogue – roamed our neighborhood with abandon from morning till night. He was incredibly athletic and, contrary to his reputation as a worthless trouble-maker, was a voracious reader and gifted student – the latter characteristic being a sore subject with me as any of my good grades were earned with much more effort.

Timmy adored Joey and was clearly his shadow if not his lackey. Small for his seven years, he easily rode atop the handlebars or shared the banana seat of his brother's Stingray bike while holding a football or kickball. Joey habitually organized pick-up games of both with neighborhood chums – or rivals. One of the latter was Pat Bickle, also known as "Fat Pat" due to his portly size; or "Frenchie" due to his insatiable love of fries. He was already pestering people when I arrived at the pool and settled on a sun-kissed, grassy knoll.

Frenchie, in my estimation, was the embodiment of Baby Huey, the popular cartoon duck who was likewise oversized, dopey and worked excessively hard to fit in. He never knew how to capitalize on any genuine acceptance, instead turning into a cry baby the moment he didn't get his way. None of us could stand him. And one of Joey's favorite pastimes was goading him into a hissy fit. Joey was faster and undoubtedly smarter than Frenchie. But sometimes when Frenchie caught Joey off-guard he'd let him have it, often by sitting on his chest and slapping him silly while likewise spitting on his face. Few people cared to intervene, mostly preferring to let them beat each other up, some showing outward pleasure over Joey's comeuppance.

Today's unofficial contest was off the high-dive, essentially a cinch for Joey who possessed the fearless agility of a top gymnast as he performed high-flying, somersaulting dives. Frenchie was a clumsy master of only the cannonball – the higher the spray and the more tsunami-like wake the better. His blubber bouncing with each exaggerated step, Frenchie would leap off the board's end with Olympian flourish. But instead of flying in well-executed flips á la Joey, he would tuck one knee up to his potbelly and hold his nose before landing in the water with all the force of an Apollo splash down.

"Hey, Fat Pat, you big lard ass," Joey hollered at Frenchie following one such jump. "Next time leave some water in the pool for the rest of us."

With seeming indifference, Frenchie climbed on to the pool deck and sat on a bench while quietly watching Joey perform a daring, double back layout, entering the water like a hot knife through butter. Staying put, he intently studied Joey as he climbed the high dive's ladder again. However, as soon as my brother neared the top rung, Frenchie swiftly butted his way past a dozen other kids and mounted the board directly behind him. Just as Joey was about to launch himself into the air, Marty spotted the impending doom and sounded a shrill warning from below.

"JOEY! FAT PAT ALERT!"

But it was too late. Bouncing hard on the opposite end, Frenchie catapulted Joey off the board into an uncontrolled flop. Nearly everyone poolside watched in wide-eyed horror as he hit the water on his stomach, the sound of it like a brick hitting cement. I held my breath. Joey slowly emerged and by his face I could see the sting from the water's smack paled in comparison to the one of anger and humiliation. Frenchie's theatrical laugh from up above meant one thing: Baby Huey was a dead duck.

Before Joey could even exit the pool, Frenchie had consumed him inside the watery hollow of another cannonball. Oddly though, as the water receded it was only Joey I saw. He was smiling rather perversely and I quickly realized why. While kneeling on Frenchie's shoulders and grasping his hair, he was riding him like a bucking bronco. Repeatedly dunking his head with one hand while pretending to brandish a lasso with the other, Joey started singing about spurs that jingled, jangled and jingled. It was excruciating to watch Frenchie repeatedly gasp for air only to be promptly plunged below.

"JOEY," I screamed, "GET OFF OF HIM!"

He ignored me. In a flash, the lifeguard flew off his chair and into the pool. Seconds after bringing a sputtering Frenchie to the surface he kicked Joey out. It was an ominous sign that my brother willingly obliged. Deviously smiling, he quickly rounded up his friends and left. Soon John and I became the new center of attention and were surrounded by curious acquaintances who eagerly held and played with him — including one girl who stuck her half-spent lollipop in his mouth to see if he'd like a lick while I took a quick dip. The calm was short-lived.

"GAIL!" Marty breathlessly returned to find me. "We need your help!"

"With what?" I answered circumspectly.

"Absolution kickball!"

My eyes narrowed. "What on earth is 'Absolution Kickball?'"

Marty excitedly carried on. "Joey got busted by Father Jack giving Frenchie a pink belly, and right now it's Joey's only chance for staying out of hell. At least for today!"

"And you want *my* help keeping Joey Kenealy out of hell? Call me when it freezes over."

"Gail, please. You gotta help us," he whined, then explained what happened.

After leaving the pool, Joey and company waited patiently to ambush Frenchie; their prey making it ridiculously easy. Frenchie had left the pool alone and while eagerly consuming a Good Humor Bar paid scant attention to his surroundings. After crossing Pallotti's ball field and rounding the school's corner, he was abruptly pinned to the ground by the small, vengeful mob.

"Wanna know what a real belly flop feels like, Fat Pat?" Marty recounted Joey asking. Then, without haste, Joey straddled Frenchie's porcine body and began harshly slapping his bare stomach. Apparently Frenchie barely flinched. Instead, he worked up a big loogie and hocked it hard towards Joey's face. From his grounded position, however, his snot bomb lacked appropriate velocity and returning to earth landed back on his own chin.

"I nearly barfed," Marty feigned a gag. "And you know what? The second I let one of Frenchie's arms loose he did just what you might expect. Went right for the Good Humor Bar. Too bad for him Joey got it first.

"'You want your ice cream?' said Joey, then picked it up and rubbed it on Frenchie's fat gut."

Frenchie was no stranger to this kind of torture and his defense was always to scream like a stuck pig. According to Marty he wailed as if being roasted alive. Rather unluckily for Joey's syndicate, Father Jack, a young priest at St. Mary of the Mills happened to be nearby when he heard Frenchie's frantic yowl. Immediately he pulled off the offenders and helped the supposedly hapless victim to his feet.

"Have you lost your minds?" Father Jack snapped. "What could have possibly gotten into you boys? Is this any way to treat another human being?"

"But *he's* not human," Joey muttered.

The priest scowled, then turned sympathetically to Frenchie whose face was covered in snot and dirt while his bright, pink stomach dripped with chocolate and vanilla. "Are you okay, son?"

"They're so mean to me, Father," Frenchie cried. "They're always picking on me, and I never do anything to deserve it." Screwing up his face, he worked hard to release reluctant tears. "My ice cream," he cried. "Look what they did to my ice cream."

Even Father Jack, not so far removed from his days of youthful exuberance, apparently seemed a bit skeptical of the boy's plight. Still, Frenchie persisted.

"Boys, I think you owe this young man an apology."

Dead silence followed.

"I said, I think you boys owe this young man an apology."

Guttural noises erupted.

"Speak up, please."

"Sorry," Joey muttered with forced contrition.

"That you're not human," Marty quipped.

"I must say," the young cleric interjected while scratching his thick, red hair, "that this can hardly be the work of our Good Lord. What kind of nonsense is this fighting and belittling one another?"

This was hardly nonsensical to Joey who evidently kept his mouth shut.

"Isn't there something more constructive you can do?"

Again, dead silence.

"Would we like to take care of this in confession?" Father asked, his voice lowering a notch.

"Sure," Marty said with mountain-moving sincerity. Joey sneered. The only Jew in the bunch, Marty once went to confession pretending to be Joey. Sitting behind the partition, he had rattled off a litany of tall-tale sins which he later recounted with great amusement, likewise informing Joey about his need to recite a dozen Hail Marys and Our Fathers each day for a week. Oh, and to return all the money he stole from the cash register at the Millstein's bakery. As retribution, Joey flushed Marty's yarmulke – handcrafted by his great grandmother – down the toilet.

Fortunately ignoring Marty, the suddenly enlightened priest spotted a ball in Timmy's hands. "I have an idea! Let's use our energy in a positive way. How about a game of kickball?"

Likely believing it was this over dozens of Hail Marys and Our Fathers, Joey quickly agreed. "Great idea, Father," he said, "but there are only seven people here."

"Well, that's a good start. And I can pitch for both sides. Go round up some other kids and meet me in the back field in one half-hour. Sound good?"

All agreed. Quickly parting ways, Frenchie, Joey and Marty took off in search of talent.

"Gail, we need you. Otherwise it's a forfeit." Marty continued begging me.

"Marty, I have a baby to watch. Plus I am barefoot and in a bikini."

"No one will notice."

"I hope you rot in hell, too."

"Come on. I'll tell my parents to give you two free bear claws the next time you're at the bakery."

Bear claws. Now he was talking. Rationalizing that the baby was sleeping and that I could still work on my tan, I agreed. Stuffing John back into my bicycle basket I headed to the field. It turned out I was to be of little help against Frenchie's top pick: his older brother, Bobby Bickle, the real neighborhood bully and a star kicker on our Catholic Youth Organization football team. Joey coveted that spot as much as he disliked Bobby.

"No fair," Joey angrily declared, "he brought a ringer."

"You had an opportunity fair and square to round up your team," said Father Jack, then turned to me. "Young lady," he lightly admonished, "do you by chance have some clothes to put on?"

No, I shrugged, prompting Joey to quickly strip off his T-shirt and toss it my way just before Father Jack flipped a coin in the air. "Heads or tails," he asked Joey as I slipped on the grungy garment.

"Heads," Joey responded. And so it was. Joey started us in the field.

"Have you ever heard of clean laundry?" I sneered at my brother as I headed to the outfield, holding my nose for emphasis.

"What? That shirt is clean. I wore it swimming in the Patuxent yesterday. Which means my underwear is clean, too."

"Loser."

"Takes one to know one."

That exchange was about as energetic on the hot, parched field as it would be during the first five innings of this match-up. At least until the top of the sixth when, with bases loaded, Bobby Bickle kicked a home run and taking a dramatic slide into home plate deliberately knocked over Joey, our catcher, while loudly challenging him to "top that."

Joey did precisely so, livening up the game by scoring a home run during his next turn. Our elation, however, was short-lived as the score stayed 4-1 until the last inning. We felt further doom when Bobby hit another ball that seemed destined for the moon.

"I've got it, I've got it!" Marty hollered near me in the backfield. Squinting his eyes while looking above, he seemed momentarily blinded by the midday sun. "Holy crap! Where is the ball?" Miraculously, it landed on his chest. Instinctively he wrapped his arms around the ball, thus shutting out Frenchie's team from scoring again and actually giving us a shot at redemption in the bottom of the ninth. Soon, however, with two outs we were still down.

Alas it was my turn and the outfield was astir. Due to playing in my bare feet – and no doubt because I was the only girl – I could see all the guys inching forward as if this game were over. Father Jack rolled a powder puff ball my way, which I hit hard and over everyone's head before it bounced in the backfield. I was safe at first. Two other single hits followed and now, with bases loaded, Joey was up.

"C'mon Joey," we all encouraged him from our respective plates. "You can do it! We can win this!"

While striking the earth with his sneaker like a bull pawing the ground, my brother surprisingly missed the first pitch, then somehow losing his balance landed on his butt.

"Game's over, you wuss," Frenchie cackled from behind the fence at home plate.

Picking himself up, Joey turned around and spat in Frenchie's direction. "Shut up, lard ass."

"Father Jack, did you hear that?" Frenchie cried.

No, he hadn't. In fact, he wouldn't hear anything for a while afterwards, as at that moment he'd already pitched another fast ball. Turning and seeing it coming at him, Joey awkwardly kicked it. But instead of sending it afar, the ball traveled low and hard into Father Jack's face knocking him over and out. Now, seeing that the man was passed out cold with blood trickling from his nose, a more compassionate person – or even one just slightly more sensible – might have immediately rushed to his aid. Not so my brother.

"Run!" Joey yelled as he sped to first base. "Move it!"

In less than thirty seconds we rounded the bases, thus winning the game 5-4. After high-fiving Marty and spitting on Frenchie, Joey went directly to the pitcher's mound to assess his celestial future. During this time Frenchie disappeared, shortly returning with Monsignor Wilson. Watching the portly pair march stiffly our way, I jumped on my bike with John still asleep in the basket and hightailed it home. Poor Father Jack had suffered a broken nose and was carried off the field on a canvas stretcher to Warren's. Joey arrived home soon thereafter looking like a wimpy rag doll with monsignor's hand firmly gripping the scruff of his neck. As I stood back listening, I wasn't sure what was worse: my mother's drunken state or monsignor's harsh expostulation on her son's sinful aggression.

"This young man's actions exceeded all standards of decent behavior and I'd like to see to it that he is properly punished."

My mother nodded at monsignor. "We're all going to hell in a hand-basket," she finally slurred, and then unexpectedly belched. Watching monsignor's mouth gape and his nostrils flare, I believe that we both detected the faint scent of smoldering wicker. I could only pray that Joey was the sole occupant of that hellbound vessel.

"Monsignor," I calmly stepped forward as if I'd been home all along. "I will have my father call you as soon as he gets back from work."

Finally releasing his grip on my recalcitrant brother, he huffed. "That would be advisable."

"Jesus, Mary and Joseph," my mother said through hiccups while watching monsignor shut the gate. "The next thing you know, Mary Joyce will be coming home pregnant."

Chapter 6

My father was so mortified over Joey's behavior that he forbid him to leave the house for the next forty-eight hours — a seeming life sentence for my brother. To worsen matters, my mother foisted John's care upon him while I went out. As I left, Joey was holding the fussy baby in his lap while reading *Twenty Thousand Leagues Under the Sea*, lowering the book just enough to reveal a contemptuous and nasty leer.

"Loser," I silently mouthed to him before sweeping out like a free bird.

Nadette lived just a few blocks away, and so I arrived shortly after 7:00 p.m. Hoping to see my crush, I'd spent two hours in between feedings and diaper changes doing my nails, make-up, and hair. I was always self-conscious that the more vibrant genes of black hair and blue eyes had been deposited in my older siblings. Still, and though sleep deprived, I looked and felt the best I had in weeks. My shoulder-length, brown hair with sun-kissed highlights was flipped up at the ends, while my bangs feathered out from a headband that matched a homemade pink, sleeveless shift. To tie it all together I wore pink sandals and my favorite "Cherry Blossom Pink" lip gloss.

"Wow! You look really pretty!" Nadette said as she excitedly answered the door. "Now close your eyes."

"Why?" I nervously asked.

"Just close your eyes," she insisted while taking my hand. My pulse quickened. I did as instructed, allowing her to lead me along.

"SURPRISE!" a chorus of feminine voices sang forth.

As my eyes and mouth popped open, I quickly scanned the room. What a disappointment. All I saw were the beaming faces of nine girlfriends surrounding an old, white wicker pram about the size of a Volkswagen Beetle. It was brimming with gifts wrapped in various shades of yellow and blue.

"What on earth? It's not my birthday."

"No, silly," said Nadette. "It's a baby shower! We found this at Things Gone Buy!" she exclaimed, which accounted for the rather run-down state of the acquisition. Things Gone Buy was an oversized, second-hand store on Main Street, doubling as a consignment and pawn shop operation. It was owned and operated by Red Maloney, a.k.a. "Baloney" Maloney.

"Don't you just love it?" Dottie piped up. "A real, old-fashioned baby buggy!"

"Thanks, you guys," I said, hoping to mask my dismay that John O'Neill wasn't expected after all. "My family will really appreciate this."

"You do like it, don't you?" Nadette asked, as if sensing my reserve.

"Well, yeah," I said. Truthfully, I couldn't care less. In fact, I felt doomed. To them, taking care of a baby was all fun and still a thing of make-believe. Not so for me, and I hated it.

"Forget the buggy! What you'll *really* love is this!" said Melinda reaching inside for a heavy rectangular box.

"Thanks, Mel," I half-smiled, noting her sly grin as I unwrapped a bottle of rum.

"When he has his bottle, you can have yours!" she laughed.

"Waahh!" cried Liz, then grabbing it screwed off the cap took a bold swig. "Here," she said, with a puckered mouth and squinted eyes while handing it back, "your turn."

I hesitated. I'd never had hard liquor before, but believing if it was good enough for taking the edge off my mother's pain, then why not mine? There was nothing tentative about my first sip. I angled the bottle over my mouth and let it in.

"OUCH!" I cried, after harshly choking. "That burns."

"That's what this is for," Nadette chimed in, retreating from the kitchen with a tray full of glasses filled with ice and cola. Thankfully her parents were away for the weekend, leaving Nadette alone to "behave herself," she'd informed us.

"Who wants a real drink?" she inquired.

All hands shot up.

"I don't think that'll be enough rum to go around," she said, then setting down the tray reached into the pram for a similarly wrapped box. "This one's from me," she grinned. She also possessed a fake ID and was probably at the liquor store while I was at the pool.

And so it began, a night of unfettered drinking and smoking with my friends. Following the liquor's debut, I opened the other gifts. There were footie pajamas from Karen, a couple of blue receiving blankets from Sheila, some adorable outfits from Gloria and Maureen, and even Dr. Spock's baby book.

"Actually, you don't need to read it," Nadette grinned. "I already did and can tell you everything you need to know."

I didn't have to ask why. I already knew. She was baby crazy, which made her boy crazy, as she'd already determined that her sole reason for living was to be a mother. She was an only child and loved the raucous atmosphere in my family so much that — and especially before all the recent madness broke loose — she often spent more time at my house than hers.

"Is there a chapter in there on making babies?" asked Tina.

"How about landing a boyfriend first?" Dottie weighed in. "Any advice for her in that department?"

"Yeah," said Nadette, "keep stuffing your bra!"

We all laughed at the hopelessly flat-chested Tina.

Nadette retrieved another beautifully wrapped package from the pram. I opened it, and welled up on unexpected emotion.

"I made it myself," she said with surprising modesty.

"Nadette," I gasped, holding up a beautiful baptismal gown. There was remarkable detail in the stitching; it was a garment crafted with love. "You really made this?"

"Uh-huh. So that you'll ask me to be his godmother."

I think I might have laughed, and I think I might have agreed. Mostly what I remember was my head suddenly spinning.

"I don't feel so hot," I blurted.

"Uh-oh, post-partum blues," Melinda joked, prompting me to snap.

"Shut-up, Mel. I did not have a baby. And he's not *my* baby," I stammered. "I'm just the one stuck taking care of him. I should be out having fun with my friends *all* the time. Instead I'm up *all* night taking care of someone else's child. No one cares about *me*."

The room fell silent. I began to cry and suddenly felt like I wanted to puke. I got up from the sofa, but stumbled. I was more intoxicated than I'd ever been in my life, and while my brain spun in one direction, my emotions spiraled out of control in the other.

"I love you guys," I slurred. "I really do. But I hate this situation. Can you imagine? I feel like my life is over."

Nadette placed a reassuring arm around my shoulder. "That's what your friends are for," she said affectionately, while casting glances around the room. "We all love and care about you, don't we girls?"

I believe I heard a yes chorus. I took one more step in the direction of the bathroom, but lost control. Soon my dinner, some thirty-two ounces of rum and cola, plus numerous chips and dip, were now in puky evidence atop her parents' brand new orange and yellow shag carpet.

"Egads, I'm so sorry," I said to Nadette, who was holding my hair and rubbing my back. Though intensely humiliated, physically I felt much better. "At least it matches the carpet," I said before offering to clean it up.

"Don't worry about it," said Nadette, very charitably putting me in her bed so that I could sleep off some of the rum's effects.

"Did Dr. Spock teach you about that?"

"About what?"

"Caring for drunk children."

Softly chuckling, she clicked off the lights; a gesture which was kind and likewise cruel, as only an hour later and just when I was a world away, she nudged me awake.

"Gail," she said, "It's nearly midnight. You need to go home."

It took me several moments to gain my bearings. Nadette's full-sized bed was infinitely more comfortable than mine. Plus, I was blissfully alone the brief period of time I slept. Finally sitting up, I smiled at her.

"You're the best friend anyone could ever have," I said. "I'm sorry I puked on your rug. And yes, you can definitely be John's godmother."

"Thanks, that means a lot to me. And don't worry, I already cleaned up the barf. My parents will never know. Are you okay?"

"I'm good. I'll make it home fine."

"That's not what I meant."

"Honestly," I replied while standing up, still feeling woozy. "Tonight came as such a surprise, and not just because of the baby shower. For some dumb reason I thought maybe John O'Neill would be here."

"I'm sorry to have disappointed you," she chuckled.

I hugged her. "Never. I really appreciate what you all did. It's just, I don't know. My life is completely different and it's not because of anything I did. Truthfully, right now, I can't imagine that any boy would want to date me if I'm bringing a diaper bag and a crying baby along."

"You can always leave him with me."

"The boy or the baby?"

"Both," she chuckled again. We then tiptoed through the living room where all the other girls were sound asleep, and on out to her front lawn where she'd already parked the gargantuan pram. It was an awkward and creaking thing to maneuver at first, especially with one hand as I casually pushed it along while smoking a cigarette with the other. I was familiar with every square inch of our neighborhood and could have made it home blindfolded – even pushing the pram. In addition to the network of sidewalks in front of each house, a grid of alleyways existed in the back, which was where everyone's garbage was collected. Hence, I could tell whose house I was passing by the nature of their trash or the items hanging on their clothes lines. Presently I was passing Mrs. Logan's backyard. Widowed with grown children, she was someone I'd profiled as a fat drunk simply because of the usual assortment of empty liquor bottles in her garbage, plus undergarments nearly the size of pillowcases frequently suspended from her clothesline.

Strolling past the Fisher's house bordered by perennial blooms, I could smell their roses and then spotted my particular favorite – some Black-Eyed Susans. Passing by their well-groomed boxwood hedges, I took in their luxuriant smell. Now at the end of McCormick Alley, I clumsily steered the pram around the corner, only to stop in cold shock at the sight of my own house. A police cruiser was parked out front. And as a light-house stands beacon in a tempestuous storm, every light was aglow inside telegraphing a serious atmospheric change.

"Holy cow!" Flicking away my cigarette, I hurriedly pushed the pram home and then abandoning it in the front yard quickly entered the foyer. There, huddled in our living room, were four of my cousins and their mutt, Brandy. Frankie was holding John while Paul and Raymond sat on either side of him. And while Paul and Raymond were quietly crying, their infant brother was wailing. His bawling, however, did little to mute the tense arguing of my parents in the kitchen.

"It's out of the question," my father insisted above the din.

"What's going on, Frankie?" I asked my distraught-looking, seventeen-year-old cousin as I reached for the baby. Frankie was a lanky, young man with a sweet, handsome face. His straight black hair fell partially over his piercing blue eyes, presently hollowed and frightened as he handed him over. John must have sensed it was me – his mother – as he began simmering down the instant I held him near.

"My father held up a liquor store," Frankie nervously answered.

"What?! Where?"

"Laurel Liquor."

Frankie had just lost his mother and now, ostensibly, his father. Yet my immediate concern was about my continued purchasing power in the neighborhood package store. If they connected the dots I might never be able to use my fake ID in there again. "Laurel Liquor? You're joking, right?"

"No."

"Where is he now?"

"On the run. He won't get far. Apparently he only got about two-hundred bucks."

"Is that why the ....?"

He nodded while finishing my sentence. "The cruiser is out front?"

This was like hearing the captain of the Titanic tell everyone to stay calm as the ship cruised through some rather large ice cubes.

"Frankie, that's really..." I was about to say awful, when the pitch of my mother's voice cut me off.

"Please, Joe, *please*! I cannot do this to my sister. We *need* to keep them together."

"I am not discussing this any more this evening. Period."

My mother responded to my father in muted tones, obviously trying to get in the last word. Still, we could hear them.

"Mary Claire, stop. Do you understand?"

"Where are Joey and Timmy?" I asked to break up the ensuing silence.

"In bed."

Figures, I thought, that Joey would pass off John at the first possible chance.

"Where's Patty?"

"Upstairs."

The baby started screaming again, so I boldly entered the kitchen to grab a bottle. Surprisingly, my mother was a step ahead of me as one was presently heating up in a pan on the stove. Not so surprising, both parents were unaware that the water was boiling. Upon seeing me her eyes lit up as if I, her only trusted ally, would suddenly help set my father straight in her pleas to permanently keep my cousins.

"That rat bastard held up Laurel Liquor," she whispered darkly.

"Mary Claire!" my father snarled over her foul language.

"It's the God's honest truth, Joe. He's a rat...."

His stiff look cut her off. I ignored them both while retrieving the bottle, now needing to run it under some tepid tap water to cool it off.

"What is that?" my mother asked, ignoring him and looking down at my knees.

"What is what?" I replied, trying not to slur my words. She pointed to my hemline where a grody chunk of my barf was smeared into the dress.

"Oh, the baby. He puked just a minute ago."

"Well, we should be able to get that out. Did you have fun?"

My father, unaware that this type of detached discourse was typical for us, looked at her like she had two heads. "Would you please feed that baby?" He snapped at me.

I promptly inserted the nipple into John's gaping mouth and quickly retreated to my room. As the door was shut and the light was on, I gently knocked. With no answer, and assuming Patty was asleep, I quietly entered the room only to find her sitting on Mary Joyce's bed lightly rocking back and forth while holding fast to a cardboard shoe box.

"Patty!" I said, with feigned cheer. "What a nice surprise!"

Though mentally disabled, she was no one's fool. In spite of the darkness that lurked in their house, it was often Patty who shined. She was all about love and Aunt Cate had adored her daughter. Presently she was pale, unkempt and — like her siblings — appeared to be scared stiff. Her shoulder-length hair was brown and straight, like mine, only it was greasy and her bangs were pathetically choppy. I assumed she'd cut them herself. Her clothes didn't match. Or perhaps they did to her, as she'd at least managed to get the plaid shorts and striped shirt in the same green color. It was impossible not to feel pity for her.

Still holding John, I gently sat down beside her. "Everything okay?"

She stayed mum while steadily rocking. Finally looking over at her one-month-old baby brother she softly spoke. "I want my mommy," is all she said.

Chapter 7

"These children are staying here. Period."

The following morning Uncle Francis was still at large and my parents were still arguing over what to do with his children. My mother openly anguished over the prospect of Cate's children living hither and yon, while my father wondered how they'd manage on his income with twice as many children in a house with only one full bathroom. My parents might have been alone in the kitchen, but their privacy ended there.

My mother volunteered to go back to work.

"Not a chance," my father thankfully interjected. "It's hard enough keeping track of my own five, let alone five more, including an infant and Patty, who is a retard."

At this point all of us were sitting in the living room listening to the entire exchange. My father's insensitive comment made us all look at Patty who, sitting on the sofa between Joey and Paul, was still holding fast to her mysterious shoe box. She'd not spoken another word since telling me she wanted her mother.

I'd never heard anyone but her father so callously call her retarded. Everyone knew it was so, though Aunt Cate was the last to admit it. Even after Patty was forced to repeat kindergarten and the first grade.

"What's a retard?" she suddenly asked.

Terror struck our eyes while candor became stuck in our throats. What was there to say? That life had basically slipped her some kind of intellectual mickey and that she was pretty much doped for good? No one answered, so she repeated the question. Joey, in his infinite wisdom, answered first.

"That's what you are. It means you're really dumb."

"I'm not dumb."

"You," said Joey, "are a retard. So *you* are *really* dumb."

"Shut-up, you jerk!" I hissed.

"What?" he whined. "It's true. Patty is a dumb retard."

With that, Patty climbed off the sofa and headed upstairs where she positioned herself on Mary Joyce's bed and stayed until it was time to leave for Mass.

It was quite a sight to see the newly extended Kenealy clan walking to church. There were ten of us in all, including the baby, whom I foolishly carried rather than push in his newly acquired pram, and only because he bawled whenever I put him down. Perhaps because I was so hungover he felt heavier by the step. Or maybe I was feeding him too much. To make matters worse, it was already a hot day and he was very fussy.

Just behind the church we passed Cate's grave, impossible to miss with its ochre-colored mound and freshly cut flowers that my mother regularly snipped from neighbors' yards. So far no one had complained, although I felt certain that would change after Mrs. Harper's prized gladiolas came into full bloom.

Once inside St. Mary's, we filled two entire pews. Just a day before it would have seemed impossible to imagine this sight of related misfits all kneeling and asking for God's compassion at once. I suppose if any family deserved even a sliver of mercy it was us. Especially when we looked up and saw Father Jack miraculously joining in the processional with monsignor. Upon seeing him, my mother crossed herself again and silently prayed. To worsen matters, and just when the baby finally simmered down and Father Jack had begun reading the Gospel in a horribly nasal tone, a great commotion erupted at the back of the church. By sound alone I could tell that a dog had gained entrance and was struggling for traction on the cool marble floor. "The Lord is my German Shepherd," Joey sniggered as mad barking ensued.

Would instant disintegration be asking too much? Charging up the aisle and at last finding her clan was Brandy, with our mutt, Mr. Bojangles nipping, at her tail. With her black fur and white chest resembling one of the sisters in full habit, Brandy frantically wedged her way into our pew.

"Ahhhh, for Pete's sake. Who left the gate open? Get 'em outta here," my father growled.

Joey, most likely believing this was a sign from God that he should skip Mass, wrangled a barking Mr. Bojangles and while jostling by me prompted the baby to start howling anew. The notion of Joey taking complete advantage of the situation while I was the truly sleep-deprived and hungover soul suddenly made me furious. Particularly as he was grounded and just grabbed a "Get Out of Jail Free" card by the collar. Reasoning that John's disruptive, piercing cry was reason enough for me to split, I stepped into the aisle.

"Gimme the dog," I commanded. "I'm taking him *and* the baby home."

"Not a chance."

"Give him to me," I persisted over John's fervent squall.

"No!"

Frankie was now beside us struggling with a recalcitrant Brandy.

"Joey Kenealy, if you don't give me that dog..."

"Uh-hum," a voice louder than mine echoed from the altar. Now looking at all the people looking at me, I slowly turned to meet monsignor's penetrating gaze. "Might I suggest that all three of you go home with your charges and perhaps return for a later Mass?" he impatiently admonished. I think I nodded in agreement. But mostly what I noticed was that this red hot mess was taking place just beside the First Station of the Cross. *Jesus is condemned to death.*

My mother wouldn't even look at us. And my father, no doubt, was wondering how much more to put in the collection plate as he looked at me darkly while jerking his head to the left: scram – *NOW*, was the clear message. As the baby wailed, Joey, Frankie, the two dogs and I bolted.

"See what you did?" I snarled at Joey catching up with him inside the narthex.

"Me?" he snorted angrily, still firmly gripping Mr. Bojangles. "You're the bossy big-mouth who started this. Have fun in your next confession, you philistine."

We quickly departed with me carrying John and Frankie hauling a fifty-pound, collarless Brandy. Joey promptly let Mr. Bojangles loose, then began running down the street with the dog nipping at his heels. Sure enough, before Frankie or I returned home, Joey was off riding his bike with Mr. Bojangles running behind. Frankie locked up Brandy in the backyard and joined me on the front porch swing where the baby had passed out in my lap. I was now smoking a cigarette and drinking a soda to battle my hangover – now exacerbated by profound mortification. Could I ever show my face at the pool, the local liquor store, or church again?

"You doing all right?" Frankie softly asked.

I shrugged.

"Do you want me to take John?" he offered.

I took a drag off my cigarette before answering. "Nah. It'll wake him up and he'll probably just start crying again. I've never known a baby who cries so much."

"I know how he feels," he said dryly, which made me chuckle.

"Yeah, me, too."

He half-heartedly smiled. "I'm really sorry about all of this."

"Why? It's not your fault."

He sighed. "We don't have to stay here, you know."

"That's crazy. Where would you go?"

"I don't know," he sighed again. "I just don't want to be a burden."

I fell silent. What was there to say? My father had already broadcast that message to him and his siblings. Frankie politely excused himself and disappeared into the living room where he buried himself in the local sports pages. Before long the rest of the crowd returned.

"Proud of yourself?" my father indignantly asked while passing me by.

My response was to rat out my supposedly-restricted brother. "Joey took off on his bike."

He released a loud, exasperated snort but didn't say another word. In fact, no one knew what to say or do – especially my cousins who hunkered down in the living room again too afraid to move. My mother went upstairs to presumably change while my brooding father made bologna sandwiches. I was still sitting on the front porch when I heard the loud racket from inside.

Clunkety-clunk. Clunkety-clunk. Bump-bump-bump. Clunkety-clunk.

Something hard was banging each step. Shortly, the front door opened and my mother briskly exited with a large, beat-up suitcase in tow. Still in her Sunday best she was preparing to walk down the front steps when my father bolted outside behind her.

"What on earth is going on here?" he demanded.

She stopped. "I'm leaving," she replied with utter conviction. "If those children can't stay, then I will go and live with them."

"You can't just leave," my father protested.

"Oh, yeah? Watch me," she said, her anger and accent mixing into full-plated Irish armor.

"Wait a minute! Stop!" my father cried as she turned and started toward the gate. "Let's talk about this."

"There's nothing more to talk about," she said, stiffly marching away. "You can bring the children over after I've cleaned their house."

Without warning a red taxi appeared. My mother waved in acknowledgment after the driver gently tooted the horn. My shocked father needed only a second longer to absorb what this meant.

"You're serious, aren't you? You would really move over there?"

She now turned to face him. If I knew one thing for certain about my mother it was not to mess with her when she sucked in her breath and held her head high. My father knew better, too. And while he might be fretting about her threatened departure, I was more concerned that she would leave the baby behind with me. Very sensibly, my father's stance softened.

"Okay. They can stay. But I'm setting the rules, and they will be strict."

They locked eyes in a way only two truly committed people are capable of doing; as if a certain look possessed by the other was the key to unlocking a deeply buried vault containing the truth.

My father didn't flinch. Unaccustomed to such a high level of brinkmanship, my mother sat down on her suitcase and burying her face in her hands began to cry. "Thank you, Lord," I think I heard her say through a muffled sob. Between that momentous decision, the collection plate, and now the waiting cab driver, this was turning into a very expensive morning for my father. I saw him give the man a couple of dollars before seeing him off. After briefly hugging my mother, he brought her and the suitcase inside and soon returned to making lunch.

Oddly, neither of them made any grand pronouncements to my cousins. What was there to say? *Your mother is dead and now your rat-bastard-good-for-nothing-drunk-son-of-a-bitch-felon-of-a-father is at large and if you don't move in with us the authorities will determine your futures.*

Soon we were all washing down bologna and mustard sandwiches with lemonade when Joey returned with a dozen bear-claws from the Millsteins's bakery. Instead of upbraiding him for his unapproved absence, my father serenely bit into one of the almond-covered pastries while matter-of-factly declaring to my cousins that he, Frankie, Joey, Paul and Raymond would shortly leave for the O'Brien house – literally on the other side of the tracks – to get their stuff, including two sets of bunk beds and an old crib. Furthermore, my mother and I were to clean out the sewing room and turn it over to the O'Brien boys. It was also determined that the baby would continue sharing my room with me. He never mentioned Patty, but the presumption was she would share my room, too.

Patty. Oh, yeah, Patty. It took us a few hours to realize it, but she'd made a decision to leave, too.

Chapter 8

John was now very hot to the touch and quite cranky, besides. Mostly because I was preoccupied with him, it wasn't until late afternoon that I realized Patty was AWOL. Assuming she was with her brothers, I tended to John alone upstairs. A cool bath brought him temporary respite. But fifteen minutes later he was highly agitated and felt inflamed again. Clearly he was running a fever. Given my lousy hangover, that Uncle Francis was still at large, and that my parents were either coping with the cops or his kids, I felt uncomfortable dumping another thing on them. And so I kept this latest development to myself.

His cry was now full of misery. To comfort him I cranked up the air conditioning unit in my room, then rocked him to sleep atop the afghan blanket crafted by his mother. Once he nodded off in my arms, I dared not put him down for fear of waking him up. Instead I cradled him for over an hour in a rocking chair I'd dragged up to my room from the front porch.

As we gently swayed, an unexpected ambivalence about him began slowly permeating my senses. In spite of my intense resentment about becoming this orphan's keeper, I suddenly marveled at his itsy-bitsy fingernails and the tiny dimples at the base of each finger, realizing that should nature take its course the infant boy in my arms would grow into a man at least thirty times larger in weight. It filled me with wonder that I was once this tiny and vulnerable.

It was impossible not to feel compassion for this innocent baby who, beyond the grasp of the blanket in which he lay, would never know the warmth of his mother's touch. And, as far as I was concerned, would want nothing to do with his father. Odd new feelings of affection towards him surfaced; the chair in which we slowly rocked serving as a petri dish of unexpected love.

I tenderly stroked his head, imagining how handsome he'd become as a man with his black hair and long dark eyelashes fringing blue eyes. As I continued to inventory his features, I noticed his breathing was increasingly junky and shallow. Furthermore, that his chest seemed to sink in with each breath. Deciding it was clearly time for some adult intervention, I gingerly placed him in a laundry-basket-turned-bassinet and left him there as I searched for my mother. I found her out in the back yard hanging up a load of wash.

"Gail," she jumped. "You scared me. I'm worried to death that good-for-nothing Francis will show up with a gun in his hand."

"Ma, something's wrong with the baby."

"What now?" she said, pinning up a sheet.

I explained the symptoms. Gratefully, and for the first time in a month, she seemed sober.

"It sounds like a cold comin' on. You should give him a cool bath."

"I already did."

"Hmmm. Run hot water to steam up the bathroom, then sit him upright in your lap. That should open him up. Also, grind up a baby aspirin and put it in his formula. Is Patty up there with you?" she added.

"No. I haven't seen her for hours. I thought maybe she'd joined Dad."

"What? I just assumed she was upstairs with you!"

Immediately suspending her activity, we took off to find her. While we double-checked my bedroom, John awoke and began his pitiful crying again. My mother touched his forehead.

"Oh, if it's not one thing, it's another," she said. "Give him that baby aspirin," she commanded before disappearing in search of Patty. I picked him up. He was boiling hot. I tried the aspirin-laced formula, but he wasn't having it. The steamed-up bathroom did little to help.

And while I dealt with this brewing crisis, my mother was facing another one herself as Patty was nowhere to be found. A search of our immediate surroundings proved fruitless. None of the neighbors had seen her, and my frantic mother feared the worse – that she'd wandered unescorted to the Patuxent River or, just as frightening, that Uncle Francis had nabbed her. My mother promptly called the police who quickly fanned out in search of her along the river's edge and throughout the neighborhood.

I nervously called Nadette. "Can you come over and watch the baby?" I said, sounding panicky.

"Of course. Is something wrong?"

"Yes. Please hurry."

Within minutes she arrived. "My Uncle Francis held up Laurel Liquor last night and the police are still looking for him. His kids are moving in with us, but now my cousin Patty is missing, and something's wrong with the baby. Please keep the house locked and don't let anyone in."

Nadette's eyes widened as she gulped. "It's not safe here. I'll take him to my house."

"What do you mean? The cops are everywhere. Besides, I need you here in case Patty comes home. I'm sure she's just wandering around the neighborhood," I said with feigned assurance. We rarely locked our house up, but Nadette bolted the door the moment I left.

Indeed, Patty was in the neighborhood and wandering. Alone and in the solitude of St. Mary's chapel – the last place any one of us thought to look for a lost soul – Patty had returned to the site where she felt the last true connection to her mother. Having slipped unnoticed out of the house with her shoe box, she'd walked back up to the church. Once inside, Patty finally removed the box's lid wherein she kept her mother's rosary beads, along with a yellowed photo of herself as a toddler sitting happily on Cate's lap. Reaching underneath the photo, Patty removed the patent leather shoes she'd worn for her First Holy Communion. Nearly a size too small, she managed to put them on, her shoes tapping loudly on the marble floor as she walked a continuous loop around the Stations of the Cross.

"Hail Mary, full of grace," she repeated again and again, along with the portions of the petition that she remembered. And then, "Thank you God for bringing my mother back."

Coincidentally, I had just entered one of the church's balconies to say a prayer to St. Anthony, the patron saint for lost things and missing people, and his heavenly brother St. Jude, the patron saint of hopeless causes, when I spotted her. From my quiet perch, I could see that she was not alone. After her ritual of delivering communion to the sick, Sister Perpetua was returning the remaining Eucharist to the tabernacle. A longtime resident of the nearby Pallottine Convent, she was the principal at St. Mary of the Mills School which I'd dutifully attended from kindergarten through eighth grade. When school was out, she spent more time at local hospitals and nursing homes tending to parishioners' personal needs. Typically in the summer she wore her white habit, but Sundays were reserved for the full black regalia. At the ornate marble altar she stood as an imposing and mystical symbol of her Pallottine order.

Genuflecting after locking the tabernacle, Sister Perpetua turned to leave the sanctuary when she noticed Patty. She did not recognize this child, nor did she see me in the shadows. Patty was now frozen in fear, unaware that Sister Perpetua was a warm and much beloved figure in the community. While her expectations were high, she was as patient as they came and rarely sharp in her criticisms. Nevertheless, she was not someone with whom to trifle.

"Hello," Sister smiled warmly.

Patty didn't blink.

"Can I help you?"

Sister Perpetua moved a bit closer, seeming to take in the oddity of Patty's mismatched green outfit and white patent-leather shoes, not to mention the rosary beads, photo and shoe box.

"May I ask your name?"

Yes, she nodded, remaining speechless. Sister laughed softly, clearly realizing that Patty had given an appropriate answer to her question.

"Okay, then, my name is Sister Perpetua. What is your name?"

"Patty," was her barely audible response.

"Patty. A pretty name for a pretty girl, wearing such pretty shoes."

"They hurt."

"Perhaps they're too small."

Again, Patty quietly nodded yes. Intrigued that she was opening up to Sister, I remained silent.

"Patty, may I ask you another question?"

"Yes."

"Are you here alone?"

At first she nodded yes, then slowly shaking her head no, turned toward one of the stained glass windows. "My mother is here. She's buried in your back yard."

Sister lightly gasped. "What do you mean, *my* back yard?"

"Out there," Patty pointed in the cemetery's direction. "My mother is buried out there."

Sister glanced in that direction. "I see," she said slowly. "And what is your purpose *here*?"

"To bring her back."

"Hmmm. But you just indicated that she's dead."

"Yes," Patty affirmed.

"If so, then you understand she's with God now. Right?"

"Jesus came back from the dead. So can she."

Sister briefly turned this over in her mind, then guided Patty to a pew where they sat down. "Patty, I imagine that your mother was a very special person, because God wanted her back home in Heaven sooner than anyone expected. And do you know what? I believe your mother is talking with God right now. In fact, she is asking Him to protect you. And God is listening, perhaps needing me to tell you that you are deeply loved and protected by both Him and your mother."

"If God is listening then tell him to send her back."

Sister did not mince words. "Patty, you will one day see your mother in Heaven. But God is not sending her back."

"Is that what God is telling you?"

"That's what God is telling me."

Slouching down, Patty absorbed this bad news. "Then *I* want to go to heaven. Tell God I want to be with my mommy."

A heartened expression transformed Sister's intelligent face. Knowing nothing of Patty or her mother's plight, she gently responded.

"Dear, sweet Patty. God knows that. And He promises that you will one day join your mother in Heaven. But God is also telling me that it is not *your* time to go there. You know what else? He is taking very good care of your mother. She feels very loved and is safe and happy with God."

Patty contemplated this. "That's good because my father was really mean to her."

Sister somewhat startled at this, and even more so at what came next.

"Sister Perpetual, everyone says I'm a retard. Which means I'm really dumb, right?"

Perhaps amused by the innocent name derivation, Sister briefly smiled as she looked heavenward over this new and wildly unexpected challenge.

"No, no, dear child," she continued with great warmth. "In fact, I suspect you are quite smart. But if it helps, I'll tell you what it means. You see, God gives each and every one of us unique and special gifts. For example, some people have very strong arms," she said flexing her own arm for added emphasis, "and they can build houses. Other people aren't so strong, but they have fast fingers and can play the piano," she went on as if performing at an invisible keyboard.

"So the strong man builds the house the piano goes into. And the girl who plays the piano moves into that house and makes beautiful music for everyone to enjoy. Each person shares their own wonderful gift with the other, and this helps to make one another happy. Now what do you suppose your gift is?"

Patty naively shrugged her shoulders. "I can count to one-hundred."

"Well, that is certainly a talent! And I'm sure you have many. But your true gift is much greater than that. Do you want me to tell you what it is?"

Patty's eyes brightened as she shook her head yes.

"Your gift," Sister said with kind deliberation, "is your wonderful heart. You see, while your mind may work just a little bit slower, your heart works twice as fast. And believe me, that's a big gift from God. Slowness of heart makes people mean or sad." Sister lowered her eyes, bit her lip, then sighed. "Patty, did ever your mother tell you that you were special?"

"Yes," she nodded.

"And indeed, you are. So remember this, if ever someone says you're 'retarded,' what they're really saying is that you are special because God gave you an extra big heart to help make them feel happy and loved. Perhaps, then, you should give that person a hug because it will make them feel happy."

This message of love prompted Patty to slowly inch closer to Sister Perpetua. Peacefully they sat until setting down her shoe box, Patty turned and looked up at Sister. "Can you please tell God I miss my mommy?"

Sister fell speechless, then while lovingly wrapping an arm around Patty's shoulder and tenderly stroking her brow, she nodded yes. This sympathetic gesture was all it took for Patty to bury her face deep in the folds of her habit, allowing Sister to rock and hold her near as the child openly and wholeheartedly wept over the loss of her mother.

Chapter 9

Sister Perpetua wasn't present at the 10:00 a.m. Mass, so having missed out on our earlier family folly she was unaware of Patty's relationship to me. Finally, and softly intruding, I made my presence known.

"Gail," she smiled. "And to what do we owe the pleasure?"

"Hi, Sister. I see you've met my cousin."

"Ahh," she reacted with a satisfied nod as if connecting a challenging puzzle piece.

"Patty, we've all been really worried about you. You should have told someone where you were going."

Patty sniffled, and instead of responding to me wiped her face on Sister's sleeve. Perhaps from so many years of dealing with snot-nosed kids, Sister seemed nonplussed. Silently, Patty removed her shoes and placed them back in the box along with the rosary beads and photo. Now barefoot and prepared to leave, she stood.

"I suspect there is much you can tell me," Sister remarked, also rising. "In the meantime, go gently and please let me know if there is anything I can do to help. Good-bye and God bless, Patty. I hope to see you again soon."

Patty quietly nodded.

"Thank you, Sister," I politely responded, and taking Patty by the hand left without another word. However moved I might have been by Sister's compassion, and whatever halo I pretended to wear in her presence, quickly vanished outside.

"Patty, why in the hell didn't you tell someone at the house where you were going?" I growled at her. "Seriously. The last thing we need is another troublemaker in the family."

Instead of answering, she dropped my hand and pulled her treasure box in tight. The events of the past twenty-four hours and her defiance so annoyed me that I promptly stopped and positioned myself directly in front of her. "Young lady, did you hear me?"

Her head hung low, she mumbled a response.

"Look up at me when you're talking," I said, now sounding more like Sister Beatrice, a bulldog of a nun whose bark was the same as her bite. She was a fifth-grade teacher who would chew you out and threaten to rap your head with an unabridged dictionary if you so much as looked at her cross-eyed.

Patty glanced upwards with fast tears spilling down her face. This time I heard her loud and clear. "It's not my house and no one there cares about me."

Her comment startled me. Was she wise enough to perceive this as possible? I always assumed if one were mentally disabled it meant they were not only slow to learn, but slow to feel, and thus easier to ignore. I'd certainly ignored her while caring for John. The one who loved her most was dead and her father had utterly abandoned her. My mother was an emotional wreck and my father had not only spoken poorly about her in front of everyone, but he'd not even spoken to her. And her own brothers were either preoccupied with their own needs or were simply too young to notice hers. My sinking heart took an unexpected pivot. Truly, she was lost.

"Patty," I spoke softly and sincerely, "You're wrong. Do you know why? Because I care about you. Which is why I went looking for you. We're sharing a room now which means we're like sisters. And sisters care for each other and always look out for one another."

"Like Sister Perpetual?" she meekly asked.

"Well, not like *that* kind of sister," I remarked, last night's drunken remnants still stirring inside me. "I'm talking about Mary Joyce. And I'm so happy to share my room with you, too," I startled myself by saying as I had no earthly idea how this forced arrangement might work. "And you know why? Because just like Sister Perpetua said, I also believe you are very special."

She hugged me, and in spite smelling like a wild onion, I pulled her in and held her tight. Looking down at her chopped, greasy, uncombed hair; then considering her grimy, ill-fitting clothes, and bare, dirty feet, it made me wonder when she'd last bathed. Cate would have never let her out looking like this. And given my mother's pathetic condition, it was not surprising that she'd overlooked Patty's basic appearance. It was then that something more profound struck me: I missed *my* mother, too.

"Patty," I stepped back, choking up on my own emotion, "I'm really sorry for your loss."

Squatting down, I took hold of her hands and looking up at her spoke more soulfully. "I mean this with all of my heart. I can never replace your mother. But I can be your best friend. And you can be one of mine. But you have to promise me something. And that is that you will *always* let *me* know exactly where you are going because I need to know. Your disappearance today really scared me."

My orphaned cousin, my new roommate, my new sister, my new best friend convincingly nodded her head. We had a deal. I sealed it by hugging her again.

"You know what MJ and I like to do together?" I said now standing up. "We like to fix each other's hair and paint each other's toe nails. Will you let me style your hair and paint your nails? I'll even get you some new clothes. Deal?" I said, realizing there went some of my savings.

Once more she nodded, only this time I could see her eyes light up. Reclasping hands, we casually walked the few blocks down to my house where it appeared the troops were still out looking for her.

"Oh, praise God, you're home!" Nadette frantically said upon seeing us. She was holding John who wore only a diaper. His eyes were closed and he appeared limp as a noodle. Forsaking any niceties to Patty, she jumped right in. "No one else is back and John's burning hot and getting worse by the minute. I called Warren's and told Sallyann the symptoms. She said it would be best to get him to the Emergency Room at Children's Hospital right away."

"Why not Warren's?" I asked about the nurse's advice.

"She said that Children's would be better equipped to deal with him. It could be pneumonia."

"Pneumonia?" I repeated incredulously. "Babies don't get pneumonia."

She carefully handed John over and she wasn't kidding. Though passed out cold, he was hotter than before and his chest heaved with each labored breath.

"He could die without proper help," she said gravely, promptly leaving to get her car. Fortunately she possessed more common sense about infants than I obviously did, as well as a driver's license and a hand-me-down car from her parents. Shortly she returned, furiously beeping the horn of that 1958 Buick Riviera. Patty and I climbed into the sprawling front seat. And with John on my lap, now too sick to even cry, Nadette sped off.

For once I was grateful that she always drove too fast. Before long we were at Children's Hospital in Washington, D.C. — a state of the art facility. And not a minute too soon. By the time we arrived he was barely breathing and everything next happened in a blur. The oxygen mask. Blood being drawn. A chest X-ray, the IV drip, the constant attention from doctors and nurses. John was desperately fighting acute bacterial pneumonia and it wasn't clear if he'd make it another day let alone another minute.

I'd left a note at home for my mother informing her that Patty had been found and was with me, and furthermore that we were off to Children's Hospital. Presently, I called her from the nursing station.

"Ma, you and Dad need to get here immediately," I said determinedly when she answered.

"For Pete's sake, Gail, what's going on? What happened to Patty?" she frantically asked.

"Patty's fine. She was up at the church with Sister Perpetua. But the baby," I said, my voice cracking. "He's dying."

Her pent-up grief erupted in a haunting wail that reverberated through every bone in my body. I pulled the receiver away from my ear, if only to protect my own soul from being sucked into more darkness. Suddenly I heard my father's voice.

"Mary Claire! Mary Claire! What's wrong?" he yelled in the background before grabbing the receiver. "Gail, what is going on? Where's Patty?"

"She's fine, Dad. She was up at the church with Sister Perpetua and now she's with me. But it's the baby. He has bacterial pneumonia and may not survive the night." I spoke so matter-of-factly that I barely recognized the authority in my own voice. "We're in the Intensive Care Unit at Children's Hospital."

Soon my parents arrived; my mother's face was swollen from crying and my father looked more anguished than ever, especially when quietly informing me that Uncle Francis was spotted – this time holding up a bank.

"It happened in Columbia," he whispered, looking downward as he spoke, apparently to prevent upsetting my mother any further.

"Columbia, Maryland?" I asked of the newly opened, planned community just up the road from Laurel.

No, he shook his head. "Columbia, South Carolina. Plus, he stole a car after their family station wagon broke down somewhere in Virginia."

"Three major crimes in three states in less than twenty-four hours? If he put half as much effort into being a normal person he'd be....well, normal," I whispered harshly.

Our conversation was interrupted by the arrival of Dr. Dyer, a handsome pediatric pulmonologist who began debriefing by parents. My mother was still in such shock over the most recent turn of events that she could barely keep up with the doctor's assessment. He was blunt, but thorough.

"His condition wouldn't be nearly so bad if you'd taken appropriate action much earlier. It's possible this child might not make it. Do you have any questions?" he concluded.

"Yes," my mother said, then squarely faced Nadette. "Can you stay with Gail for a bit while she looks after John? We need to feed Patty and the boys."

Suddenly I felt just as abandoned as the baby. I looked my mother directly in the eye, a place where I could generally predict my short-term future and saw something I'd never seen before: nothing. My mother simply couldn't handle another loss and was leaving this one up to me. I turned imploringly toward my usually stalwart father. He closed his eyes and hung his head. I was on my own.

"Well, of course, Mrs. Kenealy," Nadette said, now wrapping a loving arm around my shoulder. "And don't worry. Everything's going to be all right."

"Call me if anything changes," my mother said. I knew what she meant.

Patty pleaded to stay with me. I took her aside. "Do me a big favor, okay? When you get back to the house tell Frankie that I've asked him to keep an eye on you and that I'm coming back as soon as I can. And don't go anywhere without telling him first."

"Are you staying here because John is going to die?"

What was I supposed to say to this surprisingly precocious child with a knack for bluntness? I hugged and reassured her that *I'd* be home soon, solemnly watching the three of them disappear.

"Are you okay?" Nadette softly asked.

Of course I was not okay. I couldn't imagine why all of this was happening and at once. It was so overwhelming. We'd barely been given the chance to take in Aunt Cate's death before her five children were rendered parentless. And now the final living legacy of that beautiful woman was near death himself. *No, I will not let that happen*, I thought, as an odd mixture of love, anger and determination began brewing inside me – the raw substances of some badly needed courage.

"I'm fine," I finally said.

And so we stayed, keeping an agonizing bedside vigil beside my orphaned cousin, my newest brother, my unofficially adopted son, and Nadette's unofficial godson. At one point when I'd drifted off to sleep in a chair, Nadette nudged me awake. She was standing beside his incubator holding a miniature paper cup filled with water. "We need to baptize him," she declared.

My eyes grew wide as my pulse quickened. "Why? What's happening?" I jumped up.

"Nothing's changed. But he needs to be baptized."

"Where are we going to find a priest at this hour?"

"We don't need a priest."

"Says who?"

"It says so in the Catechism. In an emergency – and I think this counts – any baptized person can baptize another."

"Since when did you become so...so...Catholic?" I stammered, embarrassed at not remembering this myself. We'd shared the same religious education since kindergarten. How did she suddenly get so smart?

"Do you want me to be his godmother or not?"

"Well, yeah, of course."

"Okay, then tilt his head a little, please."

Nadette crossed herself before petitioning God to bless the water as I, ever so slightly, tipped his head back thinking that he looked like an alien baby with his tiniest conceivable oxygen mask. With unexpected reverence, Nadette poured small amounts of water on his head saying, "John Aloysius, I baptize you in the name of the Father, and of the Son, and of the Holy Spirit." Next, reaching into her pocket she pulled out a small bottle of Jean Naté cologne and, as if it were a sacramental chrism, doused her fingertip then gently traced a cross on his forehead.

"This is a sign of the Holy Spirit. You are now blessed and marked as one of God's own forever."

In multiple ways I'd always underestimated my friend. She was a boy crazy goof, a perennial underachiever in school and, in my opinion, an oddity as an only child of Catholic parents. But today, and particularly by this gesture, she revealed an impressive and deeper sensitivity than I'd ever witnessed in her before. The only reason it fell short of truly mature was because she was chewing gum the whole time.

Gently setting John's head back down, I took hold of one diminutive hand as she grasped his other. Leaning close to him she whispered, "God loves you, John Aloysius. And I promise you're gonna make it. Just hang in there."

I startled, and will swear until my last dying breath that he responded by ever so gently squeezing our fingers back.

"Did you feel that?" Nadette burst out.

Yes, I nodded.

"You see," she said smiling and softly stroking John's head, "God really does love you. And so do we."

"Thank you," I whispered. Now choking on emotion and shedding hopeful tears for him, I looked her in the eye and spoke straight from the heart. "One day you will make the world's greatest mother."

Chapter 10

*J*ohn made it through the night. And into the next. By the third day his color was restored to a more healthy pink and his temperature had almost returned to normal. It was 105 degrees when we'd arrived.

With rare exception I never left his side, and my mother never returned. Instead, Nadette remained intermittently present, bringing me some fresh clothes and toiletries while regaling me with stories of our friends. Melinda was grounded for two weeks after being caught smoking in her bathroom at home. Tina got fired from Baskin-Robbins after giving out too much free ice cream, but scored a job at the Tastee-Freez an hour later. "Obviously they didn't check her references," she said, adding, "She'll probably get fired from there, too." I concurred.

Normally I would find this gossip engaging, especially given that it was about our mutual friends. But I was exhausted and somehow it seemed so mundane. That is until she mentioned having seen John O'Neill at the community pool.

"Really? Did he ask about me?"

Nadette sighed. "Gail, you're not gonna like this, but he was with Helen."

I sighed. A year older, Helen Hartley, with her robust chest and blonde good looks went to Holy Trinity Academy, a private school in nearby Baltimore. Unless needing instant public flattery, she always acted snooty towards us "Pallotti people," as I once heard her call us. She'd actually attended St. Mary of Mills through eighth grade and used to live in our neighborhood. But as her father prospered, they moved to an upscale development of newer homes in the neighboring county and her parents promptly enrolled her in the most exclusive Catholic girls' school in the state – probably hoping to protect her virginity. Good luck with that.

60

"So."

"What do you mean, 'so?' Doesn't that bother you? It would bother me."

"But how do you know they were even together?"

"They kissed," she said.

"You saw them?"

She nodded her head. "They were in the pool together. She was in a teeny-tiny, purple bikini. And you know, with those big bahoombas of hers. Well just suffice it to say that every guy at the pool was gawking at her."

I sighed again. My athletic frame and mousy brown hair were no match against that Barbie doll. "Thanks for making me feel so great."

"Sorry. Anyway," she continued, "I saw her swim up to him underwater and emerge like some mermaid, then make-out with him right there for the whole world to see."

"Well that doesn't mean anything. Maybe he didn't really kiss her back."

"Are you crazy? Yes he did."

While looking past my shoulder she began furiously fishing in a pocket for her lipstick, then swiftly applied a coat. Before I could tell her that she'd missed the mark, Dr. Dyer was beside us.

"Dr. Dyer," she said, casting a clownish grin. "Nice to see you."

"Thanks, Nadine."

"Nadette," she smiled. "Short for Bernadette. You know, like the Four Tops song."

He half-smiled. "How's he doing?" he asked, picking up John's chart. In spite of his handsome looks, it was apparent from the stubble on his face and his tired demeanor that he'd been working a long time.

"Much better, thanks," I said. "His temperature is stable at 99.5. His color looks good and I've changed three diapers so far today. He even had a small bowel movement."

"Very good."

"Can we go home?"

"No." He then turned to Nadette. "If you don't mind, I'd like a word alone with Gail."

Nadette blushed. "Oh, sure," she said, nervously cracking her gum while scurrying out of the room.

"Gail," he started and reflectively paused. "We've discussed this before, but in reviewing John's history it's clear he left the hospital far too soon after his birth, especially considering the trauma his mother experienced. Normally he would have stayed in the hospital much longer for observation."

"I know," I declared. "It was my mother's choice."

"Yes, I understand. And I hope you don't think I'm nosy, but who exactly is responsible for taking care of this baby?"

"Why?"

"It's important to know he's receiving appropriate follow-up care."

"He will."

"From whom?"

I rolled my eyes then stared blankly at a wall.

"How old are you?"

"Fifteen."

"Fifteen? Well, you could have fooled me. I mean, I would have pegged you as being at least a couple of years older."

What a dreamboat.

"Gail, for the sake of his ongoing care, it's critical that I know who's actually taking care of this baby."

I glanced down at my nails. The pink polish I'd applied a few days earlier to impress John O'Neill at Nadette's party was all chipped. My clothes were wrinkled and my hair was pulled back in a dirty pony-tail. I probably smelled, too.

"Me," I finally answered while meeting his concerned look.

"I thought so. And how are you supposed to handle that?"

"Why are you asking me this?"

"Because you're still a child yourself."

Unexpected indignation welled up inside me. It wasn't just a baby I was taking care of, it was my entire family.

"Dr. Dyer," I said, now standing up. "My parents aren't here because, as you know, John's mother just died. And, FYI, his father up and left.

So now we have John *and* his four siblings living in our house. Oh, and did I mention that we already have five children in my immediate family? Which, actually, is *the* point. We are a family and we look out for each other. This baby is loved and will be damned well taken care of, just as I am loved and damned well taken care of.

"And one other thing," I said, surprising even myself with this new-found tenacity. "You were right."

"About what?"

"You are nosy."

"Well, I think we're done for now." He shook his head in seeming defeat, and after returning John's chart left without another word.

"Is everything okay?" Nadette asked, returning to my side after Dr. Dyer brusquely passed by her.

"Yes," I said sourly. "I just can't wait to go home."

I stayed in the hospital with John for two full weeks, during which Dr. Dyer never peppered me with personal questions again. Instead, he spent time reviewing the more clinical aspects of John's care. I suspected that even after John was ready to go Dr. Dyer kept him there, wanting to make sure that both of us were truly fit for release. In truth, John and I were both healing. Even though I was sleeping on a cot and eating crappy food, I was at least free from the domestic chaos. Plus, shifting my focus towards keeping John alive helped to briefly alleviate the anger I felt towards my mother.

Each day I gained deeper appreciation for his needs and survival instincts. I also learned that while most babies are vigorously programmed to thrive, everything around them is a potential threat. Even without my mother's supervision, I should have known better about simple things like proper bottle sterilization and keeping him protected from the sun. I dared not mention how I carelessly transported him in my flimsy bicycle basket, nor how I allowed some random child to stick her lollipop in his mouth. Or worse, how I always smoked in my room, and often while feeding him. I felt incredibly ashamed about treating him like a rag doll and for exacerbating the hardness of his life. It may not have been my choice to care for him, but it was my decision now to see that he survived.

And Dr. Dyer went out of his way to help us both. John soon began putting on weight. At last filled with renewed energy, his expression grew ever more alert. He even grinned, and his large eyes seemed to truly recognize me.

"Listen kid," I whispered softly one evening when alone and gently rocking him. "I need you to know something. Neither of us planned it this way, but from now on we need to hang in there for each other. You hear me?"

He looked up at me, drowsily blinked his eyes and peacefully drifted off to sleep.

Chapter 11

Fortunately Dr. Dyer wasn't there to pepper my father with personal questions when he came to fetch us. My Dad simply signed the release papers and we were free to leave.

"Ready to go?" he asked, as though picking me up from some party. Holding John, his diaper bag and my overnight satchel, I nodded my head in quiet disbelief. On the way home we exchanged simple small talk.

"How's Ma?"

"She's coping."

Translation: drinking.

"How are the kids doing?"

"Everyone's getting along," he said, matter-of-factly explaining that he'd given everyone a job to do and so far they were doing it.

He wasn't kidding. When we pulled up to the house I did a double-take. As opposed to their shaggy appearance when I'd left, the lawn and shrubberies were very neatly trimmed. One missing shutter had been replaced and all of them had received a fresh coat of paint. The porch itself and even the swing were painted anew. Suddenly I heard loud banging and laughter ringing from out back.

"What's going on?" I asked.

"Go see for yourself," my father slyly grinned.

It was a jaw-dropping sight. In my absence he'd embarked on a spectacular tree house building project with all the kids. Two towering oak trees in close proximity to one another now boasted their own cottage-like, wooden structures, connected by a bridge from which Frankie and Raymond were presently installing a slide. As Patty and Timmy were busy painting exterior walls, Paul and Joey were laughing aloud inside the first tree house while hammering into place three sets of built-in bunk beds. The second unit was constructed as a gathering room, its entrance through a shabby screened-door leading to a beat up kitchen table with mismatched chairs – all junk yard scores. Clearly wanting the kids to have a fun, safe place to hang out, my father had also wired the structures with electricity, promptly making me wonder just how long it would take for Joey to turn the edifice into an under-aged gambling parlor. Regardless, the fact that everyone was sharing a sprit of industry was uplifting to witness, as the project seemed to have instilled some badly needed fervor into their souls.

"Hey, Gail," rang an enthusiastic chorus upon seeing us. Frankie quickly hopped down.

"Welcome home," he spoke tenderly while stroking John's forehead. "How is he?"

I suddenly choked up realizing how perilously close we'd come to a different conversation, also noting how comfortably Frankie used the word 'home.'

"He's good."

Frankie gently hugged me. "Thank you."

Fighting tears, I nodded appreciation. "Thank you, for helping out here," I softly reciprocated. He nodded sympathetically. We got each other. Suddenly John started whimpering in a way which I knew meant he was hungry.

"Well, I better get him settled in," I said, but first turned to my father. "Where's Ma?"

"The construction noise was getting on her nerves, so she's been up the street helping Mrs. Logan."

"What's wrong with Mrs. Logan?"

"She broke her hip."

Instantly I seethed. No doubt my mother was helping the old sot drink her way back to health. "Just so I understand," I surprised myself by snapping at him. "I'm at the hospital for two straight weeks of *my* summer vacation taking care of John while she's helping a neighbor who, by the way, has her own family? I thought she left me alone at the hospital so *she* could take care of *our* family. And don't let this surprise you, Dad, but Mrs. Logan is a drunk."

My father fell tensely silent.

John's cry suddenly morphed into what sounded like a crow's caw — meaning he was mad to boot. Without another word I retreated into the house, only to stop in cold shock once inside the kitchen. It was as clean and organized as I'd ever seen it. The red linoleum floor was freshly cleaned and waxed, there were no dirty dishes anywhere, and for once the kitchen table wasn't covered with junk. Frankie soon joined me.

"Did my mother do this?"

"Nope. Your old man," he stated succinctly.

"My *father* cleaned the house?" I said incredulously.

"No, actually we did. He supervised."

My eyes widened and I was all ears. "Would you please hold him?" I said, handing Frankie his brother. Frankie cradled him while elaborating.

Apparently calling upon his days as an enlisted sailor, my father had become a convert for strict order, now insisting that each and every bed be properly made before anyone set foot out of his or her bedroom. Adding to his newfound discipline was the banishment of random piles. To prove his grit, stuff lying around on any given night was gone the next morning.

"And I mean gone!" Frankie added. "He even threw out Joey's favorite football and my transistor radio."

"Is any of my stuff missing?" I anxiously asked.

"I'm not sure. I picked up a lot of what I thought was yours and hid it under your bed before he got to it."

John started howling. "I know how you feel, kid," I said. Joining Frankie at the kitchen table, I took the baby and slipped the bottle into his gaping mouth. Within seconds he calmed down. "At least *someone* is looking out for me. Thanks, Frankie."

"No problem. Just be careful," he continued. "Before we're even awake he'll load stray items on to his truck and toss them into a random dumpster on his way to work. He's already done it four times. So far he's trashed board games, wet bathing suits, one skate board — and even a broken TV which Joey swore he could fix for the tree house. We finally got the message and cleaned up our acts."

"That stinks," was my response. Looking past Frankie and into the dining room I could also see that the dingy wallpaper was gone and replaced with a fresh coat of soft yellow paint.

In truth, despite of all these extra people in our house, at first glance it had never been fresher or tidier.

"Then you probably won't like the bathroom schedule either," he continued with a hint of sarcasm. "Turns in ten minutes or less. Starting times change each day to make sure that no one is perpetually left without hot water. The only one allowed to take a bath is your mother. And any time exceeding your ten minutes will be deducted from your next scheduled time slot. Also, if the bathroom is in use, barging in is forbidden. You either have to use the toilet in the cellar or pee in the backyard bushes."

"Ten minutes!" I lamented.

"Don't worry. Joey thinks he's clean enough after swimming in the Patuxent and said he'll sell his shower time if anyone needs it."

"How much?"

"Two dollars for ten minutes."

"TWO DOLLARS!" I exclaimed. "That's four hours of babysitting! I hate him."

Still, I hope my father didn't catch on as I wanted to keep my options open. Not that he would object to Joey's resourcefulness, just his smell.

After watching John vanquish his formula, I looked up at Frankie. "Are those the only changes?"

Beneath shaggy bangs, I saw his blue eyes surprisingly twinkle. "No. There's one other mandate."

"Please tell me it's not daily Communion."

"No, not the Lord's Supper, but ours. His rule is that anyone over the age of eight is responsible for preparing at least one family dinner each week. With MJ and Tommy away, this means you, me, Joey, Timmy, Paul and Raymond."

"What about Patty?"

"No."

"And my father?"

"No."

"And my mother? I take it she's off the hook?"

Yes, he shook his head.

My father, because he worked so hard, and Patty for what seemed like obvious reasons, were declared exempt. But my mother? This hardly seemed fair.

"He's quite strict about this, too," Frankie continued, watching me now burp John. "If you forget it's your night to cook or if dinner isn't ready by a certain time, everyone goes to bed hungry. No exceptions. And no inviting the Colonel to dinner, either."

Frankie reported that it only took two episodes of growling stomachs for everyone to fall in line. "Tonight is Timmy's turn to make dinner," he added while playfully rolling his eyes. In other words, I should keep my expectations low.

"Frankie, I've been eating hospital food for two straight weeks. How bad could it be?"

That night it was so bad that even Patty openly complained.

"I can cook better than this," she blurted while eating one of Timmy's over boiled hot dogs. I looked over at Timmy's slightly dejected, freckled face. Looking down at my limp hot dog, baked beans from a can, applesauce from a jar, and tater tots from a frozen box, I had to admit she had a point.

Joey contemptuously laughed. "As if."

"'As if' what?" she demanded.

"As if you could cook. You're retarded."

"No, I'm not!" Patty adamantly responded. "I'm special."

"You're 'specially dumb and retarded," said Joey, who was swiftly rapped on the back of his hand by the heavy end of my father's knife.

"OW!" Joey exclaimed. "That hurt!"

"Ow, nothing. Do you think your comment didn't hurt?" my father rebuked him. Had my mother been home she might have weighed in, too. Except she was still "caring" for Mrs. Logan.

"Come here, Patty," my father gently encouraged her. His eyes were striking and could be icy blue one moment and sky blue the next. Having seen Joey get upbraided, Patty was afraid to move. But my father's look appeared soft and warm so I coaxed Patty his way, feeling pinched by emotion as he hugged her. The irony was not lost on me that just a few weeks earlier he'd openly denigrated her disability. I suppose he'd unexpectedly drawn closer to all the O'Brien children during my absence; particularly so during the tree house construction. Patty smiled appreciatively as if relishing this unexpected slice of affection. Certainly her own father had never hugged her so.

"One day," my father said, "I promise you will be a great cook. But for right now, let's just leave it up to the other kids."

"Why?" she put him on the spot.

"Well, because you're not exactly reading very well yet. I bet that after this school year you'll be able to read recipes. Then you can cook. How's that?"

"Timmy doesn't really cook. He just heats. I can do that."

"Hey, that hurts *my* feelings," Timmy defended his efforts, most likely hoping my father would whack her with his knife, too.

"Son, you did a fine job this evening," my father affirmed. "Thank you."

Timmy smiled triumphantly, and Patty may have carried on except that my mother literally stumbled into the conversation. After pushing open the front door, she tripped over her own feet and fell hard on the foyer floor.

"What the bloody hell?" she loudly exclaimed, completely unaware that we were all watching from the dining room table. Standing up, her lanky body waving like a Slinky toy, she worked hard to steady herself.

"Uhm, Mary Claire," my father cautiously spoke. Her head turned slowly in the direction of his voice, and after catching sight of us all her wobbling body followed suit.

"Gailec," she exclaimed, using a favorite nickname. "How lovely. You're back from the hospital," her words slurred. "Did they treat you well?"

I was speechless.

"Did you bring the baby home?" she chirped. He was presently asleep on my lap.

My father promptly joined her and while whispering something in her ear began guiding her up the stairs, ostensibly to put her to bed.

"Oh, I'm so glad the baby's home," she said behind Dad's back, then waved. "Good night all!"

How in the hell did my mother morph into such a fall-down drunk? I didn't know what was worse — that she had succumbed to this or that my father was so unbelievably tolerant. His newfound discipline with the kids might be keeping the house clean and food on the table, but it was only whitewash as her bumbling display proved there were much darker things that needed conforming. I looked at Frankie hoping to find some measure of reassurance. His face was clouded with similar disbelief.

The next day was no different. She was right back at Mrs. Logan's.

Chapter 12

Feeding John and getting him to bed at customary times was not only essential to his well-being, but also mine. Especially as there was no expectation of help from my mother. Thankfully Frankie did his best to keep an eye on the boys, while Patty always stuck close to me. And so it was in joining me on a walk with the baby a couple of days later that we ran into her new friend.

"Sister Perpetual," Patty said gleefully. "Look at my shoes," she boasted about her new patent leather Mary Janes from Things Gone Buy.

"My, my," Sister said. "They're beautiful."

Patty grinned.

"How's everything going, Patty? Are you making new friends in the neighborhood?"

Ignoring Sister's question, Patty quickly brought up what was foremost on her mind.

"Everybody at home but me gets to cook."

My heart suddenly pinched. Not because she wasn't allowed to cook but, like Frankie, she now called our house her home.

"Well, then, it's one less chore for you," Sister smiled.

"But I want to be a cook," she politely insisted.

"I see. Well, perhaps you could be a cook's helper."

"No one wants my help. Is it because I'm retarded? I told them I was special, like you said. Joey just said that I'm 'specially dumb.'"

"Really?" she looked at me. "Remind me to have a word with him," she said circumspectly. "Now tell me exactly what it is you'd like to cook."

"Dinner."

"Sister," I interjected. "My father has implemented a new rule in our house that every kid over the age of eight is responsible for cooking at least one dinner a week."

"Then why not Patty?"

"My father said it's because she can't read very well yet."

Sister Perpetua, ever the schemer in God's good graces, grinned. "Well, there are other ways you can learn to cook. Follow me."

Patty would have followed the woman to Jupiter, and clasping her hand they crossed the street together as I followed behind with John's pram. We entered the old, three-story convent adjacent to Pallotti's High School, a former girls' boarding school at the turn of the last century. Their present number of residents per bathroom ratio was similar to ours: there were thirty of them to just three full bathrooms. There was a kitchen and dining hall on the main floor, along with a small chapel, plus a common room. We lacked the chapel, but then they didn't have a tree house. Soon we were in the convent's kitchen.

"Sister Marguerite," Sister Perpetua smiled at a charming young woman also robed in a white habit. Though French, as a novitiate she had chosen to serve in the United States, landing her first assignment at St. Mary's where she was soon to teach first grade. But for now she was the convent's cook and in the process of preparing dinner.

By chance it turned out that Sister Marguerite was a fabulous chef, producing more heavenly meals from that speckless kitchen in one month than all the Sisters had probably eaten in a lifetime. The immaculate nature of the kitchen had less to do with the Blessed Virgin Mary – a statue of which kept a vigil from the window sill – and more to do with Sister Marguerite's creative and amazing level of organization. Her kitchen was pristine and neatly stocked with multiple pans for boiling, baking, browning, braising, and blanching. Her alphabetized seasonings stood sentry in charming glass bottles on two open shelves above an industrial-sized steel oven. In front of a sunny window and secured between two cabinets was a package string from which hung various, drying herbs and a long braid of garlic. The window itself was a work of art. Sitting above a deep, white porcelain farmer's sink it was adorned with a simple, white lace valence. A marble windowsill held three identical clay pots, each brimming with fresh green herbs. And, of course, there was the Mother of God smiling serenely and approvingly on it all.

The center island, a large stainless steel table, was graced with a cheerful green pitcher containing a colorful bouquet of zinnias, while a multitude of fresh vegetables lay ready for her guillotine. Something fragrant was already simmering in a pot and freshly-baked brownies had just come out of the oven. I'd never been inside such an inspiring kitchen, and I must admit it was quite uplifting.

"Sister Marguerite, I would like to introduce you to Gail Kenealy and her cousins, Patty and John."

"Bon jour, Gail and Patty," she mellifluously answered. "How nice to meet you. My name is Sister Marguerite." She wiped her hands on her long, white apron, then shook our hands. "And you," she said endearingly while bending over the old, wicker pram, "must be monsieur."

She and the baby beamed at each other.

"Look at my new shoes," Patty enthused.

"How lovely!" she smiled.

"Sister Marguerite, Patty has expressed an interest in cooking," said Sister Perpetua. "And I was wondering if perhaps you might not need an extra pair of hands in the kitchen. You know, to help you with *whatever,*" she suggested while casting a telepathic look, "might need to be done."

"Oh, oui!" Sister Marguerite cheerfully rejoined, now clasping her hands together. "I would love an apprentice. In fact, I could use some help right now!" She looked Patty square in the eye, adding, "You know what today is, don't you?"

Patty's face was blank.

"Today," she said with emphasis, "is Friday. Which is a traditional fish day. So tonight we are having fish! Would you like to help me make some very special soup for tonight? It's called bouillabaisse. Mon amie, have you ever heard of bouillabaisse?"

No, Patty shook her head at the diminutive nun. I did the same.

"Repeat after me," Sister Marguerite spiritedly instructed her. "Say bull."

"Bull," Patty responded tentatively.

"Wonderful! Now say bull-*yah*."

"Bull-*yah*."

"Very good! Now repeat after me. Bull-yah-*base*."

"Bull-yah-base."

"Ah, très bien!

"Ahh, tray bean," Patty parroted, prompting both nuns to good-naturedly laugh.

"Very good," said Sister Marguerite. "You will be speaking French and cooking great food before we know it!"

"Bull-ya-base," Patty proudly repeated.

"How wonderful! I can already tell you are a very special girl."

Patty, now programmed to respond to such a compliment, hugged the petite nun who was barely taller than she.

"Yes, you are very special indeed," Sister Marguerite said after warmly embracing her in kind. "Now shall we get you an apron? Say 'oui,' just like you and me, we. In French that means yes."

"We," Patty grinned.

"Très bien!"

"We, tray bean, bull-ya-base," Patty chirped.

"Oh, my goodness, you're becoming fluent in French already!" said Sister Marguerite, while tying an oversized, white apron around Patty's pudgy waist and handing her a small basket of ripe tomatoes.

"You see these? In French a tomato is called 'la tomate.'"

"La toe-maht."

"My, what a smart girl. Now, Mademoiselle 'Pa-tree-cia,' today I would like your help washing les tomates. Oui?" she playfully nudged her.

"We!" Patty grinned.

Sister Perpetua smiled at the happily engaged pair. "Gail, do you mind if she stays here for awhile?"

"Not at all," I smiled back, delighted by Patty's industrious spirit. "And, thank you," I added realizing that no one but those two celestial co-conspirators would have ever guessed the good things to come, as the Pallottine Convent had just found themselves a very eager sous chef.

Chapter 13

Testosterone now seemed to ooze from the walls in my house. With the exception of Frankie, there was nothing over which my brothers and cousins wouldn't compete. They would challenge each other to see who could stay awake the longest. Or get up the stairs the fastest. Then down again. They were always looking to shave time in hopes of winning, and seconds mattered in these endeavors.

One afternoon, a few days after our visit to the convent, I happened to glance outside and caught sight of a human tumbleweed rumbling across our back lawn. There were arms and legs throwing punches and kicks everywhere as the boys moved in one fast, hellbent cluster while beating each other up. Periodically someone would come up for air, then dive back in. My father would never tolerate this kind of behavior but, as usual, he was working. My mother was likewise absent, having returned to Mrs. Logan's. And Frankie was out looking for a job.

I might have left this electrified mass alone to roll across our back lawn, except when I heard Patty screaming from its midst I swiftly stepped outside.

"Stop it, Joey," she cried. He was pulling her hair, so she clocked him in his smart-mouthed jaw — thankfully saving me the task. Otherwise worried that Patty might truly get hurt, I would have let her go at him a bit longer.

"Stop it, all of you!" I screamed while running outside, then setting the baby down on the lawn dashed boldly into the melee. "Someone's gonna get hurt."

Evidently I was too late because Paul had a bloody nose and it looked like Timmy already had the makings of a black eye. Quickly I pulled them apart, firmly standing guard so they wouldn't bunch up again.

"What is going on?" I demanded.

"Nothing," Joey angrily replied.

"You mean to tell me that you were actually beating each other up over nothing?"

"She started it," Timmy said, pointing an accusatory finger at Patty.

"Yeah," said Joey. "She told us she's a better cook than any of us. Said she knows how to make boo-boo-base, or something stupid like that, better than any of us. Patty doesn't know how to cook. She's retarded."

With that, Patty kicked Timmy, then Joey, prompting the human tumbleweed to take off again. I must admit a certain pride over her assertiveness. Nevertheless, I forcibly broke them up again, but apparently not soon enough, for two of Patty's front teeth were broken: one on the top and one the bottom. A trip to the dentist would eventually follow. But in the meantime, and that night at dinner, Patty made an announcement – her newly configured teeth causing an unexpected lisp.

"I 'shink itsh' important for everybody to know I can cook. And tomorrow night 'ish' fish Friday and I am making dinner. 'Jush' wait and 'schee,'" she declared, then quietly sat back down.

All the boys started snickering. Actually, all but Joey who was grounded for a week over knocking out her teeth. He was told by my father that if he so much as stepped even one toe outside our yard, and other than to attend Mass, that he'd be locked in the house for the rest of the summer.

"Well," said my father, keen to the fact she'd been helping at the convent. "If Patty wants to make dinner, then by all means Patty should make dinner. And we will look forward to whatever it is she makes."

My father's gesture made me glow. Patty, with the dimmest prospects among us for a bright future, was determined to prove she was as good as the rest and had softened his heart enough to at last encourage that chance.

Indeed, the next day was "fish Friday." Determined to prove herself, Patty arose before anyone else in our house, and prior to leaving for the convent set the dining room table. There was nothing but cereal bowls, improperly sequenced flatware and haphazardly folded napkins on each place mat. However, in Patty's mind she was preparing for a king's feast and so added a vase with roses and dandelions snipped from our yard.

Even flowering weeds were an embellishment not a single one of us had ever cared to provide.

Though the boys hung out at the river and in the tree house most of the day, Patty went to the convent. At last my father came home, took a quick shower, and then along with my mother sat at the table.

"How strange," she observed in a loopy manner. "Lovely, but strange."

"Where's everyone else and where's Patty?" my father asked. "She told me yesterday that dinner will be served at 6:30 and that everyone should be seated at the table."

At 6:20 there was considerable commotion as the troops began drifting in famished and ready to humiliate poor Patty. As I settled the baby into a laundry-basket-cum-bassinet in the corner, my father made them all wash up first, then at the appointed time we sat down and waited.

"Could you please pass the salt with those dandelions," said Joey at 6:40, just as there was a light rap on the front door.

"Oh, Sister Marguerite," I heard my father politely speak as he answered it. "How nice to see you. And Patty," he said curiously. Seconds later the pair emerged with Sister Marguerite looking all business in her full black habit and rosary beads hanging from the tied strings of a starched, white apron. Patty, in her adorable, quirky manner was similarly attired. Her own white apron from which her mother's rosary beads were suspended, covered a simple black dress. She wore black tights, her black Mary Janes, and for greater authenticity had fashioned a veil out of a white pillowcase held to her head with several bobby pins.

"Bon jour," Sister Marguerite smiled. "How lovely to see everyone. I hope you have a hearty appetite because mon amie, Mademoiselle 'Pat-tree-cia,' has cooked up a dinner most délicieux for you."

"Bon jour," Patty mimicked her.

"Bon jour, Pa-tree-cia," we feebly, and with odd reverence replied.

Stunned silence followed as Sister placed a large soup tureen on the table nearest my father. Patty had come in carrying a good-sized wicker basket laden with warm baguettes and covered in a blue and white checkered cloth. The boys, including Joey, momentarily restrained themselves from making any snide remarks. Could Sister possibly be fooled into believing that this polite behavior was normal in the Kenealy house?

"We will have dinner in a moment. But first, I was thinking that perhaps we might want to say grace," said Sister.

We concurred, bowing our heads, crossing our hearts, and folding our hands, expecting Sister to begin the prayer. Instead, she turned to Patty and asked, "Who should lead us?"

"Joey," she snidely answered.

We all glanced up in time to see Joey grimace. He crossed himself, muttered a few indistinct words, crossed himself again, then loud enough to be heard said, "Amen."

Sister wasn't impressed.

"My friend, I did not hear you. Would you please say the grace once more for all of us and the Good Lord to hear?"

Joey cleared his throat. "In the name of the Father, Son and Holy Spirit. God is good, God is great, and we thank him for our food. AMEN."

"Amen," we sang, crossing ourselves again.

"Perhaps, Monsieur Joey, we should try the following version," said Sister dutifully bowing her head after giving the nod to Patty.

"'Shank' you, shishter. Blesh ush,'O Lord, and 'theesh' your 'giftsh,' which we are about to 'resheive' from your bounty. 'Schrough Chrisht' our Lord. Amen."

Another "amen" chorus, another sign of the cross. I noticed my father's approving glance at Patty, who was now making a move to collect everyone's "soup" bowl. Carefully placing the stack before Sister Marguerite's petite yet commanding form, Patty spoke, and with great elan I might add.

"Tonight, in honor of fish Friday," Patty started.

Joey, never able to contain himself, butted in. "Patty, haven't you ever heard of Vatican Two? We don't have to eat fish on Fridays anymore!" he stated provocatively.

"'Shush' up, Joey," Patty lambasted him, "and let me finish what I was 'shaying.'"

Sister wisely moved behind Joey and placed a firm hand on his shoulder.

"As I was 'shaying,'" she continued, "In honor of fish Friday, we're having fish. And tonight I made a fish 'shoop.' It's called 'bull-yu-baysh.'"

"See, Gail, I told you she wanted to make boo-boo-base," Timmy imperiously stated from his perch atop the Yellow Pages.

"Mmmm, it sounds most délicieux!" Raymond said sarcastically. Frankie eyed him darkly while nudging him hard to be quiet.

Sister Marguerite returned to the soup tureen and removed its lid, allowing a nicely pungent and spicy saffron smell to emanate throughout the room. It was rather enticing. Ladle by ladle she served up portions of soup, while Patty cheerfully passed the bowls and doled out the bread.

"Sister, won't you join us?" my father asked.

"Merci, Monsieur Kenealy. But the answer is no. Tonight I am here to assist the chef," she said in her upbeat manner.

Patty finally took her place at the table, at which point we commenced eating. Our family history was full of strange and random moments. And this was clearly one of them. No one said a word. And not because we didn't have anything nice to say, but because we were so absorbed in consuming this oddly delicate but hearty dish that we didn't feel like talking. Not a one of us was disappointed with this French classic comprised of herbs, seasonings, vegetables and a variety of fish. Nor with the crisp, beautiful bread – fresh and homemade with the love and help of Patty's hands.

I tasted a bit of lobster and then what would turn out to be monkfish along with some trout. There were tomatoes and onions, garlic, dill and olive oil. It was a melange of things I'd never tasted in one mix before, but it was most "délicieux."

"Patty," my father finally spoke through the energetic clatter of spoons hitting bowls, "What kind of soup is this again?"

"'Bull-yu-baysh.'"

"I must say, young lady, I'm quite impressed. You really *can* cook."

Finally, Patty had managed to silence all her critics with a stew not unlike this motley bunch – a unique blend that somehow managed to work.

"Yeah, Patty," said Joey, the first to finish and ask for more.

I looked over at Frankie, whose face expressed something more satisfying. "Patty," he spoke softly, "Mom, would be so proud of you."

An awkward silence ensued, as we were all so careful not to mention Cate in my mother's presence. Perhaps the combination of alcohol *and* bouillabaisse calming her troubled soul, she quietly and agreeably nodded her head.

"'Shanksh,' Frankie," Patty smiled affectionately at her older brother, creating an unspoken understanding. For so long it was Frankie who'd literally kept their bodies and souls together by preparing meals when no one else was capable or cared to do so.

"Sister," my father asked again, "Won't you please join us?"

"Merci, Monsieur, but I am expected back at the convent. Au revoir!" she chirped as she exited the dining room, but not before lightly bowing in front of Patty. She'd just about left the house when her mellifluous voice carried forward from the foyer, "Oh, and bon apetit!"

Indeed.

Chapter 14

The following day when Patty and I went to return Sister Marguerite's soup tureen, we were met by a very unexpected visitor: Frankie. He loved to cook and was so inspired by the previous day's events that he was already in the kitchen to witness the culinary oasis for himself.

"Hey!" Patty said, still dressed in her mock nun's habit. "No 'boysh' are allowed in here."

Sister Marguerite promptly defended him. "Patty, this young man wants to learn to cook just like you."

Where once her cooking skills had been jeered, her favorite brother now emulated her. Still, she persisted. "But no 'boysh' are allowed here."

"They are allowed in the kitchen, just nowhere else," Sister winked at her.

Patty absorbed this as if it were up to her to provide ultimate permission. "But jush so you know, I'm the bosh here."

Frankie heartily laughed. "Of course, you're the boss. So, with your permission may I join you today in learning how to make chicken cacciatore?"

"'Chicken—catsh-a-schtory?'" Patty genuinely tried repeating. We chuckled. But then, in her inimitable and loveable manner, she garnered the last laugh. "Do you know where chickens 'catsh a schtory?'" she asked.

"Where would that be?" Sister smiled.

"In a cook book," she grinned. We all cracked up, and I fell evermore in love with her realizing that she not only possessed an ability to feed the masses, but to humor us as well.

"Trés bien!" Sister giggled. "Anyone who can make me laugh is always the boss in my kitchen."

And that did it. Patty allowed Frankie to stay and make 'chicken-catch-a-story' with her before he was expected to begin a new job. Having no interest in this culinary exercise, I politely excused myself and pushing John in his pram headed over to the pool where I was met by an electrified Nadette.

"Guess what?" she asked.

"John O'Neill wants to marry me?"

"Maybe."

I swallowed. "Did he say he liked me?"

"Well, no. And I haven't talked to him. But there's a party tonight and I heard he's going. That's a start."

"For real?"

"Someone junked an old hearse near Apple Hill Farm, so the Murphy brothers are throwing a 'get dead drunk' party. You gotta come."

"A hearse? Was anyone left behind?"

"No, no dead bodies. But seriously, I heard John O'Neill is coming. And I know you're dying to see him."

I groaned.

"I thought that was pretty good," she wryly smiled, lighting up a cigarette. "Come on. Just look your best and join me. Pleeeaaasseee."

"You know I can't do that. Who's going to take care of the baby?"

"There are five-hundred people living in your house. Can't one of them watch him?"

"That's not the only problem. You know my Dad won't let me go to a keg party in some dark, remote woods."

"Don't tell him. Just say we're going to the movies."

"That's a lie."

"Seriously? Since when did that stop you?"

I hesitated. She was right. But lately I was always on the younger kids to stop lying to me or to one another, and suddenly doing so to my father had a different significance.

"I'm not going to do that."

"How will you ever marry John O'Neill if you stay home all the time? No wonder he goes out with Helen. SHE'S AVAILABLE."

"Did you have to put it like that?" I groaned, peeking in on John, who was sound asleep. To hasten my tan, I slathered on some baby oil and before leaning back in the pool chaise bummed a cigarette. The notion that Helen Hartley was stealing my fun while I was caring for a brood of children struck a raw nerve. "I'll ask Frankie," I finally said while exhaling.

I immediately felt guilty. And not for abandoning the kids, but because I was excluding Frankie from the frivolity. After showing up at the convent to get a head start on tonight's dinner, he was scheduled to start working at the Laurel Meat Market on Main Street. Unbelievably, just a few days earlier he'd actually sought *my* permission to accept the position. After the other kids had gone to bed and I was feeding John his last bottle for the night, he approached me.

"Gail," he said after gently tapping on my bedroom door.

"Come on in," I whispered, for Patty was already asleep.

"Thanks," he said, tip-toeing into the dimly-lit room. Sitting on the edge of my bed, he smiled sweetly as I sat in the rocker feeding John. "I have something to ask and something to say. Which would you prefer to hear first?"

"Is this like a good news, bad news thing?"

A warm, boyish grin encased his face. Frankie was blessed with his mother's good looks, but also a bit of her vulnerability. If not for the fact that he was insanely shy around girls, he could probably have any pick of them.

"It's all good. At least I think so."

"What's up?"

"I've been offered a job as a stock clerk at the Laurel Meat Market. You know, doing odds and ends kinda things."

"That's great," I smiled affirmatively.

"I haven't accepted it yet."

"How come?"

"Well, I decided I would take the job only under two conditions. The first is that *you* say it's okay, and the second is that you agree to let me pay you for helping out with the kids."

His selflessness dumbfounded me.

"Before you answer," he added, "there is something I need to say first." He looked downward again, then back at me with glistening eyes. Suddenly choked on emotion, he could barely talk.

"Just look at you," he softly said. "You're feeding my baby brother. In his mind, you're his mother. You've given up your summer to take care of us. And then your own mom is..."

Now my eyes unexpectedly welled up.

"I'm sorry. I didn't mean to make you cry. It's just that what I needed to say first is thank you. This has been the most painful time in my life — in all our lives — and I'm really sorry that we ruined your summer. And I want you to know how grateful I am for all you've done. I meant what I said, I won't take the job without some understanding between us. First, that you're okay with me doing this since I'll be gone a fair amount. And secondly, that you let me share my wages with you."

As John began dozing, I carefully removed the bottle and rocked him anew while pondering what Frankie had just shared and what his offer truly meant. Yes, I had missed out on a lot of carefree fun. But just as important, I'd lost the chance to earn and save money this summer, so his gesture meant I could at least make up some of the difference. Still, his losses were far greater.

"I'm not taking your money, Frankie," I finally responded.

"Then I won't take the job."

"Be serious."

"I am, because otherwise I wouldn't feel right and I won't have it any other way."

"Well, *I* won't have it any other way. We're a family and we take care of each other."

"Precisely. Which is why *I* need to take care of *you*."

I shook my head in downright wonder over his maturity and generosity. "Frankie, I don't think I've ever known anyone as, as...," I inwardly chuckled as his magnanimous gesture somehow conjured up the image of a brave knight.

"As what?" he insisted.

"Gallant."

He stifled a laugh. "Hardly. So it's a deal?"

"It's a deal. What else are you going to do with your money?"

"Well, like you," he smiled with genuine warmth, "I'm also saving my money for a car. But one day, what I really want, is to open my own rib joint. Frankie O'Brien's House of Ribs," he beamed over his specialty and our favorite. "After," he chuckled, "I get a job working for the NFL!"

Superficially one might think this orphaned child a bit off-kilter over these lofty goals. Not only an amazing cook, Frankie was an ardent football fan and successful volunteer coach for the Catholic Youth Organization. A former player himself, after becoming outsized by his high school team-mates he satisfied his love of the game with his impressive coaching skills. An avid reader of the sports pages, Frankie possessed an encyclopedic mind for statistics and was knowledgeable about national, college, and local teams. He could correctly tick off the names of coaches, their strat-egies, strengths and weaknesses, and which players were truly worth a damn. Apparently this talent helped him win three sizeable betting pools when choosing Heisman Trophy winners. He idolized Vince Lombardi, the most successful coach in professional football, and had previously shared a secret desire to one day work for "The Man," as he called him.

I reflected on all this as I approached him about going out with Nadette that night. It was following dinner – a delicious batch of "chicken-catch-a-story" with a fresh salad and home baked brownies for dessert. My mother had already gone to bed and my father was working. We were clearing plates.

"Can I talk with you?" I asked conspiratorially.

He looked around. "Sure. What's up?"

"Would you mind watching Patty and the baby tonight?" I continued whispering. "I want to go out with Nadette."

He chuckled. "Sounds like trouble. Where are you going?"

"Oh, I don't know. Some party," I said, reluctantly.

"Does your father know?"

I shook my head.

"Is that a good idea?"

"No. But I'm desperate for a night out."

"Well, then, don't let *me* stop you!"

I would later wish that he had.

Chapter 15

"*I* love Frankie," Nadette said when I called to share my plan.

"Yeah," I guiltily concurred. After hanging up with Nadette, I sought out Joey as I needed to purchase his shower time. Sensing my urgency, he put a one-dollar premium on it. I paid.

I showered, curled my hair, then sat beneath a hooded dryer in my bedroom, during which time I plunked John down on a blanket to amuse himself while I painted my toenails. He was on his tummy and raising his head in my direction. As he grinned, I cringed. More guilt.

Patty soon joined us plopping down on the floor beside John, her pillowcase veil deepening my sense of sin. "Where are you going?"

"Nowhere."

"Then why are you getting 'dreshy?'"

"I'm not getting dressy."

"You're getting 'dreshy.'"

"Well, I guess I... just feel like looking pretty. Do you want me to paint your nails, too?"

"Hmmm," mother superior replied, first checking out the color. She disapproved of my Fire Engine Red and took a pass.

"Gail, what do you want to be when you grow up?"

"Oh, I don't know. I guess a mother."

"But you're already a mommy."

"What do you mean?"

"You're 'John'sh' mommy. And you're like a mommy to me. I love sharing a room 'wish' you," she added, clearly enjoying this kind of bonding. I felt horrible. Nothing would stop me from going out, but her comments made my heart sink further.

"I love sharing a room with you, too," I smiled back. "Listen, it's getting late. You need to get ready for bed."

It was actually a half-hour early for Patty, but she obliged and shortly thereafter wearing pajamas and clutching her rosary beads, she was in bed. With my hair still in curlers, I retrieved one last bottle for John, dimmed the lights and then rocked and fed him while Patty said her goodnight prayers. She petitioned God to bless every living creature in our house, thanked him for taking care of her mother and finally asked God to help her own father, "Wherever he 'ish' because 'hish' heart 'worksh' way too 'shlow.'"

Like magic the two of them fell fast asleep. Tiptoeing around, I put on a pair of pressed white shorts and a sleeveless, blue-and-white gingham shirt that I tied at my waist so to give a peek of my abdomen. A trek in the woods called for my more practical Keds, but with newly polished toenails I opted for my favorite white sandals. After applying mascara and some lip gloss, I carefully brushed out my hair and was pulling it back in a ponytail when a devilish thought arose.

To hell with Helen Hartley, I thought while glancing in the mirror.

Instead I flipped my head over, and for the first time ever slightly teased my hair before allowing it to fall full and loose around my shoulders. It looked pretty. Suddenly feeling emboldened, I spritzed on some Chantilly perfume and added more lip gloss.

My father came home a bit later than expected, so I anxiously listened from upstairs as he served himself some leftovers, took a shower, then finally went to bed. Soon after ten o'clock, I peeked outside my bedroom door and could hear his steady snoring. I knew my mother was passed out, too. Grabbing my cigarettes, I gently tiptoed down to Frankie's room and lightly tapped on the door. He cracked it open.

"It must be someone special you're going to see," he grinned and whispered.

"Sort of. Not really. Well, maybe."

"You look pretty. Good luck. What time will you be back?"

"Not too late. There are two bottles in the fridge."

He nodded. "Have fun."

Quietly, I slipped outside and joined Nadette who was waiting for me on her front porch. A rare bird in our neighborhood, Nadette was the only child of Catholic parents, which more than once prompted her to quip, "They stopped trying after giving birth to such perfection."

Perhaps. But I always thought it was because they valued their freedom and being able to afford trendy things like new orange and yellow shag carpeting and late model cars. Her father was the manager at Citizen's National Bank on the corner of Fourth and Main. He always had money, or at least easy credit.

"Where are your parents?" I asked.

"Out," she said taking a drag off her cigarette.

"Lucky you."

"Says who? You look really pretty, by the way."

"Thanks. Are you sure John will be there?"

"Sean Murphy said that he'd invited the entire football team. And John's on the football team, so I'm assuming John will be there."

"I thought you said for sure he'd be there. The only reason I'm going is to see him."

"Isn't it enough to have a night out with me? Or in your case, even a night out?"

"Yeah, but ..."

"Let's go," she said. Turning around I headed straight for her car. She stopped me. "I'm not driving tonight."

"Why not?"

"'Cause it's a "dead drunk" party and I plan on getting dead drunk. Aren't you? Besides, I promised my parents I wouldn't drink and drive," she said, now stomping out her cigarette.

"They know you drink?"

"Oh, puh-lease. I've been using my fake ID for over a year to buy them alcohol. Come on, we're wasting time."

"I don't think that's something to brag about."

"You think?" she concluded the topic.

No strangers to Laurel in the dark, we made our way down to Route One then walked the two-mile distance to Apple Hill Farm chatting, smoking and carrying on like old times. Soon after traipsing down a dirt road in a remote wooded area, we heard the echo of raucous laughter.

"Great balls of fire!" Nadette blurted as we approached the scene. Multiple flashlights were aglow with at least three dozen of our schoolmates gathered around the back of an old, beat-up hearse – the rear door of which was propped open while a keg sat in the cargo hold. I could see a swath of ripped, red velvet hanging loosely from the ceiling, while tattered and yellowed lace curtains covered the windows. The sight of it would be creepy enough during the day, let alone the dark of night.

Melinda sighted us first. "Look who it is!" she shined a flashlight our way. It felt so uplifting to be warmly greeted by a swarm of old friends.

"Gail! How are you? Where have you been?" I repeatedly heard.

"I'm really sorry about your aunt," a few people offered sincere condolences.

"I heard what happened," one nitwit joined us, adding, "You look *really* great after just having had a baby!"

"I did not have a baby!" I defensively fired back, then set her straight.

I looked around the crowd, but didn't see John O'Neill. His absence was disappointing, but being out with my friends again made me soon forget. Nadette was just about to pour me my third beer when she suddenly began speaking like a ventriloquist. "Don't look now."

I immediately turned and out of the darkness he appeared, alone and more handsome than ever. John was quickly surrounded by admirers – girls and guys alike – leaving little room for me to exercise my newfound assertion.

"I told you so," she said. "Aren't you going to talk to him?"

"Yes. But let him come to me first."

"Oh, the old hard to get routine. How's that been working for you lately?"

"Shut up."

"Do you want me to mention that you're here?"

"No, don't be stupid. He'll see me." But after finishing my fourth beer and third cigarette, he still hadn't broken from the small mob. Realizing a greater urge, I stumbled off to the woods alone to pee.

Presumably out of everyone's sight, I pulled down my shorts and under-wear and attempted a position so as not to piss on myself, but immediately lost my footing and tumbled backwards down a small embankment and into a shallow ravine. It wasn't such a long trip to the bottom. But in the dark, I didn't know when I would stop rolling and my shrill cry for help along the way made it seem like I was falling to the center of the earth. In seconds there were six people coming to my rescue. John reached me first.

"Are you okay?" he earnestly asked.

"Yeah," I said, somewhat dazed while reaching for his outstretched hand.

Oh, my god! Oh, my god! He's holding my hand!

"Does it feel like anything is broken?"

"I don't think so. I'm okay, really."

With that, he secured his footing then gently pulled me up.

"What happened?" he asked.

"I guess I kinda fell," I slurred.

"Uh-hum, Gail," I heard Nadette as Melinda's flashlight shone upon us from the ridge. I was so enthralled by John's heroism that I intentionally ignored her.

"Gail," she snapped as the others began to laugh.

John bent down close to my face, and now determined to outmatch Helen, I impulsively planted my lips upon his for a kiss, which he briefly and kindly reciprocated before moving his mouth near my ear.

"If you'd like," he whispered, "I'll stand in front of you while you pull your pants up."

No, a thousand times, no. In my drunken stupor and love-struck oblivion I had not bothered to secure my shorts. With John as my shield, I pulled everything back in place while wishing like hell I was at home and in the confines of my bedroom feeding his namesake a bottle.

"All clear?" John asked.

"I'm good," I contritely rejoined. He turned around and kind of smirked. "Here, let me help you," he offered, then promptly began pulling woodsy debris out of my hair.

Nadette quickly joined us, her stifled amusement only worsening my mortification. "Gail, are you okay?"

"I'm going home," I declared.

"Now? The party just got started."

"Yes, now."

"But I'm not ready to leave."

"Then I'll go home alone."

"No you won't," John interjected. "I'll get you back there. I've got my Dad's car out by the main road."

"I'm okay," I insisted.

"I will not let you walk alone. Come on, let's go," he said taking hold of my hand.

"See ya," said Nadette, her voice ringing with optimism while he guided me up the hill. As her flashlight illuminated our path, I turned and looked. She was likewise making wild gestures for me to call her. Hoping John didn't see, I stuck my tongue out at her and kept going. Shortly we were away from the crowd and on the moonlit dirt road leading up to Route One.

"Seriously, are you okay?" he asked warmly while still casually holding my hand. I was so absorbed by the size and tenderness of *his* hand and by feeling so safe, that at first I didn't answer.

The best part about a secret crush was that in my mind everything always worked in my favor. We were the perfect couple and everything was easy-peasy. He loved me, I loved him. We never argued. We'd go to prom. One day we'd get married and live happily ever after.

In reality, I'd always been petrified to talk to him first because then the dream might die. When we actually spoke, our conversations were brief and always general in nature. Regardless, I would later dissect every word and nuance for deeper meaning. It might have been the alcohol's liberating effect, or Nadette's admonition that Helen was always available, but a surprising and unabashed sincerity arose.

"Truthfully, I'm not okay. I'm drunk. And I'm embarrassed. Actually, I'm really drunk and I'm really, really embarrassed."

"I could tell, I mean about the drunk part. I just want to make sure you're not hurt in any way."

"Naw," I nonchalantly responded, then chuckled at the absurdity of it all. "You didn't happen to notice if my underwear said 'Saturday' on it, did you?"

Still holding my hand he threw his head back and heartily laughed. "No."

"Well that's something to be thankful for because if it said 'Thursday' then you might think of me as a slob."

He laughed some more. "Honestly, I wasn't paying attention to any of that. I was more concerned you might have been injured."

"Does my pride count?"

"Brace yourself. Everything will hurt worse tomorrow."

"Are you speaking from similar experience?" I chortled.

"No. It's a little easier for us guys, if you know what I mean."

I now had eight males in my family — seven of them potty-trained — with one bathroom and two toilets. I was enlightened by images of the boys periodically pissing in the backyard bushes.

"By the way," he said turning more somber, "I heard about your Aunt's death, your Uncle, and then about your cousins coming to live with you," he said compassionately. "I'm really sorry."

"Thanks. How'd ya' know?" I asked as if it were all a well-kept secret.

"I saw Tommy at the beach last week and he filled me in a little bit."

"A little bit" is right because a little bit is all he knows, I thought about my older brother who was living life large and had no clue just how bad things were. Like MJ, Tommy had basically ignored us all summer.

"Football practice starts next week, so he said he'd be home soon. Is he back yet?"

"Nope, and I don't know when to expect him, either."

"I see," he said, and probably detecting a note of indifference changed the subject. "So how's your summer been?"

"Rotten. I haven't been to the beach once," I offered as if that were my only setback.

"That stinks."

"How about yours?" I asked, eager to change the topic myself.

"Pretty good, I guess. I made some trips to look at colleges."

My heart sank. In one year he'd be gone. "Really? Where?"

"Oh, here and there. I looked at Maryland, of course. And then the University of Virginia – which I really like – and a few others."

"UVA, huh? You want to be a Cavalier?"

"Yeah, but it's too rich for my family's budget. I'd have to get a big scholarship. Any idea where you want to go to college?"

"Not really," I said, actually thinking, *wherever you go.*

I wanted to ask him about Helen. I wanted to ask him if they were serious. I wanted to tell him there was a baby at my house named after him. I didn't. Shortly we were in his car and at my darkened house. He offered to walk me up to the front door when I told him it wasn't cool. "My parents don't know I'm out."

He softly laughed, his dimples folding in deep.

"Well, then, good luck slipping in. Should I wait just in case?"

"No, they always leave the house unlocked. By the way, I'm sorry I kissed you."

"You are?"

"Well, I mean, it was kind of impulsive and inappropriate and I was just, I was just..."

With that he leaned over and pecked me sweetly on the cheek. His nearness was intoxicating. "Except for the fact that I'm not a smoker and you are, it was a mighty fine kiss."

Humiliated once more, I got out of the car. "So you think I taste like an ashtray?" I boldly asked while leaning through the car window.

He grinned. "Yeah, a little. Good night, Gail. See ya' around."

"Good night, John Aloysius-you're-incredibly-delicious-O'Neill," I whispered as he drove away.

My humiliation was not to end there. I tried opening the front door, but it was locked. The back door was shut tight, too. I mildly panicked realizing my father had probably gotten up and, after noticing I was gone, decided to force me to knock on the door. I felt dejected. Is this what to expect should I ever runaway?

Instead of making a spectacle by knocking or trying a window, I climbed into the tree house and curled up in a sleeping bag on one of

the bunks. But not before smoking what would truly be my last cigarette. When dawn broke I tried the back door again, this time finding it
unlocked along with a note from my father on the kitchen table.

*Gail, please let me know where you are going the next time you head out at
night. Love, Dad.*

Chapter 16

*I*t was just about noon when she walked in the door. With her raven hair, dark tan, violet eyes and gorgeous body, Mary Joyce Kenealy was truly a beautiful girl. Her personality was perpetually sunny and in her view every day was Saturday.

My mother cried at the sight of her, not fully aware just how much she'd missed her eldest daughter. They'd last seen each other at Aunt Cate's funeral, during which my mother had been wholly preoccupied. After which Mary Joyce promptly returned to the beach.

Now eighteen-years-old, she had one more week before starting at Salisbury State College where she hoped to receive a degree in early childhood education. Her natural sweetness made her particularly well suited for that kind of work. This was apparent as she spent considerable time chatting with Patty who described her new friends at the convent, her new shoes, her new baby brother, her new shoes again, and then how hard it was to take a shower in ten minutes. While patiently listening to Patty, MJ lovingly held and fed John, bonding with him almost instantly. I felt surprising jealousy when he grinned at her ticklish prompting.

At dinner – over Patty and Frankie's leftover "chicken-catch-a-story" – she talked about life at the beach and described it as the best experience she'd ever had. Her disposition was so Pollyannaish I believe she'd say that about shoveling manure. Anyway, she'd made nearly $3,000 waiting tables at the renowned Phillip's Crab House. My parents were ecstatic. Again, I was jealous.

She shared funny stories about carefree living in a house with five other girls who, like her, worked hard on their tans and flirting skills all day at the beach, then flaunted said tans while flirting for tips at the restaurant each night. So what that she'd hauled heavy platters of crabs and pitchers of beer. Her arms were remarkably toned and her skin was perfectly tanned.

Mary Joyce was one of those people for whom everything came easy and who always seemed to get all the breaks. I'd always emulated her in every conceivable way, eagerly wearing her cast-off clothing if it meant that I might look more like her. No one ever raved about my beauty like they did hers, and occasionally I'd been told of some resemblance. It was a weak compliment, but better than none whenever the comparison was made.

When at last the entire family had gone to bed, and Patty and John were fast asleep in our room, she jumped in the shower. Contrary to our new bathroom rules, I brazenly walked in just as she climbed out. It was hard to miss the small patches of glaring white skin in the shape of a bikini upon her darkly tanned skin. It was also hard to miss that she'd put on some weight – mostly, it seemed, in her boobs. MJ never flinched over being naked around me, particularly as privacy was a rare commodity in our lives. Suddenly, though, she startled and quickly threw a towel around herself. "What do you want?"

"To use the toilet," I casually replied, as if we hadn't shared this room a thousand times before.

"I thought the new rule was ten minutes to ourselves."

"Sorry," I said, leaving truly surprised and wondering how she'd managed any privacy at the beach with five other teenaged girls in a one-bathroom house.

Shortly, we were ready to settle in. As Patty was asleep in MJ's bed, we agreed to share mine. But not before getting caught up.

"So, how's your summer been? Have you seen that cutie, John O'Neill, at all?"

Aunt Cate was dead. Uncle Francis remained at large. Our mother was emotionally crippled. Plus there were five more children and another dog living in our house. Nothing in *her* sunny world seemed to have changed, so why wouldn't she pick up where we'd left off? Only because she'd asked about my favorite topic, I seamlessly rejoined.

"You won't believe this," I recounted with fresh embarrassment the incidents of the previous night, telling her about my half-naked, drunken stumble into the ravine, of John's rescue, and then later of sleeping in the tree house. Giggling uncontrollably, MJ buried her face in a favorite stuffed lion to keep from waking the others.

"Do you even own day-of-the-week underwear?" she asked, wiping away tears of laughter.

"Nope."

This set her to laughing anew. "And you really quit smoking? For ever and for sure?"

"Yep," I said adamantly, then grew more serious. "Now let me ask you a question. Why did you stay away all summer?"

Her expression darkened as her voice grew defensive. "I didn't want to lose my job."

"Don't you think they would have understood that your family's going through a tough time? Besides, I'm sure you could have gotten a waitressing job here."

"I suppose. Truthfully, Gail, I had more important things I was dealing with."

Her demeanor shocked me. Mary Joyce, the good girl. Mary Joyce, the one whom our mother held up as a shining example of virtue. Mary Joyce, who seemed closer to our mother than any of the other children. It just didn't sound like her talking.

"More important than your own family?"

Instead of answering she quietly massaged her abdomen.

"You might not have noticed just yet," I pressed her, "but Ma's drinking pretty heavily."

"What do you mean, 'heavily?' Are you sure?"

"It's bad. She's even mixing booze with her morning coffee. Sometimes she sleeps half the day. Even when she's awake, she leaves me in charge of everybody. To make things worse, Mrs. Logan fell and broke her hip, so Ma's been going over there to help her."

"That fat, old drunk?" she said incredulously.

"Yeah, and when she comes home she's *really* loopy. Big surprise, huh?"

"What does Dad say?"

"We haven't talked about it specifically, but it would be hard to miss. Especially two nights ago after Ma had been at Mrs. Logan's all day, then fell flat on her face just walking in the door."

"Well, even *I've* done that!" she chuckled. "Besides, you bared your butt to the world in a drunken fall last night. How different is that?"

"Seriously? We're teenagers. She's a forty-two-old mother. In fact, the *entire* family watched from the dining room table. You know what Dad did? Without a word he got up and put her to bed. He doesn't know how to handle it."

"Wow," she said nonchalantly, then in her customary effervescent manner added, "Well, you're doing a great job keeping the house clean."

Un-be-liev-a-ble. I just told her our mother was a newly minted drunk and that I was burdened with taking care of all the children. Yet her only reaction was to compliment me on good housekeeping.

"Does a seal of approval come with that stupid comment?"

"Why are you being so mean?"

"Because I'm taking care of a baby and I barely have time to take care of myself, which can make my life really sucky. If the house is clean it's because Dad has turned into a drill master where certain things are concerned."

"Hmmm," she obliviously responded, then got up and gazed at John in his crib. "Don't you love babies?" she asked, clearly not hearing "baby" and "sucky" in the same sentence. "I do," she added, her voice still dreamy and optimistic.

"Are you nuts? Wait till you have to take care of one all the time! I'm an expert now and I can tell you it's exhausting."

"It's different when it's your *own* baby," she reacted with benign authority. "I mean, think about it. A child you've created with someone you love. What greater thing could possibly exist than to bring two souls together into one beautiful baby?"

I must say that her level of blithe ignorance in the matter was matched only by a higher level of sleep-deprived awareness in me. I knew now as a cold-hard fact that there was no harder job in the world than raising a child. Period.

"Gail," she whispered conspiratorially. "Can you keep a secret?"

"Sure."

"No, I mean *really* keep a secret?"

"I've always kept your secrets. Why wouldn't I now?"

"Because this one is bigger than any other secret I've ever shared with you before." I could tell by her brightened eyes and tone of voice that my fidelity mattered, but only a fraction less than the news she was busting to share.

"Promise?" she pushed.

"Promise," I said, deeply curious.

She was wearing a pair of white baby-doll pajamas with short pants that showed off her shapely legs. Not far from me, she lifted up the top and lowered her pants just enough to show her belly.

"Look at this," she glowed. "I'm going to have a baby of my own!"

After all the shocking developments over the past few months it scarcely seemed possible that anything else could render me speechless. But I was tongue-tied. Now that I could see her abdomen more closely it was obvious. It resembled a frog's slightly swollen vocal sac. Soon it would be one big balloon attached to her body. She grabbed my hand and placed it below her belly-button. "Say hi to your new niece or nephew."

I instantly recoiled. "You're pregnant!" I exclaimed so loud that Patty stirred, but fortunately didn't wake.

"Keep it down," she hissed. "I don't want Ma and Dad to know. At least not yet."

"Just exactly when are you planning on breaking the news to them?"

"After they've had a chance to meet my husband," she said coyly.

My voice edged higher. "'Did you and Bobby elope?" I asked of her longtime beau.

"Shhhhhhh!" she whispered mischievously. "It's not Bobby's baby."

It was like she'd just spoken to me in Chinese. I sat in stunned silence.

"Did you hear me?" she said excitedly. "It's *not* Bobby's baby."

"I thought you loved him forever and ever."

"That was true until I met Steve, who is actually my fiancé. Steve changed everything," she said with more dreamy optimism.

Until this point, almost everything Mary Joyce Kenealy had done in her life I had wanted to do in spades. Suddenly, I felt the upper hand. "Please tell me that this is not happening," I said rather soberly.

"Aren't you happy for me?"

"No. You're pregnant, you're not married and you haven't gone to college. When exactly did you meet Steve?"

"Senior weekend."

"How pregnant are you?"

She coyly glanced down while biting her lower lip.

"Oh, no," I said, quickly realizing she was nearly four months pregnant. It really was like talking with a foreigner. "Who exactly is this Steve guy?"

"Well, he's a golf pro."

"As in he's 'on tour' golf pro?"

"Yes! He plays in the PGA," she gushed.

"Let me guess. You met him at the Ocean City Putt-Putt and fell in love after watching him sink a fifteen-footer under the dragon's butt."

"Stop it," she chastised me. "He just graduated from the University of Maryland and was on their golf team. But I know he'll be the next Jack Nicklaus. He's just as handsome, too," she carried on. "Why aren't you happy for me?"

I answered her question with two of my own. "When are you getting married? And what about college?"

"I'm not going. At least not right now. Instead, I'm – or rather we're – moving to Florida. I'm going ahead of Steve to find an apartment and get everything ready for the baby. He'll join me in November after he's done with the tour. Then we'll get married."

"So, pregnant and on your own until then? Ma and Dad will do cartwheels over this one."

"I'll be fine!" she enthused. "And I know they'll be so happy since it's their first grandchild! Oh, wait till you meet Steve. You'll love him. And you'll love having a place to visit in Florida," she added like a game show hostess hawking a prize trip.

"MJ, I know as much about professional golf as you do. Still, doesn't it seem odd that he'd be touring up until November? Are there even tournaments in the winter?"

"That's why we're going to Florida!"

"And exactly when are you planning to get married?"

"Maybe December."

I closed my eyes and did the math. "I'll take that wedding gown in a size seven-to-eight months-pregnant. MJ this is insane."

I was furious. Hadn't my parents suffered enough anguish lately? Learning that their oldest child was pregnant out-of-wedlock would devastate them. I at least had the good sense and enough empathy to know this.

"Listen, I'm not suggesting that you lie to Ma and Dad. But maybe you could go easy on them."

"What are you saying?"

"That you hold off telling them the truth," I said forthrightly.

"Why?" she became defensive. "That's not being very honest."

"Right. Which is why going to Florida is a *really* good idea. And instead of telling them about Mr. PGA, just say you changed your mind and decided to go to a small college in Florida – one that you'd always dreamed of attending and where you could keep your tan. And then, with that $3,000 you earned this summer, and with whatever your 'fiancé' chips in, you go ahead and set up house down there. Tell them you're studying all the time. They don't have to know that you're majoring in home economics. Big time."

"I hate you," she blurted and started crying. "Why are you so nasty? I thought *you'd* be happy for me."

This was nothing of what I'd expect from her. She was a different girl now sitting on the end of my bed. Or, perhaps, it was a different me sitting opposite her.

"What do you know about this Steve guy?"

"He has a last name, you know. Barelli."

"As in Barelli Construction?" I muttered.

"I think," she nodded, wiping away a tear. "He said his father is in some construction business."

The Barelli family was an institution in the tony town of Chevy Chase. And it wasn't just 'some' construction company they owned. It seemed they'd built half of the state of Maryland. I knew this because when doing morning crossword puzzles I typically scanned the news. Had Mary Joyce read more than the funnies she would have known that old man Barelli was a wealthy builder and philanthropist often featured in the business and society pages. In fact, he was apparently a devout Catholic and his company was involved in ongoing construction projects at the Basilica and Catholic University in Washington, D.C.

"Where's your ring?" I asked, now needing more evidence than a slightly pregnant belly of this pending union.

She got up from the bed, fished a gold ring with a diminutive diamond chip out of her purse, slipped it on her ring finger and held her hand up to my face. "See," she stated. "It's really real. And I am really going to be Mrs. Steven Dominic Barelli."

"Wow," I said with sheer disbelief. "His family is worth millions and all you got was that piece of crap?"

"I hate you," she repeated. "Why are you being so mean? It's because you're jealous, aren't you?"

"For the first time in my life that's not true," I said with absolute confidence. "I just don't approve. You got pregnant before you were married and you don't even know this guy. My guess is that you were attracted to him because of his money."

"You're wrong."

"Oh spare me."

"No, you're wrong. I had no idea who he was or where he came from or how much money he had. He is really, really cute, though," she said, with a hint of whimsy. "Anyway, one night after drinking Mai Tais at a beach party, we took a walk and that's when he started sharing his dreams with me about making it big in the PGA. I was so impressed. And he said with someone like me cheering him on he felt like he could really make it big. Then one thing led to another and the next thing you know...."

"He sank a hole in one," I interjected.

"Yeah." She surprisingly agreed while tenderly rubbing her abdomen. "But things happen for a reason, you know. God has a plan for me and must have wanted us to be together and for me to have this baby."

"MJ, just for the record, I don't think God's plan to be fruitful and multiply should be confused with consuming fruity alcoholic drinks and having sex with strangers."

"You're a fine one to talk," she snapped. "Just last night you were half-naked and kissing John O'Neill after getting drunk. What do you have to show for that? At least *I'm* engaged," she said, defiantly flashing the ring in my face again.

"And pregnant. Besides, John is no stranger and I've loved him forever."

"Well, Steve and I fell in love at first sight. So there. And *we're* getting married."

"You don't even have a wedding date. By the way, where is he now?"

"Phoenix. I think."

"You *think?*" I said incredulously.

She shrugged her shoulders.

"You don't really know where he is, do you? Is he supporting you in any way? Has he given you any money to get 'everything ready for the baby?'"

She didn't respond.

"So while you're carrying his baby along with two-ton trays of food and beer he's at some cushy club – and God only knows where – playing golf? I hate to disappoint you, but this guy doesn't even know you and he's not supporting you. How could he love you?"

Clearly I struck the rawest nerve. Suddenly she began sobbing and yet again buried her face in the stuffed lion. Fortunately Patty and John remained sound asleep.

"Now what's wrong?"

She answered, but with her head hung low I could barely hear her.

"What?" I pressed.

She looked up, now clearly speaking the fragile truth. "I'm scared. I mean, *really* scared," she paused, waiting for my reaction. Her entire countenance had changed, rapidly shifting from sunny and low eighties to board up your windows and evacuate. I leaned closer, as barely whispering she revealed more.

"He rarely calls me and he never writes. I only saw him three other times over the summer. The first time was when I told him I was pregnant. Right away he wanted me to have an abortion. But I said no. So then the next time was when he proposed and decided we should move to Florida. He made me promise to keep it all a secret because he's worried about his professional image. Which I totally understand. It could end up in the news and that's the last thing we want. And then when he said good-bye to me at the beach."

I repeated my earlier question. "Did he at least give you money to help you out?"

"No," she blubbered on, her elastic hope stretching even thinner, "I can't believe this is happening to me. I don't know the first thing to do." She lowered her head again. "I feel so ashamed. I can barely take care of myself. How can I take care of a baby?"

My sister rarely asked my advice on anything beyond how she looked. Being three years older she was presumably wiser on all matters in life. Now just inches apart on my narrow twin bed, I felt a new chasm between us as I had the answers she sought. I knew firsthand the frustration, angst, anger, tedium, sacrifice and overall hardship that arises in caring for a baby. The needs of all the other children in our house were just as great. The only difference was that I wasn't changing their diapers ten times a day. They all required steady supervision and nurturing, and I'd learned that being a parent was flat-out the hardest job in the world with enormous overhead and no time off. I knew better than ever now that there was a time and a place for everything. And that having someone's child out of wedlock — and worse, someone who didn't truly know, love and care about you — could be one of the fastest routes to potential self-destruction, as well as damage to an innocent baby's life. Crawling through the other stuffed animals, I hugged my sister, at the same time realizing how strange it was that a new life was growing inside her. We were both crying now.

"Tell me, honestly," she said, finally reaching for a tissue, "what is it really like taking care of a baby?"

I took hold of her hand and tenderly kissed it as if trying to break the fall.

"MJ, I'm not going to sugar coat this. It is *soooo* hard. Remember how we used to play with our dolls on the front porch, then leave them there while we ran off to do something else? It's nothing like that. You can't just take off on a whim and leave a real baby to do what you want. Right now – when he's asleep – is basically the only break I get. Otherwise, I feel like I have a barnacle stuck to my body that sucks all the energy out of me."

"But what if he were your own baby? You would love him and want to be with him all the time, right?" she said. We both leaned our backs against the wall and looked over at John peacefully sleeping.

"I guess, I mean I don't know. But what I do know is that whether you're taking care of your own baby or someone else's, the baby's needs always come first. Right now I am completely sleep, tan and fun deprived. Basically my life is one big diaper change. Nadette sometimes helps, and Frankie also pitches in. But now he has a job at the Laurel Meat Market and Nadette is free to have fun and has the best tan. And because Ma is utterly drunk and depressed and Dad is always working, it's up to me to make sure this baby survives. In fact, that all the children are cared for."

It was my turn to grab a tissue. "It's really hard," I cried. "Every day has felt like I'm taking a pop quiz I never studied for; sometimes I pass, sometimes I don't. Even when they're healthy, babies are extremely needy. And it's doubly hard when they get sick. I lived at the hospital for two weeks in July when he had pneumonia. I felt so horrible. I'd been treating him like a rag doll. Thankfully he's okay. But he could have died or suffered lifelong disabilities because I ignored some of his most basic needs."

Her eyes widened. "I had no idea you were dealing with all of this. And why would you be expected to know how to care for him? You're just a kid yourself."

"No, of course, you didn't know about this. You've been at the beach waiting for that jackass to carry you off into the sunset. And there you are, basically a kid yourself and about to give birth to a barnacle."

"Stop being so bitter with me."

"First, if I sound bitter it's because I'm burned out. Don't forget, babies turn into bratty children. Patty is a piece of cake compared to Raymond and Paul. Think about it. In the span of one month those kids lost both their parents. I know they're relieved to be here. But they're suffering and it doesn't take much to provoke them into fighting with each other. Joey and Timmy are no better. Whenever Dad or Frankie are around they generally behave. Otherwise, they all have ways of torturing me and each other. It makes me crazy."

"But I believe if you give them unconditional love they will love you back."

"You're really clueless."

"Yeah, maybe," she gently leaned her head upon my shoulder. "But I'm an unwed, pregnant teenager and I have to believe in something," she said, fresh tears falling. "I've even thought of putting this baby up for adoption."

"You can't do that!"

"Why not? You just called my baby a barnacle. You make it sound like the worst thing in the world."

"I'm sorry," I sighed. She was right. All I'd said was true. Still, in just a few short months I had shared several happy milestone's in John's life. I felt thrilled when he was released from the hospital after his near-death experience, particularly after personally witnessing his healing and growth. To see it continually unfold before my eyes was another side of the story, and simply a continuation of what had begun deeply protected within Cate's womb. It was all pretty miraculous to me. Realizing MJ's need for genuine encouragement in this very real dilemma, I softened my tone.

"I'm sorry, I really am. I didn't mean to be so harsh. And I hope you will never have an abortion or put your baby up for adoption. There are a lot of good things in store for you."

"Like what?"

The answers flowed. "You know what I didn't expect? How my heart could melt over just one gummy grin. Or how incredibly strong and peaceful I feel when rocking John to sleep knowing he feels safe in *my* arms. And then I think of how amazing it is that while I'm holding this itty-bitty baby right now, one day he'll be a full-grown man. All that beautiful potential exists right there, right now. It just needs to be nurtured to maturity.

"In the meantime, that nurturing means constant attention, and you really do need to want and love that baby unconditionally to give it your best. Even if you're not with it, you'll be thinking about it. So it's easy to feel resentful and burned out, like I tend to get. Especially if you don't have much money or help. Because then you're always struggling and sacrificing all your fun and maybe even personal potential for the sake of someone else. That's all."

She blew her nose. "I get it. Taking care of a baby is hard work and a pain in the ass. Still, if it's yours, then it has to be different. I already love my baby. And *he*," she added, glancing over at John, "is so lucky to have *you*." She looked back at me. "I wish you would come to Florida with me."

It was tempting.

"Thanks, MJ. Listen, I'll help you however I can. Do me a huge favor though. Help Ma and Dad first by waiting a little bit longer before telling them. It's been a living hell for both of them these past few months. Besides, Ma is already treading in the deep end, and I'm afraid she'd sink to the bottom over this news."

Blind to any other solutions, I encouraged her current plans. "So I guess you should just go to Florida, then tell them everything when they can meet Steve in person. At that point I think they'll be far more prepared to accept the news. Especially when you tell them the part about Steve being really rich," I said, fostering false hope myself that this wealthy, handsome guy would actually take care of my hopelessly naive sister and their innocent baby.

"I love you, Gail."

"I thought you hated me."

"I did. But, really, I love you."

"Care for some pickles with that opinion?"

The next morning at the breakfast table, Mary Joyce was feeding John his bottle when she suddenly blurted that she had some really exciting news to share with my parents. My father put down his paper. My mother set down her spiked coffee. My stomach flipped.

"What is it, sweetheart?" my mother serenely responded.

I held my breath as my sister looked at me before speaking, then began telling the most bald-faced lie I'd ever heard.

"Well, I know we hadn't discussed this before. But there's a college in Florida with a wonderful early childhood education program. And guess what? I applied and I got in! Plus, I got a full scholarship!"

I suppose if you're going to lie, then why not make it big? Right now my parents' ignorance was a blessing as they had no idea that colleges did not admit students or award scholarships this late in the summer. Now glowing, my father didn't even bother to ask the name of the school as all he'd heard was that he didn't have to pay for it.

"Oh, praise the Lord!" he said. "I knew you were smart. But not, well...that's great news, honey."

My mother was on her feet and wrapping her arms around MJ's neck. "Oh, I'm so proud of you. I mean, really, really proud of you." It was the first time I'd seen her express any kind of true joy in months.

"So then you're not going to Salisbury State next week?" my genius father inquired.

"No, Dad. I'm heading south. Today, in fact. I'm so excited."

"This is the best news I've heard in ages!" My mother went on. "And just think. You'll have the most fabulous tan all year long."

Priorities.

"Absolutely!" MJ beamed, making me wonder if she and my mother were sharing the same flavored coffee.

"I'll have to come visit you," I said gamely.

"Anytime, Sis."

"What town is it in and what's the name of this college?" my father finally got around to asking. Again, I held my breath. Was it hoping for too much that the floor would suddenly cave in?

"Our Lady of Perpetual Help," my sister astutely responded. "It's in uhm...it's uhm, in a small town near...uhm...Tampa."

"So is it on the west coast of Florida?" he asked.

"Yup, I think so. I've got all the information packed up in my car. I promise I'll write," she radiantly smiled, now burping John.

"Our Lady of Perpetual Help," Dad said thoughtfully. "I've never heard of it. But it sounds like a good Catholic school and I'm sure that you will graduate with top honors."

"Thanks, Dad!" By her enthusiastic tone, I think even MJ believed that to be true.

"This sounds too good to be true," my mother began crying, then took a big swallow of her coffee.

"I'll say," said Dad. "Gail, maybe you should think of applying to school there, too."

"I dunno, Dad. The admission standards are pretty stiff," I grinned, then silently said a prayer.

Our Lady of Perpetual Help, please help us.

Chapter 17

It was a Saturday morning. And almost as soon as Mary Joyce rolled out in her old, red Ford Fairlane, Tommy rolled in. Raven-haired, violet-eyed and more bronzed than her, he'd clearly been working out over the summer to bulk up for his final football season at Pallotti.

"How's it goin', Sis?" he pecked my cheek then started gagging. I was in the bathroom changing one of John's fermented diapers. "Barf! How can you stand that?"

"It's no different than anything else I deal with around here," I said, my mood more sour than the diaper.

"That bad, huh?" he chortled, sitting on the tub's ledge. "By the way, I brought two friends home from the beach."

I glowered. "More isn't merrier around here. Just where were you planning on putting them?"

"Back in their own beds. I'm talking about Joey and Timmy."

"'Joey and Timmy?'" I repeated incredulously. Yes, he nodded with a mischievous twinkle in his eye.

"What are you talking about? Joey told me yesterday they were spending the night at the Millstein's."

"Yeah, the Millstein's beach house. I picked those two knuckleheads up while they were hitchhiking on the main drag in Ocean City."

"*Hitchhiking?*" *My eight and twelve-year-old brothers?*

"I came home a day early to bring them back. What a waste, considering no one missed them."

"Could this family get any more dysfunctional? Thank God you saw them. And please don't tell Ma or Dad. They have their own share of woes right now. By the way," I said, steering him toward my primary concern. "MJ just left. Did you see her at the beach very much?"

"Not really. My life guard station was fifty blocks north from where she lived, and then she worked nights. Occasionally I'd run into her at a party on her night off. She doing okay?"

"I suppose. This might come as something of a shock to you, but she's moving to Florida instead of going to Salisbury."

"Really? Why?"

I deeply sighed. "Different program. Apparently a full scholarship somewhere else."

"Far out. Ma and Dad must be happy. But what about Bobby? He must be broken-hearted."

"I would imagine. Though she didn't talk as much about him as she did some guy named Steve Barelli."

"The dude whose father owns Barelli Construction?"

"So you know him?"

"Yeah, well, sort of. His family has a huge beach house near my guard station. I met Steve a few times with his fiancée."

My blood ran cold. "His what?"

"His fiancée. Really preppie chick who went to Stone Ridge and then Sweet Briar College. She grew up with him in Chevy Chase. Connie Sullivan. They've dated for years. She's got quite a rock, too."

John squirmed as I pulled rubber pants over his fresh diaper. I handed him over to Tommy. "That son-of-a-bitch," I muttered while angrily dunking the soiled cloth diaper in and out of the toilet.

"Why do you say that?"

"Oh, apparently he asked MJ out a couple of times and she kind of fell for him. He told her he's touring with the PGA and that they'd see each other when he got back."

Tommy held the baby up to his face. "Even you don't believe that, do you?"

John grinned on cue. I deposited the diaper into a pail, washed my hands and then took him back. "So you're saying he's *not* touring with the PGA?"

"He told me he's working on lowering his handicap, then maybe he'll qualify. It's all bullshit. His only handicap is the amount of pot he smokes. The guy's a total dope fiend."

"So he's done with college?"

"No. He dropped out and is supervising one of his father's construction projects in D.C. His fiancée's father is also in construction and he's loaded, too. Anyway, I think they're getting married this October."

"I hope that Connie chick realizes what she's getting herself into," I snapped, now believing there was no way in heaven or hell that Steve Barelli would ever marry our sister, nor that he was worthy of her.

"I don't think it's a question of what, but how much. The Barellis are worth tens of millions. MJ must know that."

"Tommy, I love our sister. But honestly, she's amazingly naive. The answer is no, she didn't."

My heart was breaking and I desperately wanted to come clean. The fact that our pregnant sister just took off to Florida to bet her savings on a murky future with someone who was clearly a lying jerk made me want to puke.

"Tommy," I said heavily. "Life has changed a lot since you left, and not for the better. I promise to clue you in more later. But suffice it to say Ma's a wreck and Dad's coping."

Standing up, his six-foot frame towering over me, Tommy surprisingly wrapped his arms around me and John then tenderly drew us close. "This summer hasn't been easy for you, I can tell. Is there anything *I* can do?"

I'd never felt such compassion emanate from him. There in the small bathroom, embraced in a group hug, I fell apart. Still, my personal problems paled in comparison to what Mary Joyce was facing. Struggling to keep my promise to her, I pulled myself together.

"Thanks, I'll let you know," I said, restraining from adding, *would it be asking too much for you to break Steve Barelli's arms and legs before stuffing a dozen golf balls down his throat?*

Instead, I mentioned my immediate plans. "Nadette, Melinda and Tina are on their way over and we're taking Patty and the baby to the pool. Wanna come?"

"Sure. What about all the other kids? Do you want me to bring them?"

"If you can round them all up, that would be great."

Shortly, I was packing John's pram for our trip to the pool. The buggy was big enough to haul Dumbo. Nevertheless, it worked well as there was plenty of room for him, his paraphernalia and all my pool stuff. Plus, the cavernous canopy protected him from the sun – my carelessness with the latter clearly contributing to his near-death experience. I'd learned from Dr. Dyer that my exposing him to the sun had exacerbated his emergent pneumonia by dehydrating him and raising his temperature even more. Plus, I'd done little to nothing to protect his sensitive skin or eyes. What an idiot.

During John's hospital stay I had read Dr. Spock's book cover-to-cover. The significance of sterilizing bottles, proper infant hygiene, keeping him on a schedule and making sure that his head and neck were properly supported came graphically to light. It was horrifying to think how I'd stuffed him into my flimsy, wicker bicycle basket with such disregard for his well-being. As I packed two bottles into a small cooler, my senses snared on what lay ahead for Mary Joyce. I felt fresh despair, as if I'd just stuffed my pregnant sister into a bicycle basket with scant regard for her well-being or the blistering sun.

"His family has a huge beach house near my guard station. I met Steve a few times with his fiancée."

I thought of Mary Joyce's joke-of-an-engagement ring compared to Connie's "rock." Even if she did marry him, MJ would be stuck in a loveless marriage with a two-faced jerk. At least she might have the benefit of Barelli's money. Still, I'd rather she have the love.

From the kitchen I heard a knock at the door. Tommy answered it.

"Oh, my Gosh! Tommy Kenealy? Well, the beach was certainly good to you, wasn't it? You look fantastic!" I heard Nadette gush. I left the kitchen to find my three friends in the foyer, along with Patty who was in her bathing suit and ready to go.

"Thanks, 'Dette," Tommy grinned slyly, using his longtime nickname for her. She broadly grinned back, still unaware that it was his shortened version of space cadette.

"Have you been working out?"

Tommy blushed at the flattery. "Yeah, kinda. I'm trying to get in shape for football."

"Well, then go Panthers, go. By looking at you I can tell we're gonna have a killer year."

The two had known each other since grade school, so I dismissed the effusive praise as harmless.

"All right girls," I chimed in after settling John into the pram. "Are you ready to go?"

Nadette ignored me. "Tommy, are you going to join us?"

"Yeah, in a bit."

"Swell. We'll hold a spot for you," she said, probably having imagined him to say, "Yes-I'll-be-there-and-I'd-like-to-ask-you-to-homecoming-and-by-the-way-will-you-marry-me?"

After we left the house all she could talk about was Tommy.

"Your brother is gorgeous. Do you think he could ever like me? Puh-lease, put in a good word for me."

"Nadette, don't you think this is a bit weird? He's like a brother to you."

Yesterday it was Dr. Dyer. Today it was my brother. Tomorrow – well all I knew was that it better not be John O'Neill.

"How about a quick stop at Guvelli's?" I deliberately changed the subject. Patty jumped at my impulsive suggestion – something I soon regretted. As I struggled to get the oversized pram inside the ice-cream shop, the cow bells over the door announced our arrival again and again and again. Most amused, I'm sure, was one very unexpected patron who snidely smiled. It was Helen Hartley, accompanied by a young girl. They both wore bathing suit cover ups, apparently on their way to the pool, too.

"Oh, hello," she said with instinctual snobbery. "How's it going?"

"Good," Nadette, Melinda, Tina and I casually echoed as Patty wandered off to ponder her choices.

"This is my niece, Cammie," she said animatedly. Cammie sweetly grinned. Admittedly the young look-alike in her pink cover-up, flower-topped flip-flops and blonde pony tail was pretty adorable.

"Hi, Cammie. How are you?" I politely asked.

Helen cut her off. "I had heard you had a baby," she said derisively. "I guess girls like you can't really go back to school, huh?"

Her comment shocked me less with its ignorance and insensitivity than the realization of what Mary Joyce was truly facing. My own sister would have to contend with people treating her with such disrespect. Nadette openly sighed, and I could see by her undisguised look of contempt that she was about to let Helen have it.

"What's the baby's name?" Cammie sweetly interjected.

I was about to answer when Nadette jumped in. "John. John Al-o-y-sius," she replied, emphasizing every syllable of his middle name.

"Nice name," Helen nodded. Then it hit her. "John Aloysius. As in John Aloysius O'Neill?"

"Yes," said Nadette, demonically drawing out his name again, "As in John Al-o-y-sius O-Ne-ill."

"Is he the...." Helen choked, then angrily turned on me as if just receiving confirmation that I was, indeed, that kind of girl.

"Did you go out with him?"

"Well, what do *you* think?" Nadette kept at it. "Just look at this baby."

Helen removed her sunglasses and bent over to study his face. She nervously glanced at me then continued to inventory him. "He certainly has John's black hair and long eyelashes. But this isn't possible. I mean, how is it that I didn't know anything about this?"

"It's all true," said Nadette. "And I'm the godmother. We even had a baby shower for Gail, didn't we girls?"

"Yes," my Greek chorus concurred.

"This cannot be!" Helen retorted, her voice turning dark and menacing. "John O'Neill is *my* man. Do you understand? And I better not ever see you with him or there will be instant hell to pay," she fumed at me. Then without even paying for her soda or candy, Helen grabbed Cammie by the hand and stomped out.

"Shoplifter," I shouted as the cow bells clamored in her wake. "I'm telling monsignor," I laughed, amused that her priority was to protect her ongoing interest in John as opposed to dealing with the possibility that he'd cheated on her and sired an illegitimate child. But as my friends chimed in, a new dilemma dawned. Nadette was the only one with whom I'd confided the inspiration for the baby's name. Not only was John O'Neill destined to learn of his namesake, but of his presumed paternity, as well.

"What an imbecile! Did you see the look on her face?" Nadette laughed, then quickly caught the look on mine. "Uh-oh."

"You know, I think it's too hot for the baby. Maybe I should go home," I said anxiously.

"Nonsense," Nadette confidently countered. "Don't let that witch bully you."

"What?" said Melinda. "Did you actually name him after John O'Neill?"

"Are you crazy? Of course not," Nadette asserted. "Those are only the two most Catholic names in the world, which is why Gail's *mother*," she emphasized, "named him that. Let Helen spread whatever rumors she wants. We know the truth. That's all that matters."

Then she turned to me. "She's trash. Ignore her."

Which was impossible. She was already at the pool with her groupies when we arrived. Presently her mouth was going a-mile-a-minute while casting steely shots my way. Shortly after settling on to some turf of our own, and just when I was in the middle of feeding John a bottle, Nadette softly poked me while quietly singing the new hit tune, "Come on Down to My Boat Baby."

I instinctively glanced up, falling speechless at the sight of Tommy strolling in alongside John O'Neill, both wearing Ray-Ban aviator sunglasses. Each guy was barefoot and wearing swim trunks, and both were tan and shirtless showing off six-pack abs and powerful pecs. My younger brothers and cousins were in lockstep behind them. Even Frankie, taking a rare afternoon off from work to join us, strode in with the group.

Helen jumped up at the sight of him. "John, over here!" she said, as if he were expected. John utterly ignored Helen. Instead, he waved hello to me.

"Hey, Gail," John smiled warmly upon reaching us. "How are you?"

"Good, thanks. Nice to see you again," I gulped, looking briefly at Nadette. The recent wounding of my pride in the woods was diminished only by the new threat stirred up by our creative sniping at Guvelli's.

"This must be your aunt's baby. May I?" John asked, holding out his hands. I gulped again. Glancing nervously at Helen, I removed the bottle and carefully handed him over. "Baby John" immediately whimpered, but "Big John's" gentle bouncing calmed him down. In fact, the baby even cooed – something I did in silence while staring at the taut muscles in Big John's arms. I held my breath as he took the bottle from me and began feeding the baby. It was a rush watching such tenderness that seemed to come as naturally from our star quarterback as his fierce instincts on the gridiron. Nadette abruptly nudged me again, which is when I saw the lightening bolt heading our way. In a two-piece white bikini, Helen Hartley, who'd been watching us eagle-eyed from the opposite side of the pool, was fast marching toward us. For someone so petite she was remarkably top heavy and used her breasts like anti-ballistic missiles – something capable of deterring competition. She was clearly thrusting her weight now as she stopped just in front of him.

"John Aloysious O'Neill! Is that your bastard child?" she demanded to know.

"What?" he responded harshly.

"I know that's your baby," she stated, wildly wagging a well-manicured finger at him. "That's what that, that…hussy told me," Helen said, now pointing an accusatory finger at me.

"What?" he repeated.

Helen snorted. "Just how stupid do you think I am?"

I scarcely dared to breathe.

"I'm beginning to wonder," he said perplexedly.

"This is *your* baby, isn't it?" she said with burning rage.

"*My* baby?" he curiously shot back, protectively cradling John.

"Well, it's pretty damned obvious. He looks just like you."

Nadette sniggered.

"Are you out of your mind?" John asked.

"Oh, please don't insult me. He even has your name."

John turned and looked at me. I shrugged my shoulders and meekly nodded my head yes.

"So what's the big deal if he has my name?" he said coolly, still feeding John.

"So then it's true?"

"Well, Helen, truthfully..."

He never got to tell her the truth, or even some wonderful lie as Helen cut him off.

"You low-life," she said, then looking at me added, "That goes for both of you."

With that — and flipping her ponytail for added emphasis — she abruptly returned to her eagerly waiting friends.

"What a psycho," said Frankie.

"You have no idea," John said, finally handing Baby John back to me. "As a 'joke' she started sending me pictures of engagement rings and wedding dresses right after our second date. I've been trying to avoid her most of the summer, but she wouldn't have it. Is anyone sitting here?" he asked about the empty chair beside me. No, I nodded, my tension melting into giddiness.

"So," he asked. "Is it true? Is his name really John Aloysious?"

"Yes," I affirmed.

"After me?" he chuckled.

"According to my mother, he's named after the saints," I said, grateful that Nadette kept her big mouth shut.

"That's reassuring. Because to name a child after me would be a curse," he laughed again.

With no obvious interest in perpetuating Helen's drama, he focused his attention on our group. "I've met everyone, but you," he smiled warmly at Patty. "I'm John O'Neill. What's your name?"

"Patty," she beamed.

"Oh, Patty," he said. "I've heard many nice things about you from Tommy."

She fell speechless while staring at him.

"Do you play football?" he asked.

"Yesh," she smiled. I'd never seen a football in her hands. But then, I never thought she could cook, either.

"Well then, come on," he said, and grabbing Joey's football led her by the hand and jumped into the water with all the other O'Brien and

Kenealy kids jumping in from behind. Only Frankie and Joey came close to matching John's or Tommy's true accuracy for throwing the ball. It didn't matter. For the better part of an hour they all eagerly tried. During which time Helen managed several attention-grabbing jackknives off the high-dive. What followed next came as no surprise.

"Help, help, somebody, *PUH-LEASE* help!" she cried loudly after executing her last dive and coming up for air. Her top had *accidentally* fallen off and she had no intention of getting it herself. Instead, climbing half-naked out of the pool and with hands cupped over those blimps, she begged for someone else to rescue the skimpy garment. It was like watching two slices of American cheese held together by a string sink to the pool's bottom. At one point she looked directly at John, who nonchalantly tossed the football to Paul.

Probably most disappointing to Helen was that Frenchie, also at the pool, took the bait. After cannon-balling in and retrieving the prized top, he came up grinning only to have Helen snatch it back without saying thanks. She then further disappointed him by going to the girl's locker room to put it back on.

Now one might have thought she was done with her theatrics for the day. But no. Knowing full well that she had everyone's attention, Helen climbed the high dive again. I watched with muted glee as Frenchie, most likely feeling humiliated and vengeful, nonchalantly climbed the diving board right behind her. As soon as Helen reached the end of the board – and as only Frenchie was wont to do – he jumped hard on the opposite end, thus sending Helen flailing stomach first on to the water. The resulting belly flop appeared to have knocked her breathless.

Commotion ensued. A lifeguard blew his whistle for everyone to clear the water then promptly dove for the seemingly lifeless Helen. Wrapping his arm across her chest, he swam with her to the safety of the pool's edge and, along with one of the other male life guards, lifted her limp body out.

"She's not breathing," he immediately determined, then promptly put his mouth over hers. Even witnessing it, I couldn't believe the audacity of her next move. Miraculously coming back to life, Helen threw her arms around his neck, and turning his genuine life-saving gesture into a selfish farce, French-kissed him. At first he startled, as if he'd truly rescued her from the dead. But as the onlookers laughed, his demeanor withered.

"Gotchya," she giggled. He did not laugh back. And while Helen basked in the limelight, I noticed a *truly* motionless body with a blonde ponytail floating in the opposite end of the pool.

"TOMMY!" I screamed pointing at Cammie. Within seconds he had hoisted her out of the pool, pumped the water out of her bloated belly, then promptly administered CPR to the truly breathless child. Soon she began gasping, then choking.

"Call an ambulance," Tommy shouted, even though she appeared to be okay.

"Cammie, CAMMIE!" Helen screamed while running over, immediately blaming John. "This would have never happened if not for you!"

Even I felt tempted to slap her across the face. John, however, got my licks in for me. He didn't say a word. Nor did he slap her. He merely pushed her into the pool. Rising to the surface, she began wildly cussing and screaming at him. "You absolute, good-for-nothing, loathsome jerk! What was that for?" she bellowed.

"To shut you up," he said.

Shortly, paramedics arrived and carted her innocent niece off to the hospital as an overly dramatic Helen escorted her and, of course, wearing only her bikini.

"Ding, dong. I believe that bitch is dead," mused Nadette.

"Broomstick, please," I snickered back.

In a fairy tale twist, I would soon feel as if I were wearing the ruby slippers. When leaving the pool, John voluntarily joined me as I pushed the wicker pram in the direction of home while Patty walked between us.

"Uhm," John said with surprising shyness directing his attention to me, "Listen, I was wondering if you might not want to go out with me sometime?"

"'Shure,'" said Patty smiling up at him enthusiastically.

John grinned broadly. "Okay," he said. "Then we have a date?"

"Tonight?" Patty queried.

"Well, I was thinking maybe in a couple of days from now," he looked over at me.

"Okay," Patty answered. I nodded along with her.

"Good. How about Tuesday? I'll pick you up at say, 7:00 o'clock."

"'That'sh' during my 'bash-room' time," Patty declared matter-of-factly. "Can you make it 'sheven-shirty' o'clock?"

John pinched his nose to keep from laughing. "Then 7:30 o'clock it is. Tuesday night," he said, winking at me.

At long last, a date with John O'Neill. Bells were pealing. The witch was dead.

Chapter 18

Patty ducked into the bathroom as soon as my father left for work on Tuesday morning. She wasn't leaving anything about her appearance and tonight's big date to chance. Risking a breach in our mandated shower schedule she sneaked in a luxurious bubble bath. Afterwards, and to the best of her ability, she set her hair in curlers where they remained for most of the day. Later she asked me to paint her nails pink and to brush out her hair. To no avail I tried coaxing her out of her wardrobe choice.

By 6:30 p.m. she was ready for her date with John. She looked adorable in her Easter best – a pink chiffon dress, white gloves, white socks with lace, black patent leather shoes and a matching purse. Atop her freshly curled brown hair was a matching straw bonnet adorned with artificial flowers. For the better part of an hour she sat patiently on the front porch swing awaiting her date's arrival. Trying to spare her feelings, I told her that John was also taking me out tonight, but that he considered this a wonderful opportunity to get to know her, too.

"'He'sh' my boyfriend," she hissed.

"Well, yes, he's a boy. And he's your friend."

"So, 'he'sh' *my* boyfriend."

There was no arguing her cockamamie logic. As the baby napped, I preened, and Patty waited. Meanwhile, the phone rang. My nails were wet so I ignored it. It rang some more.

"Will someone please get that?" I hollered from the living room. Shortly, I'd be grateful that no one else had answered, particularly my mother who was also asleep. Finally bolting for the kitchen, I gingerly picked up the phone.

Hello!" I said with exasperation.

"Gail?"

"MJ?" I startled.

"Oh, I'm so happy to hear your voice," she said. "I'm here."

"Where's here?"

"New Port Richey, Florida, where my car broke down. Not far from Tampa."

"Are you okay?"

"Yeah."

I detected scattered clouds in her sunny voice. "Are you sure you're all right?" I whispered heavily.

"Yeah, I suppose. Thankfully my car could be fixed. Anyway, while it was being repaired I looked around town. It's kinda pretty here and the people are really nice. Plus, there are a couple of golf courses, which Steve will like. I think I'm going to stay."

"Does Steve know this?"

She paused.

"MJ?"

"Yeah, I'm here. And no, only because I can't reach him. He's never there when I call. I've tried several of the places where he told me he was touring, but no one seems to know where he is, or even who he is. You know those golf pros, they're always on the go," she said dourly.

"How are you feeling?"

"I'm exhausted."

What else would you expect from a clueless, pregnant teenager who had just driven through six states by herself only to have her car break down in an unfamiliar place? Her response was refreshing only because it was honest. I felt tortured knowing she had no one there to support her and, worse, that she was doing this for the love of a phantom fiancé. Suddenly, a disembodied operator interrupted our conversation. "Please deposit thirty-five cents for the next three minutes."

I heard two coins drop. "Gail, I'm at a pay phone. Hurry. Grab a pen and paper and take down my motel information."

I quickly obliged.

"I'll write when I have a permanent address. I love you. Bye," she concluded.

"MJ, wait!"

"What? I'm out of change!"

I paused. Was it too soon to tell her that Steve was a lying dope fiend and that his "touring" was mostly from girl to girl, one of whom he'd gotten pregnant and the other he was about to marry?

"Gail, are you there?"

"Yeah, MJ. I love you, too," I said, suddenly fighting tears. "Bye for now." The phone clicked from afar. Presently even the prospect of a long-awaited date with John O'Neill did little to bolster my spirits.

Later, and sharply at "seven-thirty o'clock," I was presentably dressed and giving the baby a bottle when John arrived, stopping short at the porch when he saw Patty. I keenly observed them through the open living room window.

"Hello, Patty, how nice to see you. You look very pretty. Are you ready for some ice cream?" A practiced older brother of two sisters, his sincerity was believable.

"'Yesh,'" she politely answered. Then standing up to greet him, she solemnly curtsied. John admirably bowed in response.

"You know, it would be a shame if you got ice cream on those gloves. Perhaps you might put them in your purse," he kindly suggested. Who knew what else was in that handbag. But not wanting to disappoint her boyfriend, Patty did as he suggested. Before they left, John rapped on the screen door.

"C'mon in," I said casually, though feeling positively electrified as he entered the living room. Being settled on the sofa with the baby it was hard to move. I just looked up. He seemed more handsome than ever to me. His black hair and tan showed well against a white-oxford, button-down shirt with rolled-up sleeves. He wore khaki pants and loafers with no socks – something typical for him. But there was a discernible difference. Was it too much to believe it was genuine warmth? Plus, I detected a hint of Old Spice.

"Hey, Gail," he grinned and playfully winked. "Well, Patty and I are off to Guvelli's. We'll be back in just a little while."

"Take your time," I said approvingly, watching John Aloysius–you're-incredibly-delicious-O'Neill clasp Patty's hand then open the front gate for her. Still feeling dreamy, I had just burped the baby and was about to put him down for the night when a bloodcurdling scream erupted from the back yard. Moments later Raymond ran through the back door looking for me.

"Gail," he screeched. "Joey's dead."

Raymond was the more conniving one in the O'Brien bunch. He'd inherited his father's wavy brown hair and narrow eyes, along with a sharp nose and tongue to match. As with Joey, it took diligence to keep him in line.

"You're joking, right?" I nonchalantly replied.

"NO, I'M NOT!" he urgently insisted. "He flubbed his landing doing a flip out of the tree house. He's not moving."

Clutching the baby to my hip, I quickly dashed outside only to see a motionless Joey lying face-up on the ground with one ankle swelling like a grapefruit. Quickly setting the baby down on the grass, I knelt beside him, grateful to hear him moan.

"Joey!" I screamed, truthfully more concerned over a potentially botched date than his well being.

"JOEY!" I hollered, "WAKE UP!"

He moaned again and blinked several times, trying to focus.

"Joey, who am I?"

No response.

"Joey, what is my name?"

Still, no response.

"Joey Kenealy, if you don't wake up I'm going to kill you. WHAT IS MY NAME?"

"Gail," he condescendingly muttered.

"How many fingers am I holding up?" I queried, placing three fingers in front of his face.

"Can't you count? Five."

"Raymond, go get my mother," I commanded.

I was doomed. Under any other circumstances I would have taken complete charge. But not tonight. I had my long-awaited first date with John O'Neill and I needed her help. Due to my father working an emergency moonlighting job, Frankie working late, and Tommy also being out on a date, Joey had agreed to babysit the kids; for a steep price, of course. As Raymond disappeared, I looked up at the tree house porch where Paul and Timmy were speculatively watching.

"What happened?" I asked, needing to hear their version.

"He did a back flip off the bridge," said Paul.

"Why?"

"We dared him. Bet five dollars he wouldn't do it."

"Losers," I blurted. "Get down here now and get the wheelbarrow out of the shed!"

Following my command, they quickly slid down to the lawn and went about their task at the same time my mother emerged with Raymond. Barefoot and wearing a rumpled night shift, she looked completely spent.

"Ma, it looks like Joey may have broken his ankle. He could even have a concussion. You need to get him down to the hospital."

She said nothing.

"Ma, did you hear me? Joey's hurt."

She was more dazed than my brother. And as the others scrambled to hoist Joey into the wheelbarrow and prop his leg up on a pillow, I stood and quietly faced her in what felt like a futile vacuum of hopelessness. She obviously couldn't care less about her son's welfare, nor mine. I tried absorbing the reality of her utterly intoxicated state. I had no idea who this person was anymore. The core instinct of a mother's love and the previous vitality for life were all seemingly washed away by the whisky with which she ritually tried drowning herself. My night was ruined.

"Do you have any idea just how wretched you are?" I darkly whispered.

A mixed look of disorientation and disgust crossed her face, and she blurted one of the meanest and most ironic things I think she'd ever said to me.

"Why can't you be more like your sister?"

I swallowed hard. I could have easily summoned hatred. But truthfully, I found her to be utterly pitiful — more painful, it seemed, than feeling contempt.

"Go back to bed, Ma," I said sadly. Silently, she obliged.

Scooping up John and depositing him in his wicker pram, I instructed the boys to follow me. Oblivious to my plight, they began pushing Joey with great determination out the front gate. Paul had one handle, while Raymond held the other, both mimicking the sound of a siren as they moved swiftly along. Timmy fell in step, too, with Brandy and Mr. Bojangles barking madly at his heels. Preparing to make a right turn toward the hospital, I ordered the makeshift rescue squad to stop.

"Hold it," I said, "First we have to go to Guvelli's."

"You want ice cream when I'm dying?" Joey suddenly perked up.

"I'd be happy to hasten the process," I growled, actually relieved that he was coming back to his senses.

"Murderer."

"Killjoy," I responded, continuing to exchange barbs with him as I steered the group to Main Street where Patty and John had nearly finished their ice cream sundaes. John later told me they were in the midst of a heart-to-heart talk when he saw us barreling down the road.

"I cooked dinner 'lash' night," Patty had cheerfully told him during their conversation.

"Really? What did you make?" John replied, easily promoting her happy chatter while taking a big bite of his own confection.

"Tuna 'cash-er-ole.' Shishter' Marguerite taught me how to make it."

"How nice. I know they must love having a special girl like you to help out in the convent."

Patty grinned, then unexpectedly got up from the table and briefly hugged John. "'Shanksh.'"

Returning to her seat, she went on about her favorite subjects, including Brandy and Mr. Bojangles, the horrible shower schedule in our house, and then of her mother. "Did you know my Mommy 'ish' dead?"

"Yes," John said with genuine compassion. "And I'm so sorry about that."

"I miss her."

Before John could formulate a sensible response, she carried on. "Did you know that my father ran away?"

John stopped eating and gathered his wits. "Yes, I did know that. Do you miss him, too?"

"No. He hated me."

"How could anyone hate *you*, Patty? You're so sweet."

"He would 'alwaysh' hit me. One time he got 'sho' mad he locked me in the 'baysh-ment.' But my Mommy let me out. 'Sho' he hit her."

John calmly set down his spoon, allowing his heart and ice cream to melt at once.

"Patty, I want you to make me a promise, and I will make a promise back to you. Okay?"

"Okay."

He took her hands. "Promise me that if anyone, and I mean *anyone*, ever touches you or threatens to hurt you again that you will tell me. I don't care who it is. You just tell me and I promise you that person will never be mean to you again. Do you understand?"

"Even if 'it'sh' Joey?"

"Even if it's Joey," he said, now squeezing her little hands.

"Okay," she said assuredly, then resumed eating her ice cream.

"Do you know how to use a telephone?" John asked.

"'Yesh.'"

He went to the counter and shortly returned with a piece of paper. "Put this in your purse. It's my phone number and you can call me any-time you need help. Okay?"

"Okay," she said, then read it aloud. John had no idea how much Patty loved numbers and that before sticking it in her purse had memorized it. It was then that John glanced out the front window beside their table, only to witness our makeshift ambulance brigade coming at them full steam ahead. I could see Patty do a double-take herself. They promptly joined us.

"John, we have a slight diversion," I said breathlessly. "I think Joey's ankle is broken."

"What happened?" he asked looking at my brother's propped up foot, his other leg dangling over the wheelbarrow's edge.

"He flubbed a back flip out of the tree house," Paul enthused. "We dared him."

"Hey!" Joey perked up, "I did the flip and you guys owe me money!"

The other boys guffawed. "As if," said Raymond tapping Joey's ankle, "You flubbed it."

"OWWW! You jerk!" Joey cried.

"Where are you going to dump him?" Patty innocently interjected.

"Might I suggest the Patuxent?" I sharply responded.

"Really?" she replied optimistically.

"Murderer," Joey groused again.

"Killjoy."

Realizing how harsh I sounded, I softened my tone. "We're actually on our way to Warren's," I said to Patty.

"I'll come with you," John surprisingly offered, then gently taking Patty's hand ordered the troops to march. While briskly proceeding along Main Street we approached the Laurel Meat Market, and just as Frankie surprisingly emerged. The dogs began furiously sniffing his jeans.

"What on earth?" he said disbelievingly, looking exhausted after working overtime.

"Hey, Frankie," Joey meekly waved.

"What happened to your ankle?"

"Hurt it flipping out of the tree house," Joey nonchalantly bragged.

"What? You idiot!" Frankie promptly chastised him. "I thought you were going out for place kicker this year." Possessing a deep belief in Joey's athletic potential, Frankie had secured a CYO team transfer so that he could coach him this season and was chomping at the bit for practice to start.

"Sorry, coach," Joey's voice lowered, as if now on his death bed.

"I don't believe this. You realize what a sissy you look like being carted around in a wheelbarrow like this? Gail, you should have stuffed him into the baby carriage."

"Trust me," I stated, leaving it at that while gently rocking the pram to quiet the whimpering baby.

"You guys can all go home. I'll take him up to Warren's."

"Are you sure?" I said.

"Yeah, absolutely," he responded. "Thanks guys," he said relieving the attendings, then effortlessly lifted the wheelbarrow himself while flexing muscular arms that had become even more toned since working at the meat market. Apparently it was a daily custom for him to haul hundred-pound slabs of beef off the refrigerated truck and into the store to be butchered.

"By the way, John," he added, "Good to see you again. And Patty," he sweetly remarked, "you look very pretty."

"'Shanksh,' Frankie," she beamed. "'Shee' you later," she said, watching as he carted Joey away.

"Never a dull moment in your house, is there?" John chuckled.

"That's putting it mildly. Listen, I'm really sorry. But I think we'll have to wait till some other night to go out. My father's gone, Tommy's out, and my mother is..."

"Nonsense. I've got the car for the night," he gently interrupted, then picking up the fussy baby cradled and bounced him lightly in his arms. The oldest of five children, he was accustomed to family chaos, though certainly none of the drama we shared. "I say we all head over to the Laurel Drive-In and catch tonight's performance of *The Sound of Music.*"

"With everyone?"

"Of course," he grinned.

I had already seen the blockbuster hit when it was released two years earlier. But I would venture to say that none of my cousins had seen it.

"Are you sure?"

"It's not dark yet. We still have time."

And so, piling in the front seat with John were Patty, the baby and me, while Paul, Raymond and Timmy staked out spots in the back of the O'Neill family station wagon. Once at the Laurel Drive-In, John indulged all of us with sodas and large tubs of buttered popcorn. At one point during the movie it was hard to tell who was singing "Do-Re-Mi" louder – Sister Maria and the Von Trapp children, or Patty still in her Sunday attire and probably having the most happy and memorable evening of her life.

Later, when arriving home, my father greeted us with the same startled expression as Captain von Trapp displayed over the antics of his own children. With the windows rolled down, we pulled up in the O'Neill's station wagon still singing "Do-Re-Mi" at the top of our lungs.

"Hello, sir, nice to see you," said John politely after climbing out of the car. "How's Joey?"

"He'll survive, though I'm not sure about the rest of us," he said with mild aggravation about that development. "It was a busy night at the hospital and they're still waiting for X-ray results. You about ready for another football season, son?"

"I'll say," John warmly grinned, adding, "Well, Mr. Kenealy, thanks for loaning me your family tonight. I hope they had fun. I know I did."

"No, thank *you*," my father said sincerely, while shaking his hand and patting him on the shoulder. "That was a mighty fine thing you did."

Later, as I settled Baby John into his crib, I smiled down at him and contentedly whispered, "You know something kid? You really are named after one of the saints."

Chapter 19

I had just settled into bed with the lights out and window open when I heard Frankie's voice. I was wide awake and quietly reliving every second spent with John O'Neill; my lopsided crush now morphing into something totally unexpected – reality. It was such a magnanimous gesture he'd performed by taking all of us out for the evening. He handled the younger kids with kind respect, laughing along with them when they made fun of his horrible singing, also cracking them up with his equally bad jokes. This included a spate of knock-knock jokes, one of which went over the heads of the younger ones, but wasn't the least bit lost on me.

"Knock-knock," he started.

"Who's there?" we chimed back.

"Cantaloupe."

"Cantaloupe who?"

"Cantaloupe tonight, Dad's got the car!"

"Not true," I promptly replied. "You've already got it!"

"Wanna elope then?" he broadly grinned while dipping a finger in one of my dimples.

Yes, yes, a million times yes.

I peered outside when hearing Frankie's voice carry through the air. My father had updated me before I headed to bed that Joey's foot was badly sprained, plus he'd suffered a mild concussion. Because he was forbidden to walk on his affected foot for about a month, and had to lie low to protect his head, it meant some of us were destined to become enslaved.

"Still, that was a really dumb thing you did," Frankie said while pushing the wheelbarrow through the garden gate as Joey hobbled behind on crutches.

"That's only about the hundredth time you've told me so."

"Because you don't seem to get it," Frankie sharply retorted.

"Get what? You keep telling me I'm going to miss football. Big deal."

"That's what you don't get, Joey. Eighth grade CYO football *is* a big deal. Scouts come out from some of the most elite prep schools during the season looking for someone with your kind of talent and potential. If you work at it, you could end up playing football at a really good high school."

"What's wrong with Pallotti?"

"Nothing. But I'm talking about an entirely different league of competition. I'm also talking about an ability to get noticed by a really good university and maybe even land a scholarship. You don't think you need it, so you don't see it. But I do. You're smart as hell, you're tough as nails, plus you can block hard, run fast, *and* kick the ball. For all we know you could be the next Paul Hornung," he said, referring to Notre Dame's Heisman Trophy winner and recently retired star player on Vince Lombardi's indomitable Green Bay Packers.

"I mean it Joey. Don't let yourself down, because you'll live to regret it. You've got too much going for you."

"So do you," Joey said, faintly attempting to bolster his cousin's ego while lifting both feet off the ground and playfully swinging between his crutches.

"No, I don't. I don't have your versatility or star potential. But you," he paused watching as Joey foolishly tried turning a pirouette on one crutch, then tumble hard on the lawn.

"Ouch!" Joey hollered, briefly trying to leverage his bandaged foot in an attempt to grasp the stray crutch.

Frankie didn't budge.

"Are you going to help me or not?"

"No," Frankie said brusquely.

"Asshole," Joey loudly charged, then impulsively whacked Frankie in the shin with the crutch still in his possession.

Still, Frankie didn't flinch.

"I take that back. Actually you're an asshole and a pathetic orphan."

There was a long, uncomfortable silence. Still, Joey persisted. "You think you're better than everyone, don't you? Help me up, dammit."

Surprisingly, Frankie obliged. Pulling Joey up off the ground he handed him both crutches, then leaned closely into his face.

"You don't take me seriously. But you should, because I'm right. I think you're amazing and have everything in the world going for you. Except you behave like a spoiled child who thinks he's Peter Pan and can fly out of trees. Keep that up and you will find yourself in Neverland. Which means you will *NEVER* amount to anything in life."

The two stared fiercely at each other before Frankie spoke again.

"Let me know when you decide to grow up," he added. "But just remember, I'm not cutting you any breaks. You're gonna learn to walk a straight line on those crutches and get back into fighting shape if you want to play on my team." Then shoving him back to the ground, he left to return the wheelbarrow to the shed while leaving Joey sprawled on the ground in front of the darkened house.

Neither of them had noticed my father sitting alone on the porch swing drinking a beer. Joey was still grounded while essentially licking his wounds when Frankie reached the darkened front porch. He startled at my father's voice. "It's about time someone knocked some sense into that boy."

"Sir?" Frankie jumped.

"I agree with every last thing you said. Joey has a smart mind, but an equally smart mouth. And just so you know, from my perspective the true definition of 'pathetic' is wallowing in self-pity on my front lawn," he spoke loud enough to be overheard.

Joey was now sitting up and staring angrily at them both.

"And in case he doesn't have the good manners to do so, at least I want to thank you for skipping dinner to help him. You're a good kid, Francis O'Brien. And so long as there's a single breath left in my body you will never be an orphan."

"Thanks, Uncle Joe."

"Good night, son."

"Good night, sir."

Soon I heard the two of them inside the house, flat out ignoring Joey and leaving him alone outside as they each headed to bed. It had been a long time since I'd heard my brother cry. He wasn't sobbing, just sniveling. Finally gathering the crutches, he managed to pick himself up off the lawn. But instead of coming inside, he went to the tree house and somehow managing to hoist himself up the ladder, it is where he spent the night.

Chapter 20

The next morning required another trip to Warren's Hospital, but for reasons unrelated to my headstrong brother. It was for John's routine check-up.

"Well, young man," said Doc Warren with good-natured authority, "you appear to be right on track."

Doc Warren, with his peppered gray hair and wire-rimmed spectacles, was a thoughtful, well-regarded physician, and one of the gentlest souls I knew. He even made house visits as needed.

"How much does he weigh?" I asked.

"Ten pounds and ten ounces! Not bad for a slightly premature baby who suffered pneumonia. You must be doing something right," the kind doctor said while picking him up from the scale. "How are his bowel movements?"

"Far too many."

He raised a curious eyebrow.

"I'm joking," I shot back. "I'm changing at least ten to twelve diapers a day. Most have pee. Still, that's ten to twelve too many for me."

He chuckled while setting him on the exam table. After warming the chest piece on his stethoscope, Doc Warren placed it on John's bare back, prompting him to squirm and whine in protest. "Help me out here," he said, enlisting me to hold John as he skillfully listened to his breathing.

"His lungs sound very good. And his bowel movements are regular, right?"

"Yes. Morning, noon and night."

"Well aren't we the comedienne!"

"I'm serious."

137

"What are they like?"

"Smelly."

"No, I meant the consistency."

"Goopy, but not runny."

"That's good. Then keep him on that recommended formula. How's he sleeping?"

"No later than eight o'clock each night he gets a bath, then a bottle, and usually goes right to sleep. Around midnight he wakes up for a brief feeding, then sleeps till 4:00 a.m., when he usually wants a full bottle. Then he'll sleep for another two to three hours. I think he's doing much better now that he's actually sleeping in a crib."

"You mean he outgrew the laundry basket?" he teased. Then while looking into John's ears he abruptly switched gears. "How's your mother handling his schedule?"

I clammed up while watching him look down the baby's throat and then check his reflexes. "All's well. Good going, young man!" He said handing him over. "Go ahead and get him dressed."

I did as instructed while the doctor made notes on his chart. Finally setting it down, he sat in a chair across from me.

"You've got a lot on your plate, young lady, don't you?"

"Yeah, but he's a good baby. You know what's interesting? He recently discovered his hands. He's not a thumb-sucker — yet. But he loves nibbling on his fingers, and then mine."

He persisted. "Gail, I'm talking about your mother. She's not well. I saw her at the pharmacy the other day and she looked spent. In fact, it took her a moment to figure out it was me. She told me she was there to pick up a prescription for Mrs. Logan."

I sighed. "Then you know what I'm dealing with."

"I think I do. Aside from that daredevil brother of yours, what's going on there?"

"A lot. We'll get through it. Are we done?"

"No. I want to know how *you* are doing?"

"I'm fine. I manage." *Well, in spite of the fact that my mother is a miserable drunk; my brother could have killed himself last night and, I almost wish he* had; that my father has to work all the time leaving me in charge of seven children, including this baby who truly believes I'm his mother, I'm just fine. Really. By the way, Mary Joyce is pregnant. Some good news, though. I quit smoking.

"You let me know if you need anything. Otherwise, I'll see you next month. And Gail," he added warmly.

"Yes?"

"He's lucky to have you in his life."

"Thanks, Doc," I nodded in genuine appreciation as he left the room.

Certainly I felt pleased that John's health was stable. As for myself, I realized that unless my mother got her act together, then there was no end in sight to these routine check-ups. I even wondered if Mary Joyce and Steve wouldn't get married after all, and furthermore if they wouldn't want to adopt him. Irish twins – MJ would be up for that. At last, I'd be relieved from all the drudgery and John would get all the attention he deserved. His life story began playing out in my mind.

You see, John. Your mother died giving birth to you. Then your drunken, abusive father didn't want you and immediately offered you to the Daughters of Charity to put up for adoption. Fortunately, before the Sisters took you away, your Aunt Mary Claire kidnaped you from the hospital and stuffed you inside your fifteen-year-old cousin's sock drawer for safe-keeping. Gail was only supposed to help take care of you for a few days. But shortly afterwards your aunt had a nervous break-down, so Gail had to care for you full-time. She was pretty clueless and didn't treat you very well to start. In fact, because of her, you nearly died from bacterial pneumonia. Afterwards, Gail started paying better attention to you. That is, until school started again. Then she had parties and proms to attend, and you became an even bigger burden. So she handed you over to her older sister, Mary Joyce, who was pregnant out of wedlock at the time. And so that brother of yours is really your second cousin and that's why...

He obliviously smiled and sweetly touched my face, prompting me to gently kiss his forehead while realizing how guilty I might be of perhaps creating lasting emotional injury.

Fortunately, before the Sisters took you away, your Aunt Mary Claire kidnaped you from the hospital and stuffed you inside your fifteen-year-old cousin's sock drawer for safe-keeping. Which is when your cousin, Gail, fell hopelessly in love with you like she was your own mother, and refused to let anyone else help. And that's why...

I kissed his forehead again, and began to cry. "I love you, little man."

Finally pulling myself together, I left the office, placed him in his pram then headed directly to my next stop for the day – our community library. Like just about everything else, it was within walking distance to my house. Which was a good thing as our homework was principally conducted at the dining room table, where bickering for space and quiet generally super-seded anything academic. As a result, I'd spent many nights holed up in the library until closing to get away from the quarreling. Ironically, many of my friends would show up, which was equally distracting.

But there was nothing social nor humorous about my trip there today. Though it was a gorgeous, sunny day and I should have been planning a trip to the pool, I was at the library early Monday morning with John.

"Why Gail Marie!" the cheerful, part-time librarian chirped upon seeing me. Everyone in town was familiar with Mrs. Sullivan. She was a plain-looking woman who always wore her brown hair in a tight chignon bun. "It's not the night before a book report is due," she chortled. "What on earth are you doing here? And who is this precious young man?" she sweetly asked while peering over her reading glasses and down into the pram.

Her winning demeanor was misleading. She was actually a sanctimo-nious woman with a deceptive knack for interrogation. She'd first put her victim at ease by starting with innocuous questions, then she'd gently dig deeper and deeper – always in a pleasant manner – until she struck a raw nerve and extracted some kind of deeply personal confession. You could tell by the smug grin on her face that two things had been accomplished: Mrs. Sullivan had experienced a gossip orgasm and that your reputation was in danger of getting screwed.

"This is my cousin. His mother died so I'm helping to take care of him."

"Oh, Lord have mercy. I'm so sorry to hear that. We've been vaca-tioning in Michigan this summer, so I had no idea. Obviously this was recent. Is there anything I can do to help?"

"That's very kind of you. Actually, I'm here to see back issues of *The Washington Post*."

"What are you looking for?"

"Well, I'm not exactly sure when it might have appeared, if at all. But I'm looking for an engagement announcement that might have been published sometime this year – most likely before July."

"That's only a few dozen issues," Mrs. Sullivan said. "It shouldn't be hard to find. In fact, I love reading the social pages. Give me the names of the new couple and I'll even help you look."

"Steve Barelli and Connie Sullivan."

"What are the odds?!" she gushed. Then, placing a hand atop her chest, added, "You don't need to waste a single second reading the papers. Connie Sullivan is the daughter of my husband's first cousin and is the most precious young lady!! How do you know them?"

"What are the odds?" As in, what are the odds that hell is freezing over this very moment? I wanted to say. Though thirty minutes away, the extremely affluent town of Chevy Chase seemed ice ages removed from Laurel. So why would it possibly occur to me that their common surnames should be any indication that Mrs. Sullivan and the bride-to-be were related?

"Are you going to the wedding?" she excitedly carried on as if blue birds-of-paradise were suddenly flitting about us. They might have been chirping for her. But I felt like one had just crapped on my head.

"Uh, no. I'm doing this for my sister. She left for college and she wanted to..."

"Oh, Mary Joyce. How is she? Is she settled in at Salisbury State yet?"

This woman most likely had one conversation with my sister about college and could probably tell *me* Mary Joyce's GPA, the date she received her acceptance, and exactly what day and time she was expected to arrive at school.

"Uhm, no ma'am. In fact, Mary Joyce changed her mind and is going to college in Florida instead."

"Really? Which school?"

I hit my forehead with the palm of my hand. "It's a small school and I can't remember the name of it off the top of my head."

She dug deeper. "Do you at least know the city?"

I skewed my mouth sideways and looked upwards, then for dramatic effect sighed. "It's near the beach is all I remember."

She obliquely smiled. "Darling, just about everywhere in Florida is near the beach. Give it a minute, I'm sure it will come to you. Now what did she want to know about Connie and Stevie?"

"*Stevie?*" Yech. Any wisdom I might possess about dropping the whole matter right then and there was dissipated by a harsh truth that would eventually be known. I looked down at John who was the most innocent creature I'd ever known, realizing his fate had also been forged by a lying, abusive father.

"Apparently Mary Joyce met Steve at the beach and he...uhm...and they...uhm, Stevie, that is, talked about their wedding plans and said he wanted her to be a part of it." My heart was now racing and my tongue felt like a Twizzler stick over speaking this twisted truth – particularly while interacting with the town's tattler. I mean, it was all true. Mary Joyce did meet him at the beach, they did talk about *their* wedding plans, and he supposedly wanted her to be a part of it. My logic relieved me, so I carried on. "But she gave Steve her Salisbury address so the invitation probably went there. She's just trying to plan ahead."

"Well, I suppose I could give them Mary Joyce's new address – if only you knew which school she was attending," she sarcastically remarked. "Why don't I just have them send another one to your home address?"

"Oh, no, please, MJ wouldn't want to trouble you or them. We'll figure it out. Do you know when they're getting married?"

"On October 14th. Oh, my, what a wedding this is going to be, too! I would *walk* up from Florida if I had to in order not to miss it," she raved some more. "And this Saturday night there's a big engagement party for them at the Chevy Chase Club. Shame, my husband and I are out of town this weekend, so we can't go. I really love those kind of fancy parties.

"That Connie, I'm telling you. I've known her since she was a baby and she is the most darling girl," she blathered on. "They've been dating for years and Stevie's so lucky to have her. Her father made a lot of money in the construction business himself and is going to throw one heck of a wedding for them!"

My stomach churned. "So what do you think of Stevie?" I bravely asked.

"Oh, he's a charming young man. They make the perfect couple. They have both been raised so well. He's a good golfer and had wild dreams of touring professionally. But his father insisted that he work in the family construction business, instead. Which is a smart idea, if you ask me, because he's certain to make much more money doing that than playing golf.

"Well, I certainly hope Mary Joyce can make it to the wedding. I'll be sure to keep an eye out for her. At least *she* will be able to tell me where she's going to college!" She devilishly laughed.

I managed a slight grin. "Thanks for your help."

"My pleasure. And, I'm so sorry about your family's recent loss."

I nodded, realizing she was more interested in the upcoming nuptials of a high-society couple than she was over the loss of my aunt and her orphaned infant. I dared not mention Uncle Francis's escapades, nor that he was still at large believing that information would bring on a full-fledged gossip orgy. I left the library and headed straight to Nadette's.

"Hey!" she cheerfully greeted me at the front door in pink curlers, pink baby doll pajamas, and matching pink, furry slippers. Her face was lathered with cold cream so all I could see were her eyes and mouth — from which was dangling a lit cigarette as she was trying to protect her freshly painted nails.

"Want one?" she asked.

"No," I said adamantly. "I quit."

Before carefully removing the cigarette she took a long drag, then blew the smoke in my face. "You're no fun anymore."

I immediately started coughing.

"You wouldn't be coughing if you were still smoking. What's up?"

"I've been invited to an engagement party at the Chevy Chase Club this Saturday night and I was wondering if you would like to go with me? You'd have to drive, of course."

"An engagement party at the Chevy Chase Club? As in *the* Chevy Chase Club?"

"Yes, *the* Chevy Chase Club in *Chevy Chase*, Maryland."

"Is Tommy going, too?"

"No. Which is why you'll have to drive."

"No sweat. What time and what do I wear?"

"Fancy."

"This calls for new clothes!" she said excitedly. "By the way, who's getting married and how do you know them?"

"Oh, just some kids of old family friends."

"I didn't know you knew any rich people. Why isn't Tommy going?"

"He doesn't know them as well, so he wasn't invited."

"Well, at least he can see me all dressed up when I come to get you."

"Yeah, sure."

"Does he like me?"

"Yeah, sure," I repeated, sounding detached, my mind absorbed over the news of "Stevie and Connie" and wondering what this meant for poor Mary Joyce.

Her expression soured.

"No, no. I didn't mean it like that. Of course he likes you, you're his old friend. I'm sure you'll look beautiful and Tommy will think so, too. By the way, he might like you better if you didn't smell like an ashtray." Fortunately John started fussing. "Gotta go. He's hungry," I said, then turned to leave.

"Are you at least saying nice things to Tommy about me?"

"All the time," I said, now half-way down her front walkway. "Oh, and pick me up at 6:00 o'clock. Okay?"

"Okay," she replied somewhat dejectedly.

Hurrying home, I walked into the house only to find Joey sprawled out on the sofa, his crutches leaning up on the armrest along with his injured foot. Wearing the same clothes from the previous day, his black hair greasy and messy, he looked like a dirt ball and was apparently using his injury as further excuse not to bathe.

"Are you okay?" I asked.

"No," was all he said. I could tell by the tone of his voice that he meant it. Somehow, sympathy wasn't the first thing I felt. Particularly when I saw that Patty of all people had gone to the kitchen to fetch him a glass of water along with his pain medication and a couple of Twinkies.

"Here," she said, then like a little mother tenderly stroked his brow.

"Thanks, Patty," he said, his mouth curling up slightly at one end. At first I thought Joey was taking complete advantage of Patty. Despite the fact that Joey never failed to remind her that she was retarded and even though the gaps in her front teeth were due to *his* aggression, I realized that Patty was the only one who seemed to truly care about his welfare. Still, I planned to keep a very close eye on them for any signs of maltreatment.

John was growing even more agitated, and I had not yet warmed his bottle when the phone rang.

"Gail," Sister Perpetua said after hearing my voice. "How are you?"

"Okay, thank you," I startled, surprised it was her.

"And what about Patty? How's she adjusting?"

I glanced over at her rearranging the pillows upon which Joey's foot was propped.

"She's fitting in."

"That's good to hear. We've grown quite fond of her at the convent. Listen, the reason I'm calling is that I haven't heard from your parents. Are Timmy and Joey coming back to St. Mary's?"

"Well, yes, of course," I said.

"I have incomplete registrations for both of them. Is your mother planning on taking care of it?"

"Sister, do you mind holding while I get her?"

"Not at all," she politely responded.

It was 10:30 a.m. when I knocked on her bedroom door.

"Ma," I said, from the other side. There was no answer.

"MA! Sister Perpetua is on the phone for you."

"Tell her I'll call back," she snapped. Her response seemed particularly harsh considering Sister was someone with whom she'd worked closely on the PTA ever since I could remember. Without hesitation, I opened the door, then gasped at the sight and smell. My parents' room had always been bright and Spartan. There was a matching bedroom set

145

with a queen-sized, mahogany frame, two bedside tables with a brass lamp on each, and a shared bureau. The walls, the linens, bedspread, curtains and even a hooked rug on the hardwood floor were all white, making prominent the crucifix above their bed.

But now the room seemed dark and dangerous, with a swirling plume of smoke rising above Christ's head. There was my mother in her rumpled cotton night shift on the edge of the unmade bed, long, dark roots chasing her dyed-red, disheveled hair. She was smoking a cigarette with one hand while holding a coffee cup with the other. An open bottle of whisky stood on the night table.

"Oh, my god," I whispered upon seeing her pale, sickly pallor against her electrified hair, unable to understand how she'd morphed into this. Until now, I had never known that alcohol possessed such a dangerous rip current, capable of swiftly carrying away even the strongest swimmer in its fierce, random force.

"Tell her I'll call her back," she said haltingly. "What does she want, anyway?"

Utter disbelief consumed me. And not just because of her sickly appearance and outright disrespect for Sister Perpetua, but also because of the notion that my father was sleeping with this wretch every night.

"Who are you?" I half-whispered.

"What do you mean 'Who are you?' I'm your mother." She lightly coughed, then took a drag from her cigarette. "Is there something else? Otherwise I'll call her later."

"No," I said, my voice anchored with unfathomable pain. "I'll take care of it." I left, closed her door and just stood there trying to process the dark forces of depression. Was my father capable of saving her or had the currents carried her too far? This was the woman who had begged him to let my cousins come and live with us, only to abandon them – and us – as soon as they had settled in.

I know who you are, I thought, feeling deep sadness. *I just don't know where you are.*

I headed downstairs and picked up the phone trying to speak over John's hungry cry. "I'm sorry to keep you waiting so long, Sister. But my mother is really under the weather," I bit my lip over this white-washing. "Is there anything I can do?"

"Sure. Come get the paperwork for your parents to complete. Also, were they planning on sending your cousins to St. Mary's as well? If so, we need school records transferred and registration forms filled out for them, too."

I felt my heart sink even further at the prospect of this administrative task during the last week of summer vacation. Clearly Frankie would be returning to Laurel High for his senior year. But I'd barely given a thought to his siblings, assuming that my parents would take care of everything. I cleared my throat of welling emotion. "Uhm, Sister, I'm kind of in the dark about this. And besides," I added meekly, "I know my parents can't afford the tuition for all of us."

"Poppycock," she stated firmly. "I've already discussed this with Monsignor Wilson. Your parents will receive a substantial break on everyone's tuition. Of course, it's extra for the uniforms and supplies, but there are ways to work that out, too."

"What about Patty?"

"Oh, Patty. What a love. She's a great helper in our kitchen and a true gift from God, if you ask me. Unfortunately, and I mean this, she'll have to attend the public elementary school where they have the proper resources to teach her. Just make sure she's enrolled in Religious Education."

"Yes, Ma'am."

"Well, what about it? When can I expect you?"

"I'll be up shortly. Thanks for calling, Sister," I said, then after hanging up the kitchen phone placed my arms above my head and leaned against the wall.

I'm not sure how long I stood there like that. Paradoxically, I felt relieved by her foresightedness, as if for a change someone was actually thinking ahead for me. But then a complex brew of anger and frustration surfaced. My life had forever changed and it sucked. I stared at my bare feet on the red linoleum floor, the remnants of Cotton Candy Fluff polish on my overgrown toe nails a reflection of myself – neglected, chipped, and exposed. My toenails I could polish, but what about my life?

John was now screaming mad, prompting me to grab a bottle out of the fridge and place it in a saucepan of water on the stove to warm up. They say a watched pot never boils, and clearly this was the case as John's demanding pitch heated far faster than the water.

Shortly my mother's voice pierced through the din. "Gail? Where are you? What's the matter with that baby?"

In an attempt to get both of them to simmer down, I hurriedly and clumsily reached for the bottle, and in the process knocked the pan of near boiling water off the stove. Crashing loudly to the floor, the glass bottle broke into a million shards. And as I was wearing shorts, the hot water sprayed on to my bare legs. I screamed. And not just because of the searing pain. Picking up the pan I banged it uncontrollably and repeatedly on the counter top.

"What is going on down there?" she yelled. Her footsteps were heavy on the stairs, and seconds later she stood before me, menacing and frail at once.

"I hate you," I yelled back. "What did I do to deserve this? I hate you. I hate YOU! My life is over," I shouted, then began to sob. In saner times I would never have spoken to her like that. Also, in saner times she would have instantly tended to my wounds – emotional and physical.

"Who do you think you're talking to?" she asked.

"You, dammit! I hate you. I hate what you are and I hate what you've done to me. You're worse than Uncle Francis."

I don't know what was more intense: John's hot howling or my mother's cold stare. She angrily stepped forward, scaring me to believe she might even hit me – something she'd never done before.

"What has gotten into you?" she finally spoke in a low, exasperated tone. "Quit acting like a baby and get John his bottle."

"You don't get it, do you?"

"Get what?" she charged back in her heavy brogue. "That John's screaming his little head off and somehow I'm to blame because you dropped his bottle and think your life is over. Do I have to do everything around here?" she asked, then opening the refrigerator door pulled out another bottle – one that I'd prepared – and without heating it marched into the living room to feed him as Patty and Joey solemnly watched.

148

Sinking down in the milky sea of glass, I sat on the floor and, head in hands, just sobbed. I would have liked to have sat like that for a while, absorbed in my own self-pity. But John began to wail in such an unfamiliar and urgent manner that, picking myself up, I instinctively headed toward him only to be met by my mother eager to pass him my way.

I didn't say a word. I simply reached out and took hold of him, in an instant calming him down. She handed me the bottle, and quietly I retreated to the bathroom where I filled the tub with cold water then sat on the edge and drenched my burned legs while crying and feeding him.

I rocked him as he drank, finding unexpected comfort in the warmth of his little body. At last, when he was finished, he looked up at me and grinned. It wasn't a partial or even a gassy grin. It was a broad grin emanating from roots of very simple contentedness. If only we could all live in such innocent bliss.

"Hello," I weakly and unenthusiastically smiled, the sound of my voice perking him up even more. He began playfully waving a little hand across his body. Then, still smiling, he made soft guttural noises as if he were telling me something special. My concerns surprisingly melted as his large eyes shined bright, and the warmth of his gaze unexpectedly tempered my angst. At one point he reached up and wrapping his tiny hand around one of my fingers pulled it toward himself, then happily stuffed it in his mouth. In his little mind we were clearly one and there was no hint of pain in the heart of the one who held him.

Shortly, Patty tapped on the door and entered the room. She didn't say a word. Instead, just like earlier when she'd tenderly brushed Joey's brow, she quietly and lovingly did the same to mine.

Chapter 21

Shortly after packing his diaper bag, I strolled with John up to St. Mary's school where Sister Perpetua greeted me with a pile of paperwork, then joined me in the cafeteria to help search through the "gently used" garment bin for school uniforms.

"My goodness, Gail, that's quite a sun burn," she said looking down at my pink-splotched legs.

"Yeah, I guess I should have been more careful," I replied, picking up a white button-down shirt with a blue stain on the cuff. "This should fit Timmy. And he likes to paint, so I'm sure the other cuff will match soon enough."

"May I ask how your mother is doing? I never see her at Mass anymore."

I didn't respond.

"Is everything okay?" she gently persisted.

"Sister Perpetua," I started, then hesitated. Regardless that it was something beyond my control, I found it embarrassing to admit to either the kind family doctor or this genuinely concerned nun that my own mother was a fall-down drunk.

"Her sister's death has been really hard on her," I finally confessed. "Plus, her brother-in-law committed a series of armed robberies afterwards and is still on the run. My mother's not coping very well."

"I had read about the hold-up at Laurel Liquor and I deducted the family tie. I'm deeply worried about all of you. How are *you* doing?"

I closed my eyes while fighting tears. Her question beckoned the truth, my truth, that I felt like my mother's loving spirit and my winsome youth had been buried alive in Aunt Cate's grave. I wasn't sure why I would open up to her and not Doc Warren. But I did.

"Honestly, Sister, I'm not doing very well, either. My mother has checked out. And now that our family has doubled in size, my Dad's working all the time to help feed us. Meanwhile the kids can get kinda crazy and I'm pretty much in charge. My older cousin, Frankie, helps a lot. But it's this baby that's my biggest concern. There's really no one else willing to take care of him, and if not for me he'd starve. I don't know what will become of him once school starts," I said, the tears now escaping. "I can't be there for him all the time, and I know my mother won't take good care of him."

"Please, have a seat," Sister calmly responded, directing me to a nearby metal folding chair.

Pulling John's pram beside me, I did as instructed. The long, white fabric in Sister's habit elegantly draped around her and softly pooled on the floor as she sat in a chair opposite me. Truthfully, all I'd ever tended to notice about her intelligent face before was that it was lightly wrinkled. For the first time, however, I observed behind her wire-rimmed spectacles pretty hazel eyes fringed by thick lashes. Her high cheekbones and heart-shaped mouth all bore traces of genteel beauty. It made me wonder if she'd ever dated before becoming a nun and what would make her choose this life over marriage to a mortal.

"I know this isn't what you want to hear, but it bears asking," she began to compassionately present her solution. "Is there any chance your parents would consider putting this young man up for adoption? I know there are plenty of families who would be happy to give him a nice home."

I had already turned this over in my mind. Yet the thought of abandoning him severely pinched my heart. "Sister, this baby," I started, then blinked back more tears. "No," I blurted. "I would rather drop out of school than give him up," I added, unwittingly carrying my mother's emotional torch for her dead sister.

"Hmmm, I see," she spoke cautiously. "What about Mary Joyce? Perhaps she could postpone college for a year to stay home and help take care of everyone until the situation stabilizes."

"She's moved to Florida."

"Florida? For heaven's sake, why would she do that when your family life is in such turmoil?"

"Because she's pregnant," I impulsively blurted, then swallowed hard while wondering with wide-eyed shock what I had just done. Not only had I betrayed Mary Joyce's confidence, but I'd done so with the last person she'd care to know.

"Mary Joyce is what? Pregnant? Is she married?"

"Oh, Sister Perpetua," I immediately lamented. "I promised Mary Joyce I wouldn't tell anyone. Please don't tell my parents!"

"No, I will not tell your parents. Mary Joyce is eighteen and is considered to be an adult. But I have to say, her behavior strikes me as selfish and immature. Who is the father? And are they married yet?"

No, I somberly shook my head. "He proposed to her, but he's actually really engaged to someone else."

Her eyes darkened. I'd seen that look before when a student was about to be censured, and I knew that she was not someone with whom to trifle.

"He's *what?*"

"His name is Steve Barelli, and from what I understand he's going to marry a girl named Connie Sullivan on October 14th."

"And Mary Joyce approves of this?"

"She doesn't know."

"And why not?"

"I haven't told her yet," I responded meekly.

"And why not?" she repeated.

"Because I just found out. And," I added sadly, "because I've been trying to save my parents from the pain."

"Were you ever planning on sharing this news with Mary Joyce?"

"Yes, of course. But I was going to at least wait until after this weekend. There's an engagement party at the Chevy Chase Club for Steve and Connie this Saturday, and I'm planning on confronting him there first."

"Oh, my goodness. This is not to be believed. And your goal is to take this on yourself?"

Yes, I nodded.

An absorbing silence followed as Sister tried composing herself, even closing her eyes and clutching her rosary beads. Finally she sighed, her tone circumspect.

"How far along is she?"

"About four months."

She lightly gasped. "And what does *she* know of this young man?"

"Not enough. He told her he's touring with the PGA and will join her in Florida when he's done for the year. I found out he's not even a professional golfer," I boldly added.

"Tsk, tsk, tsk," she clucked her tongue while shaking her head in clear disappointment, sounding as if she were summoning a horse or, perhaps in my family's case, the cavalry. "Gail, I am angered and utterly heartsick for you and your family. There seems to be no end to the hardship. And you, well, you are loving and generous beyond your years."

"No, I'm not. I hate this. I hate my life. I miss my friends and I miss my mother. I don't know why this is happening to me."

Her tender response surprised me.

"I know this might be hard to conceive, but I truly believe you are living in a state of grace right now. I suspect that God is caring for you in ways you cannot even imagine nor have even asked for. Be grateful for that and give thanks."

"Thanks for what, Sister Perpetua?" I impetuously replied. "My Aunt Cate's death? Her husband's crime spree? Their children's abandonment? My mother's drunkenness? The fact that this baby nearly died? Mary Joyce's pregnancy? If those are things to be thankful for, then thank you, thank you, thank you, God."

"You will stop that nonsense this instant," she immediately rebuked me. "There is little benefit to feeling sorry for oneself and certainly none in showing such contempt for our Lord. Just because you aren't getting your way doesn't mean that a way is not being made for you. You must have faith in the mystery of God and in his divine plan. I recognize the challenges you face, and they are not trivial. One step at a time I will do what I can to help you. In fact, we have another novitiate coming next week who is supposed to be a teacher's aide. I'll ask mother superior if perhaps this young woman can watch the baby while you're in class. This will only be temporary, of course."

I pressed my luck. "What about cheerleading practice after school?"

She was undaunted. "Like I said, one step at a time."

I brushed aside a run-away tear. "Promise me you won't tell my parents about Mary Joyce?"

"Yes, I promise. I know you are looking out for each of them, and I admire that," she spoke sincerely.

Though no less confused about God's quirky and mysterious ways, I was suddenly feeling embarrassed about my impulsive remarks to one of his kind ambassadors.

"I think I should head home," I said while standing up. She did the same, while throwing yet another morsel of morality at me.

"I know this might seem odd coming from me, but there is an old Yiddish proverb that I want to share with you." With that she took my hands and then gently spoke. "When the father gives to his son, both laugh; when the son gives to his father, both cry." She squeezed my hands before letting go. "Clearly you are being called upon to give to your parents. And you should do so with a grateful heart."

I nodded with half-hearted appreciation. I knew what she said was supposed to be profound and should be sinking in. But all I wanted was to leave and have a cigarette. Being the love-struck fool that I was, that was no longer an option, so I decided on getting ice cream instead. "Thanks, Sister. I'll get back to you with the paperwork and the tuition," I said, then departed to Guvelli's.

Later that evening, after all the kids and my mother were in bed, I found my father sitting alone on the porch swing. Typically he would have gently swayed while slowly drinking a single Pabst Blue Ribbon beer as my mother – in saner days – nestled beside him as they shared the day's events. Tonight, however, he was drinking a can of soda and wasn't even rocking.

"Dad, can I join you?"

"Sure," he half-grinned at seeing me, then scooted over. He'd recently taken a shower and smelled fresh and clean.

"Nice night," he said nonchalantly. "Is the baby asleep?"

"Yeah. By the way, I took him in for a check-up this morning and he's doing really well."

He patted my knee. "That's good to hear."

"Yeah, I know. Can you believe summer's almost over?"

"You ready for school?"

"No."

"I was never ready either." My father had finished high school by the skin of his teeth.

"Dad, we need to talk."

"Sure, what's on your mind?"

"Well, first of all, Sister Perpetua called today. No one in our family was registered for school yet."

He scratched the back of his head and let out an exhausted sigh.

"Don't worry. I took care of it. Well, sort of. I picked up all the paperwork and some uniforms. But I need you to sign everything. Plus, I need a couple of checks from you."

"For how much?" he gruffed.

"It's not so bad. Monsignor offered to let me and Tommy attend Pallotti for the price of one. It's two-for-one at St. Mary's for Joey and Timmy, too."

"That I can do."

"And then only $100 for Raymond at St. Mary's. Paul will be a ninth-grader this year. So you can either send him back to his public junior high or Pallotti at a discount."

"Hmmm. Tough call financially. Still, something tells me he could really use the more disciplined structure at Pallotti. What about Patty and Frankie?"

"This is Frankie's last year at Laurel High, and Patty will have to attend Laurel Elementary where they have the right resources to teach her."

"How about the baby?"

My stomach clenched as I prepared to broach the next topic.

"Dad, I need to talk with you about someone else, first."

"Who's that?"

"Ma."

He took a deliberately long sip of his soda.

"You know what I mean, right?"

"I know," he said warily. "Your mother's not well."

"She's not well because she's drunk."

"She's drunk because she's not well."

"Can't you help her?"

"I've tried."

"Try again."

He grew defiant. "It's not that easy, Gail. She won't listen to me. She won't listen to anybody right now. Ever since Cate died she's become hostile and insulting. It's impossible to talk with her."

That pretty well summed it up. And I was at least shrewd enough not to suggest he wasn't doing his best. My mother might be unraveling, but my father was working tirelessly to keep up his end of the bargain. We sat in dispirited silence, each contemplating this sad turn of family events. I leaned my head on to his shoulder and into a quiet reservoir of solidarity.

After a spell, we began to gently sway. "I told Bill at the liquor store to shut her off. But I can't babysit her, and all he cares about is making a sale. I've even told Mrs. Logan that your mother has too much going on in her own house to help her. I don't know what else to do," he lamented. "I've reminded your mother that this isn't what Cate would want. I've told her that everyone's suffering without her." He looked askance before speaking again. "God, I miss her," he said, his voice trembling, a rare tear escaping.

"Me too, Dad," I choked back emotion. "Still, I don't get it. How could she have fallen so hard and so fast?"

"Somehow she blames herself for Cate's death."

"Why?" I straightened up and turned toward him.

"Cate was a wreck and really wanted out of that marriage. Last year your mother was trying to help her find a place to live. Francis figured out what was going on, which is when he turned all sweet on her. At least long enough to get her pregnant with John. Then he got ugly again." He paused, perhaps wondering if he'd shared too much. "You know, those two gals lost both their parents at a young age. Being the older sister, your mother took charge. Now she feels like she not only lost her only sibling and let her best friend down, but she failed their parents as well."

I reflected on this. I already knew my mother had wanted Cate to get out of that marriage. I also knew their mother had died from leukemia when they were respectively thirteen and nine years old, and that afterwards my mother did her best to bridge the maternal gap in Cate's life. It wasn't easy, particularly a year later when in 1938 their father found work as a welding foreman with a prominent American ship builder and moved them from Belfast to Baltimore. I knew about the difficult adjustment period. But also how they'd eventually — and happily — settled into life as "Americans." Until, that is, an untimely heart attack killed my grandfather. My mother was barely eighteen and had just graduated from high-school. Instead of going to college, she got a full-time job as a stenographer and finished raising Cate. During this time my father began courting my mother and was intimately familiar with their circumstances.

Gently interrupting my thoughts, my father went on. "Where your mother was practical and had common sense, Cate was carefree and a bit naive. Your mother could see through Francis before they ever married, but not Cate," he uncharacteristically delved in. "He was a good plumber, fun-loving and church-going, so Cate thought her future with him was secure. Coupla' times though, when they were dating, we went out to dinner with them. One time when the bill came he suddenly realized he'd left his wallet at home, so Cate paid. The second time it happened, your mother knew it was an issue. She tried talking to Cate about it, but your aunt was snowed and the next thing we knew they'd run off to Atlantic City to get married. Turns out she was pregnant with Frankie."

My heart caved in. Ironically, I was desperate to protect *my* carefree, naive, and pregnant sister. Here my father was candidly sharing adult problems and perspectives with me for the first time ever — particularly those involving my mother — while I was likewise anguishing over how to protect them from pain I just learned contained a familiar thread. This conversation, like my earlier one with Sister Perpetua, sparked a strange inward permutation, as if the training wheels on my youthful soul were suddenly off. I was on a crash course into adulthood and it evoked none of the glee I'd anticipated. I'd always envisioned being a grown-up as something like living in an amusement park with no lines, always fast and always fun. You could do what you wanted, when you wanted, and no one would stop you. Only now, I felt strapped-in and stuck upside-down on a broken ride. The thrill was gone. I just wanted off. My father wasn't helping.

"He was fun-loving all right," my father sarcastically added. "And it wasn't long before we learned he was a binge-drinking slacker and a serious gambler who spent Sundays at the race track. Their first year together he went through all of Cate's inheritance. Then he lost one job after another. Couldn't keep his mouth shut and was always getting fired. Cate ended up working full-time at a grocery store while she was pregnant with Frankie to support them. Poor Cate, she was so sweet. And miserable from nearly the beginning of that marriage. The only thing that made her happy were those kids." As he fell silent, all I could think of was Mary Joyce's exuberance for her unborn child. I heard him sniffle. He was crying again.

"Early on your mother told Cate that God would forgive her for leaving such an abusive swindler. She begged her to get out. Every time Cate would work up the courage to leave, he'd pretend to clean up his act. So she'd stay."

"Dad, I don't understand. If you knew Uncle Francis was so abusive, then why didn't you want the cousins to live with us right away?"

Shame seeped into his voice. "I thought maybe it was something between him and Cate. I really couldn't imagine a man mistreating his own children."

"Even after he tried giving them away?"

"Look, I panicked. It's a lot of people to be living under one tiny roof and on my salary. But even though my hand got forced, they're family and I'm glad they're here with us now. I just wish they'd find that SOB Francis. I can't help but sleep with one eye open, and I know everything he's done is tearing your mother up."

"I know what you mean about Uncle Francis. Still, Ma got what she wanted. The kids are here and, for the most part, happy."

"Yeah, but Cate's dead and she feels like it's her fault," he reiterated.

"So they go from living with one drunk to another. It doesn't make sense. If she loved Cate so much, why wouldn't she want to do everything possible to love them and be there for them?"

"She can hardly talk about it, your mother. But she was holding Cate's hand the moment she died. Whenever that baby cries, all your mother sees and hears is Cate gasping for her last breath just as that baby made his first."

I thought of our earlier clash and how my mother tried to feed John his bottle, only to instantly pass him off when his wail grew hot and pitched. Just moments before I was struggling to find pity for her. Yet now all I wanted to do was comfort her. My heart began aching for John, too, realizing that the only one who seemed to truly love him was me; an accidental love at best.

"Does she blame John for Cate's death?"

"She's never said so."

"But she wants nothing to do with him."

"That sounds so harsh."

"It makes sense."

He heaved an exasperated sigh. "We're gonna get through this," he uttered.

"How, Dad?"

"I have faith," he said, "that God *will* get us through this."

I wondered if he would feel the same way knowing about Mary Joyce's condition.

"Really, Dad? Do you think? I seriously wonder about God and his mysterious ways. Truthfully, right now, it feels like a never-ending game of hide-and-stupid-seek."

I was taken aback by my second burst of outspokenness for the day, and fully expected a disappointed response. Instead, my fairly undemonstrative father lightly chuckled as he wiped away another tear. Then he picked up my hand and kissed it.

"Well, it's no mystery how grateful I am for all that you are doing. Besides," he added, "I get the feeling that God is doing his level best to keep this family together, and thankfully found strength in *you* to help get the job done."

Chapter 22

Fortunately Mary Joyce left behind a spaghetti-strapped, aqua-blue, chiffon dress that fit me perfectly. I know it looked more striking with her black hair than my brown. But something about wearing her dress provided me with a sense of armor; I was going into battle and I needed all the protection I could get. I'd solicited Frankie's help with the kids – something he willingly agreed to do – giving me several free hours to get dressed and go out for the evening.

"Wow," said Patty upon entering our bedroom. "Are you going to a birthday party?"

We'd spent half the day at the dentist's office, so with her new caps she looked and sounded much better. She was not so happy, however, with the decision to send her to Laurel Elementary instead of St. Mary's and insisted on wearing their parochial uniform to the public school. To accommodate her, I went back to the gently used bin and found two plaid – albeit badly stained – jumpers. Though school had yet to start, she was already wearing one with a striped T-shirt beneath it, along with her patent leather shoes and pillowcase veil.

I smiled. "It's just a regular party, and thank you for the compliment."

Her demeanor darkened. "Are you going with John?"

"Nope. Nadette."

"Can I go?" She chirped.

"Oh, no honey. I wish I could bring you. But this is not a party for children."

"I'll wait for you in the car."

I laughed. "Well, Patty, if I could, I would bring you. But we're going to the Chevy Chase Club and they won't allow children to wait in the car either."

She jumped on her bed alongside Brandy, presently curled up there and watching us both. "Then I'll wait up for you."

"That's fine," I said, knowing how fast she usually fell asleep. "And, since you'll be awake, would you mind helping Frankie with John? I don't think he's as good at changing diapers as you are."

"Sure," she smiled, though her diapering skills were lacking, too.

"Thanks, Patty. I knew I could count on you." She beamed.

While spraying on a light cologne mist, I heard a knock at the front door. "I'll bet that's Nadette," I said, glancing at myself in the mirror one last time – and yes, I approved. I kissed Patty's forehead, grabbed my clutch, then headed downstairs. Indeed it was Nadette, whom Tommy was already ogling. She was wearing a sophisticated, straight-cut and sleeveless satin dress with a collarless, short-sleeved jacket and matching sandal heels all in a soft shade of peach. The dress's peek-a-boo side-slit emphasized her long, shapely legs. Her pale blonde hair, make-up and nails had just the right touch – not overdone but just enough to magnify her prettiness. She looked intensely gorgeous.

"And where exactly are you two going?" my father asked.

"A party at the Chevy Chase Club," I said.

"Really?" he looked at me incredulously. "And how does one get an invitation to a party at the Chevy Chase Club?"

"From friends of *your* family," Nadette piped in. I held my breath.

"*Our* family?" His eyes widened.

"Listen, Dad, we're running a bit late. I'll fill you in later."

"What time are you coming home?"

"I'll be back by midnight. And don't worry, Frankie and Patty are watching the baby."

"*That's* not the baby I'm worried about," he said, his voice mingled with pride and concern. "You two be careful out there. And no drinking," he said, his eyes darting between us.

"Yes, sir," Nadette piped up.

"You girls have fun," Tommy said, then pecked both of us on the cheek – though he loitered slightly longer on Nadette's. She blushed.

"Good night, everyone," I said, grabbing her by the arm before she could say or do anything dumb.

"Did you see that? Your brother kissed me. Do you think he likes me?" she gushed as we climbed into her Buick – a big, blue, boat-of-a-vehicle with tail fins, white-wall tires and a steering wheel larger than the lid of a garbage can.

"Wanna cigarette?" she asked, pushing in the lighter and producing a pack of smokes from her purse.

"No, thanks." I said, still mum about quitting because of John O'Neill.

"You sure?" she said, putting one in her mouth.

"Positive," I said, now checking my image in the car's vanity mirror.

"Ow!" she suddenly screamed, then madly veered on to the shoulder of the road.

"What are you doing?" I screamed back.

"Dammit! I just dropped the lighter. It bounced off my calf and now it's rolling around my feet."

"I'll get it! Just watch the road," I pleaded, then immediately sunk to the floor where I snatched the cool end of the hot metal tube from near her feet.

"Both of us could die young because of your smoking," I said handing it over as she steered us back on the road. She lit her cigarette, then returned the device to its dashboard chamber. Because she didn't want to ruin her hair, she'd kept the windows rolled up. Shortly, the smoke started choking me. "Do you really want to smell like Oliver's Tavern tonight?"

"Rich people smoke, too, you know. In fact, they invented cigarettes to make money off all us poor people."

"Says who?"

"Says Sister Mary Elizabeth. And it's in our history books. When the English finally beat the Spanish Armada in 1587, and could settle in the 'New World' without a fight from them, what did they find? Indians growing and smoking tobacco. The early settlers got hooked on it and started selling it in Europe. Before long they had vending machines everywhere."

"That is so not true."

"Yes it is!"

"Everyone knows the Spanish Armada was defeated in 1588."

"Really, Brittany Britannica?"

"In fifteen-hundred and eighty-eight, the Spanish Armada met its fate."

"Oh, I'm sorry. You're actually Humpty Dumpty," she said sarcastically then rolled down her window and tossed out her cigarette. "By the way, just whose party is this?"

"It's an engagement party for Steve Barelli and Connie Sullivan."

"Do you even know them?"

"No."

"I didn't think so."

"Why?"

"You said they were family friends, but your father was clueless. Besides, you never mentioned them before. You're up to no good. I can tell."

"Why do you say that?"

"I know you wouldn't have invited me if you didn't need an accomplice. You weren't even invited, were you?"

"No," I confessed.

"Wait a minute. I spent all day getting ready and twenty-three dollars on this dress to crash a party?"

"Pretty much."

She started giggling. "I love it. And even if you'd told me the truth from the start, I'd still have spent all day getting ready and even *fifty* dollars on *this* dress. I mean, think about it. An engagement party at the Chevy Chase Club can mean only one thing."

"Good food?"

"Better than that. Fine men."

"'Men?'" I startled, imagining Nadette flirting with someone my father's age.

"You know what I mean. Boys. A little bit older and a lot richer. Boys who turn into rich men."

"I thought you liked my poorer brother."

"Yeah, but I'm not sure he'd ever really like me."

"I wouldn't be so sure about that," I replied thinking how his eyes nearly popped out of his head a short while ago. Fortunately, the conversation shifted as from the radio the Mamas and the Papas began singing one of our favorite songs, now telling us to go where we wanted to go. We merrily sang along with them, each of us feeling more grown up than ever as, all dolled up and on our own, we were going where we wanted to go. Shortly we were crooning along with Frankie Valli, who couldn't seem to take his eyes off of us, and then with Neil Diamond when he told us we'd be women soon.

The radio volume and our jolliness ebbed a half-hour later when we hit the light at the intersection of Bradley Boulevard and Connecticut Avenue in Chevy Chase. There at the southwest corner sat the imposing and exclusive club with its porticoed entrance and fieldstone buildings that seemed to stretch half-a-mile. We both gulped.

"Do you feel like we're not in Kansas anymore?" asked Nadette, sounding nervous as she pulled into the driveway. While her car was perfectly at home in our neighborhood, we were soon to learn our first lesson about the manor born and their preference for late model and far sleeker cars.

I took a deep breath. The mere sight of the building – a bulwark against the likes of us – made me feel sick. How could Mary Joyce possibly expect to compete with this? It wasn't a matter of old money versus new money; it was old money versus no money at all.

"Nadette, promise me you'll be on your best behavior."

"Tell me again why we're here."

"No."

"How badly do you want me to behave myself?"

"More than you can imagine."

"I'll do my best. Just tell me why we're here."

"I will when the time is right," I said. Checking my image in the car's vanity mirror once more, I applied a fresh coat of lip gloss and sighed nervously as the valet opened my door.

"Thank you," I said very formally, while climbing out of the car and on to the first step leading into the club.

"Promise me?" I heard Nadette say.

I turned, but it wasn't me she was talking to.

"I mean it. Don't let anything happen to this car or my mother will kill me."

"Don't worry," said a young, clean-cut, parking attendant. "I wouldn't let anything happen to the car of the prettiest girl here."

Nadette blushed. "You're so sweet," she cooed. "What's your name?"

"Ronnie," he grinned.

"Nadette," I hissed, and jerked my head, indicating I wanted her to move it instead of flirting with the hired help.

"Thanks, Ronnie," she teasingly smiled, then dropped the claim ticket in her purse like an old pro before finally joining me. "Do you have any idea where we're headed?"

"Yeah. I called the club earlier today to confirm. Upstairs ballroom."

Once inside the foyer, we both stood still. I'd never seen furnishings so rich nor ceilings so high, their imposing height a good match for this lofty crowd. The area was crowded with young and old alike, many greeting each other like lifelong chums. As no one paid particular attention to us, we silently absorbed the sights and sounds.

"And I thought *I* had a good tan," she whispered.

"C'mon," I said beneath my breath. "Let's go."

Fortunately she clammed up and followed my lead. It didn't take long for us to find an expansive staircase leading to the second floor where it appeared the party-goers were headed.

Nadette had been right. There were a lot of very fine men – dozens of young, handsome preppies conducting themselves with a fun and breezy grace. Fortunately, we'd gotten the dress code right and so far fit in with a sea of perfectly attractive people, in perfectly tailored clothes with perfect teeth and perfect hair finding their way to the perfect food.

In addition to the sumptuously laden buffet tables replete with roast beef carving stations, there were big bowls of ice-cold shrimp, and servers in crisp uniforms passing out delicate hors d'oeuvres. Ignoring etiquette, we each helped ourselves to a heaping plate of just about everything, then stopped for more en route to an open bar.

"What do you want?" Nadette asked, her mouth full of shrimp cocktail.

"A ginger ale, please. I'll meet you back here in just a minute," I said, needing to survey the room.

I might not have seen Steve Barelli right away, but it would have been impossible to miss the bride-to-be. Connie Sullivan was the cool, thin brunette with a glow-in-the-dark rock on her left hand. Her dazzling smile added to the effect. I'll admit she was quite a package deal – rich and beautiful. And then I saw him. Without any introduction, I knew who he was.

First, he warmly shook the hand of whomever she was talking with, then slipped his arm behind her back and gave her a little peck on the cheek. He was every bit as handsome as she was pretty, and I suddenly found myself wrapped up in the fairy tale existence of this couple. He seemed charming, and regardless of his financial status I could see why Mary Joyce was attracted to him. With his sun-kissed blonde hair and all-American good looks, I could also see the resemblance to Jack Nicklaus.

I anxiously licked my lips then drifted his way. I was standing just behind one other well-wisher when he caught my eye and smiled at me somewhat knowingly. I smiled back. I had no interest in talking with Connie, and so I waited until her attention was again diverted before sidling up beside him.

"Hello, Steve."

He smiled flirtatiously. "You look familiar. How do I know you?"

"Does the name Mary Joyce Kenealy ring a bell?"

"Mary Joyce?" he startled, studying my face.

"No," I blurted. "I'm Mary Joyce's sister and we need to talk."

His look grew dark and defensive. "I'm busy. It will have to wait."

"No," I said firmly. "We need to talk now."

"Stevie," Connie suddenly interrupted. "This is my uncle from Connecticut I've been telling you all about. Uncle Bill, this is Steve Barelli, and...."

Steve shot me a dark look before returning his attention to his truly betrothed. Just as I slithered away I heard Nadette's voice.

"Gail, there you are! I've been looking all over for you."

I quickly gulped the ginger ale she handed me. "There's rum in it," she grinned.

"Oh, great," I choked slightly on the after-taste. "Please tell me you're not drinking."

"Is that the happy couple?" she asked, diverting my question. Still planning to keep secret my true intentions, I nevertheless took her by the arm and moved us out of earshot distance from them when we were suddenly interrupted.

"Nadette," I heard the young man's smooth voice. I turned to see one of the fine, classically-dressed, preppies with a beguiling smile. It was like staring right in the face of what could have been the poster boy for anything from Eagle Scouts, to a famous astronaut, to the future president of the United States.

"Oh, hi, Charles. This is my friend Gail."

"Nice to meet you, Gail. Nadette and I just met at the bar. Do you two happen to know Connie from Sweet Briar?"

Nadette swiftly butted in. "Sweet Briar? No offense to Connie, but please. We still have two more years at Princeton," she responded so assuredly that I almost believed her.

"Really?" he smirked.

I took a nervous sip of my drink.

"You two are in high school, aren't you?"

"What makes you think that?" Nadette stupidly grinned.

"I'm kind of smart that way."

"Where do you go to school?" she asked.

"Princeton."

Nadette didn't miss a beat. "How is it we've missed each other?"

"Probably because no girls go there," he threw his head back, laughing snootily.

Humiliation consumed me and I felt my face flush. "Will you excuse me, please?"

"Sure," they said. He seemed more interested in her, anyway, so I left them and wandered out through some French doors to an expansive balcony overlooking the emerald green golf course. Clearly we weren't in Kansas anymore, and I truly felt like there was no place like home. I could hardly believe these people had suffered any of the hardships in their lifetime that I'd already packed into one summer. All I could think about was my poor sister and how offensive it was that she was deemed good enough to screw, but not to marry. Feeling overwhelming heartbreak for her and deep disdain for Steve Barelli, I marched back into the ballroom.

Now that he was on to me, he darted in the opposite direction whenever I got near. At one point I brazenly got close to Connie acting as if I might start talking with her instead. Seeing me, he quickly squired her away to the other side of the room. I played cat and mouse with him like this for nearly an hour, when it dawned on me that I hadn't seen Nadette in a while. Changing tack, I started looking for her, but she wasn't in the ballroom. I headed to the hallway and when passing by two older women leaving the powder room heard one comment about how these young kids just can't hold their liquor. I darted inside and heard Nadette before I even saw her peach shoes sticking out beneath the door of the marble-walled stall.

Buuuuhhhh.

"Nadette?"

"GM?" she said, using her drunken nickname for Gail Marie. "Is that you?"

"Yes, are you okay?"

"Uh-huh." *Buuuuhhhh.*

"Oh, my god," I said. The stall door wasn't even locked, and pulling it open I found her kneeling before the toilet. I quickly pulled back her hair and held it in place as she puked some more.

"How much have you had to drink?"

"Just one."

"Just one?!"

Buuuuhhhh. "Just one right after the other." *Buuuuhhhh.* "With Princeton."

Two more women came into the bathroom, so I promptly closed the stall door. "Oh, this is just great." I whispered harshly. "I thought you promised your parents you wouldn't drink and drive. How can you possibly drive home?"

"I'll be okay." *Buuuuhhhh.*

This was a disaster. I did not have my learner's permit with me. "Nadette, you need to work this off."

"Happy to," she said, then finally stood up. There was barf on her dress, face and hair. Feeling panicked, I waited until the others had left the room before I opened the door and escorted her to a sink to rinse off.

"Oh, that feels sooo good," she slurred while splashing cold water on her face. I held my breath as another guest entered the room, then jammed a hand towel bearing the club's fancy insignia into her hands.

"Quick! Wipe your face and follow me," I commanded, remembering that down the hall from the ballroom there were smaller, vacant dining rooms. We made our way to the darkened corner of one where I got her to lie down beneath a skirted table.

"Don't go anywhere without me," I admonished her.

"Promise," she said, and within seconds passed out in a semi-fetal position using the towel as a makeshift pillow.

Timing in life is everything. No sooner had I entered the ballroom again in search of Steve Barelli when I witnessed the arrival of another party crasher: Sister Perpetua who, in her full black habit and stiff demeanor, had people clearing out of her way faster than the Red Sea parted for Moses.

"Good evening, Sister," people spoke while taking a respectful step back.

"Sister."

"God bless, Sister." One person after another humbly acknowledged her as she coursed determinedly through the ballroom crowd, her furious pace giving the impression of a black-clad Whirling Dervish.

How could she do this to me? I angrily wondered. Much as I wanted to protect Mary Joyce myself, this was beyond embarrassing. And realizing that whatever was about to take place was now out of my hands, I attempted to steer clear of her.

"Monsignor Flanagan," she said finally stopping when she came upon the apparently familiar face. He was standing nearby me. "I'm looking for Steve Barelli. Can you point him out?"

The presumed officiant of the wedding smiled warmly. "Sure, Sister, he's over there," he said, pointing Steve's way. "Nice young man."

"We'll see about that," she said curtly, making her way to him in seconds flat.

"Are you Steve Barelli?" she abruptly broke into his conversation.

"Yes, Ma'am."

"We need to talk."

"Right now?"

"Yes, right now."

"Is there a problem?" Connie piped in.

"I should say," said Sister in a most deprecating way.

"No, no," Steve reassured Connie. "We'll be right back." With that, he stepped away with Sister beside him. "I don't understand. What is this all about?"

"Young man, where is your father?"

"He's, uhm, he's here somewhere."

"I suggest you go find him."

"Would you mind telling me what this is all about, first?"

"I will not. You go get your father this instant."

Steve complied, shortly returning with his father – a good looking, but somewhat smarmy, man. "Sister," said Mr. Barelli, a cocktail in one hand and a cigar in the other. "And to what do we owe the honor?"

"I need to have a word with both of you. Is there somewhere we can speak in private?"

Even with my back turned toward them, I knew this meant trouble. Darting out of the room as quickly and inconspicuously as possible, I headed to the empty dining room where Nadette was thankfully sound asleep.

"Nadette," I nudged her, hoping she'd stir. She moaned and rolled over.

"Oh, for crying out loud," I said realizing it was utterly fruitless to think she'd be driving home. "Nadette," I poked her again, then startled as I heard the doors to the darkened room open. Shortly a light popped on, prompting me to crouch while peering around the table's skirt.

"Here, have a seat," Mr. Barelli said, pulling out a chair for Sister Perpetua at one of the other round tables. She refused the courtesy, so Steve sat down instead.

"How can I help you?" he asked while setting down his cocktail. Grabbing an ashtray, he took one last drag before stubbing out his cigar.

"I am here to tell you that there will be no wedding, Mr. Barelli. At least not between your son and Miss Sullivan."

"I'm sorry, Sister, I don't quite follow you."

"Perhaps your son can tell you why."

Steve shrugged his shoulders. "I don't have a clue what she's talking about, Dad."

"Does the name Mary Joyce Kenealy ring a bell?" she asked.

Steve started to shake his head no, but Sister's hot glare forced it to change direction. Yes, he nodded.

"Son, do you know her?" Mr. Barelli asked.

"Yeah, I think so."

"You think so, or you *know* so?" Sister unhesitatingly interjected. "Because she's pregnant. With your child."

"Steve, please tell me this is not true," Mr. Barelli stated, his eyes darting between them.

"I guess. I mean, maybe it's my baby."

"How dare you insult me with 'maybe it's my baby,'" Sister castigated him.

"Sister, please have a seat," Mr. Barelli suggested. Again, she declined.

He turned to his son. "I'm sure we can work this out. Steve, what's going on here? Is this true?" Mr. Barelli asked again, nervously sitting down himself.

"Yeah, I guess," said Steve.

"Did you or did you not get this Mary Joyce girl pregnant?" his father insisted. This time Steve looked his father in the eye and shook his head yes.

"Dammit, Steve! This is a disaster. Why didn't you tell me about this before?"

"I don't know. I barely know her. How do I know if it's even *my* baby?"

"So do you admit you had sex with her?" Sister Perpetua sharply asked.

"Yes."

"Did she tell you she was pregnant?" she persisted.

"Yes."

"And you proposed to her, then just let her move off to Florida in false anticipation that you would marry her?"

"Wait, wait, wait!" Mr. Barelli jumped in. "How pregnant is she?"

"Just a little," said Steve.

"A little?" Sister Perpetua harshly laughed. "In the same way, perhaps, that you are just 'a little' engaged to Connie Sullivan? For the record, this young lady is in her second trimester."

"Is she here?" Mr. Barelli asked.

Pure contempt for him arose in me. Clearly he was more concerned about the unfolding social consequences than his grandchild's well-being.

"No," Sister replied. "She is down in Florida awaiting your son's arrival when he finishes touring with the PGA."

"See, I knew this was some big mistake," he said with genuine relief. "I don't have a son touring with the PGA." Her look seemed to decimate him. Suddenly it sank in as he turned toward Steve. "You told her you were touring with the P-G-A?"

"I wanted to impress her."

"That's some impression you left," he snorted incredulously. "Sister, pardon my saying so, but I do need to play devil's advocate. Is it possible that she's not really pregnant and that she's after him for his money? Or, if she is, that it's not his child and she's trying to get his money? We're worth a lot, you know, so that wouldn't surprise me. And who is this girl, anyway?" he added derisively.

Sister's face and mood darkened even more. "I find your attitudes to be sinful and outrageous," she immediately chastened them. "We are talking about a fine young woman from an upstanding family. Not to mention you are questioning my own veracity."

"Steve?" his father said inquisitively. "So, is it true?"

"I guess so. I mean, yeah. But I don't really know her. She's really pretty, though," he added as if somehow it would at least make his father understand.

"That," Sister Perpetua harrumphed, "is precisely the problem. They didn't even know each other and they had sex. There are consequences for that kind of behavior, Mr. Barelli. And I am sure that if I take this up with the Cardinal he will agree. With everything."

Mr. Barelli blanched. "Sister, please. We don't need that kind of trouble. Listen," he said now reaching inside his suit jacket for his ever-ready remedy. "Will it make any difference if I write the poor girl and her family a check?"

"And then what? Have your son proceed with getting married to someone else, thereby abandoning his child – YOUR grandchild – and its' 'poor' mother?" she mocked him. "I think not."

Mr. Barelli shrugged his shoulders. "I don't know what else to do."

"I'll tell you what to do, or else I'll do it for you. You tell Monsignor Flanagan that there will not be a wedding. And then you send your son down to Florida to join Miss Kenealy and let the two of them sort this out like the adults they are supposed to be."

Suddenly, the banquet room door banged opened and Mrs. Barelli barged in. She did not sound pleased. "What is going on here?" she angrily demanded. I had observed her in the ballroom and she came across as a snobby bitch with a practiced put-down air. Clearly in her youth she had been a more attractive woman. But as is often the case with women so endowed, they do whatever they can to preserve that youthful look even when they gain weight and the style no longer suits them or the day. At one point, her luxuriant red hair might have been the centerpiece of her appearance. Now, dyed and teased into the most ridiculous proportions, it looked like a nesting place for numerous feathered creatures. In addition, a presumed girdle barely diminished her girth, making her pink Chanel suit look more like bouclé sausage casing.

"We're talking to Sister, uhm, Sister..." offered Mr. Barelli.

"Perpetua," she said matter-of-factly.

"Honey, this is Sister Perpetua from..."

"Laurel."

173

"Sister Perpetua from Laurel just came to pay us a visit. Isn't that nice?"

"Sister, thank you for joining us," Mrs. Barelli said with contrived politeness. "But my husband and my son are ignoring our other guests and I won't have it."

"Honey, you need to give us a moment longer," Mr. Barelli implored.

"You can talk later. I need you out there – now," she ordered, thrusting her weight upon the situation.

Mr. Barelli stood up. "Excuse me, Sister," he said very considerately. "I'll be right back."

Speaking in a low, obviously threatening tone, he pulled Mrs. Barelli aside and closer to my hide-out. "I said, you need to give us a moment longer."

"I don't care. What possible business could she have that is more important than our guests? This is a very special event in our son's life. People are asking for him."

His voice grew sharp. "It appears the only special event we can anticipate right now is the birth of our first grandchild."

"Connie's pregnant?" she startled. "She can't be very far along, and the wedding is in a matter of weeks. She'll still fit into her dress. We'll just say it's a honeymoon baby," she said, quickly calculating the social costs.

No, he shook his head.

"Why not?" she insisted. "The timing works out."

"Because," he said through gritted teeth, "It's not Connie's baby."

If Mrs. Barelli was smart about anything, it was that she knew her place in this society had everything to do with proper appearances and his money.

"Do I need to get the checkbook?" she whispered darkly.

"I've got it."

Her expression intensified. "Then I expect you to take care of it." With that, she put the steam roller in reverse and retreated from the room.

"Like I was saying," said Mr. Barelli as he turned to Sister and Steve.

"No, like I was telling *you*," Sister Perpetua interrupted. "There will be no wedding. At least not between your son and Connie Sullivan. I am not asking. I am telling you. I insist he put his selfish, immature behavior to an end to do the right thing by Mary Joyce Kenealy and their child. Am I clear?"

"Steve," said his father, "please go join your mother."

Steve bolted.

Mr. Barelli retrieved a pen from his coat pocket and was positioning it atop a blank check. "Sister, those two kids don't even know each other. What harm would it do if we gave her money to support herself and the baby — a baby that we don't even know for certain is his? And then allow my son to go ahead and get married to Connie — whom he and the rest of our family truly loves — as planned? I think that would work best."

Without responding, Sister Perpetua did an about-face and marched toward the door.

"Sister Perfecta....*please*, wait."

She halted and slowly turned, the wrath on her face looking like it could have stopped the bulls in Pamplona. Barelli withered. "We'll work this out. I promise I'll send him to Florida first thing Monday morning."

"Tonight."

"Okay, tomorrow. And we'll get this worked out. I promise."

With a quietly devastating look, she studied him for any signs of insincerity. His pen was now poised once more above his checkbook. "Don't you need a new convent, or something?" he meekly asked.

"Yes. We do," she replied, essentially shoveling the first pile of dirt. "But before we discuss that I will confirm that your son is on his way to Florida. Tomorrow. Even if it means I have to drive him to the airport myself. If not, I will call the Cardinal. Tomorrow. Now do I make myself clear?"

A call to the Cardinal could clearly send his construction projects up in smoke. Mr. Barelli put the pen down looking like one of her unruly students who'd been caught in some sinful act. "Yes, Sister Perfecta."

"Per-pet-u-a. My name is Sister PER-PET-U-A," she chided him once more, then swiftly left.

"Per-fec-ta. Per-pe-tu-ity. Poop-de-doo. Whatever," he snorted once she'd closed the door and he his checkbook. Again, timing is everything. As he rose to leave, Nadette groaned. I put a hand over her mouth to keep her from saying anything. She promptly puked into my hand.

"Oh, gross," I said loudly.

Barelli was over us in an instant.

"Bad shrimp," I said looking up at him scornfully.

"You girls been in here the whole time?"

Yes, I nodded.

"You heard everything?"

Yes, I nodded.

He reached for his wallet.

"Here," he said, jamming two one-hundred dollar bills into my barf-covered hand. "You didn't hear anything did you?"

"My name is Gail Kenealy," I said, now handing the barf-covered bills back. "And Mary Joyce is my sister."

He raised his hands in an "I surrender" gesture and quickly left the room.

Shortly, we did too. After stuffing Nadette into the back seat of her car, I adjusted the driver's seat and the mirrors, then for good measure I crossed myself before pulling tentatively out of the parking lot.

"Ship to shore," she piped up from way in the back seat before passing out again. "Promise you won't tell Tommy?"

"Promise," I said, my mind on more important things as I turned the big, blue boat on to Connecticut Avenue.

"You're the best friend a girl could ever have." Then silence.

Thirty minutes later – and thankfully without incident – we were back in Laurel. At her insistence I left her alone in the back seat.

"Good night, Nadette," I said. Then, removing my high-heeled sandals, I walked barefoot in the dark back to my house, wondering just what on earth would happen with Mary Joyce and if she would ever forgive me for opening my big mouth.

One long week later I got my answer.

Two letters arrived, both of them from her. One was addressed to me, the other to my parents. Her pretty handwriting stood out on the pink stationery she'd chosen, which made me wonder if she was hoping for a girl. The postmark said "New Port Richey, Florida."

My mother tore her letter open with all the zeal of someone who'd just won a sweepstakes. In her eyes Mary Joyce wore wings. I quietly held tight to mine.

"Oh, oh, oh!" my mother exclaimed. "She loves it. She truly loves Our Lady of Perpetual Help." I had no idea my sister could be such a world-class liar.

"Mary Joyce says that she's made lots of friends. And that she'll be home for Christmas."

It was the happiest and most lucid moment my mother had experienced in weeks. I cringed at the notion of Mary Joyce walking in the door with an awesome tan but hugely pregnant.

"How nice," I responded. Retreating to my room with John on my hip, I set him down on my bed and opened Mary Joyce's letter to me.

"*Dear Gail,*

"*I lost the baby.*"

My heart sank to the floor.

"*But I'm doing okay. A few days after we talked, I had really, really bad cramps and was bleeding heavily, which I thought was odd since you're not supposed to have a period when you're pregnant. The pain so bad that I went to the emergency room. Later that night I had a miscarriage. It was awful.*

"*I tried calling Steve after it happened,*" she continued. I could barely bring myself to finish the sentence, "*but couldn't find him anywhere. I left him several urgent messages and told him where to reach me. Then, last Sunday he called and flew down to be with me for a couple of days before leaving to rejoin the tour. He's trying so hard to make it big.*"

Another world-class liar. No wonder they were attracted to each other. Still, my sister had faced a debilitating loss all alone. I read on.

"*I realized after all this how I'm really not ready to be a mother. Besides, I also realized that while Steve is awfully cute, all he can talk about is himself. I asked him if we would still get married. He said he'd think about it. What a jerk. I told him we were through.*

"*He took it really well. In fact, he insisted on giving me a check for $5,000 from his PGA winnings to help me out, which was nice. He also asked me to keep this whole thing just between us. I guess that's okay, so I'm only telling you because I trust you.*

"*Anyway, though I'm really sad about the baby, I do have some good news to share. There's a wonderful little college not far from here! I visited the campus and really like it. I talked with the admissions director, and given my good grades at*

Pallotti, I'll be able to start school at Trinity College in the spring semester. They said some famous preacher named Billy Graham even graduated from here. Neat, huh? The tuition isn't too bad, and I'll probably be able to get a scholarship. So now I have nearly $8,000 in cash and probably a scholarship!

"In the meantime, I'm recovering well. I also got a job as a waitress and then found a nice apartment with a pool! I've made some new friends and I actually like it here. At Christmas, I'll tell Ma and Dad that I didn't like Our Lady of Perpetual Help and decided to transfer.

"I hope you're doing okay. Give Patty and John extra hugs from me, would you? And please, please, please write me. Better yet, come visit! Your loving sis, MJ."

I read through her letter once more, stopping at the part about Billy Graham, when two things struck me. First, how my sister remained hopelessly ill-informed. Other than the Pope, Billy Graham was only the most famous preacher on the planet. And then, how she'd mentioned God's plan when she first shared the news about being pregnant.

I reached over and stroked John's head. No, perhaps MJ wasn't ready to be a mother. Neither was I. But still, she'd lost something precious. Her baby was, after all, a member of our family we would never know and I felt the loss, too. Now picking up John, I hugged him tight and cried, wondering even more about God's plans. If he was so great, then why all the suffering? Why weren't all the believers sane, happy people all the time? Some of them— my mother included – were truly miserable. Was that part of God's plan? So why on earth would Sister Perpetua think it necessary to thank God for all this misery?

I did not know. The only thing I knew for sure was that Mary Joyce was in a happy place and relieved of any obligation to Steve Barelli, whose dark behavior was white-washed only by his family's money. Perhaps *that* was God's plan, for MJ to land in Florida and in a place that made her happy.

So, *Our Lady of Perpetual Help*, I thought. *Wherever you are, thank you.*

Chapter 23

*I*t was our first day back to school and chaos ruled. Of course my father had left early for work while my mother slept in. And so, on the opening day of my junior-year in high school, I awoke to feed and change a nearly three-month-old baby while likewise getting his special needs sister squared away, being forced to take care of myself only at the last minute. It wasn't a pretty sight when I first glanced in the mirror, either. The circles beneath my eyes were darker than my summer tan, and I hadn't curled my hair. Instead, I pulled it back in a pony tail while wondering what John O'Neill would think of me looking like this. I hadn't heard from him since our date at the movies, so I also wondered if the whole scene in my house hadn't scared him away.

While Patty eagerly wore a uniform where none was needed, I reluctantly slipped on my own – which wasn't even ironed – and eventually made my way down to the kitchen where Raymond and Timmy were fighting over a box of cereal. And not its contents, mind you, but over who got to read the riddles on the package while eating breakfast. Sharing was a foreign concept to those two.

No one's lunch was made. And at the rate we were moving, it would be suppertime before that task was complete. After losing control of the cereal box, Raymond began belly-aching about wearing St. Mary's mandatory bow tie. "I hate this thing. It makes me feel stupid," he declared while ripping it off and stuffing it in the pocket of his pants. It was pointless for me to react as shortly the nuns would have him appropriately bedecked. I could only wish one of the nuns were in our kitchen right now, as the minute I turned my back Raymond jumped up and grabbed the cereal box, which started the squabbling anew.

Paul, on the other hand, seemed quietly pleased with the uniform mandate, including the necktie he was required to wear with his white button-down shirt and gray slacks. Last night he'd carefully laid out his entire uniform, including the new socks, shoes and belt my father purchased for him after treating him to a hair cut. We could finally see the kid's eyes. He and Frankie looked so much alike, except that Paul had recently suffered an outbreak of acne over which he was painfully sensitive.

"Oh, my gosh!" I gushed at the sight of him. "You look so handsome!"

Paul blushed as I impulsively kissed the top of his head.

"What about me?" said Joey, in his rumpled shirt and haphazardly affixed bow tie.

"Like I said, Paul, you look so handsome."

Joey responded by sticking out one of the crutches on which he was still dependent. Seeing it coming – and while holding the baby – I miraculously hurdled it.

"Way to go, Bozo. Are you trying to kill an innocent baby?"

"No, just you, the bigger baby."

I sneered, then nearly wet my pants as a deep voice boomed behind me. "Sit down, all of you!"

It was Frankie, who was neatly dressed and ready to go. Everyone, including me, startled.

"Do you have any idea what time it is?" he admonished us, while commandeering the cereal box. "You have ten minutes to finish breakfast, wash your dishes, and get out the door," he said, pouring cereal into Raymond's bowl. "Where's your bow tie?"

"In my pocket. I'm not wearing it."

"You know what the nuns do to kids like you, don't you?" Joey interjected with his brand of enlightenment. "They hang you from the flagpole in your underwear."

"Shut up!" said Raymond while fishing in his pocket, allowing Frankie to help him get the accessory back on.

"There are no lunches," I said.

"Good grief!" Frankie grimaced, promptly pulling out a loaf of bread, some peanut butter and jelly, quickly slapping together bag lunches for everyone. Only because of him were we late getting out the door by only a few minutes.

Before guiding Paul to Pallotti, Tommy led Joey and the younger boys to St. Mary's, while Frankie dropped Patty off at Laurel Elementary on his way to Laurel High. After packing the baby along with his diaper bag and my school junk into his pram, I began pushing him up the street toward the convent where the newly arrived novitiate was expecting us. En route John started squawking, so I popped a pacifier in his mouth realizing how hard it was to believe that just one year ago I was heading to school with Nadette while jabbering about cheerleading, John O'Neill, cheerleading and John O'Neill. Back then I had a serious tan, curled hair, pressed clothing, a lunch made by mother, and I was perfectly happy.

I was soon greeted at the convent with cheerful delight by Sister Aileen. "Oh, my goodness," she broadly grinned at the sight of John. "He's gorgeous."

"Thanks," I beamed. "I'm Gail Kenealy, his...cousin."

"It's a pleasure to meet you both. Sister Perpetua has filled me in a bit. Why don't you tell me about him and his schedule," she said lifting him out of his pram. I felt a pang of jealousy.

"Well, his name is John. John Aloysius."

"After the saints?" she said echoing my mother's pride.

"Of course."

"How lovely. And just how old is John Aloysius?"

"Almost eleven weeks."

"Practically a newborn," she gushed some more. "What else?"

"Well, he's already been fed and changed. His next poop is usually between 8:30 and 9:00 o'clock. After that, he takes about six ounces of formula, followed by his first nap. Then he'll sleep for an hour, sometimes two."

"Very well," she said glancing at her watch.

"Then you have to change him again, but it's usually only because he's peed."

"Okay."

"After his nap he loves to lie on the floor and play with his hands. I'm not sure if he knows they're connected to his body or not, but he thinks they're great fun. He's not a thumb-sucker – at least not yet. But he does enjoy his pacifier."

Sister nodded and smiled.

"After he plays on the floor for a bit," I proceeded, welling up with unexpected emotion and disquieting feelings of guilt, "I usually rock him while feeding him another bottle. And lately," I paused, "well, lately he just kind of happily studies me during his feedings. And then I burp him, and then I take him for a walk, and then, and then…"

I burst into tears. "I didn't expect this to be so hard."

"I can see that," she said reassuringly, handing him over so that *he* could comfort me. "And I hope that you will trust me to take very good care of him."

"Of course," I said, wiping tears away with the back of one hand. "It's just that we're so attached that it's hard to imagine trusting anyone else to take care of him. Even a nun."

"I understand," she said. "What time is your lunch break?"

"Eleven-thirty."

"Why don't you join us for lunch, then?"

"Oh, thank you so much. I'll do that," I said. And at last gathering my wits, I kissed him good-bye, then headed out the door and up to the high school.

There were happy faces everywhere and all the usual high-energy chatter and clanging of lockers preceding the start of class. Typically I'd search for my friends and try to find one with a pack of cigarettes or gum – perhaps both – and indulge myself with one or the other – or both – before school started. Gathering in outdoor cliques, we'd sneak a smoke and catch up on one another's gossip before the warning bell, then dash off to class with seconds to spare before the last one rang. I wasn't feeling very social today, particularly after passing a tight-knit group of gossipy, uppity sophomore girls.

"That's her," one of them said. Dispirited as I was, it took a minute for it to register that they were talking about me. Stopping a few yards away, I turned to see five faces with wide open yaps now staring back.

"'That's her' *what?*" I asked with emphatic sarcasm. "*Her* backpack? *Her* ponytail? *Her* majesty?"

There was a chorus of synchronized gulps. No one spoke.

"I'm sorry, but I must be hearing things. I could have sworn one of you said, *'That's her,'* when I walked by. Is there a problem with something? Because if there is, then today is your lucky day."

"Why?" the bravest of the bunch spoke first.

"I'll tell you why after you tell me why you said, 'That's her,'" I spoke in their syncopated rhythm.

"We heard you had a baby over the summer. And then we saw you pushing a carriage this morning. That's all."

Isolated from my own support system of close friends and family, I felt none of the pleasurable zeal I did when misleading Helen Hartley into believing I was John's biological mother. Instead, the enormity of my situation arose, for it seemed not long ago I had been similarly guilty of blithe ignorance, gleefully judging and poking fun at anyone I perceived to be less fortunate than I. Which was everyone.

"Gosh, Gail, I'm sorry," the spokesperson said, as the group watched me fight fresh tears. "Is there anything we can do to help? I mean, I'd be happy to babysit some time. And by the way, you look super great for having just had a baby."

"Yeah," one of the others piped in. "And besides, I have a cousin who's looking to adopt if you want to give it away. Is it a boy or a girl, because she'd really like a girl."

"At least you didn't have an abortion," chirped another. "I would never be able to show my face in public again if I did that," she said, proudly displaying her Catholic colors. "By the way, who's the father?"

I took a deep breath, then placed an arm around her shoulder and then that of one other girl. "No, I did not have an abortion. And not because I didn't think I could ever show my face in public again," I said looking idiot number one in the eye. "I did not have an abortion because I was *never* pregnant. You see, he's not *my* baby, he's my cousin who was orphaned after his real mother died during childbirth."

There was a synchronized gasp.

"Also," I added, gathering steam and addressing idiot number two, "I'm sure your cousin is a lovely person. But as it's a boy, I guess she wouldn't want him. However, I would love it if any of you would be willing to baby-sit sometime. That is, if your own babysitters will let you do it."

Synchronized sneers followed.

"You said this was our lucky day," the bravest one reminded me. "Why?"

"I was being sarcastic," I muttered as I turned and headed straight into home room. Thankfully, I was alone there till just before the first bell rang, during which I darkly sulked. Who would have thought one year ago – heck, even three months ago – that I would start school worrying about feeding schedules, dirty diapers, and the emotional well-being of an infant. My own well-being felt jeopardized, and suddenly I felt an impulse to just drop out of school and stay home with John. Shortly the teacher and several students arrived. Nadette rolled in just before the last bell.

"Gail," she said, breathlessly plopping down. "Where've you been?"

"I had to take John over to the convent. One of the nuns is watching him."

"What's wrong?" she said, seeing evidence that I'd been crying.

"I'll be alright."

She gave me an unexpected, but very reassuring hug, then proceeded to share some good news. "Guess what?" she said. "John O'Neill just asked about you."

"Really?" I perked up.

"Yeah, he asked me where you were."

"He did? Really?"

"Ye-ah!" she excitedly shot back.

"Did he say it like he liked me? Or more like," I spoke more mundanely, "where's your pathetic sidekick Gail?"

"It sounded to me like he likes you!"

Suddenly I was back in school.

Chapter 24

"Thank you so much, Sister Aileen," I said relinquishing John from her care at the end of the school day.

She smiled warmly. "He's a lovely baby. We had a wonderful time, didn't we young man?" He seemed content, reigniting a certain jealousy in me that he'd adjusted so well. I packed him into his pram, stuffed my book bag and his diaper bag in there and off we went. Feeling like I wanted some time alone with him, I impulsively strolled over to Guvelli's before heading home to help all the other kids slog through dinner and homework. While leaning on the marble counter and contemplating my choices, a familiar voice arose. "Gail, what a nice surprise."

I turned and startled to see Sister Perpetua. "Oh, hi Sister," I said politely.

"How did it work out with Sister Aileen?"

"Good, thanks."

"I'm glad to hear that. How's your mother doing?"

"Same."

"Hmmm," was all she said. After acquiring our cones, we left the store where she invited me to join her on the wooden bench outside. School may have begun, but summer wasn't over. It was sunny, a perfect seventy-seven degrees, and a warm breeze lightly rustled some nearby trees. Typically any regret I felt over the end of summer break would vanish in my unlimited enthusiasm over the first day of school and the fun to come. Fun, however, was no longer a seamless promise in my life.

"Cheers!" she said, spiritedly tapping her cone against mine.

"Cheers," I responded without verve, then took a bite of my peppermint crunch ice-cream.

"How heavenly," she declared after biting into her own confection.

"Isn't everything heavenly for you?" I asked with subtle sarcasm.

"Hardly," she sighed, then took another bite. "I had a trying day."

"I would imagine the first day of school would always be chaotic for you."

"True. Actually, though, I just came back from delivering communion to a dying friend."

"I'm sorry," I said more tenderly.

"Thank you," she solemnly responded.

Quietly, we consumed our ice cream. In truth, I still felt so sore with her over betraying my trust that I didn't know what to say. Then, as if reading my mind, she spoke.

"By the way, have you heard from Mary Joyce recently?"

"Yes, I got a letter from her. She uhm, she...well, she lost the baby. I meant to come and tell you, but I've been kind of preoccupied," I stated, slightly rocking John's pram. He was dozing off.

"I already heard the news."

"Really? From whom?"

"Steve Barelli's father."

I tried suppressing a sigh. It was futile. My eyes rolled at the same time.

"Gail, as promised, I kept the information safe from your parents. And I hope you will forgive me for this, but I did take the matter up directly with Mr. Barelli because, as far as I could see it, the only wedding that should be taking place was between his son and your sister. At the very least I needed to know that Mary Joyce and the baby were being taken care of. She is a part of my family, you know, at least my parish family. And I felt a deep obligation to help her."

"I know."

"So you agree that I did the right thing?"

"What I'm saying is, I knew you took it up with Mr. Barelli. I was in the same room when you spoke to him."

Her face contorted. "How is that possible?"

"I was hiding."

"From me?"

"Not specifically. Remember I told you I was going there myself to confront Steve. I went with a friend who got sick and decided to rest under a table in that same room when you all showed up. I overheard everything. First I betrayed Mary Joyce's trust by telling you. Then *you* said you wouldn't tell my parents. But by talking to Mr. Barelli, who knew what would happen? If you can't trust a nun, who can you trust?" I blurted.

She turned slightly to face me, then responded with a tempered softness. "Gail, I am as genuinely sorry for betraying you as I am saddened that Mary Joyce lost the baby."

I blankly looked ahead while continuing to eat my ice cream. She carried on.

"But as you know, Mary Joyce's condition would have eventually spoken for itself, so I thought it best to act sooner rather than later. Particularly as Steve would soon be married to another. As an adult – and especially as a nun – I have a lot more authority than you in most circumstances. Clearly this was one of them."

She had a point. "He gave her five-thousand dollars," I said matter-of-factly.

"Really? That much?" her voice pitched.

"Yeah, apparently so."

"I hope she'll invest it wisely," she said tightly.

"I guess my spilling the beans wasn't so bad after all."

"I would say so. Thanks to you, we also have a sizeable contribution towards a new convent. Surely God works in mysterious ways."

Suddenly I felt less intrigued by the prospect of a new convent than I was about God's "mysterious ways." I'd heard that refrain so much lately, and the only thing more mysterious to me was why anyone had to suffer their way through all these Lord Almighty mysteries. My sister might have gained freedom from premature parenthood. But she lost a baby and got emotionally burned. I took a few bites of crunchy peppermint bits and rich vanilla ice cream before making a brazen inquiry. "Sister, would you please tell me exactly why God is so damned 'mysterious?' And why I should accept that as a good thing?"

She obviously heard me, but in silence continued consuming her Rocky Road. Perhaps I offended her. Still, I persisted. "Don't you think more people would praise God and find religion if he were right out there making everyone obviously happy? So why all the mystery and all the suffering? To tell you the truth, with everything that's been happening around me, I'm beginning to wonder if God even exists."

She quietly finished her ice cream cone. Then after delicately wiping her mouth with a napkin, she lightly brushed her hand over the rosary beads hanging from her neck; her way, perhaps, of gathering strength against my tsunami of expressed doubt.

"I've had my doubts, too," she finally said.

What?! The waves were now crashing on *my* shore. It was okay for me to second guess God, but not her. I felt a sudden sense of propriety about Sister Perpetua, about every priest and nun in our parish. After all, didn't we, the parishioners, pay them to always dress and act the part and hadn't they better not ever deviate from the script? My faith might be shakable. But the same seemed impermissible for her.

"Seriously?" I uttered.

"Yes," she replied firmly. "Suffering is complicated. If God so loved us, why would he allow misery in any form? Particularly in permitting his own Son to be persecuted."

This had to be a trick question. I'd asked a presumed expert for an explanation and she was asking *me* for the answer. Thankfully, I wasn't left hanging for long.

"Perhaps you might recall Hebrews Four, fourteen through sixteen. Just because we suffer it doesn't mean there isn't salvation, or that mercy is not on the way."

I nodded my head feigning recollection of the passage. I was clueless. She carried on.

"The truth is, by living in a free will universe we can choose to do, say, and consume whatever we want. As a result, if we're not careful we can create a lot of needless suffering through our personal choices. Every choice has a consequence, and the connection to suffering when selfish or sinful behavior is involved is pretty apparent.

"Look at Mary Joyce, for example. It's not difficult to figure out how one gets pregnant. Plus, she made the choice to have sex with someone she hardly knew. If that isn't a set-up for trial and tribulation, then I don't know what is. Not to mention the impact it has on an innocent child born into a world of uncertainty. Sadly, Mary Joyce learned what happens when the knight in shining armor abruptly takes off. Or in her case, was never truly there to begin with."

"But how could she have known about him?"

Sister cast a withering look. "It did not take much for you, Nancy Drew, to find out his true story. Had your sister shown proper restraint she might have saved herself a lot of trouble."

"You make it sound like it's her fault."

"Because she *is* partly to blame. Chances are alcohol was involved. She got loosened up and then let loose with a near-stranger. Or to put it in terms du jour, she had a fling. Funny thing is in a situation like this, after everyone's sobered up none of that loose behavior amounts to anything more lasting than, perhaps, *a child*," she added harshly. "Then to her surprise he does his level best to ignore the situation. Instead of acting like a real man, he decides he'll just wait to see what happens. Maybe she's not really pregnant. Maybe she'll just go away, have the baby and never bother him. Maybe, she won't even have the baby. And my personal favorite, how do I even know it's mine? Or, and most pathetically, he breeds false hope by acting like a man till the baby's born, then realizing what it takes to be a real father disappears.

"I've seen this before. Because then the young woman – and I use that term lightly for I think it suggests a level of maturity – will cry foul and hold that baby up as evidence that life is hard and unfair. Now she behaves like a victim, believing that she and her child are entitled to ongoing care and financial support by everyone else. How fair is that when – had the couple practiced a modicum of self-control – the pregnancy was preventable in the first place? They've just created a unique, innocent child. One of life's greatest treasures who, by its very nature is needy and, by the way, is the true victim in the equation. Where's the mystery in that?

"The truth is, you can celebrate Mary Joyce's small financial windfall all you want. But not her moral downfall. I hope she's learned a valuable lesson from this. You, too."

Her response infuriated me.

"You know what? You make it sound so obvious. Just like la-la-la, make the right choices, and la-la-la, angels will sing, and la-la-la, life will be hunky-dory. Mystery solved. But suppose you don't have the right information to make the right choices? Or you find yourself in a bad situation not of your choosing? Oh, as if that never happened in the history of the world. Steve Barelli's not blameless, either, you know."

"No, he is not. Frankly, I view him as a dreadfully manipulative and selfish soul. But don't forget that Mary Joyce was once my pupil. And though she is a bit naive, she is certainly *not* dumb. You young girls are much more promiscuous, if you will, and she learned the hard way that there are consequences to every behavior," she harrumphed. "I know I don't need to explain to you how people get pregnant. But understanding why and with whom is different. I know of many successful marriages that started with a child created out of wedlock. I also know the odds of marital success are vastly improved when two people invest the proper time getting to know each other before making a lifetime commitment, and certainly before having children together."

"You know what, Sister?" I impulsively replied. "My Aunt Cate did the right thing by getting married after *she* got pregnant. But, guess what? It turns out she married an abusive con artist who made her life miserable. Five children later she's dead, he's an outlaw, and look who's taking care of their kids during her junior year in high school. And you know what else? I heard that Steve Barelli is a dope fiend. And we both know *he's* an abusive, lying con artist, too. So would you really have wanted Mary Joyce to marry such a conniving rat bastard?"

Sister Perpetua closed her eyes and pinched her brow.

I immediately grimaced. "Oh my gosh! That was really crude. I'm sorry."

"No, no, don't apologize," she stated, then lightly chuckled. Her voice softened. "Your honesty is refreshing. I did not know that about Cate and

Francis, and what has become of that family is quite sad. However, we are talking about two separate things: the mysteries of God and then well-known, foolish decisions made by us mortals. Let me ask you, exactly how long did Mary Joyce know Steve before consenting to intimacy?"

"Not very long," I answered meekly.

"Are we talking days or weeks?"

I silently bounced the pram.

"How long?" she pressed.

"Hours."

"Well if that isn't a recipe for happily-ever-after, then I don't know what is!" she exclaimed while smacking her hand on her forehead.

I let out a loud, righteous sigh. "So where is God in all of this? If marriage is a sacrament, then God obviously wants us to be married, so you would think he'd make life easy for all married people. Right?"

She suddenly looked like a startled meerkat. Raising her neck high, then glancing at me through her wire-rimmed spectacles with a surprised expression, she turned and looked ahead, then back at me. I braced myself, fearful that any remaining personal fantasies about "happily-ever-after" were about to get clocked; that Prince Charming was about to go down with Santa Claus and the Easter Bunny.

"And just now who's singing 'la-la-la, make the right choices, and la-la-la, angels will sing, and la-la-la, life will be hunky-dory?' Do you really believe that?" she said with a mixture of shock and rebuke.

"Believe what?"

"That a blessed marriage was designed as a guarantee of happiness?"

"Kinda. Why wouldn't I? I mean, look at my parents. Until recently they were happy together. In fact, we were all pretty darned happy."

She positioned her hands over the lower half of her face, her fingertips on her nose as if in prayer, and took in a very deep breath. Whatever she was about to say, I had a feeling I didn't want to hear. Fortunately she wasn't righteous or dismissive. Instead, her tone was gentle and intellectual.

"Gail, just to be clear, we are talking about very different things. The sacrament of marriage as a covenant relationship with God, and marriage as a social instrument. By its very nature marriage is challenging and complex. Still, and speaking from a secular viewpoint, it is widely seen as a gold standard of social acceptance. Some people – which includes both men and women – are so needy for that kind of validation that they will settle for just about anyone and on the faintest premise of love. Their marriage can become a world of false harmony, as if always walking in shoes too small. There's a price for that when the pain of incompatibility arises. It can lead to chronic irritability and contempt, which can turn into anger and rage – all of it a potential hotbed for disastrous, abusive and sinful behavior. Does that make sense?"

Without waiting for any response from me she carried on.

"The church certainly doesn't condone abuse. But to complicate matters, if the marriage relationship sours and abuse arises, many unrealistically fear God's retribution for leaving and therefore stay put. This can have a devastating and tumultuous effect on their family and personal lives. You do understand that, right?"

That part was easy. Yes, I nodded.

"This is all the more reason why neither casual sex nor marriage should be taken lightly in the first place. It requires deep love and respect for one another and a mutual desire to allow God to enter into and inspire a relationship for it to succeed. But first, it takes time and commitment to truly get to know and understand one another. The sacrament of marriage isn't about a guarantee of happiness or an easy life. It is a covenant between God and two people who should fully understand the seriousness of such a union, as well as what a privilege it is to create or nurture new life by either giving birth to or adopting children and then carefully raising them. Life is sacred and needs to be treated with the utmost respect at any stage – particularly at its most vulnerable," she said looking down at John. "A committed couple who honor their vows should be there to support one another as well as the child, making life less challenging for all. Which is the essence of the marriage covenant and, in and of itself, can bring bliss and a nearness to God."

I got it. Particularly given how hard it had been on me these past few months as John's caregiver and also while experiencing the strain between my parents. But there was something else; something about her knowledge of this that transcended scripted doctrine. She seemed to speak from the heart. It left me wondering.

"Sister, I know this is really personal, but why didn't you ever get married? I guess what I mean is, did you ever want to be married or have a baby of your own instead of becoming a nun?"

An awkward silence grew, during which she grew pensive. Looking downward she softly spoke. "I was once married and I did have a baby of my own."

I felt like I was spiraling down into a dark abyss. Weren't all nuns pure with virginity? Didn't all of them devote their lives to God from the time they could talk? This was Sister "P" in 3D. A thousand questions came to mind. "Really?" was all I could manage.

Yes, she nodded. "I was married to a young fighter pilot who fought in World War II. We had a child together."

"Oh, my gosh. So he died in a plane crash?"

She blinked, either recalling deep pain or love. Probably both.

"No," she said somberly. "He served valiantly and came home a decorated hero. It was actually a car crash after he'd returned from Europe. We were hit by a drunk driver," she heaved a sigh and looked upward. "Obviously, I survived. But he and our toddler son died."

I felt an urge to hug her. Instead, I unwittingly rocked the pram, then just as quickly felt a self-conscious pinch as if I were rubbing it in her face that I had a baby to love and she didn't.

"I'm so sorry," I muttered, as much out of embarrassment for my personal prying as for her loss. As she quietly nodded I imagined her as an elegant, young woman deeply in love, and as the love of someone's life. Happy, confident and beautiful. I'm sure she was a wonderful wife and mother. And what about the man she'd married? Was he as handsome as John O'Neill? Had she once lived with a secret crush on him, too? Was she still in love with him today? Even though he wasn't officially mine to lose, I simply couldn't imagine the loss of John O'Neill. My curiosity still racing, I blurted, "Did you ever think of getting married again instead of becoming a nun?"

"But I am remarried. For the past twenty-one years I've been happily married to Christ. Which is why," she deftly switched back to Mary Joyce, "I became so deeply concerned about your sister and that innocent baby. As far as I could see it, no wedding was going to take place until matters of the Church and that child's welfare were successfully resolved."

Clearly she wasn't going to discuss any more of her personal business. It didn't matter, because now I was far more in tune with whatever else she had to say.

"You know what? Steve lied to Mary Joyce when he saw her in Florida."

"That's not surprising. How so?"

"He didn't say anything about Connie and continued to let her believe he was touring with the PGA. She thinks the money he gave her was from his winnings. And he told her to keep it between them, basically because he doesn't need any bad press. I'll bet he never told Connie the truth, either."

Her eyebrows raised up so high I thought they would disappear beneath her habit.

"You see, Sister, that was *my* point. People don't always have enough information to make the best decisions. Connie Sullivan thinks she's marrying the man of her dreams. You and I both know she's about to marry a living nightmare. She and Mary Joyce are both innocent people. So just whose side is God on, anyway?"

"God does not pick sides. People choose to side with God. And I can tell you who has not chosen to be on God's side. It is that positively amoral young man."

She fell momentarily silent, then turned to me and spoke with genuine mercy. "Gail, earlier you were wondering whether or not God even exists. Not I. Tonight when I say my prayers, I will be thanking God for this gorgeous afternoon while eating an ice cream cone with someone I truly admire."

"Me?"

"Of course. I think you're a remarkable young lady and that God was right to seek you out. Just like he did our Virgin Mother."

I laughed aloud. "Sister, you can hardly size me up to the Virgin Mary. That's like comparing someone who rarely sings and then always off-tune to a world-class opera star."

She smiled. "I was referring to her extraordinary sacrifices. Just as you've made sacrifices for your family, particularly for your mother and this young man. All God asks is that we show one another mutual respect, which we do through kindness and charity. Without even thinking about it, you've been following the old Golden Rule: *Do unto others whatever you would have them do to you*; which has reduced an enormous amount of suffering in your family. If everyone did that," she sweetly smiled, "We'd all get along, everyone would spread the good word and la-la-la, angels would sing."

"That sounds pretty hokey, doesn't it?"

She chuckled. "A little, but I knew what you meant. I hope you realize that the challenges you've accepted have truly made a difference. Had you not risen to the occasion, this child and his siblings might have found themselves in a dark and unfathomable wilderness. There is nothing mysterious about that. They would have likely been wrenched apart from one another and, worse, could have possibly landed in another hostile or cold environment. That happens to orphaned children more times than you can imagine. Did you ever wonder how it would feel if the tables were turned and suddenly you'd been abandoned by both parents, separated from your siblings, then forced to live with strangers while attending a new school?"

"Honestly, I always thought I was better than my cousins and that nothing like it could ever happen to me."

"But suppose it were that way? What would you hope for?"

I slightly choked thinking of my mother's plight. I ached for her in more ways than I cared to confess. "A warm, loving family, I guess."

"Precisely. Do you think it's any different for your cousins? They did not create today's troubles. Nor did God. But even in your presently frustrated manner, you've been demonstrating exactly what God and our Savior would wish from you: compassion. You don't know what has to happen somewhere else in order for you to get your way, or to receive God's grace. But God does. His higher priority may have been addressing the needs and prayers of your cousins to give them the chance to stay together as a family."

"What about *my* prayers?"

She closed her eyes and fell silent while temporarily wringing her hands. Then, turning her gaze upon me, she patiently continued. "Think about this. Even though it was a trying day, I had no intention of stopping for ice cream. I had just gotten off the train and was walking up Main Street while thinking about some pressing school matters. I heard those old cow bells and impulsively ended up here. Clearly I did not anticipate this chat nor the badly needed opportunity to say 'I'm sorry.' Something tells me that this encounter was not on your prayer list, either. But God knew of your needs and he anticipated mine. Which is why I told you once before that I believe you are living in a state of grace right now. God is taking care of you in unimaginable ways as you endure the present hardships. For this you are blessed and should give thanks."

As if on cue, the door opened and the cow bells chimed. She reached over and patted my knee. "Think about it. Our paths unexpectedly crossed giving me a chance to apologize for causing you anguish," she continued. "And I do hope you'll find it in your heart to forgive me. I was sincerely trying to be helpful. It's just that I knew that the full force of my presence at the Chevy Chase Club, and in my little black dress," she chuckled, "is what was truly needed to help Mary Joyce without directly involving your parents."

I grinned. "I suppose so. You even had me scared, 'Sister Perfecta!'"

We laughed, but she immediately fell serious again.

"Gail, if nothing else comes out of our conversation today, I want you to remember this: what may feel like a denial from God is only a delay. In order to assist in answering our prayers, He must first protect them. Give Him time to work miracles through others who are being quietly inspired to share their insights, blessings or abundance with you. Your job is to be humble, stay faithful and give thanks. In time you'll recognize what he's accomplished on your behalf – or others for whom you pray – often delivering so much more and what is so much better than you could ever imagine. In turn you will be inspired to share your blessings by being of service to others and then, perhaps, come to understand why he's so 'damned mysterious.'"

I cringed at hearing her repeat my blasphemy. "So you really do believe there's a God?" I asked, more rhetorically.

"Trust me, even I've had periods of deep doubt. But I've learned that's okay. Because I realize that those were the times when God did his best work for me and through me. I've learned to find wisdom and courage in the dark space of sometimes seeming hopelessness."

Stirring from his brief nap, John softly whimpered, prompting me to pick him up.

"May I?" she surprisingly asked.

"Of course," I said, my heart suddenly aching over the newfound understanding of her loss so long ago. I handed him over, watching quietly as the two studied each other. Before long John began yanking on the beads and crucifix hanging from her neck. They quickly found way to his mouth.

"I kiss them, too," she cooed while gently removing them from his soft grip. Standing up, she placed him back in the pram, stroked his brow and then popped his pacifier into his mouth.

"Well, I suppose I'd better head to the school and finish some business before dinner. Which," she jovially added, "I really don't want to miss. Frankie donated some lovely pork tenderloins and Sister Marguerite is working her magic with them. That Frankie is such a fine, young man," she smiled.

Emotion caught in my throat. "Thank you, Sister, for recognizing that," I said, also rising. "And just so you know, I do forgive you. In fact, I think what you did for Mary Joyce was pretty brave. So thank you for that, too."

Her eyes suddenly sparkled and her warm smile seemed to effuse gratitude. "We were both rather daring that evening."

"Yeah," I laughed. "But I suppose it all worked out."

"Hmmm. Very mysterious, wouldn't you say?"

I smiled and spontaneously hugged her.

"May I ask a favor of you?" she said.

"What's that?"

"Please pray with me."

She'd just compared me to the Virgin Mother. Yet, and in spite of the fact that I was wearing a Catholic school uniform and standing beside a nun in full habit, I suddenly felt embarrassed to pray in public.

"Here? Right now?"

"Yes," she affirmed, not waiting for any further response. "In the name of the Father, Son and the Holy Spirit," she started. Quickly, I caught up with her.

"Heavenly Father," she said, then took my hands while closing her eyes. "Thank you for the gifts and the grace that you have bestowed on my young friend, Gail. Thank you for her fortitude and loving heart. Please strengthen and heal her family. And Lord, thank you for this wonderful moment of communion with her. Please imbue this young woman with the faith and hope that she needs to better understand your love and many mysteries. And may *all* her prayers be answered. In Jesus's name we pray. Amen."

Chapter 25

When I arrived home it was apparent none of the other kids were there. However, familiar sounds were emanating from the kitchen. It was an orchestra of organization. The oven door banged shut, I heard tap water running, and then a pot being clunked down on the stove top. Best of all, I sensed something warm and wonderful was on the menu.

That's odd, I thought, realizing it was Timmy's night to make dinner. A surprising sense of relief consumed me, and I felt my spirits soar at the thought that my mother might actually be back in the kitchen devoting time to feeding her family.

"Ma," I said cheerfully, carrying John into the kitchen, then stopped short at the sight before me. Indeed, dinner was under way. But it was Frankie, and not my mother, wearing a white chef's apron and basting a pot roast. The strange calm was only because all the younger children were quietly concentrating on their homework at the kitchen table. Except for Patty, who had patches of flour sprinkled on her apron and was drizzling some melted butter over dough she'd formed into biscuits.

"Wow," I muttered.

Frankie faintly smiled at me while tapping his baby brother on the nose. "Thanks for taking care of him today."

"Don't mention it," I replied, noticing his reddened, watery eyes.

"By the way, your mother's taking care of Mrs. Logan."

"Hmmm," I responded at our code for a drinking binge. "Frankie, is everything okay?"

He looked askance. "I must have gotten some flour in my eyes," he replied, tapping John's nose again. His brother's broad, gummy grin made me think of Sister Perpetua's earlier comments, now saddening me to think of the O'Briens being wrenched apart. Truly, if anyone had helped to reduce the suffering in our family it was Frankie. Only he knew how to counter the morning's madness by ensuring that homework was done and a hearty meal was served after the first day of school. I did something I'd never done before by pecking him on the cheek. "Thanks for making dinner. I really appreciate it."

Suddenly tears started flowing. "Excuse me," he said, hastily exiting the kitchen. No one but me seemed to notice, and deeply concerned I quickly followed him to the front porch where I found him sobbing. Holding the baby with my right arm, I sat beside him on the porch swing and placed my left arm around his shoulder. "Frankie, whatever it is, I'm here to help you."

"There's nothing you can do to help."

"Well, just try me, please."

Leaning back on the swing, then reaching into his pocket, he produced a crumpled piece of paper semi-tangled in masking tape. I put John on my lap and took the mass from him. After carefully opening it, I gasped. It was an FBI wanted flyer featuring a grainy photo of his father in a bank hold-up.

"Where did you find this?"

"Taped on my locker this morning. Some jerk obviously thought it was funny. It's a good thing I was a few minutes late, because I was pretty much by myself in the hallway when I found it." Wrapping his arms around himself, he broke down sobbing again. "Oh, my god. It hurts. It all hurts so much."

I had never seen him so distraught, nor I had ever felt so heartbroken for anyone. Ever. "I'm dropping out of school," he mumbled.

I reached over and tenderly patted his knee. "I can completely understand why you'd feel that way."

He straightened up a bit, took a big breath and sighed deeply. I went on.

"You did nothing to deserve that. I can't even imagine someone being so heartless. I mean, suppose it was their father? Do you think that person would find it funny if *you* did that?"

He slowly shook his head no.

"Do you have any idea who did it?"

"No."

"You know what, Frankie?"

"What?"

"It doesn't matter."

"Why?" he sniffled.

"It doesn't matter *who* did it. What matters is that if you drop out of school now, then whoever did it will always go on being a bully and you will get stuck believing the worst about yourself. Do you want to prove to someone with no class or courage that he can get away with this? Just by showing up at school tomorrow you'll demonstrate ten times more courage.

"You wanna know something interesting?" I added, now raising John up to my shoulder and gently rubbing his little back. "A lot of people at school think that John is my baby. In fact, I had it out in the hallway this morning with a bunch of idiot sophomores who were openly discussing the fact that I'd had a baby."

"What did you do?" he sniffled, wiping tears with the back of his hand.

"Well, after I set them straight I went to Home Room and pretty much reacted the way you are right now."

"You cried?" he asked, sounding surprised.

"Yup. And I thought of dropping out, too. Like you said, it hurts. It all hurts. You know what else? It may be your father on that flyer, but he's my uncle, and you're like a brother and a best friend to me. We're family and we are in this together. And we're going to prove to all those idiots how strong our family is. Believe me, no one's life is perfect," I said, partially reflecting on those sleazy Barellis. "The important thing is that we learn how to live by the old Golden Rule."

"I hope you realize that the challenges you've accepted have truly made a difference. Had you not risen to the occasion, this child and his siblings might have found themselves in a dark and unfathomable wilderness. There is nothing mysterious about that. They would have likely been wrenched apart from one another and, worse, could have possibly landed in another hostile or cold environment."

I took his hand and squeezed it. "I'm so grateful that you all are here, and I'm particularly glad that I've gotten to know you better. As my father would say, 'You're a good kid, Francis O'Brien!'"

He lightly chuckled, then sighed again, only now with apparent relief. We sat quietly, just swaying as John dozed, each of us absorbing the last vestiges of summer. The settling sun encased us in a warm glow, while a few crickets in some nearby shade got a head start on their evening mating chirps.

"Speaking of your Dad," Frankie finally spoke. "He called and said he was running late."

I nodded my head, as his tendency to take moonlighting jobs to help foot the bills meant it was typically just us kids at the dinner table.

"Thanks for listening," he added. "I promise I'll go back to school tomorrow, at least if you do the same. In the meantime," he rose, "I'd better make sure that the pot roast isn't burning."

"Frankie," I stopped him just as he had his hand on the door. He turned. "I want you to know I feel like you're a brother to me, and I love you. I hope you know I will always be here for you," I said with great sincerity. "Always."

Blinking back fresh tears, he silently nodded his head while tapping a fist over his heart. *I love you, too,* he conveyed, but simply couldn't say. I sat for a while longer afterwards swinging his baby brother and feeling more grateful than I expected for my encounter with Sister Perpetua.

"I've learned to find wisdom and courage in the dark space of sometimes seeming hopelessness."

Later, after feeding John, I joined the kids at the dinner table where we indulged in Frankie's scrumptious pot roast. Not long into the meal there was a knock on the front door.

"I've got it," Tommy said, jumping up. "Hey man!" he congenially exclaimed upon opening it. "Come on in!"

I was holding the baby in one arm while shoving a forkful of mashed potatoes in my mouth when in walked John O'Neill wearing navy blue gym shorts, a gray Pallotti T-Shirt and flip-flops. Football practice had started and the two were eager to talk shop. It was impossible not to stare.

"Hey, Gail," he grinned.

"John," I mumbled, my mouth loaded.

Frankie invited him to sit down in my father's empty chair and join us for dinner.

"Thanks," he said, sitting down next to me. "It smells great."

Patty, who was also seated beside him, turned giddy. "John," she announced, "I started school today. And I'm the biggest one in my class. So that makes me the smartest. I also cooked dinner with Frankie. Here," she said, and picking up the bread basket peeled back a kitchen towel to reveal a warm batch of biscuits.

"Well, no doubt about it, Patty, you're one of the smartest girls I've ever known," he said, then took a bite of her homemade offering. "Mm, mmm. You're also one of the best cooks in town! This is awesome," he said, licking his lips. I knew he wasn't lying because I felt the same way after I'd consumed one which seemed to melt in my mouth. Patty was beaming. Turning to me, John held out his arms. "Why don't you give me the baby so you can finish eating?"

"Seriously?"

"Hand him over," he grinned. I did, watching in amusement as he gingerly sandwiched Baby John in a belly-down position between the palms of his hands, promptly turning the hand-off into a football play.

"John O'Neill receives the lateral pass. Look at him run," he said gently bouncing the enthralled infant. "He's at the thirty. Now he's at the twenty. Linebacker Tom Kenealy takes a dive for him, but misses. He's at the ten and....TOUCHDOWN!" he said, now holding John above his head. "Whew!" he added, screwing up his face. "Too much excitement in the end zone!"

I laughed, and taking him back sniffed his rear end. "Clearly he went for the conversion. I'll be right back," I said, briefly disappearing to change his diaper. I felt as giddy as Patty, unable to believe John was downstairs and seemingly happy to see me. While washing my hands I checked my image in the mirror to make sure no food was stuck to my face or in my teeth, then quickly ran a brush through my hair. Returning to the table, John smiled warmly and took the baby from me while carrying on a lively discussion about football, a conversation that was briefly and uncomfortably interrupted when my mother walked in the door. She paused to survey the scene, all the while smiling. "It smells good," she commented, clumsily drifting our way.

"I saved a plate for you," said Frankie, who had practice with keeping dinner warm for a stone cold drunk.

"Thanks," she continued grinning while patting him on the head like he was Mr. Bojangles. "But Mrs. Logan and I already had dinner," she hic-cuped. "Scuuussse meee!"

Was my humiliation as apparent as her inebriation? Even worse, she never acknowledged John O'Neill, instead treating him like one more face in a sea of bobbing children. She looked spent. She was thinner than ever and her hair looked electrified. It hadn't been cut, styled or colored since just before Cate died, and shot out wildly around her sallow face. She had been wearing the same black tunic top and blue pants for a week now. And unless she bathed when no one was paying attention, I think it had been a week since she'd last showered. She reached into her pocket for a cigarette, then using a lighter with a flame set higher than usual, proceeded to light one up. It was rather dramatic, particularly as she took a long drag before snapping it shut.

"Is your father home?" she asked of no one in particular while blowing smoke our way.

"He stayed at work while you got drunk," said Patty.

"Patricia O'Brien, what on earth are you talking about?"

"It's Patricia Caitlin O'Brien. And Uncle Joe works all the time while you get drunk," she succinctly stated.

"Young lady, that's the most ridiculous thing I've ever heard," she urged a smile, then took another long drag, teetering all the while.

"No it's not. He works late and you like to get drunk. Just like my father."

The room fell dead silent as eight pairs of thunderstruck eyes looked at my mother, then toward Patty, then back at my mother. Not a one of us – Frankie, Tommy, John, Joey, Paul, Raymond, Timmy, or I uttered a sound. What was there to say after Patty had dared to go where angels feared to tread?

Probably realizing the futility of the conversation, she finally said, "Well. It's been a long day taking care of Mrs. Logan. I'm going to bed."

Thankfully, she left. Through each creak of the stairs as she awkwardly made her way up, I ran the sequence of immediate events through my mind. Clearly my mother was drunk. But there was something else going on, another layer of intoxication, I thought, as it seemed that the hard edge of her misery and drunkenness were softer and sloppier than usual. She was really zoned out. We could hear her knocking around for a few minutes, and then, like the atmosphere in the dining room, it fell utterly silent upstairs.

John tried picking up the conversation by focusing again on football. "We're going to have a great season," he said, looking directly at Tommy.

Tommy hadn't been so fully exposed to our mother's behavior until now. Instead of immediately responding to John, he looked across the table at me, as if hurt and confused.

"You guys are gonna kick some serious butt," Frankie quickly rejoined, speaking specifically to John and Tommy, respectively Pallotti's starting quarterback and best wide receiver. Frankie's favorite subject was football, and the more he talked the more animated he became, the darker events of his day fading into cross-talk over who had the best high school football programs in the greater metropolitan areas of Washington and Baltimore. Finally Tommy, and even Paul, jumped in.

Built like Frankie, Paul's tall, lanky frame prevented him from excelling at football, plus he preferred basketball. Also like Frankie, he had a mind for sports and absorbed the particular details of various leagues. The two would talk sports for hours.

"I think Prep is going to win the IAC this year," he declared about the highly competitive Interstate Athletic Conference, which set them to debating anew whether Georgetown Prep, an elite, private Jesuit high school in Bethesda, Maryland, would beat their arch rival Gonzaga. A similarly elite Jesuit high school in Washington, D.C., their Eagles always gave the Hoyas a good run for their blue blood money. Inwardly I smiled at Paul. Still wearing his Pallotti uniform, his tie hung loose in a classic "I'm done for the day" look, he was one of them now – a high

205

school prep student – and by the tone of his voice alone I detected a fresh confidence.

While Patty stayed at the table simply to admire John, Timmy and Raymond quickly split to avoid any clean-up. Joey remained, though he was uncommonly subdued. In fact, at one point, and without saying a word, he hobbled outside alone. Later, and after John O'Neill left and I was bathing Baby John in the kitchen sink, Frankie went out and joined him.

"Are you okay?" I heard Frankie through the screened door. Joey was lying on the nearby picnic table with his hands folded behind his head just staring at the stars. He didn't answer, making me wonder if he'd also learned about the "Most Wanted" flyer.

"Seriously, I can tell something's wrong," Frankie pressed. "What's going on?"

"Nothing."

"I don't believe that."

"I said, nothing's wrong," Joey snapped.

"You're lying."

"What is up with you?" Joey fired back. "You think you're so damned..." he hesitated, then snorted.

"So damned what?"

"Perfect," Joey responded.

His comment was both ironic and absurd.

"So one day I'm a 'pathetic orphan' and the next day I'm 'perfect.' You know what this is really all about?"

"No, but I'm sure Mr. Know-it-All is going to tell me."

"You injured your foot showing off, you're missing out on playing football this season, and now you're blaming me. You know why? Because I had higher hopes for you than anyone else. Including yourself."

"I'm not blaming you. I just don't like hanging around assholes like *you* who think they're better than everybody else."

"Oh that's rich, coming from you."

"Oh that's rich, coming from you," Joey mocked him.

"Sit up," Frankie commanded.

Joey didn't budge.

"Sit up," Frankie said even more forcefully.

"No."

"Oh, of course. Nobody gets to tell Joey Kenealy what to do? Do they?"

Joey propped himself up on one elbow. "Happy?"

"Put your hands behind your head and touch your knees with your nose."

"That's not sitting up. That's a sit-up."

"Exactly."

Angrily, Joey did as requested. One sit-up. "There, you happy?" he repeated.

"Not till I see twenty-four more."

"I'm not doing twenty-five sit-ups for you."

"There you have it. Nobody gets to tell Joey Kenealy what to do. Not even his football coach."

"You're damned right," Joey said, climbing off the table and limping towards the back door.

"You know what's going to happen to you?" Frankie yelled behind him. Joey stopped.

"One day you're gonna wake up and realize that the best of life's opportunities passed you by. And it will probably be while you're sitting in some dingy bar nursing a keg like my outlaw father always did. Or worse, drinking alone in your bedroom."

In spite of his devil-may-care attitude, Joey was not immune to the pain of our mother's alcoholic descent. So it didn't surprise me, though I must say it horrified me, as through the screen door I watched him turn around, hop, skip and jump his way to Frankie, then cold-cock him in the nose. Frankie barely flinched. Instead, he stood with steely determination as Joey disappeared in the house.

"I hate Frankie," Joey muttered while passing me in the kitchen.

I could have cold-cocked Joey myself at that point, but immediately focused my attention on Frankie. Wrapping the baby up in a towel, I scurried outside.

"Oh, my god, Frankie, you're bleeding. Is it broken?" I promptly handed him the bath towel, which he placed against his nose. John, now utterly naked, began to pee with abandon. I could not have cared less; I just held him in a position to best avoid the spray while I assessed Frankie's situation.

"I think it's okay," said Frankie, then moved over and sat on the weathered picnic bench while leaning his head back against the table.

"Do you want to go to Warren's?" I anguished.

"No, I'll be fine."

"What is going on with him?"

"That kid is in a world of hurt right now and he doesn't know what to do. So he's lashing out."

"But at you, of all people? Why?"

"Because of what's going on with your mother. It doesn't make any sense to him. And I'm sure in his head I'm partly to blame."

I sat down on the bench beside him, now huddling the naked baby inside my cardigan sweater. Frankie looked at the towel, which was bright red in one spot, then touched his nose. The blood was still flowing, so he put the towel back, and retilting his head, spoke.

"Do you remember the summer that my Mom broke her arm?"

"Yeah, she tripped on one of your skateboards."

"No, she didn't," he stated matter-of-factly. "My father broke it."

"He what?"

"Yeah, it was no accident. Paul, Raymond, and I had been shoveling snow and cutting lawns all year to save up for new bikes. One night we counted our money at the kitchen table. We had nearly two-thousand dollars. The next day we were going to buy new bikes, then put the rest in savings. I hid the cash in my bedroom, but the next day it was missing. Patty was barely four at the time so she didn't figure as a suspect. I knew my mother would never touch it, so she suggested I ask my father.

'Did you take my money?' I asked him.

"'What does it matter to you?'" Frankie sarcastically mimicked his father. "'I put a roof over your head, don't I?'

"Gail, I swear, it was the first time he failed to land the first punch. I might have been smaller, but I was angry as hell and after he took a swing at me I cracked him in the jaw. He passed out on the floor. It turned out he'd spent most of our money drinking and gambling at the Laurel Race track. I found what was left of it – about four-hundred dollars – in his pocket. I took that money and we bought ourselves three decent bikes. There was nothing left for savings.

"Anyway, we were gone by the time he came around, so he took his rage out on my mother by twisting her arm behind her back and breaking it."

I impulsively hugged Cate's baby closer as Frankie sat upright, then checked the towel again. His nose was still bleeding, but it was now at a trickle.

"Sometimes I felt like I could kill him. Instead, I burned my aggression on the football field. Which is what Joey should be doing."

Frankie had been a successful running back in the CYO league. But once at Laurel High School, he was outmatched by several faster and bulkier players on the team, thus rendering him a second-string safety. Frustrated by seeing no action, he decided to return to the CYO – this time as an assistant coach – and for the worst team in the league. During their first season together his eighth-graders won all but two games. The following year they narrowly lost the championship game. This summer he'd transferred to Joey's team, primarily to coach him, and was now the offensive coach.

"I was hoping," said Frankie, "that this would be my winning year. Joey also needs that kind of outlet and personal victory, and he could help take us there. But not any more."

"You can win without him," I tried bucking him up.

"Oh, I know," he said with surprising confidence. "It's just that Joey will miss out. That kid's got more natural talent than anyone I've ever seen. With his athletic ability and his brains, who knows, he could end up being a Heisman Trophy winner. But he's hard-headed, immature and lacks focus. It's too bad."

He examined the towel once more. The bleeding had almost subsided. "What a day. I'm going in for some ice." He patted John on the head
and looked at me. "You coming in?" he asked.

"Yeah," I said, more in response to his comment about the kind of day
it had been.

It was rather tense between Frankie and Joey afterwards. They flat-
out ignored each other. Soon though, Joey began his version of a rap-
prochement – which was to act as if nothing had happened. But Frankie
wasn't having it. If Joey asked him a question, Frankie simply left the
room.

The following week, and still enduring the silent treatment, Joey had
my father install a chin-up bar beneath the tree house's bridge. He then
began daily upper body work outs, before long doing dozens of chin ups
at a time. Additionally, he factored in sit-ups, surely surpassing the one-
hundred mark. I watched as he repeatedly stretched his body and manipu-
lated his sore foot, doing every imaginable conditioning exercise in order
to regain and increase his strength and – perhaps – Frankie's respect.
Frankie kept ignoring him.

A few weeks later, and during a home game for their CYO team, Joey
unexpectedly suited up and made a surprise appearance, standing on the
sidelines like nothing had ever happened. Still, Frankie ignored him.

I was watching the game with all the younger kids when this happened. I also witnessed Bobby Bickle getting tackled so hard he briefly
passed out, which made a trip to the emergency room – and a replacement on the field – essential. When the game resumed, Frankie's team
had possession of the ball. With the score tied at 14-14, a fourth down
with only seconds left, Frankie looked at Joey. Bickle was his punter and
place kicker, and now Joey was his only hope for a winning field goal
attempt from the thirty-five yard line.

Joey hesitated, but not for long. Still walking with a slight limp, he
positioned himself on the field, then instead of hitting the ball squarely
proceeded with a soccer style kick, maybe thinking that it wouldn't hurt
as much. Coming in at a thirty degree angle, Joey kept his head down,
never once losing sight of the ball. Sweeping through the kick with his

injured foot, Joey sent that football sailing high over the huddled players and straight through the goal posts, never even bothering to look up until he heard an eruption of cheers.

Quietly he turned and looked straight at Frankie.

"Happy?" Frankie mouthed the word with a look of warm approval.

Yes, Joey nodded.

Yes, indeed.

Chapter 26

*I*f my mother's festering darkness forced us into a collective routine, it turned out to be school and football that galvanized it. I would like to say Baby John was the only one not playing football except, to my horror, I'd sometimes find the boys tossing him in various football-like passes. Football ruled. To each of them it was more than a physical pastime. As Frankie had declared, it was emotional; a way to ward off the demons that had robbed them of their parents.

Like my father, Frankie and Tommy demanded strict order and Spartan conditions, including beds made in the morning, dirty clothes in hampers, clean clothes stored properly, and homework done before dinner. Furthermore the boys were required to religiously maintain their shower schedules and to arrive at school and Mass on time. Football drills in the backyard and memorizing strategic plays – mostly dreamed up on Frankie's chalkboard – took place after the dinner dishes were washed, put away, and homework was done. This followed their normal practices at school and the CYO league. An assortment of players on Pallotti's team, and frequently John O'Neill, would often show up for backyard sessions or to sit in our dining-cum-locker-room chalking out their plays in a swirling sea of Xs and Os.

We still took turns making dinner. But lately, it often involved something from the Laurel Meat Market barbecued by Frankie and Paul, while Patty would help with the side dishes. John O'Neill became a more regular fixture during those meals, as he loved anything cooked on the grill. Though I chose to believe it was because of me, I know he genuinely loved the backyard camaraderie and practicing sneaky passes and winning plays with the other boys. There was a great deal of bonding in their ranks, and when my father wasn't late getting home he'd sit outside on the picnic bench and absorb with quiet satisfaction the evolution of his enlarged family. Periodically my mother would join him, but her inebriation was more obvious than a missed pass. We all rolled with it as best we could.

Cheerleading remained my contribution to our household's spirit of football. Unfortunately, however, practices didn't turn out to be so cheerful. Sister Aileen's schedule did not include coverage during post-school activities, so I was forced to bring John to practice. At first he was the center of attention, something he seemed to love. But the second we ignored him he became fussy. And one day he bellowed so loudly that the football coach blew his whistle, then a gasket.

"Would someone put a cork in that baby?" he roared.

I quickly rocked the pram while stuffing the pacifier in his mouth. Truthfully I knew John was off his schedule and hungry. Within seconds he was hollering again, which prompted the coach to storm my way. The entire football squad, cheerleaders and even members of the far-noisier marching band watched as I pushed his pram out of our stadium with the speed of a NASCAR racer. Clearly, and unless I wanted to quit cheerleading, there was no easy solution to this problem.

That evening while the boys were practicing in the backyard, I noticed Patty – still in her school uniform and pillowcase veil – standing on the sidelines cheering with pom-pons self-crafted from wads of toilet paper and rubber bands. Every time John threw or caught a pass Patty jumped and cheered, "Go, John, go!" Alternatively if Joey got the ball she would yell, "Rub-a-dub-dub. Don't make a flub."

It was then that I got the bright idea to ask for her help.

"Patty," I said sweetly just before kissing her goodnight. "You're such a good cheerleader!"

"I know. Now I'm just like you!"

"Just about! Listen, Big John needs a BIG favor from you."

Wide-eyed, she sat upright. "What?" she asked, eager to please.

"Well, you know I have cheerleading practice at the same time Big John is practicing football. I've been bringing Baby John to the field, but he gets really cranky and cries so loud that Big John can't concentrate and sometimes drops the ball. So I...actually John...was wondering if you'd like to come to cheerleading practice and watch your baby brother? Big John *and I* would be really grateful if you did. You could give the baby a bottle. Maybe walk him around the track. Whatever it takes to make him happy. Doesn't that sound good?"

"If I come to cheerleading practice does that make me a cheerleader?"

"Yes," I grinned. "It kinda' makes you a cheerleader, too."

Nothing could have pleased her more. For the next three days, Patty – in her St. Mary's plaid jumper and pillowcase veil – pushed Baby John's pram around the track while the various squads practiced their drills. She would always stop whenever she got near John O'Neill and, whether he was just stretching or actually practicing plays, would chant, "Go, John, go!"

A few evenings later I was giving John his usual bath in the kitchen sink when I glanced out back and caught Patty in the act of mimicking our cheers. It was amusing at first. But not so funny the next day at practice when she abandoned the baby and declared herself a member of the squad. Still in her plaid jumper and pillowcase veil, she was now on the track beside us.

"Patty," I tried explaining sweetly. "Remember, you agreed to watch the baby. Please go back over there," I pointed to a nearby bench beside the parked pram.

"He's asleep. And I need to practice cheering."

"I can't let you do that."

"Why? I'm a cheerleader."

"Well, that's true. But you aren't old enough to be a *Pallotti* cheerleader."

"Am, too."

"Are not," I responded more sharply.

"You told me I'm a cheerleader. So I'm a cheerleader."

"But you need to go to Pallotti to be a Pallotti cheerleader."

"I'm at Pallotti right now," she persisted. "So I'm a Pallotti cheerleader."

"Listen," I said, taking a more subtle approach. "John O'Neill *really* needs your help. Because otherwise the baby will cry and the football team won't be able to practice. And it will make Big John really happy if you help keep Baby John happy."

Her face screwed up as she contemplated Big John's need. "Okay," she finally relented.

I was relieved, but dead wrong thinking the issue was resolved.

The next afternoon was Pallotti's first home match. I packed John into his pram with a promise from Patty that she would watch him during the game. After I promised a trip to Guvelli's, she solemnly agreed to sit on the first row of the bleachers next to him and to stay put. If I'd inspected the contents of his diaper bag a little closer before leaving I would have seen what was coming.

It was an exhilarating Indian summer day, sunny and with temps in the low seventies. It felt fantastic to be joining my friends and comrades for some good old-fashioned fun. The marching band blared and drums snared. The crowd was large and boisterous and my spirits were high.

"Two, four, six, eight. Who do we appreciate? Panthers! Panthers! Panthers!" my squad cheered, when a strikingly familiar voice embellished the cheer with a tag of her own.

"Go, John, go!" There was Patty in the first row wildly waving her pom-pons. The crowd seemed mildly amused by her belated chant, so she repeated it.

"Go, John, go!" she inspired the crowd into echoing the chant for their star quarterback. And so did the cheerleaders, creating an impromptu line-up while singing the same phrase. Shortly, the teams appeared on the field and the crowd grew noisier. We positioned ourselves into formation and began to perform one of our practiced routines.

"P-P-A-A-DOUBLE-L-O-O-DOUBLE-T-I-I —Pallotti's twice as good!! Pallotti's twice as good!!"

The crowd went crazy, further energizing us, so we repeated the chant.

"Go, John, go!" I heard the familiar voice when we finished cheering.

"Go, John, go!" The crowd chanted back. Then broad laughter erupted.

I turned to see Patty – now beside us on the track – madly shaking her pom-pons. Setting them down, she proceeded with turning three wobbly cartwheels while flashing the pink flowered underwear she wore beneath her St. Mary's jumper, finishing off the entire maneuver with a C-jump – which in her case was something more akin to a lowercase "j."

"Go, John, go!" she concluded her antics, and as the crowd wildly repeated her chant.

"Patty," I hissed. "Come here."

"No."

"COME HERE," I growled.

"I told you I can do it."

"You're not supposed to be down here. Go back to the bleachers right this minute and watch your brother."

Instant tears fell from her soulful brown eyes. She picked up her pom-pons and blew her nose into one of them. "Why?"

Nadette, a fellow cheerleader, butted in. "Are you an idiot? She's not hurting anyone. Let her stay."

Patty blew her nose again and then wiped away her tears.

"Who's gonna watch the baby?" I sneered.

"He's right there! We can all keep an eye on him," Nadette insisted.

"Oh, all right," I relented, and turned to Patty.

"You can stay on the track, but you have to stand over there," I said, pointing to a spot just out of our way.

That lasted all of five minutes. She was either right beside us or in front of us through the entire game. Funny thing, though. We did not just win. We slaughtered the other team.

John was not oblivious to the chant and knowing who was behind it praised Patty for inspiring the crowd. He also thanked *her* for the win, letting *her* claim credit for the victory. I'd created a monster.

It happened again. The following week we won. Big. And then the next week even bigger. Though I attributed our success to the talents of John, Tommy, and the team, the fans regarded Patty as our talisman.

A view that became even more entrenched when she missed a game due to a ferocious cold and Pallotti lost 21-7 to a team they should have easily beat. The following Saturday she was back and we won the match-up.

"You know Patty," John O'Neill said after that game. "You really do bring our football team good luck. From now on, you need to be at every game, you hear me? Because we like winning. And we love you!" She beamed.

The next week was our homecoming match against our arch rival and nemesis, St. Matthew's, an uppity boy's prep school just outside of Baltimore. It was their Lions vs. our Panthers. We were out for blood, and they for their ususal self-important glory.

By now it was fall with a chill in the air. Also, by now, Patty's cheer-leading uniform included a donated school sweater with a giant "P" for Pallotti, though she chose to believe it was for "Patty." Getting into the spirit of the day, she arrived in her newly acquired sweater on top of her St. Mary's jumper, patent leather shoes and – for special effect had traded her pillowcase veil for Joey's beat-up football helmet. Fortunately Frankie and all the boys were there to keep an eye on Baby John. We were all in a winning spirit.

The team's beloved and now de facto mascot, Patty, was offered a prime position on the pre-game float which carried the homecom-ing court. Patty stood right up front beside her prince, John O'Neill– who was in his football uniform – while she enthusiastically waved her pom-pons. Clearly Patty, with her diminutive size, screwball outfit, and matching demeanor appeared a bit "off," though I would venture to say her IQ was probably higher than the average student at St. Matthew's. Particularly given what happened next.

As the float passed by the visiting bleachers and the homecoming court continued waving at the crowd, a derelict from the St. Matthew's side began chanting, "Two, four, six, eight, who do we appreciate? Retards," *clap, clap,* "Retards."

Soon, an obnoxious and rowdy band of his school friends joined in.

"Retards," *clap, clap.* "Retards."

The Pallotti students atop the float tried ignoring them. That is until someone from their crowd lobbed a raw egg that hit Patty square in the chest, thus covering her letter "P" with a drippy yellow mess. Unfazed, Patty set to cleaning it off with one of her pom-pons.

John O'Neill, however, had seen that egg from the instant it left the perpetrator's hand. And with the float still moving, he jumped off and headed straight up into the bleachers where he found the cocky kid, and grabbing him by the shirt front threatened to turn his brain into a scrambled egg. That was all the provocation my brother Joey needed.

"Fight!" he screamed, then flying out of our bleachers led the charge from the opposite side of the field where shortly all hell broke loose and fists were flying everywhere. Quickly, I ran to protect John in his pram, ready to bolt in an instant as the melee prompted the St. Matthew's crowd to charge back, thus drawing both teams into a premature battle on the gridiron. No referee, coach, or even priest seemed capable of stopping them, as heads were butting and uncontrollable punches were swinging left and right. It wasn't until the police arrived shortly thereafter that order – though not necessarily calm – was restored. It was quickly decided that the game was a forfeit for both sides and thus was not played. We were told to pack our things and go home.

"Did we win?" asked Patty, somewhat oblivious to her role in the riot.

"Well, basically we tied," I told her as we pushed the pram home along Montgomery Avenue.

Fortunately, the homecoming dance wasn't cancelled. Which was particularly good considering John had asked me to go as his date. That night he was crowned homecoming king, an improbable choice considering his impulsive move earlier that day. Much to the chagrin of the princesses, not a one of them made queen. Instead it was unanimously decided by the judges that Patty should be anointed. As her surrogate at the time of coronation, I was invited up on to the stage to receive the crown on her behalf. Passing by the princesses who'd been passed by themselves, I noticed inside those broad smiles some fangs I'd never seen before.

After the dance John and I walked home, he in his crown and I wearing Patty's. It was a short trip, but a chilly night. And being a fashion fool, I'd worn Mary Joyce's aqua-blue spaghetti-strap dress with no wrap. When I started shivering John promptly removed his suit jacket, gently placed the garment over my shoulders, then drew me in for an unexpected and exquisitely tender kiss. I'd never felt such pure warmth. A million times I'd envisioned this romantic moment. In a million years I could never have known it would feel this good. Every cell in my body seemed to pulsate with a new kind of electricity. I'm not sure just how long we stood on the corner of Fourth and Montgomery making out. But I learned an important thing about falling in love. In truth, it's all about looking up, and mostly because the person holding you inspires you in a whole new way to be bigger and better than you were the day before. With rhinestones glittering just above our heads and stars twinkling in the night sky, I fell utterly in love with John O'Neill while fully believing that he – and he alone – had hung the sun, the moon and the stars above.

Casually holding hands and laughing about the days's events, we made it back to my darkened house where John stole one more unforgettable kiss, then asked me for a favor. "Can I please give Patty her crown?"

"She's asleep."

"I know. But I think this is too important to wait."

"Okay," I agreed.

Together we tip-toed up to my bedroom where Patty and Brandy were curled up together on her bed and Baby John was asleep in his crib. I tapped Patty's shoulder. Her big brown eyes blinked, first focusing on me and then on her glorious idol in his dazzling crown.

"Shhhh," John said, holding a finger up to his mouth. Fairly dazed, Patty sat up.

"Patty, I have something very special for you," he whispered. Then, kneeling down he produced her glittering crown. "Because you've brought Pallotti so much good luck, tonight Pallotti decided to give you some good fortune back by naming you our new homecoming queen. And here's your crown to prove it."

She gasped and the sparkling look in her eyes said it all. Fake as it was, to her it was ever so real. And for a little girl with a magical soul who'd lost both parents within the past four months, the crown served as affirmation that she was, indeed, loved. With eyes ablaze, and in her oversized pink, flannel pajamas, Patty leaned over and let John put it on her head, then she heartily embraced her king.

Go, John, go!

Chapter 27

"You guys," I said to Paul and Joey one day the following week. "I'm going to High's to get some milk. Can you watch the baby for fifteen minutes?"

"Sure," said Paul.

"No problem," said Joey.

I should have know better. As football was an obsession in our house, and scrappy scrimmages the norm, then it should not have come as surprise to return and find the baby being tossed around like a human pigskin.

"Are you crazy?" I screamed at them. "I can't even trust you guys for a single minute. What if you had dropped him?"

"If?" Joey laughed.

"Twice!" Paul added, cracking them both up.

Setting down the milk, then swiftly intercepting the next pass, I quickly carried a seemingly amused John away to make sure all his parts were still in good working order. Apparently so, as there was a huge load in his diaper, something which may have prompted the baby tossing in the first place.

Another diversion in our house was Sunday NFL football and Frankie's barbecued ribs. It was always Mass in the morning and a heavenly feast in the afternoon. Upon closing time each Saturday, the kind store owner of the Laurel Meat Market would offer Frankie heavily discounted beef that was just the other side of fresh and would no doubt be green and tossed out when the store reopened on Monday. Frankie always accepted the offer, and savvy to the dangers of waiting too long would promptly cook or freeze the meat. Regardless of the weather, every Sunday afternoon Frankie would grill steaks and a mess of his popular ribs with his own "secret" sauce out on our front porch, happily serving them up to any-one who wanted to hang around and watch professional football. It was a pleasurable exertion for him to entertain family and friends, as many folks brought snacks, side dishes, and desserts all making for a welcome camaraderie.

Frankie's favorite professional team was the Green Bay Packers, mostly because of his love for their coach – Vince Lombardi – a fierce competitor, staunch Catholic, and a stand-up person. Plus, he had an eye for talent, didn't take anyone's crap and had an unmatched winning streak. As a teenager he'd also worked in a butcher shop and had hauled enormous slabs of meat from truck to hook, building up his square and solid physique in the process. Lombardi was a true icon, a role model for the day, and in all ways Frankie's idol. In fact, one Sunday afternoon while basting ribs on the grill and waiting for the Packers vs. Chicago Bears game to start, Frankie reiterated his wish to meet "The Man," or better yet, to one day work for him.

It was with some of the same passion and determination as the famed coach that Frankie pushed Joey and his CYO team members to the brink. And just like Lombardi's unstoppable Packers, Frankie's team went unde-feated, finally earning him the CYO league's elusive championship. I'd never seen two happier souls than Frankie O'Brien and Joey Kenealy upon receiving their respective trophies.

Even Tommy and John had a winning season with Pallotti. In spite of our homecoming debacle, the Panthers earned a first-time berth to the state championships where, unfortunately, we narrowly lost. Not only had every game been played out in advance in our dining room and back-yard, but each game was recapped when John O'Neill, Tommy, Frankie, the younger boys and a parade of high school players spent hours using Frankie's miniature chalkboard to recreate countless offensive and defen-sive schemes in a never-ending series of X's and O's.

Their passion blended well with mine. In time my most ardent wish came true: John and I began exclusively dating. It was unbelievable that he'd ever even noticed me, harder still to believe that given the chaos in my family he had chosen to stick around. But the oldest of five children of a firefighter dad and stay-home mom, John was no stranger to our brand of pandemonium. Though from spending some time at his house, I knew there were far more emotional fire drills at mine.

After Sunday Mass, John always joined us, helping Frankie to fire up the grill, thereby sending smoke signals through the neighborhood that game time was near. Occasionally John's father, Mac O'Neill, would come along and sit with his son and my Dad in the living room along with Frankie and all the boys. The color commentary would fly while the Paul Bunyan-sized steaks and ribs would disappear. There was great warmth and fellowship on those days, which partially inoculated me for the week against the darkness of my mother's knock-out, drag-down depression.

It was so demoralizing. Perhaps if I'd never known her as a truly devoted mother, I might not feel the loss of her sobriety so severely. Perhaps if I had never known the love she felt for her sister, whom I also loved, I wouldn't have felt pangs of empathy. Perhaps if I weren't so deeply in love with Cate's six-month old baby, then it would have been easier to dramatize the situation.

Instead, I coped. Not that I didn't try to help her. Once I even threw out her booze, which badly backfired. It made her so agitated that she actually downed a bottle of vanilla extract, its contents surprisingly high in alcohol.

It was astonishing how deeply she'd deteriorated. And even more disconcerting was how my father seemed incapable of taking any drastic steps to help her. Which is why Sunday afternoons had become a respite for me and football an increasingly important part of my own life. Fortunately, this pattern of football central at our house persisted into the professional play-off season, making the holiday transition much easier.

It was chaotic. But God love Frankie, who worked hard to make it happy and memorable. For Christmas Eve he, Patty and Paul cooked up a wonderful roast beef dinner with all the trimmings. The next day Frankie happily played Santa, having spent a lot of hard-earned money on a new, pink coat for Patty, skateboards for all the younger boys, a beautiful white angora sweater for me and new bathrobes for my parents. Mary Joyce, who came home for a week, got a new bottle of Chantilly perfume, while the baby received a large stuffed teddy bear. Finally, Frankie gave Tommy the Beatle's latest release, St. Pepper's Lonely Hearts Club Band, and then Paul an LP by some new artist named Jimi Hendrix.

"Far out!" Paul exclaimed over his new album. Nearing his fifteenth birthday, everything had suddenly turned groovy to him.

Frankie received presents in kind. But the one that struck him most was the new grill and set of utensils my father and I gave him. He was overjoyed.

Mostly for Mary Joyce's sake my mother tried feigning sobriety. But not for long. Shortly after we'd opened presents, she turned her back to the family while pretending to warm her hands by the living room's fireplace. During that time I spotted her nipping from a miniature bottle of scotch she'd stashed in the pocket of her new robe. As a self-imposed rule she typically drank in the privacy of her room or at Mrs. Logan's. But this blatant act in the same room as the children – on Christmas Day no less – sent me flying out of my chair.

"Ma, what are you doing?" I growled, stepping over the baby who was happily rolling on the floor and playing with discarded wrapping paper. Mary Joyce and Patty stopped playing some board game on the sofa to watch as I charged her way.

Finishing her slug, she screwed the cap on and glowered. "What?"

"You're drinking in front of the kids. That's what," I whispered harshly.

"Mind your own business," she said with blunt resentment. At which point I snatched the near empty bottle out of her hand, prompting her to manically charge at me to get it back. Losing her balance, she missed the mark entirely and instead fell headlong into the nearby Christmas tree. I watched in horror as both the tree and my mother crashed to the floor, leaving her tangled up in a mess of tinsel, broken ornaments, popping lights, and a scattered array of opened presents. Laying still inside that Douglas Fir trap as broken light bulbs and ornaments settled around her, I thought she might be dead.

"Mary Claire!" shouted my father, while scurrying to her aide, the dogs madly barking behind him. The first thing he did was pull the plug on the lights to prevent the tree from going up in flames. And then he reached for her. There were needles stuck to her new bathrobe and also caught up in her unkempt hair.

She was passed out cold on what was supposed to be one of the warmest holidays of the year. My father quickly determined that she was alive, though obviously not well. I had never heard him so angry as he tried shaking her awake. "Mary Claire, what in the hell is the matter with you?"

She didn't answer, but thankfully stirred as the rest of us stood still.

"I'm taking you to bed," he finally muttered. And so, while Bing Crosby crooned on the radio about tree tops glistening and children listening, my father hoisted her upon his shoulder and disappeared upstairs.

Frankie, no stranger to drunken lunacy, tried salvaging the tree along with our Christmas spirits. Standing the tree upright as a shower of glass shards and needles hit the floor, he declared it could have been worse.

"I'm not sure," I said pointing down at John, who had picked up a stray miniature from my mother's pocket and was now putting it in his mouth.

May all our days be so merry and bright.

Chapter 28

Frankie was right, Christmas Day could have been worse. Meaning my mother hadn't fallen into the new color TV – Frankie's gift to himself. Actually, it wasn't brand new as it came from Things Gone Buy. And it wasn't just for his use. Until that acquisition it seemed we were the only people in America who watched "Walt Disney's Wonderful World in Color" in black and white.

I suppose if there was one trait worth inheriting from his father it was a propensity for strategic haggling. This is my kind way of saying "con artistry." Frankie had all that potential, indeed, which was thankfully diluted by the goodness from his mother's DNA. He was a hustler for sure; and honest, no doubt. Possessing a mind like a Philadelphia lawyer he could remember the finest of details. This, along with an intuitive knowledge of how cons operated, made him one tough match for the seedier lot. I learned this when I became his unwitting accomplice where that color TV was concerned.

A couple of weeks before Christmas Frankie spotted that television set in the window at Things Gone Buy. As the shop was just a few doors down from the Laurel Meat Market, Frankie often sauntered in there on his way to and from work looking for cookware and kitchen utensils. He'd often donate good "finds" to Sister Marguerite. But before long even our kitchen rivaled the nuns' for its array of pans, interesting gizmos and time-saving gadgets. Plus, he made sure every one of us kids knew how to use them *and* to make at least three decent dinners.

Shortly before Christmas Frankie asked me to bring John in his pram and join him on a trip to Things Gone Buy.

"Hey, I recognize that cruiser," said the longtime proprietor, Red "Baloney" Maloney about the baby carriage. "Bunch of giggling girls came in here last summer and bought it. Said they was throwin' a baby shower for a good friend. Guess that little lady was you, heh?"

"Yeah," I replied as Red peeked in on John, was now sitting up on his own and playing with a few noisy toys. Meanwhile, I looked around the store while watching out of the corner of my eye as Frankie inspected a butcher's knife.

"Nice knife," he said. "Sort of like the ones I use at home with all the discounted meat I get from working at the Laurel Meat Market."

"They give you a discount there, kid?"

"Yeah. Comes in handy helping to feed our large, extended family. Ten kids, two adults, and two dogs."

Now I would say with utter conviction that Frankie O'Brien was truly principled. He made promises and threats sparingly and delivered swiftly on both. But something about bargaining over some of Red's sordidly acquired goods seemed to provide him with a sense of instant absolution. I learned that in bargaining timing was most important, and that Frankie's was impeccable. While we were living in a bear market with inflation on the rise, these two guys were all about trading bull.

"Let me ask ya' somethin', kid," Red piped up. "You gettin' deals on T-bone and 'fill-ette mig-non?'"

"Sure thing," said Frankie, closely inspecting the knife.

"Really? What's the old man charging you a pound?"

"Not nearly what you pay, I'm sure."

"Come on, kid. Whata' ya' payin'? Like a buck a pound?"

Frankie looked around as if checking for eavesdroppers, tightly nodded yes, then resumed looking at his reflection in the steel blade.

Red began to whisper. "Listen. You get me some 'fill-ette mig-non' for half-price and I'll pay you a dollar-ten a pound. You're making money, kid. Sound like a deal?"

Frankie looked deliberately puzzled, then set the knife down. "Well, yeah, except that I'm helping to feed my family," he said looking over at me and the baby. "And I get only a limited amount of meat."

"Okay, a buck-twenty."

"Thanks, Red. That's kind. I'll think about it. But like I said, the family's kind of dependent on me. In fact, I've gotta run home and cook dinner right now. I'll see ya around soon," he genuinely smiled, never once mentioning the television. "See anything special, Gail?"

"Yeah, did you see that color..."

"Colorful collection of dolls? You bet. Do you think Patty would like those?" he said, turning and winking at me.

"Yeah, collection of dolls," I quizzically stated.

Once outside, he filled me in. "Thanks for not mentioning the color TV. I don't want him to think I have any interest in it."

"Do you?"

"What, are you kidding?" he exclaimed, then clued me in on his bargaining strategy. We waited a few days longer before strolling back inside, grateful to see that the RCA television remained on display. It seemed we admired everything but that TV. At last, when we were about to leave, Frankie mentioned it.

"I'm surprised to see this is still here," Frankie casually commented.

"Yeah, me too. You know it cost over four-hundred brand new. The owner had it for less than a year."

"Why'd he sell it? Does it even work?"

"Couldn't pay his rent. Works great."

Frankie checked the price, which hadn't changed. It was $285.00, of which he suspected Red had probably paid only a fraction. "Does it have a warranty?" Frankie asked.

"Naw, not for used merchandise."

"Does it even work?"

Red promptly plugged it in and turned it on. The picture was brilliant.

"Hmmmm," was all Frankie said while carefully reexaming the butcher knife. I'd been coached to remain quiet.

"I see the price of meat just went up again," said Red, nonchalantly flipping the channels.

"Yeah, you're not kidding. How much for this knife?" Frankie asked.

"Three bucks"

"How 'bout a buck-fifty?"

"That's a damned good knife."

Frankie set it down. "Wow. Prices are going up everywhere. Including the 'fill-ette,'" he said, artfully mentioning his ace in the hole. "Makes me grateful for my job. You sure you won't take two dollars for this?"

"Okay, you gotta deal. Listen, kid," Red said, while taking Frankie's cash for the knife. "I talked it over with my wife, and we were thinking it might not be such a bad thing to fill our freezer with meat, you know. 'Specially given how prices are creeping up, and all. She was saying that maybe if you could help us out a little, maybe we could help you, too."

"Well, gosh, I don't know," said Frankie, naively. "What did you have in mind?"

"Well, you said that the 'fill-ette' is costing you a dollar a pound."

"Actually a buck-and-a-quarter now," Frankie corrected him.

Red huffed. "OK, so a buck-twenty-five. Still, let's just say you get the meat half-price and we give you a little premium on each pound. The way I see it," he grinned, "We're both coming out ahead."

"I see," Frankie smiled gently. "But I don't think my boss would appreciate that."

"Ah, the old man will never know unless you tell him. It's just between you, me and my old lady. Right? Sound like a pretty good deal?"

"I dunno, Red. What if he found out some other way and I lost my job over this? Don't forget, I'm helping to feed my family."

I knew enough about Red to sense he was pretty immune to sob stories. The race track was just a spit and a holler away. Over the years he'd done business with plenty of desperate drunks and gamblers who would pawn their mothers' wedding rings to feed their 'starving families.' But he reacted to Frankie with sincerity.

"Listen, if it makes you feel any better, pick out something, anything in the store you want, and I'll sell it to you for half-price," he said, noting Frankie's sudden interest in a six-dollar radio.

The devil had just met his match.

"Well, that's awfully generous of you. Because, you know," Frankie sheepishly added, "I could use a radio. Still, you'd have to swear to me that you and your wife would never tell a soul about it. I'm serious when I say I could lose my job."

"Kid, I'll tell you what. You get me fifty pounds of meat I can store in my freezer – and not just 'fill-ette.' But a little bit of this and a little bit of that. Good stuff, though, like T-bone and prime rib. You know. You get me fifty pounds of choice meat, and I'll give you *sixty* dollars, plus half-price on anything you want in the store."

The cost of the TV just went down to $142.50; still more than Red had probably paid for it.

"Gail," Frankie turned to me. "You swear you won't say *anything* to *anyone?*"

I vigorously shook my head no.

"Tell you what," Red spoke to me. "If it makes a difference you can pick out something for yourself or that cute baby of yours for half-price, too."

"Gail?" Frankie raised an inquisitive eyebrow.

"Well, there is that playpen for ten dollars over there," I pointed out.

Frankie nodded agreeably, then turned to Red. "I'll tell *you* what," he said. "You give me eighty dollars for the meat. Plus half-price on anything I want, the playpen for five and the knife for one dollar."

Red startled. "But you already paid for the knife."

Frankie shrugged. "I'm losing money on sixty."

"Okay, okay. Seventy dollars. Half-price on something for you, a "Lincoln" for the playpen and a buck back on the knife."

Frankie quickly did the math in his head. That was $1.40 a pound on meat for which he paid no more than twenty-five cents. This meant that he could spend $12.50 to get this man the amount of meat he wanted – 'fill-ette' included. Frankie calculated his liability in this equation to be about $85.00 for a slightly used color TV.

"I'm going to have to bring the meat in over the next couple of weeks," said Frankie. "And will you take some of it frozen?" he asked, not mentioning that he already had about half the supply stored in our family freezer.

"Sure. So you saying it's a deal?"

"It's a deal," said Frankie shaking the man's hand.

"Now you want this here radio?"

"No thanks," said Frankie. "I want the television."

Red became indignant. "You're just a kid. You can't afford the television!"

"I want the TV. You've got it priced at $285.00. Half-priced that's $142.50, minus your seventy-dollars, plus a dollar credit on the knife. Add five bucks for the playpen. So my charge is seventy-six-fifty. Here," Frankie said, reaching into his pocket and producing four twenty-dollar bills. "Now you owe me three-dollars and fifty-cents in change."

Red snorted and scowled as he scratched out the math. "How do I know you're good for the meat?"

"Well, like you, I'm a man of my word. And second, you know where I work. If I don't produce fifty pounds of meat for you over the next month – including 'fill-ette mig-non'– then you have my permission to walk into the Laurel Meat Market and tell the old man yourself that I'm gypping you out of a deal."

Red grinned. Probably because Frankie was smart, just like him. And honest. Unlike him.

"Kid, you just got yourself a playpen *and* a color TV!"

Frankie turned and winked at me, then left carrying the playpen. On Christmas Eve he returned with Joey who helped him carry the television to our house. My mother's surprising fall into the Christmas tree, and thankfully not that TV, was minor compared to what she pulled next.

Chapter 29

*T*he first thing I noticed about New Year's Eve was that it was snowing – hard. The second thing I noticed was that I'd slept in late – something I hadn't done in nearly six months.

Propping myself up on a pillow, I saw that Patty and Brandy were gone. John was missing, too. There was also the warm, familiar scent of bacon and waffles in the air. I realized a free morning was Patty's gift to me. Today was my long-awaited sixteenth birthday.

And so I lay quietly in bed for a bit longer, reflecting on my life. It was unquestionably hard, but never dull and somehow hope-filled. I'd made honor-roll twice the first semester, which was nothing short of a miracle considering the odds piled up against me. But if necessity is the mother of invention, then motherhood revealed the necessity for being inventive. I discovered that by using my time economically I could find the necessary time each day to study. This often meant spending my lunch period in the school library. Plus, there were several occasions when I rocked John to sleep after everyone else had gone to bed, holding him in one arm, a textbook in my other. I might have been sleep-deprived. But the arrival of two consecutive straight-A report cards made up for it. I wanted more out of life, and those A's were a passport to a better world.

I wanted to go to college. But where? Certainly not "Our Lady of Perpetual Help." And how? College was less than two years away and expensive. I knew my car savings would now have to help finance it, particularly as my father's salary was stretched so thin.

I rolled over and thought of John O'Neill and of the warmth, humor and normalcy he brought to my life. He was kind, gentle, and caring but did not impose his will on me – and not for lack of trying or my desire. I was adamant about not having sex – or at least not going all the way with him. No one knew better than I the hardships and sacrifices involved with creating a life too soon. And I realized that if he weren't willing to wait, he wasn't worth the wait to begin with. I was intimately familiar with the consequences of foolish choices. And as far as I could see, the dumbest choice any teenaged girl could make would be to sacrifice control of her future for a few seconds of sexual satisfaction. I wanted power over my own life, to craft a life of my own, and to make my own choices rather than having them imposed on me.

I'd learned of a huge difference between endurance and self-power. Sacrifice produced endurance, but power meant having personal control. To me, it meant the difference between tolerating and delegating. I thought of Mary Joyce and of that lying slime ball Steve Barelli. I thought of Uncle Francis's and Aunt Cate's hardships and the innocent children they'd left behind, particularly their beautiful baby who, regardless of how well he was loved and cared for might one day feel the void. I then thought of Patty: sweet, adorable, funny, charitable – and handicapped. What becomes of a child with special needs if she is born into an utterly lopsided life to a poor, uneducated, single and powerless mother?

I thought of my own mother whose descent into alcoholic madness had been partially precipitated by the unexpected arrival of five more children. Clearly there are things over which we have control. And though I loved John O'Neill with all my heart, the protection of my body and soul had grown significantly more important since the first time I'd laid eyes on him and declared myself Mrs. John Aloysius O'Neill. This, even though to me he was the greatest kisser on the planet.

And so, in the earliest hours of turning sixteen, I listened to the gentle whisper of falling snow, thinking of all things good and bad, but mostly feeling good. Shortly, there was a tap at the door. I sat up and smiled believing it might be Patty to surprise me with breakfast in bed.

"Come in," I chirped.

I startled. It was my mother, who had not entered my room in months.

"Happy birthday," she said in her smoky, languid voice. In spite of her new robe, she looked and sounded like hell. Her dark roots made her hair look like Indian candy corn, with an even, brown band beneath a shock of orange; both standing out against her ghastly white face. Plopping down on the opposite twin bed, she stared out at the snow.

"It's pretty, isn't it? Sort of whitewashes life," she said, then began to cry, reminding me of when she'd last sat on that bed and had told me about Aunt Cate. "Gail, I have to tell you something."

"Yeah, Ma," I responded uneasily. "What's up?"

"First, I'm really sorry for the way I've been treating you lately. I haven't exactly been myself."

My heart clutched.

"I need help," she added, "so I'm going away."

"You're leaving?" I barely whispered. "Where are you going?"

"Baltimore. Your father's arranged it with Doc Warren and Sister Perpetua to try and help me sober up. Doc has a colleague – some psychiatrist – that runs a fancy facility there and he's agreed to take me on. Sister arranged some financial help from the Archdiocese," she said, while wiping away a tear. "This ought to be good. Me on the cheap in a swanky nut house."

Dark images immediately came to mind of noir movies I'd seen with people in straight jackets on their way to electro-shock therapy. Afterwards their depression was cured, but only because their brains seemed to have melted from enough juice to light up the Empire State Building. Later they turned into zombies.

"Ma, are you sure you want to do this? What are they going to do to you? I mean, don't they torture people in those places?"

"Don't worry Gailec," she said half-grinning, her Irish lilt rising. She was the only one who used that term of endearment. "It'll be all right. This treatment is mostly about talking and drinking: coffee, that is, and straight up," she added with a measure of comic assurance.

I tried to laugh. Instead I broke into tears. "I'm scared for you."

Her countenance cracked. "Me, too," she muttered. "I don't know what's become of me. I know I've hurt you in ways that I never intended. I've hurt everybody. But I've been living in a whole world of hurt ever since Cate..." she stopped, unable to actually mention her death. "I miss her so much," she continued to cry.

"Ma," I gulped, "I miss her, too. We all do. But most of all, right now, we miss you."

"I know," she sniffled hard, then mused, "I miss me, too."

We both chuckled at her dark humor. "When are you going?"

"Today."

"Today? For crying out loud, it's New Year's Eve! And my sixteenth birthday," I said, utterly taken aback.

She reached into her pocket for a tissue and then blew her nose. "I'm sorry about the timing. Apparently the doctor in Baltimore called because he had a cancellation. Truthfully, I think someone who paid up ran away to celebrate New Year's Eve, so I'm taking the poor bloke's spot," she said. For months there had been a conditioned mournfulness in her face, but now a hint of her old Irish pluck was back. "I suspect the place will be packed tomorrow. So I had better get in there now if I stand a chance of getting the top bunk," she joked some more, mocking my brothers and cousins who were always arguing over who got the top bed.

We laughed, then she fell serious again.

"Your father told me after I fell into the Christmas tree that if I didn't sober up he was going to have to make some drastic changes around here."

"What did he mean?"

"He wouldn't say. But I was afraid it meant your cousins would have to leave. And there's no way I could do that to Cate or her kids."

How absurd. She'd already abandoned Cate's kids.

"How long will you be gone?"

"Long as it takes, I guess."

"Oh, Ma, you're going to be okay. I promise. And, I promise while you're gone I'll help take care of everyone."

"I know. I could have never gotten this depressed without you," she said with all sincerity. "You've done a remarkable job keeping this family together. Your father feels that way, too."

"Thanks," I smiled softly.

She fell quiet. Then picking up MJ's favorite stuffed lion from Patty's bed, she looked it in the eye for a second before propping it on her lap. Her gaze now fixed on the wall ahead, she began quietly and methodically running her fingers through it's slightly tangled, synthetic mane. I might have welcomed her silence, but not the oddity of her behavior which made me feel uncomfortable and nervous. I was about to ask her if she was okay when her demeanor and voice turned ice cold.

"He killed her," she blurted, still staring ahead.

It took a moment for the shock of her pronouncement to clear. I sensed what she meant, but asked anyway. "What are you saying?"

"Francis. He pushed and dragged her down the stairs. He killed...." she stopped, her words catching on raw emotion. "HE KILLED CATE," she cried out, then grasping the lion tightly to her chest fell to violently sobbing.

Immediately I climbed out from beneath my warm covers, grabbed the afghan blanket Cate had made, and tightly wrapped it around us. I hadn't been this close to her in a long time and I could smell her smoky breath and what I detected might be a fresh belt of liquor.

"I promised her I wouldn't tell that he'd dragged her down the stairs that night," she wailed. "And now it's killing *me*."

Not that I didn't know what to say – that much was true. But the truth she just spoke rippled with a thousand silent words; a truth leading to a better understanding of the torment she'd suffered of late. Loyal to her sister far beyond the grave, my mother had buried a dark secret. Only my mother had seemingly been buried alive with it.

She was trembling now. "Oh, my god, that night was so awful. He left her for dead on the foyer floor. She had to crawl," she started, her words suddenly drowning in torrential sobs, then finally, "I... hate... that... rat... bastard. I... hate... him! He gets away with everything, including murder."

"Ma, why didn't you tell the police?"

"You don't understand. No one would understand! There was Cate fighting for her life and begging me to promise her that if she didn't make it, that I would get her children away from him and raise them. Plus, she thought their lives were hard enough without knowing about their father.

So she made me promise to never tell them – or anyone – what he'd done to her."

Reaching up with one hand, I ran my fingers through her own wild mane and gently massaged her scalp. I could feel the vibrations of her wracking sobs. I wiped her tears, then pulled her in close. She buried her head on my chest, and with tears still flowing, finally began to calm down.

"You couldn't even tell Dad?"

"No," she whispered, finally straightening up. "I haven't told anyone. But I'm telling you now," she said, her voice quavering, "because *you* deserve to know. I promised Cate that I'd keep 'em all together. And I let her down," she said lowering her head and biting her lip.

"What do you mean, Ma? They're all here. And no one's going anywhere."

"They're here under one roof right now mostly because of you. But your father insists there will be drastic changes if I don't get help. And I know what that means. Besides, Cate didn't mean just keepin' 'em together," she choked. "She meant being a mother to 'em. Instead, there's my own child doing my job."

Her words implied what I well knew; that I'd become the de facto mother in the house. I wouldn't wish it upon anyone at this stage in their life. But oddly, this acknowledgment felt good.

"I don't know how I'll get through this," she said, choking up again. "I'm just so damned mad at him."

"I know, Ma. We're all mad at Uncle Francis."

"That's not what I meant."

"Who then? Dad?" I asked incredulously.

"No. God. Where in the hell has he been through all of this?"

"Are you asking *me* that question?" I said, half-wishing she'd saved this angry, soul-baring inquiry for a priest – or better yet, one of the psychiatrists.

"Well, do *you* have the answer?" she asked caustically. "Because I sure don't. I've been a devoted disciple all of my life and look what that's gotten me. A dead sister and a bed at an asylum."

My response startled both of us. I simply began to laugh.

"You think that's funny?" she harshly asked.

"No," I leaned over and warmly hugged her. "I don't think anything you are going through is funny. What I do find amusing is how I had the same thoughts not so long ago and pretty much let Sister Perpetua have it. I thought everything she and the church had to say was complete nonsense."

"See, then I'm not so crazy as you'd think."

"No, you're not crazy, but you are in deep pain. Other than that, you're just wrong."

"How so?" she responded sharply.

"I wondered the same thing. How could a presumably loving creator allow any of this to happen to anyone or to our family? To any family? We're good people. We work hard and take care of each other. We faithfully go to Mass. And then suddenly our lives are turned upside down. A few months ago I asked Sister Perpetua about it. And some of what she shared actually resonated with me."

"Tell me why I'm wrong, then," she said, her voice edging higher.

"Sit tight," I said, retreating to my book shelf, then returning with my Bible opened it to a marked passage.

"'Therefore, since we have a great high priest who has passed through the heavens, Jesus, the Son of God, let us hold fast to our confession. For we do not have a high priest who is unable to sympathize with our weaknesses, but one who has similarly been tested in every way, yet without sin. So let us confidently approach the throne of grace to receive mercy and to find grace for timely help.'"

Softly speaking, I gently closed the book on Hebrews Four. "Ma, I think what this says is that Jesus learned a thing or two about human suffering. Still, he never lost faith because he knew he had a job to do, which was to teach us to care for and forgive one another. Just because you're suffering doesn't mean that God isn't there for you. It just means that you have to stay faithful and be patient so that God can basically move things around in your favor. Think about it. The fact that you are able to get a last-minute spot in a place of healing because someone else cancelled is no coincidence. It's a miracle. And you better give thanks to God for that."

Holding fast to the stuffed animal, she rocked back and forth, crying now in the most inconsolable way.

"Ma, I'm so sorry. I was trying to be helpful, honestly." I wrapped my arms tightly around her again. "It's okay. You're going to be okay. I promise."

"I never thought this day would happen?" she whimpered.

"What do you mean, going to get help?"

"No, getting spiritual guidance from you."

I couldn't help but laugh. "I love you so much."

"I love you, too," she half-smiled. "What was that you just read to me?"

"Hebrews four, fourteen through sixteen. Sister Perpetua told me to read it when I was complaining about my own life. She wanted me to know that just because we suffer it doesn't mean there isn't salvation, or that help isn't coming. She was trying to convince me that I should be giving thanks to God for my strength during everything that was happening because somehow it meant I was living in a state of grace."

"Are you?"

"I guess. I mean, I've been praying every day for you to get better." The realization of my words startled me. "Yes, Ma. The answer is yes."

She lowered her head as she allowed my words to sink in. Finally putting the lion aside, she blew her nose again, then sighed heavily before leaning into my shoulder. And so we sat, just quietly watching the snow while bonding less as mother and daughter it seemed, than as friends.

"Are they doing all right?" she asked.

"Who?"

"The children."

"Yes."

"I don't know how this family would be able to stay together without you."

"I think you give me way too much credit. I couldn't function without Frankie. He's so grateful to be here," I stated genuinely. "Without him I'd be going to Baltimore with you. And it's not like Dad's not involved either."

"I know. And I love your father, too. He's a good man and a hard-working soul. And I honestly don't think he'd ever send 'em away. But he damn sure is ready to ship me off," she said, her voice softening. She sat still for a short spell, seemingly reflecting.

"How are they?" she finally spoke.

"Who, Ma?"

"The kids. I'm wondering how the kids are really doing and I think you're the only one who can truly answer that. I know Patty was Pallotti's homecoming queen, which is kind of strange since she doesn't go to school there. And I heard the boys had a good football season. The baby seems healthy, thanks to you. Frankie got a job and I see him helping in the kitchen. Mary Joyce seems happy; Tommy's thinking about colleges; you're dating that nice young boy; and so far Paul, Raymond and Timmy are gettin' along. Am I missing anything?"

How could she be observant in so many ways, yet glaringly blind in another. "Yes," I gently answered. "That each of us misses our mother."

She lowered her head, fresh tears falling. "I'm sorry. I'm so sorry. I didn't mean to hurt anyone."

"None of what happened is *your* fault. Do you hear me? None of it. Besides, without your insistence, Cate's children might have been split apart with each of them living in an unfathomable wilderness," I said, relying on Sister Perpetua's wisdom yet again.

"You did nothing wrong, Ma. Nothing," I reiterated. "The important thing is that all of Cate's kids are here under one roof, they're healthy, and you're finally getting a chance to pull yourself together."

The most curious look crossed her face. "You are so...," she stopped, then looked me in the eye, a twinkle in her own.

"What?"

"Grown up."

"What choice did I have?"

"I'm sorry."

"Would you stop apologizing? It was bound to happen one way or another. Besides, as much resentment as I might have felt, I'm also grate-ful for what I've witnessed. It has changed me, for the better, I believe.

I've learned to find wisdom and courage in the dark space of sometimes seeming hopelessness."

"What was that?"

"I'm saying I'm a better person because...

"No, the 'hopelessness' part."

"You mean, 'I've learned to find wisdom and courage in the dark space of sometimes seeming hopelessness?'"

She nodded her head while allowing the words to sink in. "'Wisdom and courage in the dark space of sometimes seeming hopelessness,'" she repeated. "Thank you. Those words, and coming from my own child no less, make me feel like there really is hope. You're amazing."

Why disenchant her now by giving due credit to Sister Perpetua?

"I have one other secret to tell you," she said, straightening up and blowing her nose again. "And I don't mean to spoil your fun."

"Oh, come on. What more fun could I have than seeing my mother off for who knows how long on my sixteenth birthday?" I tried joking.

"Well, you can drive up to visit me."

"Of course I'll drive up to visit you. I'm getting my license next week."

"No, I mean you could drive up to see me in your own car."

A rush of excitement passed through me. "What are you saying?"

"Listen, I know this is selfish of me for spoiling the surprise, but I wanted you to know that it was at my insistence that your father and I got you a car for your sixteenth birthday. Frankie and your boyfriend pitched in some, too. What nice young men," she added.

I sat in stunned silence, feeling overjoyed and overwhelmed at once.

"Seeing how MJ got a full scholarship to that Trinity College, I told your father that we should use some of her college savings on you." She chuckled. "He thought that was a great idea, setting that money aside for *your* college education.

"'No,' I told him. "'I want to spend that money giving Gail what she wants most in her life *right now*. Which is a car of her own.'" She looked down. "This was my one condition for going to Baltimore. I want to get well. I want to get back to taking care of my family again. But I want you to know that if I ever get this desperate again, you are free to leave. Those wheels will be your wings."

"You're wrong."

"You don't want a car?" she said, incredulously.

"No, I do. I really do. But truthfully, what I want most in my life is for you to get well and not just to come back and care for your family. But for you to come back to being a happy part of it." I put my hands over my face trying to control my own tears, but it was useless. "You've missed out on so much."

"I know," she whispered. "I know." And then she hugged me. And whether it was wishful thinking or a true ray of hope, I felt such tenderness from her. She was mighty and fragile at once; like a towering oak that might have lost limbs after being battered in a violent storm, but was still standing.

Finally separating, I asked the all-important question. "What kind of car is it?"

"That's a surprise."

"Oh, come on! When am I getting it?"

She zipped a finger over her mouth, then shook her head.

"All right," I happily conceded, "your secret is safe with me. And, Ma," I said, now warmly nestled beside her, "thanks."

She nodded her head, then rewrapped the afghan around us. And so we sat for a spell, just staring at and listening to the steadily falling snow, the accumulation of those flakes forming an unblemished and promising slate for a clean start.

I thought of what she'd just revealed to me about Uncle Francis. It wasn't something I didn't already suspect. And I would keep it to myself as she sorted out the realities of it in treatment. The most important thing right now was that she was finally getting the help she deserved.

"It's pretty," she said softly.

"Yeah. I love it when it snows."

Chapter 30

The younger children knew nothing about the true reason behind my mother's departure. After clearing the snow off of the family station wagon and putting chains on the tires, my father packed her suitcase and tucked it in the back seat. Before leaving, he wished me a happy birthday and new year in one breath, then kissed me on the cheek. "I'm really proud of you," he said. "You deserve to have a good day and a good year. I hope you get both."

In a world of trouble, my mother silently hugged me good-bye, then followed him to the car. I stepped out to the front porch and watched them disappear. Tommy joined me, the two of us staring blankly at the vacant, rectangular spot left behind; the dark patch of asphalt quickly disappearing with the falling snow. He didn't say anything. He didn't have to. We shared an unspoken symphony of hurt. Finally I sighed.

"Are you okay?" he asked.

"I'm good. I didn't expect this."

"Me neither. But it's okay. At least she's getting help."

"Yeah," I nodded as he hugged me. Soon, Frankie joined us, embracing us in a tearful group hug just as Paul and Joey slipped outside, too.

"What's going on?" Joey asked.

Why lie?

"Ma is off to get treatment for her depression," I replied.

"Where? And why didn't she tell me?" he asked, as if offended that he couldn't handle it.

"I'm not sure. But she is really heart-broken over how she's treated all of us. And Dad told her after she fell into the Christmas tree that she better get help, or else."

"Or 'else' what?" Paul nervously piped in.

"I honestly don't know. And neither did she. All she knew, and all I care about, is that Dad is determined to see her get well."

"Where's he taking her?"

"A treatment facility in Baltimore. Do me a favor, please. And don't share this with the younger kids. All they need to know is that she's off to help a sick relative. Okay?"

Frankie, Tommy, Joey and Paul each solemnly nodded their heads in agreement. Then Frankie, in his ever resilient manner, changed the topic.

"Listen, I'm getting ready to fire up the grill. The Green Bay Packers are playing the Dallas Cowboys for the NFL championship, and the game starts in about two hours. You up for watching it?"

"Yeah, I guess," I said. "John's coming over."

"I know," he grinned, and playfully punched my arm. "Today's match is going to be the clash of the titans. And my man is going all the way! Because, you know, winning isn't everything...." he paused, flashing a toothy grin just like his idol.

"It's the only thing," the four of us said in unison completing Lombardi's famous quote, then likewise moaned in chorus.

"Darned right," said Frankie. "This is Green Bay's sixth league championship game. God is clearly a Packer's fan, too."

I nodded. I ached. Even knowing that a car of my own would soon materialize, I couldn't stop thinking of my mother off in a pure, white snow storm to vanquish the darkest of demons.

"I hope you don't mind that I invited a few other friends over," said Frankie.

"No," I shrugged. "The more the merrier."

"Good," he smiled surreptitiously.

He wasn't kidding. Within the hour a small crowd started gathering at our house. Not only did Frankie and Paul fire up the grill on our covered front porch, but they built a roaring flame in our living room fireplace, too. At first it was only the guys who arrived, including John, with a large bouquet of flowers.

"Happy Birthday," he smiled warmly.

Not even the flowers could hide my gloom. "My parents just left," I said, fighting tears. "My mother is being committed to some psychiatric facility outside of Baltimore."

Speechless, John set the flowers down, then tenderly wrapped me inside his big, muscular arms where I fell apart. Neither one of us spoke. Instead, he just held me close and stroked the back of my head until my crying subsided, ignoring the curious looks from the others.

"Do you want to go somewhere?" he asked.

I shook my head. "I'll be all right, thanks."

Unconvinced, he held me that way for a little bit longer. At least until Patty interrupted us. "Gail, don't you like his flowers?"

I chuckled, and breaking away from him briefly embraced her. "Of course, I love them. And I love you for letting me sleep in this morning, and for helping to make my favorite breakfast. Thank you."

She grinned. Patty who was all about affection, hugged me back quite hard.

I'd like to report that the rest of the day – or even the afternoon – went smoothly. But it was a madhouse. At one point there were nearly forty people in our living room watching what turned out to be one of the most epic games ever played in football history: The Ice Bowl.

You had to have seen it to have believed it – even on television – as the Green Bay Packers hosted the Dallas Cowboys on their home turf, which had literally turned into a solid sheet of ice. With the wind chill factor it was minus 34 degrees in Green Bay, Wisconsin, where the referee's whistles might have been frozen into silence, but not the football talent. And certainly not the two coaches, the hot-tempered, take no prisoners, Vince Lombardi, against the cool-mannered, intellectual Tom Landry. The rivals had previously shared coaching responsibilities with the New York Giants, offense and defense respectively, before moving on to become head coaches at other franchises. So this game wasn't just to prove whose team was entitled to the NFL championship. It was a mythical clash between two warriors who knew each other's strengths and weaknesses better than anyone else. Even the players' icy breath made them look like fire-breathing dragons as they battled it out on the frozen tundra of Lambeau Field.

There was a lot of gambling going on in my living room, with Frankie the principal bookie and Joey his assistant. Like Frankie, Joey had a remarkable brain for numbers and could quickly compute math in his head. And I knew if there were a buck to be made that afternoon, that those two would make it. By day's end they had taken in at least one hundred bets on every conceivable angle of the game, and a few hundred dollars in earnings.

They bet on the pass completions and fumbles of individual players, and even which side the Packers would run their famous sweep – left or the right. And, of course, there was gambling on the final score, with a finish that defied any other for an adrenaline rush. With only seconds left, and Dallas ahead 17-14, the last-minute bets flew. Green Bay, in posses-sion of the ball near the Dallas end zone, might have gone for a field goal kick to tie the game. Instead, quarterback Bart Starr ran a highly unex-pected sneak to the right, ultimately giving his team a winning touch-down and a 21-17 victory over Dallas. Lombardi's team had won the NFL's Championship game and, for the second year in a row his Packers were headed to the Super Bowl to defend their title.

"He's the closest thing to God," said Frankie, speaking of Lombardi, while watching Joey count the cash and pay out bets.

"'The Man' walks on water," Joey agreed, handing Frankie his cut of the action.

Like everyone else, I had been so caught up in the excitement that I'd barely had time to feel my pain or think about the fact that it was my birthday – or even New Year's Eve – or that at some point I expected a car. With six inches of snow on the ground already, and more expected by the morning, we were having an "Ice Bowl" of our own. I was sitting beside John in the living room with the baby on my lap, feeling grateful to be inside the warmth of my house surrounded by family and good friends, including Nadette, Melinda, Tina and Dottie. Suddenly, the four of them slipped in the kitchen, with Nadette hollering, "Gail, can you help me for a second?"

"What do you need?" I yelled back.

"Why don't you go help her?" John prompted me.

"Go ahead," said Frankie.

"All right, already," I said. Anticipating what was about to happen, I handed the baby to John and made my way to the kitchen.

"SURPRISE!" the girls shouted in unison, holding a large chocolate sheet cake with sixteen glowing candles. My reaction surprised everyone – including myself. Instead of blowing out the candles, I began to cry. It had been that kind of up and down day.

Believing they were tears of joy, Nadette broke into singing "Happy Birthday" as the other revelers joined in. "Hurry up and blow out the candles! This cake is heavy!"

I wiped my tears, and made one wish, and one wish only – that my mother would get well – then blew them out. Nadette set the large cake down on the dining room table, then handed me a knife. "I get the piece with the biggest flower on it," she declared, an undying habit since our grade school days, "and you can have the piece with your name on it."

True to our tradition, she got a flower and I got my name in cursive icing. I tried jamming a plastic fork into my slice of the cake, but it stopped half-way. I tried again. Same thing. Setting my plate on the table, I poked my fingers down into it hitting something hard and metallic. "What on earth?" I said, looking up only to see all eyes upon me.

"What is it?" John teasingly asked.

"I have no idea," I nervously lied, at last retrieving the mystery object. I laughed. "Nadette, did you lose a key in my cake?"

"No," she grinned. "You found one."

"What?" I said, no sooner asking the question when I saw the answer I'd been dying to know. It was a Volkswagen key. My heart and my hand trembled. I looked up again, seeing the eager faces of Nadette, Frankie, and John.

"What's going on?" I coyly asked, trying not to betray my mother's secret.

"Why don't you go out front and see for yourself?" suggested John taking me by the hand. There was no sweeter cake or confection that could compare to that shiny, navy blue Volkswagen Beetle with white rimmed tires and a big, red bow on it. It had obviously been stored in someone's nearby garage, because it had only the faintest dusting of snow on it.

"What!" I screamed with genuine disbelief at the actual sight of it, "Is that for me?"

"Of course it's for you," said Frankie. "Happy Birthday, Gail!"

"Frankie, what did you have to do with this?"

"Not much. Your parents paid for it. But John and I pitched in for your insurance and a new set of tires."

If ever there was an affirmation that my sacrifices were worth it, this was it. I glanced over at John. "*You* were in on this, too?"

He grinned, and for the second time that day I found myself buried in his arms while crying. I hugged Frankie, too. "I can't believe my parents agreed to this. Frankie, you put them up to this, didn't you?"

"Honestly, no."

Still, I hugged him hard again.

"Don't you want to drive it?" John asked.

"If it's a stick shift I don't know how!" I laughed.

"It's a piece of cake," John quipped. The crowd laughed. He handed the baby to Frankie, washed the key clean for me, and as the others gathered on the front porch, he and I walked through the accumulating snow to the car. After firing up the engine, the first thing I did was turn on the radio only to catch Tommy James and the Shondells singing about the Hanky Panky.

"My baby better not do any hanky panky in this car. At least not with anyone but me," John joked as I struggled to put the car into the right gear. It jerked, I laughed, and drove about ten feet before it stalled, prompting our guests to applaud.

"Is it okay if I do it in someone else's car, then?" I laughed some more.

He laughed back, and after warmly kissing me whispered, "Happy Birthday, baby, and Happy New Year! I love you."

Chapter 31

I'd like to say that I barely noticed her absence as she was checked out so much of the time, anyway. But I ached for my mother. Her battle was darker than anyone had expected, and the sum of events surrounding Cate's death had created underlying emotional currents like a vicious riptide. One night, shortly after she'd begun treatment and I was up late doing homework in the dining room, my father walked in the front door looking ashen and positively crestfallen. My heart quickened.

"What's wrong?" I jumped up.

He sat down on the living room sofa, put his head in his hands and fell apart crying. I conjured the worst, nervously sitting beside him. "Oh, no. What's happened? Is Ma okay?"

His voice cracking, he finally spoke. "She's surviving. It's that damned Mrs. Logan," he cried. "She'd been sharing her pain pills with your mother for months. Miracle it didn't kill her mixing it with the booze. She's going through a wicked withdrawal."

"What? No wonder she was so loopy."

"No kidding. I just left Mrs. Logan's house. I told her if she ever gave your mother so much as a baby aspirin – let alone one of those narcotics – I'd turn her into the police. I don't care if she is seventy-eight-years old. She can rot in prison – or hell – for all I care." He retrieved a hankie from a pocket, then wiping away tears added, "I hate that man." I knew right away he meant Uncle Francis, who had still managed to evade the law.

My father was determined to see my mother get well. And every day after work he drove to Baltimore with a nosegay or her favorite candy to share his love, along with news of our comings and goings. He informed her that Frankie, Tommy, Joey, John O'Neill, and MJ – now a productive

249

student at Trinity College – all knew the truth of her whereabouts. The other children were told that Ma was away and caring for a very sick relative, a.k.a. Aunt Ida – Joey's derivation of "In Detox Action." It stuck.

Though missed, her absence allowed a new calm to descend on our house. Letters from MJ reported good grades and a serious boyfriend. Tommy – like John O'Neill – had begun applying to colleges. Both were working to keep their grades up while praying for a football scholarship. Several schools had expressed interest in them. But neither were banking on anything yet and continued to study hard and work out while awaiting decision letters. Tommy was hopeful about the University of Maryland, whereas John seemed keen on becoming an Atlantic Coast Conference rival at the University of Virginia.

Coinciding with my mother's absence was a deepening bond between Joey and Frankie. There was nothing unusual about the countless hours they spent dissecting football plays scratched out on Frankie's handheld chalkboard. But something else was afoot, and I intuited some quiet scheming between those two ambitious souls. Whatever it was, Paul must have sensed it, too. When being ignored he typically left the room, or even headed over to a nearby horse farm on his bike where he enjoyed volunteering his time to care for the animals.

Though smart in many ways, Paul was not always a disciplined student and often struggled in school. The first semester I helped him slog through several book reports, and had never seen his eyes shine so bright as the day he finally received a "B+" on a report he'd completed himself. I rewarded him with kudos and a banana split at Guvelli's, and he rewarded himself with an "A" on the next book report.

Then there was Raymond. Now eleven, the kid was an agile athlete with a sharp wit. Being surrounded by so many older, smart and motivated jocks is probably just what he needed most to stay out of trouble. Particularly as he'd recently been censured at school for talking back to his teacher – Sister Beatrice of all people! One might have thought he would prefer being hung by his underwear on the flagpole after she was done with him. Somehow, though, her harsh rebuke didn't stop him. But my father certainly did after Sister Perpetua personally called him about Raymond's second incident of bad-mouthing the nun.

"One more time," I heard him firmly say to Raymond afterwards, "and you will lose all TV privileges for the rest of the school year. And don't try me." Being hooked on *Lost in Space* and *Star Trek*, Raymond quickly cleaned up his act.

Thankfully sharing some of Frankie's enterprising spirit, he was also keen for the odd job where he could earn a little extra cash. Sometimes Timmy would accompany him as they knocked on doors looking to be hired. They would do anything – shovel snow, clean out an attic or a garage, even wax floors or fold laundry if it meant cash in their pockets. All such things they avoided at home knowing they'd never get paid.

Timmy was still very attached to Joey. And not surprisingly, Joey kept an eye on him, making sure Timmy got to school and bed on time. Plus, he willingly helped him with his homework. Given Joey's scholastic aptitude, this was a true windfall for my youngest brother who was likewise earning all A's.

Even Patty had adjusted. Charming, curious and uninhibited, I envied her distilled vision on life. She received in technicolor, but transmitted her world view in black and white. Seeing things her way often brought unexpected insight. She was doing pretty well in school, too, but mostly because Sister Marguerite sheltered Patty beneath her earthly wings. Not only was Sister providing volunteer tutoring, but in teaching her to follow easy recipes had boosted both her reading and cooking skills. Patty had truly mastered basic food prep and cooking simple fare. No one baked yummier shortbread cookies or made fluffier scrambled eggs. Periodically she surprised us by stewing up her special bouillabaisse with the help of Sister Marguerite. Like Paul, she was Frankie's shadow in the kitchen at home, and there was no end to her delights.

Finally there was the baby, who at seven months had filled out nicely. Like most of his siblings, he had dark hair and blue eyes. Similar to Patty he possessed an infectious charm. Unlike all the others, he came equipped with a set of killer dimples. Quite active, John was now crawling and loved rolling around on the floor. He was so delicious to me. And though he received plenty of attention from the others, it was my affection he craved the most.

251

And so, with all this seeming domestic tranquility and a car of my own, I began wondering about getting a real job. A very part-time position, of course. But something that would help me pay for car upkeep and contribute to future college expenses. Checking the classifieds that mid-January morning, I came across an ad for Children's Hospital. *Wanted: part-time nursing clerk. No experience necessary.*

Taking the baby with me, and still in my Pallotti uniform with white knee socks and saddle shoes, I headed over to Children's right after school.

"Can I help you?" asked the personnel assistant, a twenty-something woman with teased, blonde hair.

"I'm here to apply for the part-time position as a nursing clerk."

"It's been filled," she stated matter-of-factly.

"That fast? I just saw the ad in the paper this morning."

She shrugged.

"Are there any other jobs?"

She looked down at a slightly dog-eared list. "Cardiac surgeon," she intoned sarcastically while slyly glancing upwards. "Maintenance, level three – mostly working in the basement boiler room; emergency room nurse – that's the midnight shift," she added with deepening sarcasm, as if that were past my bedtime. "Accountant, cook, and security guard. Any of those interest you?"

"Well, yes," I chortled, thinking how ironic that anyone managing a house and taking care of sick and injured children has at least some experience with maintenance, emergency nursing, accounting, cooking, and security. "I'm good at making people eat their hearts out. I'll take an application for the cardiac surgeon position, thank you."

As if on cue and for the first time ever, John let out a big raspberry in her direction. She and I cracked up, which pleased him so much he let out another Bronx-style cheer. She howled.

"What's your baby's name?" she asked, still smiling.

"John," I grinned. "He's my cousin and I'm just a caregiver." He was now pulling my hair. "Ouch!" I pretended to be in pain, which prompted another raspberry. We laughed.

I could tell she thought I was all right. "You seem good with children," she said, then whispered conspiratorially. "Listen, there's going to be an opening very soon for a part-time clerk in the ICU. You interested in that?"

The Intensive Care Unit had been my home away from home last summer. I knew a little bit about how it and the people in it worked. "What are the hours?" I asked, untangling John's hands from my hair.

"Two nights a week. Three p.m. to midnight. The gal who has the job now is leaving after she has a baby. She's due any day."

"Really? Gloria's having a baby?"

"How do you know Gloria?" she sounded surprised.

"From spending time in the ICU last summer taking care of this little guy. She's really sweet."

"Yeah, I'm sorry to see her go."

"Is the shift still on Thursday and Friday nights?"

"Yeah. And the pay's not bad either," she said sharing the hourly wage. "So, are you interested?"

Last school year it was inconceivable I'd work a weeknight *and* give up a Friday night. But lately I'd spent many nights just starting my homework after everyone else went to sleep and somehow managed. And sacrificing a Friday night wasn't great, but it was better than any portion of a Saturday. Plus the wage was good. "I would love to apply."

"Great! Fill out this application and I'll put in a word with the head nurse."

"Oh, you mean Anne Janette?"

"Boy, you two really did spend some time there, didn't you?"

"Yeah, it was worth every minute of it, too," I said kissing the crown of John's head.

After receiving my completed application she promised to follow-up. Instead, Anne Janette called that night.

"Gail," she said. I immediately recognized her warm voice. "I am so thrilled to see that you applied for the clerical position. How are you?"

"I'm doing well, thank you."

"And how's that precious baby you were taking care of?"

"Oh, my goodness, you should see him. He's mobile and has a mouth-ful of teeth. If I take my eyes off of him for a second he'll roll away, then bite me when I grab him!"

"Well," she laughed, "He sounds blissfully healthy and normal. Besides, that's what we pay them to do, you know, grow up. Listen, I understand you're interested in Gloria's position. Are you sure you're up for those hours? You won't be able to get any studying done on Thursday nights. And you certainly won't be out having fun with your friends on Fridays."

"I'll work it out," I assured her.

"That's good to hear," she said, "because Gloria is in labor as we speak."

And so it was that Gloria and her husband had a baby girl, and I got her job in the ICU starting the very next day. I shared the news – both good and bad – with my father.

"Way to go! You deserve this opportunity," he beamed.

"Dad, there's one problem."

"Yeah?"

"The baby has separation anxiety."

"Separation what?"

"Anxiety. He gets upset when I leave him now. Like he's worried I won't come back."

He looked puzzled. "How do you know about this?"

"Dr. Spock and Nadette."

"Nadette? That's scary. Keep her away from Tommy."

I chuckled. "Seriously, Dad. John believes *I'm* his mother. He'll need a reliable babysitting plan. Otherwise he'll bawl his head off for hours."

"Well, the boys can help you out. I'll see to it."

"You say that. But they need to know there is NO passing him around like a football. NO keeping him up past 8:00 p.m. He HAS to be properly fed, diapered AND take a regular bath. NO exceptions."

"Now I'm having separation anxiety."

I laughed again. He tousled my hair. "I'm proud of you. And it will make your mother extremely happy to hear that you got that job. I prom-ise you, we'll work it out."

He wasn't kidding. Promptly calling a family meeting, he explained the circumstances, set up a schedule, then looking directly at Joey and speaking with a hint of hope, added, "This is all subject to change when your mother comes home from Aunt Ida's."

And so I took the job, even arranging to leave school early on Thursdays and Fridays to ensure a timely arrival. Fortunately, my first-day jitters were somewhat alleviated by my familiarity with most of the ward's staff. There were a few new faces. But Anne Janette made the introductions and before long I was being handed charts to file while answering phones and taking general administrative orders. I felt rather clumsy to start and made my first big mistake by inadvertently hanging up the phone on some irate doctor who called back to inform me what an idiot I was.

"What is your name?" he screamed.

"Gail," I answered nervously.

"Gail who?"

"Gail Kenealy."

"Well, Gail Kenealy, if you expect to keep your job you will see to it that my calls are not lost. Are we clear? Do you understand? I don't have time to waste on repeat phone calls."

Why then, I wondered, was he wasting so much time yelling at me right now.

"Yes sir, doctor, sir," I stammered.

"The name is Dr. McKenzie. Do I need to spell it out for you?"

"No, sir. I mean, no sir, Dr. McKenzie, sir. It won't happen again. Is there someone you'd like to speak with?" I was shaking.

"No, I already took care of it," he said, then abruptly hung up.

Marcie, one of the nearby nurses, cracked up. "I'm sorry," she said. "But you just got McKenzied, didn't you?"

"If being 'McKenzied' means going half-deaf, then yes."

"Did he threaten you with losing your job?"

"Uh-huh, I answered sheepishly.

"You've been 'McKenzied,' all right."

"He must have the worst bedside manners in the world. I can't imagine his patients like him very much."

She laughed again. "I'll say. He runs the morgue."

I gulped, realizing I'd just hung up with the Grim Reaper's mortal cousin.

Marcie placed a comforting hand on my shoulder. "We just lost a little boy down the hall," she said gently. "Dr. McKenzie is waiting for the body."

"Oh, my gosh," I startled. "How old?"

"Barely three. He had a lot of problems."

I sat in dread, knowing that any minute the gurney carrying the child's diminutive body would pass by. I actually heard the mother's wail down the hall before I witnessed his departure.

"What was it?"

"Neuroblastoma," she said matter-of-factly.

I looked puzzled.

"Rare form of cancer," she simplified it.

"What?" I said incredulously, truly unaware that the deadly disease affected such young children.

Finally, two orderlies carted his tiny, sheet-draped frame our way. Both sobbing parents were close behind. I tried desperately not to look, but my eyes froze right on to the mother's. She bore a horrifying expression, as if trapped in a burning fire from which I was helpless to save her. Shortly, the orderlies slipped the gurney into an open service elevator.

"My baby. I lost my baby," she suddenly wailed watching the doors close shut, then collapsed into a heap on the floor, her weeping husband quickly huddling beside her. Finally pulling themselves off the floor, they climbed on board another elevator. I could still hear the woman's sobs even after the car began its descent.

I felt rattled, especially recalling how I'd clearly contributed to John's near demise just a few months before. Their departed child was at least born to two parents who loved him from the start and probably did everything they could for him. I choked back emotion. Earlier I would have been sad if John had died. Today, I would be completely devastated. That he'd survived this long without assets from loving parents was nothing short of a miracle.

During this time I'd barely noticed the phones had been ringing madly and, for all I knew, Dr. McKenzie was lining up my firing squad. Somehow I managed not to screw up for the next two hours and was surprised at how quickly the time flew by when my replacement showed up. I offered a quick recap of the night's events.

"We're short two nurses and the beds are at full capacity," I started.

"Welcome to the ward," she said.

"And Jack Keaton died earlier this evening."

She sighed while sitting down. "Sad."

"There's already another patient in his bed."

She shook her head. "That's life."

Her statement startled me. I carried on.

"The new patient is a seven-year-old girl with Juvenile Diabetes."

She nodded and sighed again.

I gathered my purse and headed out, noting how quiet it was at this midnight hour. Walking by the various rooms with lights dimmed, monitors aglow, and hushed tones made me wonder about "that's life," the beds a seeming revolving door between life and death. If one were lucky — and hopefully most of the patients were — the revolving door stopped at the right place. If one were like Jack, it delivered one to Dr. McKenzie, then kept turning — its chambers not empty for long.

When I arrived home that night, there was one soft light on in the living room and another in my room. Everyone was asleep. I took a quick shower, then before climbing into bed went into my brothers' bedroom and checked in on them. I tenderly stroked Timmy's head and kissed it. Joey's soft snoring prompted me to kiss the crown of his head, too. Deeply sleeping, even Tommy looked like an innocent child. I then peeked in on the O'Brien boys, and smiled contentedly over an orchestra of gentle snoring, each one snug in his own bed in this, their new home.

I returned to my room where I mused at Brandy curled up in Patty's bed, while Patty and John were blissfully asleep in his crib. I stared in awe at brother and sister, wondering now what all their lives would have been like had Cate lived. Or, sadly, what foster care or staying in that dark, inhospitable environment with their father would have meant.

There was Patty, who'd grown a bit since joining us, crammed up inside that crib like some stowaway. I suppose in a sense she was, perhaps the crib being a ship that transported her back to a world that included her mother. I easily recalled the many hardships she'd endured at her young age, then wondered if she felt as loved amongst us as I know she made each of us feel.

I savored the sight of John in his blue terry-cloth footie pajamas, dreamily sucking on two fingers. Thinking of Jack's body being carted away and of his parents' anguish made me realize now, more than ever, that children are not so much gifts as gift-bearers, every day presenting those around them with remarkable treasures – if only one was truly prepared to receive them.

Chapter 32

The following Thursday I came home so dog-tired I wanted to flop right into bed. Instead, I showered, put on my flannel PJs, and happily climbed under the covers in my darkened bedroom. My head had barely hit the pillow when I heard a strange, diminutive cry.

"Uhn, uhn, uhn."

Panicked, I sat up. The sound was emanating from the direction of Patty's bed.

"Uhn, uhn," the soft and unusual whining persisted.

Quickly I turned on the light then promptly covered my mouth to keep from screaming.

It was Brandy. And six puppies. On Patty's bed.

Brandy barely glanced at me while vigorously licking one of her newborns. Jumping out of bed, my big toe hit on something warm and goopy on the floor. It was the crying victim: a seventh puppy who'd fallen to the floor and fortunately on to a small hooked rug between the beds. Scooping up the teensy creature, I set it down amid the others who were blindly seeking their way to Brandy's teats. I looked over at the crib to see Patty and John fast asleep and nestled together.

I don't know what was more unfathomable to me. The throbbing mess on Patty's bed, or that not a one of us had even noticed that the dog was pregnant. Basically, as Brandy was Patty's charge, I paid scant attention to her. And given all the general chaos in our house, it was a partially understandable oversight. Besides, where Patty might be ignorant about these things, I had to wonder if any of the boys would have noticed if even *I* were pregnant.

I gingerly patted Brandy's head while taking a closer look at her pups. It was a good guess that Mr. Bojangles was the dad. Three of the puppies had Brandy's distinct black and white fur. But there were four with his golden brown coat. Gratefully, all were alive.

I sat down on my bed and watched as I would a tank full of exotic fish. Each puppy was no bigger than a stick of butter; one of them clearly a runt and another a blood sucker. Intermittently, each would make its way to Brandy's head where she judiciously licked it before sending it back on a blind journey to one of her teats to join the puppy pile-up. Suddenly her body began to strain. And except for the bloodsucker, this interrupted all the others from nursing.

Quickly I entered Frankie's bedroom and jiggled his shoulder. One eye opened.

"Shhhhh!" I said. "Come quick! Brandy's having puppies."

"Liar."

"See for yourself."

Shortly, he was standing at the foot of the bed, mouth agape.

"That was pretty much my reaction," I said. We each plunked down on the edge of my bed and watched in awestruck wonder as an eighth, pure-white puppy packaged in a glistening sac made its way into the world. We held our breath as Brandy worked to rupture its dewy membrane. And, as if the Houdini of dogs, it suddenly wriggled free and breathed. So did we.

Frankie sniggered. "How in the hell did we not see this coming?"

With great exaggeration I raised my palms upward and shook my head. "Now what?"

Patty suddenly stirred. I went over to the crib. "Shhh!" I put my finger up to my mouth as she looked up, then whispered, "Come here."

So as not to disturb John, she carefully climbed out of the crib.

"Look," I said, pointing to her bed.

Patty was still a bit dazed, but quickly lit up. The sight was pure magic to her.

"Brandy, you're a mommy," said Patty incredulously, reaching over and patting her beloved dog on the head. I would almost swear to it that when Brandy saw her mistress she faintly smiled. Patty looked at me, then back at Brandy. "I'm glad I got in the crib. She told me to."

"She what?"

"She didn't want to share the bed. Tonight she kept walking around the room. Walking, walking, walking. And whining. So I got in the crib. Then she got in my bed and she was happy. I love you Brandy, sweet Brandy."

Then she reached for one of the puppies.

"No, Patty, don't touch them."

"Why? They're mine."

"No, honey, they're not yours. They're Brandy's. And she might get jealous if you touch any of them right now. We need to just let them be for a little bit."

Patty restrained herself. Then hovering over the scene counted out the puppies. Pointing to the white one she said, "Look. It's like Snow White and the Seven Dwarfs."

I chuckled at her absurd observation, then disappeared down the hall and rapped lightly on my parents' bedroom door. No answer. I rapped louder.

"Yeah," my Dad groused.

"Dad, can you come here, please?"

"Is there a problem?"

"Kinda."

"Can it wait till the morning?" he muttered. He was always grouchy when first awoken.

"Not really."

I heard his feet hit the floor, shuffle, then pause while he presumably put on his bathrobe and slippers. Opening the bedroom door, he squinted. "Is the house on fire?"

"You might wish," I chuckled.

He followed me toward my bedroom, only to stop in cold shock in the doorway. "Oh, Jesus, Mary, and Joseph."

"No," Patty quickly interjected. "It's Snow White and the Seven Drawfs."

My father closed his eyes while rubbing his hands up and down his face. "How do you suppose this happened?" he asked, finally daring to look again.

"We don't need to get into that, do we? The real issue, is what do we do now?"

He moved in for a closer inspection. "Everybody's alive and well?" he seemed to question Brandy. She looked up at him and slightly wagged her tail. He patted Brandy's head, then inventoried the puppies.

"What do we do, Dad?"

"You do nothing. Leave them be, then call Doc Benson first thing in the morning."

"What about school?"

"You have my permission to drop out," he said wryly, adding, "They're cute. Should be easy to find homes for them."

"This *is* their home," Patty sharply interjected.

My father cast me a knowing glance. "Well, unless the house *is* on fire, I'm going back to bed. Good night all," he turned, and while shuffling back to his room groused something aloud about an end to the madness.

Frankie was all grins. "You have to admit, this is pretty crazy. And his suggestion about dropping out of school works for me," he sniggered, then reflexively snatched one of the puppies in mid-air after it tumbled off the bed.

"I'll be right back," I declared, then retreated to the cellar and returned with a stack of pool towels. Rolling each of them up, we created a snug ring around the perimeter of the bed in hopes of preventing any other puppies from escaping. At about 4:00 a.m., Frankie finally returned to bed. And as Patty kept a watchful eye on animal kingdom, I fell fast asleep. When I awoke, daylight had broken, John was crying, and Patty was still kneeling beside her bed.

"That one's Sleepy," she cheerfully pointed out, seeing that I was awake.

"Which one is Grumpy?" I asked, feeling a kindred spirit. I got out of bed, did a quick puppy count – still eight – picked up John, then went about changing his diaper. The room was now a reeking miasma of poop and urine. Still, I had to chuckle thinking that, like my father, my mother would have readily summoned Jesus, Mary and Joseph over discovering this makeshift manger.

It was chaotic getting the other kids off to school when they learned what had happened. Patty flat-out refused to leave. Which was fine as Frankie and I were skipping school, too.

"Well, you have to give credit to Mother Nature," Doc Benson mused at the sight when he finally arrived. "She's the best mid-wife in town." First checking Brandy's vital signs and then private parts, the local vet then examined each of the pups.

"Everybody looks good! Only Brandy needs to go out and obviously this isn't the best whelping box. You need to find a safe, quiet place where she can nurture this brood and all can move about."

"How about the shed?" Frankie suggested. "I can clean it out. Plus it has electricity, so I can set up heat lamps. I'll even fence in a play yard!"

"Sounds like a plan, so long as it stays warm enough," Doc Benson said. "It is, after all, January."

Frankie went right to work. Following a trip to the hardware store for heat lamps and portable fencing, he stopped at the furniture store and with his own funds bought Patty a new mattress. Before long, we'd moved the old mattress outside, covered it with blankets from Things Gone Buy and created a snug bed for Brandy and her family. Frankie stapled plastic sheets in strategic places to keep the cold out. We shred newspapers for the floor, and that afternoon my father set up the heat lamps in the safest manner possible. Finally transferring each creature to its new home with its own fenced yard, we were fully prepared to let nature take its course.

Returning from school, the other kids took excited turns peeking in on the new dog den — so long as they could get past Patty who was acting every bit as maternal as Brandy. While the rest of us checked in periodically, for the next month Patty spent every possible spare moment with them delivering daily updates at the dinner table. During one such conversation, my father abruptly interrupted her.

"Patty," he interjected. "When are you going to start finding those dogs new homes?"

"What do you mean?"

"Those dogs can't live here forever, you know."

"Why not?"

"Because I simply cannot have ten kids and ten dogs living in my house."

She grew increasingly bold. "They already have their own house out back."

"For now it is. But they cannot stay here," he mildly rebuked her.

Large tears quickly coursed down her lightly freckled face.

"Way to go, Dad. Why don't you just tell Patty to find a new place to live, too?" Joey interceded, handing her his napkin in a deceptively kind way. Patty eyed Joey keenly, as if believing that were possible, and wiped her nose.

"If they leave, I leave," she defiantly popped off.

"Thanks, Joey," my father grumbled. "Listen, Patty, I don't think you understand that those puppies will all grow up to be the size of Brandy one day. Good Lord. What did I do to deserve this?" he whined, slapping his brow in exasperation.

"May I please be excused?" Patty asked. Without waiting for a response, and still sniveling, she retreated to the dog kennel where she remained for the next two hours. Later that night, and after she and the other kids were asleep, I heard Frankie knock on my parents' bedroom door.

"Uncle Joe, may I have a word with you?" he politely asked.

"Well, sure son," I could hear them through my open door as I fed John his evening bottle.

"I know this is a real dilemma, sir, with Patty and the puppies. But I need to share something with you."

"Okay."

"You see, Brandy was a stray puppy when Patty found her, and it was love at first sight."

"I'm not surprised by that," my father calmly replied.

Frankie hesitated, then carried on with a certain edginess. "My father hated the idea of owning a dog and wanted her gone. But Brandy made Patty so happy that I promised to pay for her care myself. Anyway, one night when I was spending the night at a friend's house he got really sick, so his mother sent me home. Even though it was late, I had my own key, so I let myself in. When I got there, Brandy wasn't inside. I looked all around," his voice lowered. "And it seemed both Brandy and Patty were missing."

"What happened? Did they run away together?" my father quipped.

"In a way, I guess. Because I wasn't home, my father wouldn't let Brandy in. So Patty went outside and slept with her."

"That sounds like Patty."

"It was February and 22-degrees outside," Frankie succinctly stated. "And my father had locked them out. Fortunately Patty had taken a sleeping bag, a pillow and some blankets out there. Still, they were lying on the frozen lawn, curled up inside her sleeping bag. All she had on was a nightgown under her coat. Keep in mind, Brandy was only about four months old."

I imagine my father, like me, had to catch his breath. The recent felony crimes that "rat-bastard-good-for-nothing-drunk-son-of-a-bitch" had committed suddenly seemed like misdemeanors compared to such barbarism. My eyes fell on to Patty, who was sound asleep in her favorite pink, flannel pajamas, one leg dangling out beneath warm covers. I pulled John in a bit closer, as if psychologically daring his still at-large father to ever torture another one of his children again.

"How long were they out there?" my Dad finally asked.

"Not sure. All I know is that Patty's lips were nearly blue when I carried her inside. I put both Patty and Brandy in my bed to make sure my old man didn't touch them. Thankfully he was passed out at the time. In fact, he never said a word about it. And I knew better than to say anything myself."

My father's voice lowered to a pained whisper. "Where was Cate?"

"Asleep. Apparently she didn't know. Even if she did, it wouldn't have made a difference. At least where Brandy was concerned. She would have frozen to death if not for Patty."

"And both of them if not for you."

"Maybe," Frankie continued. "Anyway, I'm just sharing this because you need to know that the problem is not what Patty has stuck in her head. It's what's locked in her heart."

There was an interval of silence, during which I'm sure my father restrained himself from openly criticizing Uncle Francis. Why rub it in?

"Thanks for letting me know. And Frankie, I want you to know something." He cleared his throat. "You're a noble, young man. And I love you for that."

Frankie, unaccustomed to such paternal praise, didn't quite know what to say. My father said it for him. "I'll go easy on her, I promise. Good night, son."

"Good night, Uncle Joe. And thanks."

The next night at dinner my father calmly broached the subject again. "Patty, can I talk with you about the puppies?"

"No."

"Well, I think it's important that you listen."

"No."

He went on. "I know this is hard to believe, but every one of those puppies has someone waiting for them. Someone very special, like you, who will love them and take extra special care of them all of their lives. You know, like you, when you found Brandy as a puppy."

Still grimacing, she grew more attentive.

"You see, dogs grow fast. And pretty soon it'll be a lot harder and cost a lot of money to take care of them. They each need more room than we can offer and a home of their own with someone who loves them."

"But I love them. And they like it in the shed. I'll even move in to the tree house to be near them."

"I know they like it there. They're warm and happy with you and their mother. But you know how Mary Joyce grew up and went away to college?"

She nodded her head yes.

"And you see how happy she is when she comes home? But she's happy to go back to her new place, too."

Patty's mouth skewed. She knew how much Mary Joyce loved Florida.

"Well, it's kind of like that for the puppies. As they grow up their needs change. And they need to change homes. But they can still visit. Just like Mary Joyce."

"How will they know where to find me?"

"If they can't find you, then you will know how to find them, right?"

266

She sniffled.

"I'll make a deal with you," he went on very sincerely. "Some people will pay money for a puppy. If you sell them, I'll match however much money you make. So let's just say that you sell them for a dollar a dog. Then you'll make eight dollars and I'll give you eight dollars. Then you'll have *sixteen* dollars! Doesn't that sound like a good deal?"

Appearing to give this proposition some thought, she sequentially tapped eight fingers on the table, then did it again.

"I guess," she reluctantly agreed.

"So will you find the puppies new homes?"

She sighed heavily. "Okay."

My poor father had no idea that his devilish son would soon be brokering this deal. Also sitting at the table was Joey, who quickly realized a potential windfall was at stake and quickly hatched a plan. Something I discovered when two weeks later he offered to "watch" John that Saturday.

"What are you up to?" I asked, smelling trouble.

"Nothing. I just want to spend some time with him and Patty. That's all."

"I'll think about it, " I said circumspectly. That Saturday he approached me again. Only this time Patty was standing behind him in her Halloween princess costume. Adding to the effect was her homecoming crown atop a cheap, black wig. She looked suspiciously like Snow White.

"We're off to sell the puppies!" she enthused, proudly adding, "Come see what we did!"

We stepped out to the front yard, and to say Joey had no shame is putting it mildly. Already inside John's oversized pram were the eight puppies, each bedecked with an appropriate pink or blue bow. Wisely, he'd put plastic and towels beneath them.

"How does the baby figure into this?"

"Everyone loves puppies and babies," said Joey. "It will help us to find them homes faster if John's with us."

"'Find them homes faster?'" I mocked him. "What a swindler. Why don't you say it like it is? This is all about the money. What's your take?"

"Why do you always have to spoil everything?" he growled.

"What's your take?" I persisted.

My scoundrel brother eyed me with fiendish contempt, but remained mum.

"I'm coming with you," I declared.

As it was a cool March day, I dressed John in warm clothes and plunked him down amidst the wriggling mass, silently conceding that even Central Casting couldn't have done better at scoring this picture-perfect scene. John was overjoyed, squealing and reaching for one puppy after the other, the pint-sized creatures licking him with abandon. My heart began to break realizing the separation each one soon faced, now believing my father had been wise to use cash as incentive. Soon, Joey knocked on Mrs. Carlson's door. But only after staging the pram and Patty in such a way as to provide maximum exposure to the interminable cuteness.

"Why, Patty!" Mrs. Carlson rhapsodized after she opened her door. A white-haired widow, she was also a proud member of St. Mary's choir, who often – and loudly – serenaded the neighborhood with hymns while hanging laundry. "Is it Halloween already?" her voice lilted.

"Oh, we're not trick or treating, Mrs. Carlson," my audacious brother jumped in. "We're here to see if you want to buy one of Patty's good-luck puppies."

"'Good-luck puppies!' And a baby!" she exclaimed. "How adorable! But what on earth is a good-luck puppy?"

"Well," Joey went on, "practically anything Patty touches turns lucky. And she's been taking care of these puppies for weeks now. So they are nothing but good luck."

"Do you think? And just exactly how much is a good-luck puppy?" Mrs. Carlson asked, rubbing John's head. "And how much for this adorable young man?" she laughed.

"Ten dollars for the puppy. We'll throw in the baby for free," said Joey without flinching, going full throttle with his charm offensive.

"Joey! You jerk! Mrs. Carlson, the baby's not for sale. Just the puppy, for ten dollars," I jumped in, now an unwitting accomplice.

"I hope you'll forgive me, but isn't that a lot to pay for a mutt?"

Patty had clearly been coached. "These puppies are named after the Seven Dwarfs. And look at the luck they brought Snow White. She married a prince."

Mrs. Carlson seemed amused. "Now which one of these dogs do you think would bring me the most luck?" she playfully inquired.

"This one," said Patty, pointing to Grumpy, her least favorite as he'd repeatedly bitten her. No question – she was Joey's apprentice.

Mrs. Carlson picked up Grumpy who deviously licked her face. She instantly fell in love.

"You know," she said, "I've actually thought about getting a dog. And this one's awfully cute. I'll be right back," she said, then disappearing with Grumpy soon returned with a ten-dollar bill. "Here you go," she said, handing the money over to Joey.

"Thank you, Mrs. Carlson. I'm sure you two will be very happy together," he said, closing the deal while pocketing the cash. Patty stroked Grumpy on the nose to say good-bye, which he reciprocated by taking a nip at her finger.

Within the next hour-and-a-half we'd managed to sell all but one of Patty's good-luck puppies, and Joey had seventy bucks in his pocket – soon to be one-hundred and forty, if not one-sixty.

The last dog, Dopey, was a hard sell. The runt of the litter, his thin fur was mottled gray, he was ugly as sin, and no one wanted him. Joey assumed they'd have to sell him for half-price – or worse – give him away. Shortly, we ran into Sister Marguerite who was returning from the Laurel Meat Market.

"Oh, my good friends," she chirped. "How lovely to see you. And John, too. Look how big he is!"

"Hello, Sister," said Patty, delighted to see her, as well.

"Hello, Sister," said Joey with unusual politeness.

"Well, Patty, you look very much like Snow White. Are you out looking for your Prince Charming?"

"No, I'm looking for homes for my good-luck puppies."

"Now what exactly do you mean by 'good-luck puppies?'"

Joey was squirming. There was simply no way he was going to lie to Sister Marguerite. Thankfully, believing her own press, Patty took over.

"I have good luck," said Patty. "And this is one of my puppies, so it's lucky. Would you like this one?" she concluded.

"Indeed!" exclaimed Sister Marguerite, picking up Dopey. "He is adorable. And I have been thinking how much I would love to have a dog at the convent," she said. "I am sure that Sister Perpetua and the others would be delighted with such a nice companion." Then, laughing in her guileless manner, added, "It would be the only boy allowed to live there! What is his name?"

"He's Dopey," said Patty.

"He's named after one of the Seven Dwarfs," Joey clarified.

"Ah, I see. I love Dopey. He's so sweet," Sister Marguerite bubbled while playfully kissing Dopey's nose. He joyfully wagged his tail and licked her back.

"Well," Sister declared, "Here's what I'll do for you. I will take him to the convent with me. And if the other sisters approve, then Dopey has a new home. Otherwise, I must return him to you. Is that okay?"

Joey, realizing no money would exchange hands but that the job was now almost done, agreed. Patty was particularly happy as this would give her a chance to visit Dopey on a regular basis.

"That's fine, Sister," said Joey, adding, "and good luck."

"I don't believe you," I said sarcastically as we made our way home. Truthfully, I was proud of my brother's gumption and ability to help Patty. But I was equally concerned that she might not see any gravy out of it.

"Do you really think Dad's gonna give Patty seventy bucks?" I asked.

"That was the deal."

"What's your cut?"

"Fifty percent."

"Fifty percent! You shark! By the way, Dad made that deal with Patty, not you. Do you think that's fair?"

"Think of all the money he's saving on vet bills and dog food."

"You made *how much* money selling those mutts?" my father later exclaimed.

"Seventy dollars. So now you owe Patty seventy dollars."

"How much ya' makin' offa this?" my father asked, looking Joey directly in the eye.

I held my breath.

"Thirty percent."

My father's look penetrated.

"Okay, twenty."

"Ten," my father said.

"All right, all right," Joey sighed with defeat.

The following week at Mass there was a buzz going around the church. Something about Sister Marguerite inheriting some money. Was it $100,000? No, more than that. Five-hundred thousand? No, it was an inheritance of nearly one-million dollars!

The week after bringing Dopey into the convent, Sister Marguerite received word that a favorite, elderly uncle back in southern France had suddenly died. It was both sad and surprising news, as it was learned he'd bequeathed a fair portion of his large estate and successful winery to his beloved niece. It was promptly announced that Sister would donate a significant amount of cash to the Pallottine Convent and the two parish schools. The lower school was getting a renovated gym, the high-school a long-awaited science wing, and Dopey – a permanent dog house.

There were other reports of how Joey, Patty and the puppies had prompted good luck around the neighborhood. One new dog owner hit it big down at the Laurel Race Track. Another one of Patty's good-luck puppy owners got a better job and another a proposal of marriage.

Sadly for Mrs. Carlson, her house caught on fire after Grumpy roughed up a box of those strike-anywhere matches. In the process, he managed to set fire to his bed which was also near the kitchen stove. Mrs. Carlson's good luck? During the ensuing commotion with the firefighters, Grumpy ran away and was reportedly last seen on Route One being kindly coaxed into someone's car with out-of-state tags.

Chapter 33

*I*t was a Monday and the day after St. Patrick's Day. Coming home from school I heard someone banging around in the kitchen. It was Frankie's night to cook. Holding John, I headed that way to get us both a snack and to see what he was stirring up.

"Hey, Frankie," I hollered from the foyer. "I thought we were having leftover corned beef. It smells suspiciously like lemon roast chicken," I stated from the dining room, then stopped dead in my tracks once inside the kitchen.

"Gailec," my mother smiled.

Her presence was so startling that it was almost like seeing a ghost. Only there was nothing deathly about her as she appeared healthy and vibrant and probably the most beautiful I could ever remember. Gone were the dark circles beneath her eyes; green eyes that now shined brightly against the lovely pink glow of her porcelain skin. Clearly her hair had been recently coiffed, her nails were freshly polished, and she wore lipstick, too. My father must have treated her to a new outfit, as well, because she was wearing unfamiliar gray flannel slacks and a nice black cardigan sweater beneath her favorite old apron. I had not seen her since she'd left, as apparently her caregivers wanted strict control over her schedule. Thus my father was the only one with visiting privileges.

"Honey, are you okay?" she asked.

I burst into tears. I'd been without her in so many ways and for so long that I'd forgotten what it felt like to be her child. Setting the baby down on the floor, I promptly placed my arms around her and wept.

"Oh, thank God, you're home. You're home," was all I could manage to say. She was wearing her favorite old perfume, the smell of which always evoked happy thoughts in me, as she only wore it whenever she wanted to be — and was usually at — her best.

"I'm home," she responded tenderly, now crying herself while gently rocking me.

"Dad didn't tell us," I finally said.

"He wanted to make sure I was truly ready," she smiled reassuringly. "I'm looking so forward to catching up with you. Your father tells me you're doing great in school, that you got a job, and that you're still seeing that nice young man. But how are you really doing? Are you okay?"

I took a deep breath while wiping away fresh tears. "I'm fine, Ma. But what about you? Did they treat you right?"

Yes, she nodded. "But it was pretty dreadful at first," she started, then stopped as John began crawling her way. Any other report about her experience became suspended in her disbelief over his size and development.

"Whenever that baby cries, all your mother sees and hears is Cate gasping for her last breath just as that baby made his first."

Now I was holding my breath as I watched her squat down near him and, in her own inimitable way introduce herself to him as if they'd never met.

"And you wouldn't by any chance be that wee, young man, John Aloysius now, would you?"

In his own charming and effusive manner, he literally rose to the occasion and helped himself to stand up by placing his hands on her bent knee. They looked each other in the eye, with each of them facing a monumental shift of truth. Grinning broadly, he began babbling while patting her knee with his dimpled hand.

"Well, it's nice to see you, too. And I'm sure you've got plenty of other stories to tell me. But first I think I know someone who might just need to have his diaper changed."

My mother then looked up at me as if seeking permission to pick him up. "Honey, will you please get those potatoes out of the pot and rinse them cold for me?"

She could have told me to put my hand in boiling hot water to fetch those "'P'daytas' out of the pot." The lilt of her voice, her healthy demeanor and happy face were all things that seemed to have escaped my consciousness as ever being real again.

I nodded my head yes, then stood in sheer disbelief as I watched her scoop John up, then disappear up the stairs while chatting amiably with him along the way. I did as she asked, then sat down at the kitchen table, savoring the moment as much as the smell of her cooking and favorite perfume. I felt privileged to be the first kid to see her, and I sensed she felt the same way, too. There was an unspoken dimension to our embrace; one that said thank you, thank you, ever so much. Soon enough the other kids arrived home, thoroughly delighted to see her and wondering how 'Aunt Ida' was holding up.

"She's doing quite well," my mother responded, leaving it at that. Fresh tears, however, erupted when she saw Frankie, and I could tell that her hug with him was also imbued with deep gratitude. She held and rocked him, too, as both of them cried.

And so it was, but not as it had always been, that my mother was home. There was a fresh determination about her to stay sober and to be the loving caregiver that she once knew herself to be. I would stay ever vigilant for the emotional fractures formerly glued together with alcohol and pills. The first true test of her resilience arriving in a fast curve ball pitched by Joey.

Joey, now thirteen and about to finish the eighth grade at St. Mary's, had gone through a significant growth spurt and was edging ever closer to my father's six-foot tall frame. At dinner one evening during the week of my mother's homecoming, he stood up. I presumed he was going to brag about the hard work he'd put into making the Shepherd's Pie we were eating, which was a new recipe for him in the ongoing cooking contests in our house.

"I have an announcement to make," he said. He looked over at Frankie, who glanced down at his plate, then shoveled in a mouthful.

"I, uhm," he stammered, "I got into Prep."

"I can see that!"my mother naively responded. "You did a lovely job making this meal."

"No, Ma. I mean Georgetown Prep."

"You what?" my father's voice rose sharply. Georgetown Preparatory School was one of the most competitive and expensive Catholic high schools in the nation. And it had seemed highly unlikely that Joey would ever have wanted to go there – let alone be considered a qualified candidate.

"I got into Georgetown Prep," Joey repeated.

"What?" said Tommy, likewise incredulous as he knew the caché of the esteemed school.

"I got into Georgetown Prep," Joey said again with uncommon poise.

"You don't just *get* into Georgetown Prep. You have to be accepted," said my father.

"Well, that's what I'm saying. I've been accepted into Georgetown Prep."

"You don't just get accepted into Georgetown Prep," my father went on. "You have to apply. And you have to be smart."

"I know."

"And rich."

"I know."

"Very rich."

"I know."

"So how is it that you applied and then got accepted into Georgetown Prep without your mother and I knowing anything about it?"

"It's something I wanted to do."

"That didn't answer my question. How is it your mother and I didn't know anything about it?"

"You were both busy," he said, looking my father square in the eye, speaking volumes with just one glance. "So I forged your signatures."

"Well, that's impressive," my father shot back. "You committed forgery to get into a Jesuit school. Good going. Well congratulations, but we don't have the money and you can't go. Though might I suggest going to Confession instead?"

"Sir, with all due respect," Joey started. Rarely did he call our father 'sir.' Plus it seemed inconceivable that even the notion of 'respect' was a part of his repertoire. Now, however, there were hints of a budding maturity from Joey that I'd never witnessed before. Clearly he'd been coached. I looked over at Frankie, whose large eyes shone in his otherwise frozen face.

"What I'm trying to say is that I've been accepted and that I'm going. And I'm going to live there."

"What on earth is going on here?" my mother jumped in. I have to admit I was beginning to wonder that myself. Did they have any idea at Georgetown Prep that my brother was a big Bozo?

Apparently they felt otherwise, as did Frankie, who had recognized Joey's abilities as soon as he had set foot in our house. Joey was everything Frankie had been at that age – smart, athletic and gutsy. What Frankie possessed in street smarts, Joey had in book smarts. He was a gifted student with the IQ and grades to prove it. Apparently he'd passed all the requisite entrance exams with flying colors. And so, below the radar, Frankie coaxed and coached him into it and even paid the application fee. Together they'd hitchhiked to the famed institution with its enduring traditions, then walked the expansive campus and toured the ancient brick buildings. In truth, what Frankie had done was to open a door for Joey through which he would have never been able to walk through himself.

Frankie later told me that Joey had fallen in love. And not just with the gorgeous campus. There was an order to the atmosphere that appealed to him on the most visceral level, particularly in the library where Joey took a deep breath and inhaled the smell of a classic education bound up in well-tended books, gorgeous old rugs, gilded portraits and worn leather chairs. Unlike the library at St. Mary's, or even Pallotti, there was a sanctity about the place and lofty expectations that stirred a new yearning in Joey. His future beckoned and he wanted in.

None of the young men in their navy-blue blazers had seemed nerdy to him. In fact, many of them appeared to be well-heeled jocks. He knew it was a financial mismatch, especially with the country club set. But he was every bit as smart and athletic, and now was just as determined to make this a part of his life.

"Joey, son, I don't mean to disappoint you. But Pallotti is my financial speed, and I can't go any faster than that," said my father.

"They're giving me a full scholarship, too."

"Jesus, Mary, and Joseph," my mother muttered. "Another one on scholarship! Joe, we're breeding geniuses," she beamed.

"And I've accepted their offer," Joey went on.

"Without consulting me or your mother? What is going on here?" My father was utterly taken aback and clearly angry.

Joey rolled his eyes and took a deep breath, his calm finally beginning to crack. He was just about to speak, when Frankie jumped in.

"Uncle Joe, please don't be hard on him. I put him up to this."

"What do you mean?" Dad sharply asked.

Frankie didn't flinch. "Some of the football scouts from Prep watched Joey play last season and were really impressed. They want him to play there."

"They offered you a football scholarship?" Dad said, his tone somewhat softening. Having worked every Saturday he'd missed Joey's entire season and had only heard how spectacularly he'd played.

"No, Dad. Believe it or not, I got a full academic scholarship."

"Well, then how can you play football and study at the same time?"

"It's never been a problem, before."

My father folded his arms across his chest, trying to absorb this development.

"Dad, do you realize what this means?" It was Tommy speaking now. "It means that Joey is going to get a chance to really make something of himself."

"What's wrong with going to Pallotti like the rest of you? First MJ takes off, you're next and then Joey leaves."

Quietly Frankie spoke. "I'm going there too, sir."

My father looked hard at Frankie. "You're graduating from high school this year. How is that possible?"

"I've accepted an assistant coaching position there. I'll be starting my new job this summer as soon as I finish up at Laurel High. I'll be able to keep an eye on Joey, if that makes you feel any better."

"Why should I feel any better? You got him into this mess in the first place."

"Dad," Joey said with assurance, "It's hardly a mess. And I agree with Tommy. It's a chance of a lifetime."

It was an odd thing. I would have thought my father would be elated that the children in his house were successfully moving on. Instead, it was making him visibly sad. I studied my mother's face, the intensity of her furrowed brow was typically a radar signal for brewing turbulence. Her face appeared surprisingly calm. "Joe, he's got a point," she said softly.

My father looked at me. "Gail, what have you got to say? Or are you moving out, too?"

"No, Dad," I shook my head. "But I will say this. They obviously have a shortage of class clowns."

Everyone laughed. Even the baby, sitting in a high chair between me and my mother, smiled at the camaraderie and banged his hands on the tray.

"Well, son," my father proudly concluded, "then I fully expect you'll be the valedictorian."

My mother got up from her seat and hugged Joey, Frankie and my father. Then sitting back down, she broadly grinned and burst into tears. "You kids are all amazing," she said with uncommon gratitude. "Simply amazing."

Chapter 34

"Good morning, Johnny boy," I cooed.

John stood up in his crib, grinning and jabbering. Now nine-months old, he was incredibly good-natured. If all children were like this I could actually see God's mysterious plans at work, as one would clearly be inspired to have more. By contrast, I'm sure the human population would have long been extinct if offspring came into existence with a teenager's disposition. I hugged and kissed him, then changed his diaper, impressed that he hadn't signaled distress over such a fetid load. Patty arose, and bounced out of bed.

"Johnny," she chirped. "Hey, sweet Johnny."

"You are such a mess," I smiled at her. She'd gone to bed with wet hair and it now looked like a plate of spaghetti noodles – every which way but straight. I mussed it up some more before kissing the crown of her head. "I think today is a waffle day. What do you think?"

"Yes, yes, yes!" she exclaimed clasping her hands together.

"Then that's our plan!" I enthused, lifting John off the changing table.

It was an early Saturday morning at the tail end of March and we had turned the corner into spring. Already in the high fifties, it promised to be a warm, beautiful day. The sun was out, crocuses and daffodils were blooming, and in the distance I actually heard someone's lawn mower crank up. I felt very content.

Together Patty and I took John downstairs and put him in his high chair so that we could start breakfast. My father had left for some odd job he was doing and my mother was still asleep. Frankie was already at the Laurel Meat Market. Tommy had spent the night at a friend's. And Joey, Paul, Raymond and Timmy were all camped out in the tree house – along with Mr. Bojangles, who'd amazingly learned how to run *up* the slide and into their midst. As usual, Brandy stuck with Patty and now followed us downstairs. Once in the kitchen, however, she stopped at the basement door and let out an unexpectedly dark growl.

"What is it, Bran?" I asked.

She barked, while slightly backing away.

"Come on," I said, leading her outside by the collar. "Time to go out."

She resisted, and so I dragged her there. Once outside she still seemed spooked and immediately sniffed around one of the basement windows. Curious now, I carefully peered inside, but saw nothing amiss.

"Must be a rat, or something," I said, leaving her out back. Nothing could have been closer to the truth. Upon reentering the kitchen my blood ran stone cold.

"Mornin', Gail."

I wanted to throw up. Horribly grubby, unshaven, and wearing my father's clothes a size too large – which he'd obviously stolen from a laundry basket in the basement – was Uncle Francis. He was holding a bewildered John, while an ashen-faced, pajama-clad Patty stood motionless beside him.

"Patty, come here," I said calmly.

He grabbed her hair. "Don't move."

Patty's face might have been frozen in fear, but the look in her eyes warned of a hot truth. Even though he appeared weaponless, the man was deadly. His presence alone was frightening. But when I noticed the kitchen phone cord cut in half, distilled terror set in.

"What are you doing here?" I nervously asked.

"I came for my son. No one's gonna shoot a man holding a baby."

The enormity of what was happening made my breathing go shallow. John looked at me quizzically, as if fully expecting me to take him.

"You can't have him," I spoke with measured caution.

"He's coming with me, dammit. Is that your VW out front?"

I gulped, and nodded yes. Patty's gaze on me was fixed and imploring.

"Gimme the keys."

How is it that with a nationwide manhunt underway for this deranged felon, I was the one to know where he was? It was astonishing that he'd slipped below the radar and right back into his home town. I might have been petrified to the core, but my thinking was crystal clear. He could have the car, but not a single one of his kids. "Give me the children first," I said calmly.

He looked at me with an odd smirk. "I see, you wanna play it that way? Then let me rephrase my request. Should I kill Patty first?"

Patty suddenly started crying, prompting Francis to ball her hair tightly in his fist. "Shut up you little dumb ass. Or you *will* be the first to die."

We both knew he was inherently evil and not to defy him. Still, I was desperate to get her out of harm's way. "Uncle Francis, I promise I will give you my car. But not until you let the children go," I said with contrived respect.

He laughed insultingly, and with a horrendous push shoved Patty hard and fast to the floor. She landed close to me, letting out only the faintest whimper as she knew better than to make another sound. I helped her up. Seeing her lip was cut and bleeding, I hugged her reassuringly while escorting her toward the door. "Go out back," I said gently. "I'll be out in a minute."

"Don't you go nowhere, Patty, or else I will kill Gail and the baby."

"Do you want my car keys?" I asked now opening the door. Patty was too petrified to move. I took her hand and while squeezing it kissed her on the forehead.

"Go ahead. I love you and I'll be out shortly." Thankfully, she left.

"Stay right where I can see your dumb ass," Uncle Francis darkly warned. She looked up at me with dread from the bottom step, blood now dripping down on her pink pajamas. With my back bravely turned to her father, I met her look, then mouthed the word "Go!" She immediately disappeared.

"What makes you think you're going to get away with this?" I brazenly asked, now facing him. "You're already in enough trouble as it is. If you take this baby, it will be considered kidnaping. Do you really want that kind of trouble, too? Besides, the baby will only slow you down."

"Since when did we get to be so smart?" he mocked me while reaching into his back pocket for a switch-blade knife which he promptly sprang open. Truly, I felt like screaming. But there was no telling what this violent and desperate man would do. I didn't want to scare John, nor awaken my mother. This man nearly did her in, so why chance a relapse? I tried reasoning with him.

"My parents will be getting up any minute, you know. Do you really want to deal with my father?"

"Ya' liar. I watched him leave the house early this morning. He even left the door unlocked for me. Wasn't that nice?"

I gulped. "Well, he must have left before I got up then."

John was now struggling to get away. I realized how strange it was that he was actually being held by his own father – and probably for the very first time.

"Look, Uncle Francis. This might be hard to believe, but I'd like to help you. Really. I'm sure what you've been through is awful. I'll give you my car, I'll even give you food and all my cash. But I'm not going to let you take John."

"John?" he acted surprised. "That's his name? I told your mother his name was Seamus."

"Seamus John," I lied. John heard his name, then reaching out his little arms tried squirming away again. I didn't move.

"Seamus Liam O'Brien."

"You have a brother named Liam, don't you?"

"Did. He's dead."

"Oh, I'm sorry. I hadn't heard. Listen, would you care for some breakfast? I was just getting ready to make waffles."

Now standing in a familiar place before a familiar face, perhaps imagining something hearty to load him up before his long run from the law, he actually contemplated my offer.

"Are you crazy?" he finally shot back. "I need to get outta here, and fast." He looked over my shoulder. "Where in the hell is Patty?"

I inched toward the door. She was nowhere in sight. "She's on the picnic bench."

"Where?" he asked, straining his neck for a better peek.

"Right over there," I motioned. He didn't budge, afraid, perhaps, that I might do something unpredictable myself.

"She'd better be."

John started wailing.

"Shut up!" Uncle Francis snapped, which only escalated the bawling. "Now get me those keys and your money. No funny business either, you hear?" He stopped, obviously thinking through what might happen if I left the room alone to get the keys. "Better yet," he concluded. "I'll go with you."

"They're up in my bedroom," I said, stepping a little closer. He reeked of grimy sweat.

"Well, hurry it up," he said, suddenly brandishing the knife in my face.

John desperately tried reaching for me. When I didn't take him his crying became panicky. "Give him to me, first," I demanded.

"Get moving," his tone darkened.

Returning the knife to his back pocket, he held John up and jerked him hard. "Shut up," he repeated. I instinctually moved in and tried wresting John away.

"What the hell do you think you're doing?" he backed off, pulling out the switch-blade again. I suddenly felt blind to the fact that he might hurt me.

"If you hurt him like that again I swear *I* will kill *you*. Give him to me. Now!"

"And I swear I will kill you if you don't get me those car keys."

"Well, then just have at it," I said with bitter sarcasm, still holding out my arms for John.

Uncle Francis startled. We locked eyes. Clearly this wasn't what he expected. Probably realizing that none of his children had ever found comfort in his arms, he actually handed him over, then just as quickly grabbed me by my hair before holding the blade's tip to my back. Burying John's head in my shoulder, I held him tight and kissed his head. He clung fast, his crying unabated.

"Let's go," Uncle Francis said, forcing us up the stairs. I dared not utter a word as we passed my mother's closed door. With John now whimpering, I retrieved my purse and emptied it on to my bed. Grabbing my wallet, he ripped it open and helped himself to forty-two dollars and some change.

"This all you got?" he asked.

Yes, I nodded.

Something caught his eye. It was Patty's shoe box sitting on a shelf, which he hurriedly opened and dumped. Out tumbled her "good-luck puppy" money, plus the rosary beads and old photo of Cate holding a younger Patty. He glanced at if briefly, then discarded it on the floor.

"You lied to me," he snarled.

"That belongs to Patty," I said.

He stuffed her cash in his pocket along with mine, snatched the keys, then looked at John. "Gimme the baby."

"No," I said. "You've got the money and the key. Now take the car and go before I scream."

"Why do you want him? He doesn't do you no good."

"Uncle Francis," I spoke, my voice low and resonant with anger as I gently set John in his crib. "If you don't leave right this minute, I mean it, I will scream at the top of my lungs and wake up every last person in this house. It's your choice. You can make your get-away now or take your chances with a mob of people who hate you."

I wasn't sure in that instant what kind of trouble I'd invited. But having gained all that I presently wanted – John and Patty's immediate safety – I seemed not to care. Uncle Francis turned to leave, then stopped. "You always was a snot-nosed, smart-ass," he said, then hauled off and slapped me across the face with such force that I tumbled backwards. I banged my head hard on John's crib, prompting him to start bawling. Uncle Francis turned to leave, which is when he came face-to-face with my mother.

"Oh, well look who we have here. If it isn't Mary Claire the Martyr."

"What are you doing here?" she spoke in a low, eerie calm.

"You really think you're something special, don't you? Taking all my children from me."

284

My mother remained still. "What do you want?"

"Money. How much money do you have?"

When she didn't respond, he flashed the knife in front of her face. "I'll take whatever you've got. Where's your purse?"

"In my bedroom."

"Go get it."

Not taking her eyes off of him for an instant, she carefully backed into her bedroom as I slowly followed. Reaching for her purse from atop the dresser, my mother quickly handed it over, but Uncle Francis wasn't so dumb as to put down his weapon.

"Dump it out on the bed," he demanded. My mother did as instructed, then opened her wallet. "I have fifteen dollars."

"Give it to me."

She handed it over.

"Don't move," he commanded, then began rummaging through their drawers, helping himself to my father's nice watch. It wasn't terribly expensive, but it was a tenth anniversary gift from my mother and something he'd worn with pride. He jammed it into his pocket. Suddenly one of the stairs creaked and Uncle Francis froze. Another stair creaked, but no one spoke. He moved toward the hallway.

"Who is it?" he demanded, now facing the doorway and defensively raising his knife as if preparing to plunge it into someone's heart. In a flurry, the other person tackled him at the knees sending Uncle Francis flying to the floor and the knife out of his hand. It took only a second to realize it was John O'Neill. I froze in horror as a bare-knuckle skirmish began with John pummeling him wherever he could land a punch, and Francis likewise getting in his share of scrappy hits. Roughly the same height, John easily had forty pounds on him. Still, Uncle Francis would stop at nothing. There were hard, bloody knocks and kicks flying left and right. Before long they were fighting near the top of the stairs. Horrifically, Uncle Francis retrieved possession of the knife.

"Say good-bye," he said, raising his arm.

"NOOOOOOO!!!" I screamed fast charging his way. But my mother beat me to him and with all the might that woman could muster pushed that "God-forgive-me-good-for-nothing-drunk-son-of-a-bitch" down the stairs. Cussing loudly and falling hard, we could hear what sounded like bones snapping in half as he tumbled and smashed his way to the foyer. Vainly attempting to pull himself off the floor, he was quickly thwarted as a team of cops with guns drawn suddenly burst through our front door.

"Don't move!" they commanded, pointing guns at him and even us. "Hands up!" they hollered. The three of us raised our hands to prove we were not a threat.

Uncle Francis was screaming in agony as it appeared he'd broken an arm, a leg and perhaps even his back. After getting the scene under control, the police and some medics handcuffed him to a gurney and he was carried away.

Now watching from the living room window as the escorted ambulance disappeared, my mother began to cry. "For the love of Cate, he's finished," she said, then began sobbing. Still trembling, I hugged her as best I could with the baby safely sandwiched between us, the two of us now crying hysterically.

Big John, who'd been outside talking to the cops while getting first aid for some of his injuries, finally rejoined us. My mother abruptly broke away from me, but only to hug him. "Thank you, John," she said trying to pull herself together. "Thank you for your amazing bravery."

John started crying, too, embracing her in kind. "Are you kidding? *Thank you.*"

Stepping back, she looked up at him. "How on earth did you know to come over here?"

Surprisingly, he chuckled. "You won't believe this, but it was because of Patty. Months ago I gave her my phone number and told her to call me if anyone, at anytime, tried to hurt her. Apparently she memorized the number and called from a neighbor's. And I called the police before I left my house."

"Oh, good Lord, where is she now?" my mother asked.

"Up in the tree house with the other kids."

We quickly retreated outside, and indeed that's where we found them, all too terrified to leave.

"Come here, Patty, let me see your lip," I called up to her.

She was crying and wouldn't budge.

"Patty, it's okay. He's gone and will never, ever hurt you again," John tried comforting her. "You were so smart and brave to call me."

"That's not why she's crying," Paul announced from the tree house porch, his arm wrapped around her.

"For Pete's sake, what is it?" my mother asked, looking up at him. "Is she badly hurt?"

Paul shook his head no.

"Patty, please come here. I need to look at your lip," I implored.

Finally sliding down to join us, she looked downward as she spoke. "Forgive me, Gail, for I have sinned."

"What on earth are you talking about?" I responded about her sweet, but absurd remark.

She explained. After calling John, she was worried her father would take the baby along with my car, and so she disabled it. She didn't have a clue what was inside that engine. But from seeing *The Sound of Music,* she knew the nuns had saved the Von Trapp family from the Nazis by doing the same thing. Thus my darling Patty had opened the car's boot and in a frenzy undid every conceivable wire that she could before retreating to the tree house to warn the boys of the unfolding danger. Savvy to their father's wickedness, none of them dared to leave without an "all clear."

"Oh, Patty, you precious angel," I hugged her. "You are *so, so* forgiven."

Shortly, and as word quickly traveled around town about what had happened, we were joined by my father, Tommy and Frankie. I had never seen my father cry so hard as I did when he embraced my mother. Frankie held tightly to Patty, and then to me and the baby. Tommy hugged and thanked his best friend before grasping ahold of my mother, to whom Timmy was now tightly clinging. Paul and Raymond soon joined Frankie, the three of them uncontrollably sobbing.

Shaken as we all were, there was a palpable relief all around. At last, the tyranny of Francis O'Brien had ended, and we could all get on with our lives knowing that he would never, ever, hurt a single one of us again.

Chapter 35

Within a week after all that hell broke loose in our house, it broke loose in the world around us. It was just after 6:00 p.m. on April 4th, 1968 – the day Martin Luther King, Jr. was shot at the Lorraine Motel in Memphis. It was a Thursday and I was working at the hospital. Word of the assassination spread like wild fire throughout the building. One of the nurses had turned on a television in a vacant hospital room, and periodically we checked for updated news on the brewing crisis.

It was frightening. Children's Hospital was in the heart of Washington, D.C., and following the shocking news of his death crowds began swelling on the streets. Less than two miles away was the epicenter of where the civil protests began. But by 11:00 p.m., the mobs turned angry and violence erupted. Burning and looting became rampant in the city, and from open hospital windows we could hear gunshots. Soon, tear gas clouds began drifting outside.

Until this point, I'd lived a sheltered existence in my sleepy little town, where even the Vietnam War seemed somewhat fictitious. But there was nothing imaginary about this latest crisis, particularly when nearing the end of my shift I saw a young boy arrive on the ward following emergency surgery for a gunshot wound. Fortunately he had made it through the surgery, but his hold on life was reportedly tenuous.

Just before my shift ended, John called. "I'm down in the lobby waiting for you."

I sighed with deep relief over this unexpected news.

"Are you okay?" he asked.

"I'm a little shaken up. I can't believe you made it here. What do we do about my car?"

"We'll worry about it later. I'm more worried about you right now."

"Thanks, I'll see you in a couple of minutes."

I told Anne Janette I was leaving, wrapped up final details and left the ICU. It was so comforting to see him. I was still on edge over the confrontation with Uncle Francis. That we had all survived was one thing. That I was watching my mother to make sure she maintained her sobriety was another. So far, and with my father's love, she was holding up fine. But now this? The world seemed to be going insane.

"You really didn't have to do this," I said, though actually grateful to see him in the lobby.

"I understand. I just needed to see you home safely," he said solemnly. In less than thirty minutes and without incident we were back at my house in Laurel, talking about all that had happened that fateful day. Once there, John asked me to sit on the porch swing.

"I have something to tell you," he said, his tone growing more serious.

My heart stopped. Had he come for me because there was bad family news to break and he wanted to be the one to tell me? "Is my mother okay?" my voice cracked.

"Yes," he said reassuringly. "Everyone's fine."

"You have me scared. What is it?"

"Actually, I have good news to share. I got into the University of Maryland. So did Tommy."

I breathed a sigh of relief. "Perfect! Just down the road!"

"And I also got into UVA."

"Oh, my gosh! Congratulations!" I said, giving him a spontaneous kiss. "You're going to be a Cavalier after all!"

"Well, actually, I'm not."

"So you're going to be a Terp?" I asked excitedly about Maryland.

"Hmmm, in a way," he replied mischievously, then softly began whistling *Anchors Away*. I looked perplexed. His whistling grew louder. And then it hit me. "You joined the Navy?"

"The Naval Academy," he grinned, then resumed whistling.

"John Aloysious O'Neill! You never even told me you were applying to the Naval Academy! No one gets into the Naval Academy. Well, I mean, at least no one I've ever known!"

To say that his acceptance into the famed institution in nearby Annapolis had come as a shock was true. But not a surprise. John was an exceptional athlete and a straight-A student. I knew the Academy's admission process was highly selective and that the school held itself to the highest standards of honor, duty, and responsibility. It was no wonder that they'd want him. I, however, did not want him to go.

"When did you find out?" I half-heartedly asked.

"I received my offer of appointment today."

"Offer of appointment? That sounds so official."

"It sounds official, and it is. I've officially accepted their offer."

The news hit me hard. "Why didn't you mention this before?"

"Truthfully, I didn't think I'd make it. I started the application process last year on a lark. Before we started dating, in fact. And much to my surprise I cleared one hurdle after another. They probably had 7,000 applicants for 1,300 openings in the plebe class this year."

"But why, John? Why a military academy?"

"Because," he replied with utmost sincerity, "Aside from serving my country, I'll get a free education, and that will make a big difference for my parents."

I understood the latter. With five kids, Mac O'Neill's salary as a firefighter left little money for college. Still, my response was sullen. I had to think about what this meant. I loved the notion that he was attending an all-male school only thirty minutes away. I loved the idea that he would look so handsome in dress whites or blues. I loved the fantasy of a Naval wedding and walking beneath an arch of crossed swords.

But I hated the fact that he would be serving a country at war with no foreseeable end in sight. I hated the fact that in spite of all the honor and glory that would accompany his Naval Academy credentials, this wasn't just college he'd signed on to. It was an acceptance of service as an active duty commissioned officer in the Navy or Marine Corps for five years thereafter. It meant living afar and calls to ports hither and yon. It also meant that if the war in Vietnam didn't end soon, John would most likely see active duty combat following graduation. And it meant, very seriously, that he might be counted among those who sacrificed their honorable spirit for what I considered to be a questionable cause.

I also felt disappointed because he did not talk to me or consider my feelings before making his decisions. It meant that if I had any hope of sustaining this relationship after my own graduation from college, there were serious sacrifices to make myself.

"Are you okay?" he asked. "I thought you'd be happy for me."

"I'm having a hard time with this."

"I can see that," he said, wrapping an arm around my shoulder.

"I guess it would have been easier if I'd known it might happen. But John, the world is changing in such fast and scary ways. I mean, Martin Luther King won a Nobel Peace Prize and got shot today. And right away look what happened. More violence. Plus, soldiers have been sacrificing their lives in Vietnam for nothing. You could go to college anywhere you wanted. So I'm not sure I understand this choice. And I'm not sure I understand how it impacts me."

"Gail, only my parents and advisors knew that I was doing this. It's a long, complicated application process, and it's pretty damned hard to get it in. I knew I stood a chance. But still, I felt like the odds were against me. And a rejection would have been embarrassing."

"But why hide it from *me*? I don't understand."

"I didn't want you to think any less of me."

I choked. "That's absurd. You're my hero. You saved our lives," I sniffled hard. "The only thing you could do now that would make me think less of you would be to go out with Helen Hartley again."

He unexpectedly laughed.

"Why is that funny? Is there something else you're not telling me?"

"No!" he said emphatically.

"Did you have sex with her?" I impulsively asked.

He laughed again, but didn't answer.

"I'm serious. Did you have sex with her?"

"Not lately, and let's put it this way. She had sex with me."

"What does that mean?"

"She wasn't going to give me a choice."

"Baloney. You could have just said no."

"Well, I know, but ..."

"But, but, but nothing."

He laughed again, only this time he pulled me in close.

"Gail, forget her. That's history. This is now. I didn't think at our age it was possible to love someone as much as I love you. In my eyes, you're *my* hero – or heroine. You never gave up on your cousins or siblings. That's dignity. Look how you handled your uncle. That's courage. Look how well you are doing in school in spite of all the hardships you've faced. That's honor. And," he softly choked, "these are also the reasons that one day I want to marry you."

Mr. and Mrs. Joseph T. Kenealy request the honor of your presence at the marriage of their daughter.....

....Mrs. John Aloysious O'Neill.

How many times had I found myself daydreaming in class, even writing out fictitious wedding invitations. Or writing my name as his. It was unfathomable that John Aloysious O'Neill had actually made it clear that he wanted to marry me.

"You mean that, don't you?"

"With all my heart. I love you, Gail. And even if I have to slog through a jungle and cross enemy fire to find my way back to you, I will."

I nestled my head on his shoulder, but only momentarily.

"What about Helen Hartley? What if she throws herself on you between now and then? She does, after all, have the biggest boobs in Prince George's County."

"Gail, she might have big boobs. But she has only half-a-heart and no brain. I wouldn't worry about her – ever."

"You're wrong."

"Why?"

"Precisely because she has big boobs, half-a-heart, and no brain."

"Well, then," he said reaching into his shirt pocket. "Remember, you're wearing my promise ring and not her."

Even in the dark I could see the glint of glitter and gold. It was a sweet ring with a cluster of very small diamonds in the middle.

"What is this?"

"My promise to be true to you. And I hope that in wearing it," he said, slipping it on my left ring finger, "that you will do the same for me. I love you Gail, and one day I truly hope to make you my wife."

Chapter 36

The world around us was truly a mess. Portions of Washington, D.C. and Baltimore suffered considerable damage during those violent protests, with a new breed of cynicism and distrust left in their smoldering wakes. It was so disheartening. Those events were as life changing for me as the promise of betrothal to John. I witnessed firsthand how neighborhoods near the hospital were utterly destroyed, hundreds of people were injured and scores of people and businesses were displaced.

Periodically I checked into cloud nine, daydreaming of wedding plans while perusing bridal magazines. A couple of times Nadette even coaxed me into the local bridal store to try on dresses.

"It's good practice," she said, while likewise shopping for maid of honor attire.

"Nadette, it's going to be a long time before we ever get married."

"Is he the one?"

"Yeah."

"Did he tell you he wanted to marry you?"

"Yeah."

"Then you're getting married. So you have the official right to try on wedding dresses."

"Nadette, my parents said I have to finish high school and go to college first."

"Why even bother with college? You've *already* met your husband."

There was no sense in shifting the conversation to a more insightful level. I was speaking to someone whose sole determination in life was to be a wife and mother. Still, like her, I was hopeful that we'd seen the worst of it. I was wrong. It seemed the smoke had barely cleared from the horrific assassination of Martin Luther King when another beloved brother fell. It was the last week of school and just days before Tommy and John were to graduate from St. Vincent Pallotti High School. When my radio alarm went off that morning, an announcer was sharing the somber news that Senator Robert F. Kennedy had died from the wounds of an assassin's bullet.

The news hit me hard. Every day I passed Bobby Kennedy's framed photo adorned with petrified palm fronds in our foyer. My mother adored him and was always praying for the Kennedy family. RFK was my great white hope for ending the war in Vietnam before my beloved John graduated from the Naval Academy. Or Tommy from the University of Maryland, where he'd thankfully been drafted into the ranks of the school's football team and not our nation's military. Like my mother, I was in love with Camelot. And though not yet old enough to vote, I embraced Bobby's presidential candidacy and was thus emboldened to feel that life truly got better for those who believed. Camelot, it seemed, lay in ruins. There was a soft rap at my door, soon followed by the appearance of my mother. She was crying, too.

"Gailec, Bobby's dead," she said with all the remorse as if talking about a family member.

"I know, Ma," I sniffled. "I heard it on the radio. It's the saddest thing."

Typically John was farm fresh and awake by dawn. But this morning he was still sound asleep. So too was Patty, both of them blissfully unaware.

"He's a fine baby, isn't he?" my mother said, now staring down at him as if the absorption of his innocence would ameliorate the shock and pain of Kennedy's horrific death. My mother had rather seamlessly infused herself into John's life, now becoming his principal caregiver. Something he accepted, but only because I was always so near. Clearly, however, they'd bonded and both were thriving.

"She's a sweet girl, too, that little Patty," my mother said, looking at the mop-topped child in the other twin bed. "And funny. She makes me laugh, that one."

"You have no idea," I said, realizing my mother had missed out on many of Patty's more amusing insights and antics. John suddenly stirred. Casting a surprised look at my mother, he stood up to greet her, babbling in his usual happy way.

"Come here, young man," she hoisted him out of the crib. He sweetly touched her face and she lovingly kissed his hand, and then his forehead; something I recalled she did with Timmy when he was a baby. In spite of her trials, she was such a good mother.

"Anything to show me from your overnight shift?" she asked, the last word pitched high in her Irish brogue. Once placed on the changing table, he promptly and enthusiastically began kicking his legs and chattering away while she chatted back and busied herself with replacing his soiled diaper – the whole time fighting tears.

"And how about some hearty, Irish oatmeal for breakfast?" she suggested. "That goes for you, too, Gailec," she added.

"Sure," I nodded.

As they disappeared, Patty awoke. Ever optimistic, she believed that rainy weather meant puddle-jumping; snow, then snowmen. Sunny, well, there was simply no stopping her.

"Gail, why are you crying?" she immediately asked.

"Oh, Patty. I just heard the saddest news. Bobby Kennedy was shot and he died."

She knew who he was from the framed picture.

"That's sad. He has a big family," she said, having been educated by my mother. "Kind of like us."

"Yeah, kind of like us."

We were soon to learn that a train carrying his slain body would bring him from New York to Washington, D.C., where he would be buried near his brother, President John F. Kennedy, in Arlington National Cemetery. The designated train would pass right by the station in Laurel.

On the appointed day of that journey, hundreds of thousands of people gathered beside the railroad tracks between the two major cities to pay their last respects. It was sunny, hot and humid, and the train seemed to move by inches rather than miles per hour. His distraught widow, Ethel

Kennedy, could be seen sitting in a straight-back chair near his flag-draped casket in the caboose of the dignified, twenty-one car train.

Probably as impressive as that somber sight was the spectacle of all the priests from St. Mary's and all the Pallottine nuns following behind in their full habits, solemnly marching down Main Street toward the railroad platform. Scores of people – shopkeepers, parents, children, Catholics, Protestants, and Jews alike, paraded behind them to pay their final respects, too. Pushing John in his pram, with Patty at my side, we fell in lockstep with them. My brothers and cousins, my parents, everyone, it seemed, joined in.

Mac O'Neill's fire brigade dressed in their finest blues, along with their comrades from the police department, stood sentry by the track. Uniformed Boy Scout and Girl Scout troops, and citizens of every conceivable age and race, rich and poor, waited patiently.

An odd silence crept over the crowd as the creaking train approached. The firefighters and officers respectfully saluted. The Boy Scouts removed their caps and placed their hands over their hearts. Even those typically prone to dark humor kept their thoughts in check out of respect for the dead at this rolling wake. I will never forget seeing the prominently chiseled, yet forlorn features on the faces of several Kennedy children gathered on the rear platform of the train, nor the saddened, tear-streaked faces of Sister Perpetua and the others in her order as they bid the man farewell and prayed in earnest that God would protect his soul.

I will also never forget how the gravity of the moment was interrupted by Joey who, in deference to the famous football-tossing family, had carried his own pigskin to the tracks. Somehow catching the eye of one of the Kennedy boys, Joey very unexpectedly tossed it his way. Breaking with decorum, the young man caught it, and in the inimitable Kennedy fashion tossed it back squarely into Joey's waiting arms. I actually thought Joey might run behind the train and continue with this farce.

Instead, holding the ball with one hand, he gave a thumbs up with the other. So too did Kennedy's kid. However brief, Camelot was back. Hope triumphing over adversity in the arc of a football as the train rumbled slowly on down the track.

Chapter 37

*J*une 11th. John's first birthday. Also, the first anniversary of his mother's death. We acknowledged that somber milestone by going to early morning Mass and then visiting Cate's grave. Even John, now walking, toddled along with us.

Though the Second Vatican Council eliminated the requirement for wearing a mantilla, my mother draped mournful black lace upon her head. Perhaps as a way of demonstrating her well-being, Patty wore her homecoming crown. My father and the boys all wore suits and I a plain gray dress. Monsignor Wilson, Sister Perpetua, Sister Marguerite and a few other sisters led us at a personal graveside prayer service for Caitlin Alana Cavanaugh O'Brien. John O'Neill, Nadette, and a few family friends joined us. My mother, Frankie, Patty, Nadette and I openly wept. My father remained stoic until the end when Sister Perpetua hugged him and my mother at the same time, less out of sorrow, it seemed, than gratitude for my mother's well-being. While the others let their emotions faintly trickle, Paul remained quiet and strangely unmoved.

Later, we focused our attention on John as Frankie fired up the grill and invited half the neighborhood over for what turned out to be a lot of backyard fun celebrating his brother's first birthday. Paul joined Frankie in basting and barbecuing a mountain of succulent ribs, but remained quiet and subdued.

Paul had started the school year at Pallotti rather determined. And though it was a struggle, he'd earned a respectable number of Bs and occasional As. However, following Joey's acceptance into Georgetown Prep, Paul's report card became a surprising catalogue of Cs and Ds. It seemed the intense bond that had now developed between Frankie and

Joey had created some kind of schism between Paul and my brother. They barely spoke to one another now.

Also, lately he'd begun to let his hair grow out, which was a sore subject with my father. Paul claimed it was to cover up his festering acne, and he promised to cut it before school started in the fall. My father still didn't approve, but consented for now.

The one thing that did seem to energize Paul lately was a job he'd taken feeding and cleaning horses at a farm near the Laurel Race Track. He loved those creatures, and once or twice talked about being able to ride them at work. I envied that perk so much that for the briefest of moments I even considered applying myself. He would often stay late and, in fact, frequently missed dinner. One evening in late June when it was his turn to cook, he didn't show up until nearly 9:00 p.m. Consistent with our house rules, no one ate that night and our fury at him loomed large.

"I'm sorry," he snapped. "I made a mistake," then muttering beneath his breath added, "It wouldn't hurt some of you to miss a meal, anyway."

My parents might not have heard that acerbic comment, but Frankie did and let him have it. "What in the hell has gotten in to you?" he later demanded.

"Nothing. I made a mistake. I forgot. Don't you ever make a mistake? No," he answered his own question, "You don't. Because you're perfect, aren't you?"

Frankie later told me that the temptation to slap him was strong. But he was all too familiar with the long-lasting psychic wounds leveled by a brief, violent outburst. Instead, he looked downward and shook his head.

"I don't know what's happened to you. Something's changed."

"Are you finished?" Paul angrily uttered.

"Yeah. But remember this. Tonight you let every single one of us down and then acted like it's no big deal. So I'm warning you. It *is* a big deal and don't do it again."

After Frankie left, Paul stayed outside for nearly an hour, sitting on the picnic table with his back to the house and his head in his hands. Finally returning inside, he immediately apologized to my parents.

"I'm sorry. And it won't happen again."

My mother unexpectedly hugged him. "It's okay to make a mistake every once in a while," she said. "God only knows, I do. Not often, mind you," she laughed. "But when I do it's a doozy!"

"Listen," she added, "If you're hung up and can't make dinner, then just call me and we'll work it out. Deal?"

He nodded, thanked her and apologized again before heading to bed. For a spell his spirits improved and he cooked on his designated night. But soon there was another change in his personality; the symptoms of a brewing crisis which introduced itself one morning in early July with an angry knock on the door. My mother and I were feeding John his breakfast and sharing coffee when it happened. It was a neighbor.

"Well, good morning Bill," my mother chirped.

"That's what you say," it was Bill Gregory, who was crotchety by nature. "See that?"

He pointed to a mangled bicycle in the front yard. "It was left out in the street and got run over. After," he added darkly, "the cyclist ran into my car, which is now scratched and dented."

My mother immediately recognized the bike. "Go get Paul," she ordered me.

I quickly retreated upstairs. "Paul," I shook his shoulder. "Mr. Gregory's downstairs with your busted up bike. What happened?"

He moaned, but didn't budge.

"PAUL O'BRIEN," my mother hollered from downstairs.

"What?" he yelled.

"Come downstairs at once," she snapped.

Paul sat upright, and I could see some serious scrapes on his cheek. "What does she want?"

"Did you crash your bike into Mr. Gregory's car last night?"

He cast a dazed look while raising a bruised, swollen hand. "Ow," he said, when moving it. Presently, it was the least of his problems. Climbing out of bed he threw on some jeans.

"Young man, did you crash your bike into Mr. Gregory's car last night?" my mother sharply asked before he was even half-way down the stairs.

He stopped. "Why are you asking me?" he spoke defiantly.

"Don't you take that attitude with me young man."

"Am I in some kind of trouble?"

"I would say so. Get down here," she demanded from the foyer holding John on her hip, fuming as he took his time. She then directed him out to the front yard. "Just look at your bike! Mr. Gregory claims that you damaged his car after crashing into it and then just abandoned it." She noticed his hand and cheek. "Is that how you hurt yourself?" she asked unsympathetically.

"Yeah, I guess."

My mother's brow furrowed. "Well I guess you'd better tell me what happened and fast."

"I don't really know. I mean it was dark outside and I was riding my bike home from the farm when someone threw a bottle or something at me. I lost control and hit his car," Paul gulped hard.

Mr. Gregory reacted harshly. "So you did hit my car. And took off. I'm calling the police."

"Wait just a minute," my mother snapped at him, then handing the baby to me stood with arms akimbo and clenched fists on her hips while squaring off with Paul.

"I don't know exactly what happened last night. But as you've fessed up to hitting his car then you'd better be prepared to face the consequences."

Paul's chin fell to his chest.

"Here's what I suggest," she said, and began brokering the apology. "After you tell him you're sorry – and sincerely – then you work out an agreement to pay all the damages. And then do it. Or else there will be hell to pay with me."

"Yes, ma'am," Paul sniffled. "Mr. Gregory," Paul said now looking up, "It was an accident. And it was dark, so I had no idea that I'd damaged your car. I'm really sorry. And I promise that I will pay to fix it."

"You have that kind of money?"

"I have a job and I promise I will pay you. Plus," he added, "I'll even cut your grass at no charge this week."

The latter gesture surprised even my mother. Mr. Gregory, who might have been angry, wasn't stupid. He was notoriously cheap.

"I want my grass cut once a week through the end of September."

"Don't get greedy on him," my mother jumped in.

"Okay, through August. And I want that money in cash as soon as I get an estimate on the damages."

"Yes, sir," Paul agreed, perceptibly relieved.

"And I want my grass cut today."

"Okay."

Mr. Gregory spoke to my mother. "As long as he pays me my money and cuts my damned grass I won't call the cops."

"He'll do it," she assured him. Paul grimaced as Mr. Gregory vigorously shook his swollen hand in agreement. Ignoring the injury, later that day he mowed Mr. Gregory's lawn.

My mother fully believed that Paul had saved himself from the rim fires of hell. But Frankie remained perplexed. Particularly when Paul showed up the next day with a brand new ten-speed bike that must have cost him every bit of two-hundred dollars. Frankie knew the cost and value of everything, and asked his younger brother how he could afford such a splurge, especially given that he owed money for car damages.

"Why do you care?" Paul snapped back. "It's my money."

"I understand," said Frankie. "But a less expensive bike would have done just as well. You need to pay that old man first. Besides, you should be saving your money."

"Just because you save all your money doesn't mean that I'm going to."

Frankie looked at him disapprovingly. "What has gotten into you? I feel like I barely know you anymore."

"Leave me alone."

Frankie, feeling frustrated and hurt, did just that. But not for long, as he later recounted to me what happened during his next shift at work when making a deli sandwich for some chatty, young punk.

"You're Paul O'Brien's brother, aren't you?"

"Yeah," said Frankie. "Who are you?"

"Gus," he replied.

"How did you know I'm his brother?"

"He told me you worked here. You two look alike, 'cept you don't have as many zits," he laughed.

Frankie wasn't amused. "What can I get you?"

"Ham and Swiss on rye. Heavy on the mustard."

Frankie got busy. "So how do you know Paul? From school?"

"Naw, from Magnolia Farm. By the way," Gus leaned in, then carefully whispered, "Tell him that was some great shit he sold me."

Frankie grew intensely hot as he knew Gus wasn't talking about horse manure. He kept his cool, but once at home I saw Frankie thoroughly search their bedroom. It didn't take him long, either, to find what he was looking for. Buried beneath Paul's underwear in a bureau drawer was a brown bag with a huge wad of cash. Frankie counted an astounding twenty-five hundred dollars in varying bills. He also discovered a large baggie of pot stuffed inside a sock. Jumping onto his own bike, he rode frantically to Magnolia Farm where he spotted Paul in a ring exercising a horse. Quickly, he hurdled the fence.

"What are you doing here?" Paul demanded.

"Do you want to explain this?" Frankie insisted, opening up the brown bag.

Paul dropped the horse's reins and angrily charged at Frankie. "Give me that!" he tried grabbing it, but missed, then immediately took an impulsive swing at Frankie's jaw. Seeing it coming, Frankie blocked the blow.

"Seriously, you stinking, low-life drug dealer. You think beating me up is going to make you a man?"

Paul went berserk and managed to kick Frankie hard in his side, causing him to briefly double over and lose control of the bag. As money flew around them and the horse ran crazy, those two traded blows until another farm hand entered the ring and kicked Frankie hard in the other side. Frankie fell in the dirt.

"What's going on here?"

"He's my brother," Paul declared.

"That's some kind of brotherly love. What's with all the money?"

"Oh, shit!" Paul yelled, and with that began scrambling with his co-worker to collect the cash, more than once having to avoid the spooked horse. After gathering the bills, Paul handed a few to the man, then taking hold of the horse disappeared into the barn.

Meanwhile, Frankie lay on the ground trying to collect his breath and angry thoughts. Shortly, Paul returned to the ring with another horse. Slowly rising, Frankie stood up, then painfully spoke. "Do not, under any circumstances, come back to the house."

"You can't tell me what to do."

"No, I can't. But I'm telling you for your own good what *not* to do. You wanna deal drugs, you wanna do drugs, then you're not coming home. For all I care you can rot in jail like Dad."

"It's not our home, anyway!" Paul furiously shot back.

With that, Frankie left the ring, convincing someone with a truck to give him a lift. I was the only one at home when he arrived.

"Holy cow! What happened to you?" I jumped up from the sofa where I'd been reading a book. Limping into the room and gasping for air, he painfully sat down in a chair. His clothes were filthy dirty and he was crying.

"I think I have a broken rib," he said.

Though only a couple of blocks away, I made him get into my car so that I could drive him to Warren's. Soon it was confirmed that he'd suffered a cracked rib. But worse to me, a broken spirit. He was deeply saddened as he recounted the fight with Paul.

It took me a moment to absorb the information, but it fit a growing pattern. Paul's personality had changed a lot lately, and not for the better. A few weeks earlier he'd spent longer than usual in the shower, which happened to cut into my time. He blatantly ignored me when I knocked on the locked door, muttering "bitch" as he finally left and passed me by. I might have let it slide until I saw the mess he'd left. Initially he refused to clean it up, and only did so when I threatened to tell my father. Not only would this mean a loss of future shower time to him. But leaving the kind of mess that he did – including an unflushed toilet, toothpaste in the sink and a wet towel on the floor – meant being grounded, as well. "Actually, you're a snitch bitch," he said after finishing the task.

"What do we do?" I asked Frankie about the current dilemma.

"I told him not to come home."

"My parents won't accept that."

"I don't care," said Frankie. "I think given a choice between harboring a drug dealer and letting him find another place to live that they'll understand."

"But he's not legal."

"He's dealing drugs, Gail. That's not legal either. Let him suffer the consequences."

Ironically, Paul took care of the dirty work himself. In fact, while we were away at Warren's he came home and informed my mother that he'd been offered a bunk at the barn, and that given his long summer hours it was probably best if he simply stayed there.

"You can't just move out," she said.

"I'm not moving out," he warmly reassured her. "I'm just temporarily staying down the street. You see, they want me to start exercising the horses at 5:00 a.m. So it's a lot easier for me. Think of it like sleep over camp. I promise I'll check in regularly. Besides, you know I love being with those horses. It fills a big, empty spot in my heart," he said manipulatively. My mother bought it, considering him especially trustworthy as he'd already paid Mr. Gregory in full for the car damages.

"You'll still be cutting Mr. Gregory's grass, won't you?"

"Yes," he assured her, then went upstairs, stuffed a duffle bag with personal possessions and disappeared without saying another word. For weeks we barely heard from him. Several times I wanted to travel over to the farm to plead with him to come home and change his ways. But Frankie insisted otherwise. He provided the younger kids with Paul's version: that he wanted to be closer to work. They missed him, but seemed nonplussed as they felt certain he would return.

Which indeed he did.

It was early August and hot as hell. One evening a few of us were watching TV when I thought I smelled something burning. I checked around the house, then glancing outside I caught sight of the oddest thing. There was Paul, standing in the back yard beside an old, rusted steel drum that my father customarily used to burn trash. Clearly he had started a fire and was methodically reaching into a brown paper bag and, bill by bill, burning his money. Quickly, I returned to the living room and cast Frankie a desperate look. He promptly joined me in the kitchen.

"What's the matter?" he said.

"See for yourself."

Frankie was outside in seconds flat. "I thought I told you not to come back here," he snapped. Paul remained speechless, while tossing more bills into the flames. Finally looking up, Frankie could see that his right eye was badly bruised and swollen shut. His nose was crooked, too.

"What happened?" Frankie insisted.

"I hate myself," Paul muttered. "I hate my life."

"Do you hate me, too?" he said more tenderly.

Paul didn't answer. Instead he continued throwing money into the fire. Frankie quietly watched as two twenties, a five, a ten and then a hundred-dollar bill quickly disintegrated.

"I'm so stupid," Paul whimpered.

"You're not stupid. You're a smart kid who took stupid chances. I hope you learned a lesson."

Paul started crying. "Here," he said, handing Frankie the bag. Paul was unhappy as hell. And for reasons deeper than his bruised eye revealed, he felt like destroying his ill-gotten gain was the only way to resurrect whatever stability there had been in his life.

Frankie set the bag down then hugged him hard. I choked watching as the two of them sobbed. Afterwards, they sat on the picnic bench for a long time talking. Before coming inside and announcing Paul had quit his job, Frankie did something antithetical to him – he dropped the entire bag of cash into the fire. To him it was blood money, and he didn't want a single cent of it circulating in their lives.

After seeing that Paul received the appropriate medical attention the next day, Frankie helped him to get a job at the Laurel Meat Market stocking shelves and sweeping floors. He did, however, encourage Paul's grass dealings for a short while thereafter. But only in Mr. Gregory's yard.

Chapter 38

I could not have ever imagined how hard it would be to say good-bye. To any of them. Tommy was off to Maryland on his football scholarship. Joey was now a freshman at Georgetown Prep. And while Frankie still lived with us, he was gone all the time due to working his new coaching job while keeping steady hours at the Laurel Meat Market.

John O'Neill was actually the first to go. Shortly after arriving at the Annapolis campus on Monday, July 1st, 1968, John Aloysious O'Neill participated in an oath-of-office ceremony, thus becoming a full-fledged member of the brigade of midshipmen. They cut his hair and clipped his wings, forbidding him to visit family and friends until Parents' Weekend in mid-August. After his induction into the Naval Academy, he might just as well be twenty leagues under the sea. Quite simply, Uncle Sam owned him for nearly a decade.

I ached for him. And I would like to say that I alone would have sunk a Trident submarine to reach him. But it was actually Nadette who talked me into heading up to Annapolis one Saturday, even though John didn't have leave and there was no hope of seeing him. Just being near the campus was good enough for me. So we jumped in my Beetle and made the short trip there.

"I still cannot believe he gave you a ring. You're as good as gold," she said, back on the subject of marriage. "He actually wants to marry you. I need to find someone," she further lamented. "By the way, are you still a virgin? I'd find that hard to believe seeing is how you're as good as engaged."

"Yes," I stated emphatically, "I am still a virgin."

"Liar."

"It's true."

"Only British queens-in-waiting and Mormons keep their virginity. And some Mormons remain virgins even after their marriage. They let all the other wives do the work, then just show up for dinner looking skinny and pretty. I'm serious."

I laughed. "So am I. You've seen first-hand what's happened this past year. It's really hard taking care of a baby. And you know how much I love John and want to have children with him. But not before we're ready. If John doesn't love me enough to respect that, then he doesn't love me."

"He bought that crap?"

"Yes."

"You mean it, then. You're still a virgin?"

"Yes, nosy."

"Wow."

"Aren't you?" I asked.

She fell silent, then shrugged. "Yeah."

"You say that like it's a bad thing."

"I know. I just don't want to get pregnant too soon, like Mary Joyce."

"Whoa! How'd you know about that?"

"I was at the Chevy Chase Club, remember? And I was also there when Sister Perpetua talked with the Barellis, remember?"

"I thought you were passed out."

"I was. But I woke up and heard part of it."

"Why didn't you say anything before?" I asked, realizing it was highly uncharacteristic of her to harbor such a secret.

"I love MJ. And I love your family. You've been through a lot, and I didn't want to make it any worse. Besides, when I saw her at Christmas it was clear she wasn't pregnant and she told me about Trinity College. I didn't know what all to make of it. But she seemed happy and why should I ruin it?"

I'd clearly underestimated her. "She lost the baby."

"I figured so. That's really sad."

"I know. But things worked out okay for her. Trinity offered her a nice scholarship."

"Still, it might not have been so bad marrying a handsome millionaire."

"You mean the lying, cheating, sleazy son of a lying, sleazy millionaire? I don't think so."

"I suppose. Anyway, I'm sorry that MJ suffered. And gossipmonger that I am, I promise, I haven't shared this with anyone."

"You know what? Thank-you, and I mean it. You know what else? I'm really impressed by your... maturity. I mean you kept your mouth shut *and* you recently quit smoking. I think I will keep you as my best friend, after all," I chortled.

"Trust me, my halo stops glowing after that. And if you really want to thank me ask John to fix me up on a blind-date with one of his new friends. I'd love to date a plebe."

"Why would you want to date a plebe? John's entire schedule is dictated by the United States Navy. Even his phone use is restricted. When he calls it's from a single phone in the hall with a line of plebes behind him waiting to use it and listening to every word he says."

At this point we were approaching the harbor in downtown Annapolis, and miraculously found a parking spot right next to the Naval Academy and near a popular waterfront crab house. It was a gorgeous evening during Labor Day weekend, with a balmy breeze and the fading sun casting a warm glow on the bustling town. The beautiful, historic spot was full of tourists and sailors who'd moored their boats in the marina. All of which made me yearn even more for John.

We walked inside the restaurant, where patrons were happily dissecting piles of freshly steamed crabs. Being told it would probably take up to one hour for a table, we sat on an outside bench to wait. It happened to be near a few midshipmen in their civilian clothes already picking at crabs and drinking beer on the restaurant's deck. One of the guys smiled at Nadette. She readily grinned back.

"Any of you guys know her boyfriend?" she said, jump-starting a conversation.

"That all depends," he answered.

"On what?" said Nadette.

"On who he is."

His buddies laughed. She took it in stride, but for Nadette, it was just long enough to determine which one bore the bull's eye.

"What's his name?" another asked.

"John O'Neill," she said demurely. "From Laurel."

"John O'Neill? From Laurel? What are the odds?" the third one said. "We know him. We play varsity football. He's playing on the plebe team," he said, meaning the junior varsity program, "and I'm damned glad I'm a senior, otherwise he'd be stealing all my thunder."

"Are you also a quarterback?"

He nodded and smiled at her. A handsome, zit-free, varsity quarterback from the Naval Academy. The target was defined.

"Really?" I said incredulously. "You really do know John, don't you?"

"Yeah, he's a great guy with a good arm."

"Is he doing okay?"

"I suppose. This is a tough time for the plebes. As I'm sure you're aware, this is the time when they start separating the men from the boys. How do you know him?"

"I'm his girlfriend."

"Then you also know it's when they separate the boyfriends from their girlfriends."

The guys erupted with laughter.

"Do you have a boyfriend, too?" the quarterback asked Nadette.

He might be able to do one-hundred chin ups in under three minutes while reciting the Laws of Thermodynamics. He might even know how to hold his breath under water in enemy territory for an untold length of time. But he was not immune to feminine wiles. Even from a minor. She slightly pouted her lips while shaking her head.

"No!" he said. "I find that hard to believe!"

She ate up the attention. "Any chance you could help her to see John?" she asked.

The three midshipmen looked at each other skeptically. "He's still a yard bird," one of them said.

"What does that mean?" Nadette asked.

"He doesn't have town privileges yet, so the only way for her to see him would be to sneak aboard or have him to go over the wall. What's your preference?"

"Neither," I jumped in, fully aware of the potential consequences.

"Well, there are ways," said the quarterback. "I'm sorry for being so rude. Would you two like to join us?"

"Sure," said Nadette. They were seated at a picnic table, and she promptly sat down beside him. The two others made room for me on their side.

"I'm Nadette and that's Gail."

"That's Hank and Bill. My name is Leonard. But you can call me by my nickname, Leon the Lion."

Nadette purred. He laughed.

"You're awfully cute," he grinned, then turned to me. "Do you really want to sneak on campus?"

"Of course, she does," Nadette answered.

"No, I do not!"

"That's not what you said in the car."

"I said it was easy to walk on campus – but that's during the day when they allow visitors. It's restricted after sundown."

"All the better," she said. "No one will see you."

"Forget it, Nadette! You're not getting me – or *John* – into trouble."

"'Forget it, Nadette!'" Leonard laughed. "Why do I have a feeling you say that a lot?"

"You have no idea," I laughed back, watching as Nadette brazenly helped herself to a sip of his beer.

"You don't mind, do you?"

"Are you old enough to drink? Otherwise, 'forget it, Nadette.'"

"I can drink," she retorted.

"That's different from being old enough to drink."

"I'm old enough," she adamantly replied, then chugged more of his beer. From a pitcher, he refilled the glass, the contents of which she readily consumed.

"Leon the Lion," she said, letting out a light burp and a little roar. "Do you have a girlfriend?"

"Yeah," he grinned.

"Pity."

"It's 'Forget-it-Nadette,' the newest cadet," he said, then playfully pecked her on the cheek. Rather than bask in the kiss, Nadette's face suddenly froze. Curiously, her eyes widened at the same time Leonard's jaw slackened. They were both staring straight ahead.

"Well, hello!" I heard a familiar voice. I turned to see a seriously tan Helen Hartley in a scant white bikini top and cut-off jean shorts that were about as long as the length of their zipper. Her long, blonde hair was loose, she wore aviator-style glasses and was barefoot.

"What a nice surprise! And how are you girls doing?"

"Helen," I gulped.

She smiled like we were happy to see one another, even leaning over to kiss me on the cheek. "I've been out water skiing on my cousin's boat all day. It was such a blast. We just stopped in the harbor to get gas and pick up some beer."

Leon the Lion managed to get his slack jaw back in alignment as he rose to meet her. "I'm Leonard. Care for some crabs?" he asked.

"I'm Helen," she sniggered. "And sure."

If I thought Nadette's radar was good, this one was capable of nuclear annihilation. Hank and Bill rose at once, each offering her their seat.

"I think I'll sit here," she said, squeezing in between Nadette and Leon the Lion before leaning over and kissing Nadette's cheek in the same spot just warmed by the handsome midshipman. "It's great to see you," she grinned. It was clear she'd been drinking already. Slightly crossing her arms over her torso so those double-D boobs pushed out like two helium blimps, she turned to me. "So, Gail, I hear that John's at the Academy. How's that going for him?"

"Good," I answered succinctly.

"And how's your sweet little baby? By the way, I owe you an apology. I got a little bit carried away thinking he was John's kid. Crazy, huh?"

I never responded to the implication that the baby was *mine*, as Leonard suddenly jumped in. "Sounds like everyone here is a friend of John's. He's one lucky man!"

"Absolutely!" said Helen, smiling broadly as Leonard handed her the largest crab on the table.

"I might need some help with this bad boy," she cooed while passing the creature in front of his face like some plastic dinosaur in a bad Japanese horror movie. "Rrrrr. He looks pretty ferocious."

"Hey, that's my line! My nickname is Leon the Lion. Rrrrr," he added the seductive sound bite.

Fortunately the hostess came and told us our table was ready.

"Are you sure you don't want to stay here with us?" Leonard asked.

"No," said Nadette, looking directly at him while standing up. "Thanks for the beer. And just for the record, I'd watch out for those crabs," she added snidely, then walked away.

"Nice to meet you guys," I politely added, then quickly caught up to her as we made our way to our own table.

"I hate her," said Nadette.

"Some things never change."

Shortly we watched as Leonard and his friends joined Helen on her cousin's boat. Later I shared this incident with John. Apparently he'd already received a recap of it from Leon the Lion who wanted to know if Helen was attached, and if he was the father of my child. John set him straight – at least where I was concerned – and hopefully regarding the wicked witch.

Mostly what John preferred to talk about was football. The season was now underway. In spite of it being my senior year, I shared his enthusiasm for the sport by spending my Saturdays attending games at either Navy, Maryland, or Georgetown Prep – all of which ended my career as a Pallotti cheerleader. When John's games were away, I joined the family in watching Tommy or Joey play.

Soon, it was late November and just before Navy's match-up against arch rival, Army, when I got a surreptitious phone call from John about the big game.

"Gail, you aren't going to believe this. Remember Leon the Lion?"

"Yeah."

"He just got expelled from school. He got caught in the campus chapel screwing – are you ready for this – HELEN HARTLEY!" he whispered excitedly. "That girl is amazing," he added, and not kindly. "THE

313

CHAPEL! Who does that? Apparently she invited him to practice a honeymoon night.

"And get this," he went on. "Since he's been thrown out, the second string quarterback rose to his place. Then he broke his wrist. And the third string...well, he pulled his hamstring. So basically, there's me," he added. "So yours truly is the starting quarterback in the Army-Navy game this weekend!!"

I was in stone-cold shock. First over the news that John was about to be showcased against Navy's biggest rival. And then, about how Leonard, nearing the end of a grueling academic program, would throw such a promising career out the window for an illicit tryst in such a sacred place with Helen.

"Gail, I can't stay on the phone, so I have to make this fast. There's a huge favor I need from you."

"Yeah?"

"The goat is dead."

"Goat? What goat?"

"Our mascot, Bill, the goat. Apparently someone sprayed weed killer a little too close to his pen and he ate poisoned grass. He died."

"I hope you're not counting on *me* to find the school another goat?"

"It's not a goat I need. It's Patty. Promise me that you'll bring Patty to the game. In her homecoming crown. Please? She always brought us such good luck at Pallotti."

I truly hadn't planned on having Patty join me during this weekend road trip to Philadelphia where the annual match-up took place. But I knew this was a command performance.

"I'll do my best."

"I know you will. I love you."

"I love you, too. See you soon."

I promptly called Nadette, who was already planning to travel with me.

"You won't believe this. Helen Hartley got Leon the Lion expelled from the Naval Academy after they got caught screwing in the chapel."

"Please tell me that's true."

"Very true."

"I hate her."

"Guess what else? John is replacing him as the starting quarterback in the Army-Navy game this weekend."

"How much do we LOVE Helen Hartley?!!"

"A lot. Also, FYI, John wants Patty to join us and to wear her homecoming crown for good luck."

"Go, John, go!"

"Exactly!"

Chapter 39

Two days later Nadette, Patty, and I piled into my Beetle and headed up to Philadelphia. Though chilly, it was a sunny day, made even more brilliant when the entire brigade of midshipmen marched into the stadium in their dress blues, followed by the Army cadets in their impressive gray, their respective bands playing patriotic and school fight songs while Navy fighter pilots flew in formation above.

And then the game began. It was a tense and scoreless first quarter. I held my breath on nearly every play, watching as John's skills were sorely tested. He gained little yardage against Army's fast and powerful defense. Finally, during the second quarter, one of Navy's running backs caught a long pass and ran it in for a touchdown. The crowd went nuts.

"Go, John, go!" Patty hollered, then turned and plainly speaking said, "I have to pee."

I didn't want to miss a minute of the game, so I asked Nadette to escort her there, during which the unthinkable happened. First, John got sacked. Not once, but twice. And then, as the girls returned from the lavatory I startled: the crown was missing from Patty's head.

"Where's your crown?"

She touched her head, then gasped. "I left it in the bathroom."

Having brought along a purse, she'd removed the crown and brushed her hair in the process leaving it there.

"We heard the crowd roar and came running back," said Nadette ruefully. "We thought Navy had scored a touchdown."

"This is a disaster! Show me where!" I implored. Then, grabbing Patty's hand I dragged her back to the lavatory. It was nowhere in sight. We looked in the trash, we looked at all the heads around us. It was gone.

"This is a disaster," I bellowed again, prompting Patty to cry.

"My crown," she lamented, "someone took my good luck crown."

The crowd roared. Army scored. I cringed, feeling as if I were letting the entire fleet down. Drastic action needed to be taken. If it meant going up and down every aisle in that stadium and scanning the heads of thousands of fanatic fans to find it, that is precisely what I intended to do. I returned Patty to her seat, then took off alone in search of the crown jewels.

Walking alone in friendly territory wearing a Navy sweatshirt was no threat. Still, after hitting ten different sections I had no luck. Taking a deep breath, I brazenly entered a section with rows and rows of Army cadets when I finally spotted some jester in the middle of the corps sporting Patty's crown. I didn't care how he'd acquired it. But I sure as hell knew he wasn't going to keep it. Marching down the aisle, then audaciously pushing my way right up to his seat, I then reached over in an attempt to wrest it off of his head.

"Hey, what are you doing?" He grabbed my forearm.

"You've got my crown. I want it back."

"I don't think so, Miss Navy."

"You stole it."

"I did not. It was a gift."

"Then whoever gave it to you stole it. It belongs to me and I want it back."

"What's so special about it?"

The Army section roared again. I turned. John's last pass was intercepted.

"Give it to me," I said. "Now."

"Forget it. This crown is bringing us good luck."

I looked imploringly at him. "Look, it actually belongs to my nine-year-old cousin. And she's..." I started to say retarded, but held back. "And she left it in the bathroom and now she's crying about it. Won't you please give it back?"

"No!"

"C'mon Navy, get out of the way," one of his classmates said to me, as I was obstructing his view.

"Now I know why you have a mule as a mascot," I fumed, "You're all a bunch of sorry asses." With that I headed back to my seat, where Patty was still in tears.

"No luck?" said Nadette.

"I found it, but the guy won't give it back."

"Some soldier has it?" she sniggered.

"Yes, one of America's finest is wearing it on his shaved head."

"I want my crown back," Patty cried.

"This is war!" said Nadette, then turned and saluted me. "Show us the way, admiral!"

It was all I needed to hear. Marching stiffly behind me into the Army section, Patty, Nadette and I went straight to the perpetrator's row.

"Now what?" said Nadette.

"Patty," I said pointing straight at him. "Go get it."

Shamelessly pushing past the others, she made her way to his seat and stood squarely in front of him. "That's my crown," she said staring down the contrary cadet.

He gulped. It was one thing to be belligerent with me in my Navy sweatshirt. Quite another to take on a special needs child.

"Here," he finally relented. "I'm sorry. I had no idea it belonged to you."

No sooner did Patty get it back in her hands and on her head than the crowd went wild. Navy was in possession of the ball and John had just thrown a long pass that placed the receiver within five yards of the end zone. I dared not move for fear of missing a single play. And so, standing in the aisle and amidst hundreds of zealous Army cadets, we watched and I held my breath as John took the snap, faked a pass then ran the ball into the end zone himself for a touchdown.

"GO, JOHN, GO!" Patty bellowed.

I glanced down the aisle catching sight of that square-headed cadet glowering at me. I stuck my tongue out at him while grabbing Patty by the hand and dashed out of the section with Nadette in tow. It was a mad celebration on the other side of the stadium where we were soon back in our seats.

In the final seconds of the game, John secured an unforgettable 21-14 Navy victory over nemesis Army. We only saw him briefly after the game and just before he boarded the school's bus back to Annapolis. I filled him in on the story of the clown in the crown, prompting him to hug Patty and thank her for taking one for the team. He then hugged and kissed me. His gratitude was not to end there. Back in Laurel that Monday, Patty answered a knock on the door.

"Flowers for her Royal Highness, Patricia O'Brien," said a young delivery man behind a towering arrangement of red roses.

"For me? It's not my birthday," she said somewhat confused.

"Are you Queen Patricia?"

"Just a minute," she said. Quickly, she retrieved her crown and putting it on rejoined him at the front door.

"Yes, I am."

"Sign here," he told her. I watched in amusement as she did so then gleefully took the vase.

"Open the card," I happily instructed her.

She smiled then read it aloud. "Go, Patty, go! Love, John."

Chapter 40

John's season wasn't the only one to reach a glorious end. Both the varsity and junior varsity teams at Georgetown Prep were having the best years ever, and Joey Kenealy was in heaven. He loved the school and the stirring it created in his soul. There were times he said, when he felt like an imposter; as though somehow he wasn't good enough to be there. But with the skillful guidance of the Jesuits he made a swift acclimation to the academic and spiritual rigors, soon realizing that he was just as smart – if not smarter – than many of the more highly privileged boys. Plus, his immense talent on the football field quelled any self-doubt, while his position as class clown reigned supreme. In short, his classmates loved him.

Folly aside, Joey had clearly matured. He loved Prep, often revealing to me his affection for the place. He'd spoken admiringly of the ancient brick buildings, the beautiful chapel, and the soft, rolling acres that surrounded the lush campus. The grand setting, in his own words, made him feel like he was living inside the pages of a rare, classic book. The structure and discipline that the Jesuits demanded was the perfect antidote for a young man accustomed to being a smart-mouthed hustler.

His temperament, however, differed on the football field. So far this season, Prep's junior varsity team had gone undefeated. They had one last game against arch-rival, Gonzaga: the only team that had beaten them the previous year. Both teams were out for blood.

To the wealthy parents arriving at game day in their Cadillacs and fur coats, this seemed like nothing more than a joyful afternoon in the bleachers to watch Junior – or was that the Third – play a team sport with presumed fairness and respect. Little did those mothers know that at the bottom of the pile their snot-nosed boys were jamming dirt in one another's faces, while attempting to poke each other's eyes, or pummeling one another's groins to the point that the next generation of Prep and Gonzaga students might be in serious jeopardy. Nor would they have ever believed the vulgarities passing from mouths typically fed with silver spoons. It was atop the gridiron – not in the classroom – where the true education of these future lawyers and corporate titans took place. It was not a match for the faint of heart, and at the heart of it was a passionate and determined Frankie O'Brien serving as an assistant offensive coordinator. Between the Laurel Meat Market in the early morning and Georgetown Prep every afternoon, Frankie was working seventy hours a week. I'd never seen him more exhausted, or happier.

My entire family – including Baby John, as well as Nadette – journeyed to Prep for the championship match-up. The crowd was rowdy and highly-charged for a blue-blood fight. My blue-collar and once skeptical father was a proud spectator, watching as Joey proved his mettle on the field as much as any other, while Frankie proved his moxie from the sidelines. Big and swift, Joey was the top running back *and* place kicker. Thus, it was evident from the start that he'd been singled out for attack by Gonzaga's powerful defense.

Interestingly, I could see from the bleachers that while Frankie wasn't in a position to call the major shots, he often telegraphed to Joey what he thought needed to be done using a range of personal hand signals. Particularly after a fair-catch interference. It didn't matter that Gonzaga was penalized fifteen yards. Joey acted pissed over missing a valuable chance to receive and run with the ball. He and Frankie locked heads during a brief time out, when Frankie apparently instructed him to watch the defensive end, number 62. He knew that to undermine the head coach's instructions might jeopardize his job. Still, Frankie confided later that night, he felt certain he was right.

"Keep your calm and watch his hands. Just before the snap, if he's running left, he raises his right hand off the ground ever so slightly as if to give himself a head start. Make him think you're going right, then go left for the hole."

Sure enough, on the next play, number sixty-two who'd already bloodied Joey, ever so slightly raised his right knuckles off the ground.

Following the snap, he charged left believing that was where the play was headed. Paying attention to Frankie's advice, Joey managed to avoid the defender, but missed the quarterback's pass.

On the next play, number sixty-two's hands stayed put and the player went straight. Joey was so absorbed now watching these nuances, that the only thing he managed to catch was the full wrath of sixty-two and a verbal licking from the quarterback.

"Kenealy, what the hell do you think you're doing?" he yelled.

"I'm sorry, man. Don't worry, I've got you covered."

"I am worried. You've got to stay focused. It's the fourth quarter, third down with two minutes left and no score. Stay with me."

The quarterback then dictated the next play.

Joey returned to the line-up. He looked over at Frankie, whose hands looked like he was signing to the deaf. At first Joey tried ignoring him, but before the snap he glanced at Frankie again.

Six fingers. Two fingers. Right hand balled up in a fist. *Number sixty-two is going left.*

Joey knew exactly what to do, and though the quarterback expected him to run right, he ran left, breaking through a brief opening in the defensive line and on down the field, where the quarterback – who was just about to be sacked – miraculously fired off a fifty-two yard bomb that Joey caught and carried to the end zone for a heroic touch-down. They flubbed the extra point, but Prep ultimately won the game beating Gonzaga six to zero, thus becoming the IAC champions for the year. I'd never seen my parents so jubilant. Even my mother rushed the field to hug the two boys. Later when I gave Frankie a ride home, he told me about being dressed down by the head coach in the locker room.

"Young man," the coach boomed. Frankie's stomach clenched. "Don't you ever pull that crap on me again. Do you hear?"

"I'm sorry, sir, I don't know what you're talking about."

"You know exactly what I'm talking about. Signaling the players with your own damned calls."

"With all due respect, sir. We won the game."

"You're not listening."

"But we, but I...." Frankie stammered, trying to defend himself.

"As I was saying," the coach interrupted with a warm grin, "Don't you ever signal the players with your own damned calls again unless consulting me first. Good work, young man. I think you have a future ahead of you in this sport. And thanks. That was my best win. Ever."

Though he wasn't fired, Frankie was still shaking. Before leaving, he made his way through the revelers in the locker room and toward Joey, who was too wrapped up in the camaraderie to notice him. Frankie left. But before joining me, he stopped by the empty chapel where he gave thanks for the big win and then asked God for one more favor. That is, if it was the Good Lord's intention, Frankie would one day find himself working beside a world-class coach in the NFL.

The Good Lord didn't have the right coaching position for Frankie just yet. But another miracle soon happened. This one involving a man who seemingly walked on water. A week following Prep's victory over Gonzaga, Frankie was in the locker room doing some end-of-season organizing when the coach called him into his office.

"I have something that may be of interest to you."

"What's up?"

"Pair of Redskins' season tickets."

"Season tickets?!"

"Yup. Dan Garson's father is so fed up with the 'biggest team of pathetic losers ever assembled – including that loser owner,' that he wants to unload his tickets in protest."

Frankie gulped. Regardless that they were perennial losers, tickets were very hard to come by. Dan Garson, a junior varsity football player with Joey, was one of the richest kids in the school. A lifelong resident of the D.C. area, Mr. Garson seemed a most unlikely person to relinquish his season tickets – regardless of the Redskins' protracted losing streak. So he called his son's football coach to see if he was interested. The coach already had tickets. But he implored Mr. Garson to let him find another buyer.

"There's only one problem," said the coach to Frankie.

"What's that?"

"The cost."

"How much?"

"He wants $500 bucks for the pair."

"No problem."

The coach blanched. "You got that kind of money, kid?"

"Will he take cash?"

The coach scratched his head. "I must be paying you too much," he laughed.

"Hardly," Frankie rejoined. The coach had no idea how passionate Frankie was about saving money and that he had serious multiples of that amount stashed away.

And thus, Frankie's Christmas present to himself were Redskins tickets for the upcoming 1969 season. We all joked with him about the acquisition.

"Good work buying that lump of coal. Even Pallotti could beat the Redskins!" Tommy quipped, adding, "And don't go begging me to spend a Sunday afternoon with you to watch them lose."

He would soon be eating his words. Two months later, in February of 1969, it was announced by the Redskins' team owner, Edward Bennett Williams, that he'd hired Frankie's idol away from Green Bay to coach the flailing Redskins. "The Man" was moving from Green Bay to Washington, D.C.

It usually took a sex scandal in politically-charged Washington to create the kind of buzz that Vince Lombardi's imminent arrival created. With the country bogged down in war half-a-world away, and a battle with spiraling inflation at home, there hadn't been much to cheer about lately. The Redskins hadn't helped. Lombardi was inheriting a rag tag team of players - diamonds in the rough — that he hoped to set into a Super Bowl ring. News that the most successful coach in football's history had decided to try his hand at raising the Redskins out of last place brought an energy and optimism to the city that hadn't been felt since John F. Kennedy's election. It was Camelot on the gridiron, and come fall Frankie would be on row twenty of the Redskin's forty yard line to witness his King Arthur in action.

Chapter 41

In the meantime, with MJ, Tommy and Joey all successfully living away, and Frankie working all the time, life for our blended family in early 1969 was certainly a bit calmer and, well, pretty normal. It did take some time for the darkness of what happened with Uncle Francis to fade. He had indeed fractured an arm, a leg and broken his back in the fall. He'd recovered from that, but his next fall was even steeper as he was now serving thirty years in the state penitentiary as a convicted felon. Thankfully he plead guilty to the most serious charges, thus sparing any of us from bearing witness against him.

All the children were holding up considerably well. Paul, now sixteen, stood six-foot two and towered over everyone else. His acne had finally cleared up, he was a star basketball player, and his good grades were on par with his newfound flirting skills. He was remarkably handsome and a hot target for the girls at Pallotti. He was now the master chef at home and had — we often commented — learned on his own to make a rib dinner on par with Frankie.

Raymond clearly picked up where Joey left off as the family rogue. He also reveled in being a class clown, and still needed constant guidance to stay out of trouble. Fortunately he'd stopped bad-mouthing the sisters. But he was a scrap yard dog on the playground, often picking fights over mundane things. Aware that jock straps were just as good at holding back misguided aggression as they were their intended purpose, Frankie signed him up for CYO basketball where — with Paul's help — the kid excelled and finally had something legitimate to brag about. Paul and my parents made a point of attending all his games and cheering him on like he was Wilt Chamberlain. He loved it. CYO Football was definitely next for him.

Timmy's chosen sport for the time-being was karate. He was all business in his white karate gi and orange belt My father was constantly bringing home wood blocks for his nearly ten-year-old son to cream, and we marveled over his excelled ability to easily chop those blocks in half with a bare hand or a quick roundhouse kick. He'd gained a new respect among his peers, and even Raymond would start running if Timmy assumed a warrior-like stance in response to being taunted by him.

And then, no single word exists to describe the depth of affection for Patty. Truly, she was like a sister and a best friend, always amusing and inspiring me with her unusual insights and observations. Sweet, adorable, loving, and happy, she was now reading as well as could be expected and was still cooking up a storm at the convent and at home. Plus, she was a great help with John — who was certainly not a baby anymore.

A rambunctious toddler with a mind of his own, at twenty months he no longer walked — he ran. His favorite place was the tree house and his favorite pastime was cruising head-first on his stomach down its slide: his fearlessness encouraged by Timmy and Raymond who derived great pleasure getting him to mimic them. Whether pretending to shoot hoops while riding on Paul's shoulders, or believing he could karate chop wood blocks, he was determined to keep up. Now talking, he loved the picture books we read him each night, effectively identifying colors and objects, happily repeating after every reader.

Best of all was my mother. Thus far she'd won her battle with addiction and was healthy and happy. Assuming primary care of John made a huge difference in her recovery, as she could now see clearly to fulfilling her obligations while honoring Cate's memory. She and my father had returned to many of their normal routines, like sitting on the front porch swing at the end of the day and sharing each other's thoughts and laughter. Amazingly, she'd even quit smoking.

All of this was a great relief to me, as I spent much of my senior year preparing for college. Nadette had already made up her mind she wanted to go to the University of Maryland where she planned to join a sorority and major in dating.

My criteria was different. The school had to be within a reasonable range of the Naval Academy, and I wanted to be reasonably close to home so that I could be there for my family if needed. Maryland would have worked just fine. But I also wanted to experience something challenging and unfamiliar, some place other than where to expect many of my friends for a change. Given my outstanding grades, test scores, personal and work history, I was offered a full academic scholarship elsewhere.

"Praise God!" my mother exclaimed upon hearing the news. "We are now four-for-four on scholarships," she said, gifts of which MJ, Tommy, Joey and I were each beneficiaries.

"Lucky Timmy," my father joked. "Maybe we'll just buy him a college!"

And so, after graduating from Pallotti in the spring of 1969 with very high honors, the choice was clear. I was going twenty miles away to join Georgetown University's first, full, co-educational class.

Chapter 42

*N*ow the fall of 1969, football reigned even more supreme in my family's world. Joey was a sophomore and still a star player on the junior varsity football team at Georgetown Prep, with Frankie still coaching offense. John O'Neill was now the Naval Academy's first-string, varsity quarterback, and Tommy was a stand-out wide receiver at Maryland. It was hell for my parents trying to keep up with the various sports schedules, including the CYO games Raymond and Timmy now played. They'd sometimes have to catch the first quarter here and the last quarter there. But one or the other always posted.

That covered football after school and on Saturdays. But there was a new twist: Sundays and the Washington Redskins. I'd never seen Frankie so energized by anything than the prospect of watching "The Man" live and in action. He planned out the entire season in advance, making sure that my father, Joey, Tommy, Paul, Raymond and Timmy each went to a game. But the first home game on October 12th he reserved for me. I drove out to Laurel and picked him up three hours before kick-off, just so we could arrive early in case Lombardi happened to appear for warm-up practice. He didn't. But soon enough when a deafening roar erupted in the stadium we knew he was there. Frankie had a pair of binoculars with him that barely left his eyes. He was absorbing everything "The Man" and his team did, reporting it all with vivid detail as if I weren't there to witness it myself. I had never, ever, seen anyone so thrilled by anything in their entire life than Frankie O'Brien after the Redskins soundly defeated the St. Louis Cardinals that day.

Still working at the Laurel Meat Market while coaching at Prep, Frankie maintained a grueling schedule, continuing to save money for the restaurant he one day hoped to own. Plus, his dream loomed large of first getting a job working on the staff of an NFL team.

Without failure we'd all catch up on Sunday nights. After picking up Tommy in my VW, we'd join the family for a boisterous dinner where Patty, Frankie and Paul practically tripped over each other in the kitchen to prepare the most hearty meals. Nadette, frequently joined us. And, occasionally, my beloved John O'Neill had a liberty pass and would join us, too. It was during one such evening in the early spring of 1970 that I noticed something different about Frankie. He'd lost weight. Not a lot, but still discernible. And contrary to his custom of cooking an elaborate Sunday feast, that day he begged out after complaining of flu-like symptoms. I had final exams coming up and tried to steer clear of him for fear of getting sick myself. Thankfully Patty and Paul had enough knowledge around the kitchen to pick up where he'd left off.

The following Sunday Frankie was back, this time firing up the grill to serve us a mountain of succulent ribs. Still, there was a subtle weakness about him, a simmering lethargy. Nevertheless, he was back to pushing himself each day at the Laurel Meat Market while finding time to help coach Prep's junior varsity baseball team. That job was a source of ongoing amusement for all of us, as he knew little about coaching baseball, yet still produced a winning team.

A few weeks later, on an early evening in mid-May when I was studying for final exams, I was interrupted by a knock on my dormitory door.

"Gail, there's a call for you," one of my hall mates informed me.

"Thanks," I said, retreating to the house phone.

"Hello," I chirped, hoping it was John.

"Gail," was all he said. It was Frankie.

"Hey, Frankie," I smiled.

"Are you busy?" he asked, his voice quavering.

"Kinda. I'm studying for my finals. What's up?"

"I need your help."

I felt my stomach sink. Frankie *never* asked for help, and his tone of voice suggested trouble. "Sure. What can I do for you?"

"I need a ride to Georgetown tomorrow. I have to be at the hospital first thing in the morning."

Now my stomach flipped. "Georgetown University Hospital? Why?"

"First," he implored, "promise you won't tell anyone."

"Tell anyone what, Frankie?"

He choked, then sniffled.

"Frankie, you're scaring me. What is it? I promise I won't tell."

He gathered himself for the punch. "Doc Warren," he started, then choked again.

"Doc Warren *what*, Frankie?"

His voice was barely a whisper. "He thinks I have leukemia."

I literally lost my breath.

"Gail, I'm so sorry. Are you okay?"

Frankie the protector. Frankie, always looking out for everyone else's best interests. Frankie, trying to comfort me with the shocking news that he may be facing a debilitating illness and untimely death.

"Where are you?" I finally managed to ask him.

"I'm at a pay phone on Main Street. I didn't want anybody at home to hear me."

"I'm coming right now. Please, just go to Guvelli's and I'll be there as fast as I can."

"Are you sure?"

"Don't let me down."

"I'll be waiting."

I'm not sure how I even gathered the courage to drive as a couple of times I had to pull over just to collect myself. Without a word to anyone, I simply left the dorm, climbed into my car, making it to Guvelli's as soon as I could. There, sitting alone on the outside bench with his head hung low, was Frankie. Softly I sat down beside him and immediately wrapped my arms around him. "What's going on, brother?"

"I don't know Gail. I ache. I ache everywhere," he began to cry. "Every joint in my body is in pain. I thought it was the flu, especially since I got a cold that I couldn't shake. I'm so tired, too," he said, tears pouring from his beautiful, soulful eyes. "So I finally went to the doctor to see what bug was going around."

I gave his shoulder a squeeze, continuing to hold him near.

"Anyway, after finding some lumps Doc Warren drew some blood. He called me today with the results. My white cell count is off the charts." He drew in a deep breath while fighting back more tears.

"Frankie, that's so inconclusive. It's probably some infection."

He shook his head no. "He shared the lab results with a specialist down at Georgetown University Hospital to get his opinion. He also thinks it's leukemia and he wants to see me right away. I'm scheduled for a bone biopsy there tomorrow. I'm really scared," he added with barely a whisper. "And I was wondering, if it's not too much trouble, could you take me there and stay with me?"

It was like sitting in a vacuum. There were the typical sights and sounds of a warm, spring evening. Families were happily chatting while going in and out of Guvelli's for a treat as the cow bells repeatedly chimed. There was the familiar bench upon which we were sitting where over the years I'd happily consumed countless cones. But now it all seemed so surreal. I truly felt that I couldn't swallow anything more bitter – ever – than what Frankie had just dished out. I had certainly seen my share of tragedy over the past few years. Frankie, however, had endured a lifetime of suffering. In spite of it, his life had never been about seeing how much he could receive. Rather it was about seeing how much he could give. How much more was expected of him? I held him a bit closer, now feeling the essence of a scared child. Finally, I spoke. "Of course," I said warmly. "I am always here for you no matter what."

He acknowledged this with a nod. Then, with both of us softly crying, we sat in silent communion as each contemplated what it all meant, during which my mind slipped back to a seminal conversation on this same bench with Sister Perpetua.

"Don't you think more people would praise God and find religion if he were right out there making everyone obviously happy? So why all the mystery and all the suffering? To tell you the truth, with everything that's been happening around me, I'm beginning to wonder if God even exists."

"*Gail,* she'd later stated, "*Earlier you were wondering whether or not God even exists. Not I. Tonight when I say my prayers, I will be thanking God for this gorgeous afternoon while eating an ice cream cone with someone I truly admire.*"

For me, Frankie personified all the best traits any human could possess, and it seemed I could not love or admire him more. I reached over and patted his knee. "You know what your sister would do, don't you?"

"No," he chortled at the thought of Patty.

"She believes ice cream fixes everything," I said, "So she'd ask what flavor you'd want."

"I'm partial to their chocolate mint," he said, wiping away his tears.

"Two scoops or one?"

"Two, please."

"On a cone or in a cup?"

"Cone, please."

I retreated inside Guvelli's, ordering up two identical cones, then returned to the bench, handing him his treat. "Cheers," I said, tapping my cone against his.

"Cheers," he grinned, then half-chuckled. "I knew I could count on you to make me feel better."

"You're going to be okay, Frankie. You're going to be okay," I repeated as if to assure myself. "And," I said, while lightly patting his knee again. "We're going to get through this."

Chapter 43

rancis Monroe O'Brien was admitted to Georgetown University Hospital on the morning of May 19th, 1970, following the positive results of a bone marrow test for leukemia. It was acute and his chances of survival slim. But he was barely nineteen, so hope prevailed that his youth would somehow provide endurance and thus longevity through the grueling treatments.

Up until the night of his departure, we kept his condition a secret, breaking it only to my father in the hour just before he headed up to bed. He was sitting alone on the front porch swing drinking a Pabst Blue Ribbon when we joined him.

"Uncle Joe," Frankie said. "Do you mind if I join you?"

"Sure, Frankie. You doing okay son?"

"Well, I'm not sure."

"Here," my father stopped rocking and patted to the empty spot beside him. Frankie joined him on the swing while I sat down on an old milk crate. "What's on your mind?"

"It's not so much what's on my mind that's the problem."

My father had expressed some concern recently over Frankie's increasingly wan appearance, attributing it mostly to his work ethic. Still, he was clueless as to where this conversation was headed, waiting instead to take his lead from Frankie.

"I am, uhm," Frankie started, stopped, and fought back tears.

"Go ahead, son."

"I'm not sure how to say this."

My father looked at me with concern, then back at him. "Whatever it is, it's okay," my father tried reassuring him.

"No. It's not okay," Frankie softly blurted. "I have leukemia."

My father cocked his head. "Come again?"

"I have been diagnosed with Acute Myelogenous Leukemia."

They both fell silent as my father closed his eyes, pinched and massaged his forehead while trying to absorb the news.

"Gail is taking me down to Georgetown University Hospital tomorrow so I can begin treatment."

My father sighed deeply, then looked at me. "Why am I only now hearing about this?" he asked tender-heartedly, looking first at me, then Frankie.

"Because I was hoping they were wrong," he said.

"Is it possible?"

"No."

"When did you find out?"

"It was confirmed a couple of days ago, sir."

"I see," my father said, his Adam's apple appearing large as he desperately fought back tears himself. "Who knows about this?"

"Around here, Doc Warren and Gail. That's it. And that's the way I'd like to leave it for now. I don't want to scare the children."

"What about your Aunt Mary Claire?"

"I was kind of hoping you could tell her yourself, sir, if you don't mind. I just figured she'd be able to handle it better if it came from you."

Silence resumed. In unison they began gently swinging.

"How are you feeling?" my father finally spoke.

"Scared."

My father reached his arm across Frankie's shoulder, drew him in then kissed his temple.

"I want you to know something. First, I think you are one of the finest young men whom I've ever known. And I mean that. If half those kids out there had half your values and courage, the world would be a far better place."

Frankie nodded, tears streaming down his face.

"And then, I want you to know that your Aunt Mary Claire and I are here for you. Whatever you need. Whatever you want. We will do whatever we can to help you. Thankfully you're covered under my insurance and any incidentals I will cover myself."

"Thank you, Uncle Joe. I appreciate that. But one of the primary reasons I wanted to talk with you tonight isn't about me, it's about..." Frankie started, then choked, needing a moment to collect himself. "I just want you to promise me that no matter what, you will always do what is necessary to keep the kids together. If anything happens to me..."

"Stop. Stop right there," my father insisted, his voice cracking and now crying himself. "Nothing is going to happen to you. Do you hear me? You're not going anywhere other than that blessed hospital to get better. And while you're gone, don't you worry for one minute about those kids. Because they will always have a home. They will always be fed. And they will always be loved. You, too."

"Thank you," said Frankie, sniffling. "You know, Uncle Joe," he added, "You are one of the finest men I've ever known, too."

Shortly my father headed up to bed. But not before giving Frankie an earnest hug and strong reassurance that everything would be all right.

Frankie watched my father disappear into the house, then excused himself from my company. Grabbing his old sleeping bag, he retreated to the tree house and surrounded by the nighttime lullaby of crickets, it is where he spent the night.

Chapter 44

It was Frankie's nature to make friends. The hospital staff adored him, and more than one young nurse regularly flirted with him. Which was good, as he began a very brutal course of chemotherapy. It was hard to believe that something so awful was designed to make patients better. But so it was. Frankie, always wanting to demoralize the opponent by scoring first, viewed it as the opening kick-off of Toxins vs. Malignancies.

"Bring it on," he told the doctors and residents after they fully described his course of treatment. It was easy to feel upbeat and hopeful when you hadn't been knocked on your ass yet by the effects of chemotherapy. Before you swam in a sea of nausea or found your pillow covered with your own rejected hair.

From then on, I hardly left him, camping out endless nights in the hospital just to hold his hand and smooth a cool compress over his forehead. The nausea nearly consumed him, while wild fluctuations in his temperature and blood pressure kept him in Georgetown.

Though I'd studied hard all semester and fortunately did well on my finals, nothing could have prepared me for the true tests to follow. Somehow I didn't care half as much about my grades as I did seeing Frankie through this passage. And while my father visited Georgetown several times in the ensuing weeks, no one beside my mother knew what was happening. According to my father, my mother was absolutely crestfallen, but bearing up well. In other words she wasn't drinking.

"Frankie, son," my father said to him during one such trip there. "At some point we need to let the rest of the family know what's going on. I think it's important that they all have a chance to pray for you."

Pale, nauseated, and exhausted, Frankie managed to laugh. "I would hope that no matter what they would be praying for me!"

"That's true," my father laughed back. "Still, at some point...."

"Not yet," Frankie insisted.

My father respectfully nodded. There was one thing about Frankie that was abundantly clear. He was a fighter and a survivor. And in his heart he believed he'd be home before a single one of them missed him.

He was wrong. Patty was making demanding inquiries. As were her brothers. But it was Joey who was most perplexed. Frankie had at least informed both of his employers about some health issues and had said that he would be gone for a few weeks during treatment. That's all they knew, though both suspected more. At the Laurel Meat Market, he'd long stopped hoisting heifers, as they jokingly referred to it, as for weeks before his diagnosis his strength had no longer been up to the task.

Frankie had quickly become a beloved – and now missed – presence at Georgetown Prep's campus. If not in the locker room or out on the field, he was frequently checking in on Joey to make sure that he had all he needed, and more importantly that Joey was doing everything that needed to be done. Joey sometimes pretended to resent the intrusions into his dorm room. But truthfully, more often than not Frankie's presence reminded Joey that if not for his efforts he'd be traveling a far different course.

One night shortly after Joey's return from Prep for his summer break, and I'd returned home to get some of Frankie's personal things, he cornered me. We were alone in the living room at the time.

"Gail," he said adamantly, "where in the hell is Frankie?"

"He got worn out, Joey. He needed a break, that's all."

"Where is he, then?"

I didn't answer.

"Mom and Dad are on egg shells. You look like shit. You're lying. Something's wrong, and I wish everyone would stop lying to me."

I bit my lip, looking upwards at the ceiling trying vainly not to cry.

"What's going on? Is he somewhere horrible like jail?"

"I wish," I said.

"What do you mean?" he barely whispered.

"He's in the hospital," I finally confessed, at once feeling a profusion of guilt and relief.

"Why?" Joey softly asked.

"Joey, he doesn't want you to know. Not yet."

"Stop it Gail. Just stop it and tell me the truth."

I took a deep breath. "He has leukemia."

There was no blow that Gonzaga's number sixty-two could have delivered that would have knocked Joey over quite the same as that news. He simply crumpled to the floor and fell apart. I knelt down on the floor beside him, but for the longest time he couldn't even bring himself to look at me he was sobbing so hard. Finally, lifting his tear-stained face out of his hands, he spoke.

"I need to see him."

"I know. And I think he needs to see you, too."

Helping Joey up off the floor, I hugged him, and we both cried our hearts out.

"Is he going to be okay?"

"No one knows. That's what's so hard. No one knows."

The next morning, when I left for Georgetown University Hospital, Joey was in the passenger seat beside me. I warned him that Frankie might not be receptive to this and furthermore that he needed to brace himself because of Frankie's appearance. We parked the car on Reservoir Road, then headed up to Frankie's room, only to be shocked by the sight of an empty bed. I immediately stormed down to the nurse's station.

"Where is Frankie O'Brien?" I demanded.

One of the nurses looked up at me. "Who are you?" she asked. She must have been new, as I didn't recognize her either.

"I'm his sister," I boldly answered.

"He's down getting some blood work done. He'll be up shortly."

"Thank you," I said, meaning every breath of it.

"He's having lab work done," I said, rejoining Joey. "He'll be back up soon."

There was the most incredulous look on his face. "Did you see that?" Joey asked.

"See what?"

"Who they just wheeled into that room?" he said pointing two doors down.

I shook my head no.

"It was Coach Lombardi."

"As in Vince Lombardi?"

"Yeah," he nodded. "I swear to you, it was Vince Lombardi. He looks awful, but there's no way it wasn't him. I'd recognize that man from a mile away. Listen," he said.

We both fell silent, inching a bit closer to the room while straining to overhear the conversation inside.

"How are you today, Mr. Lombardi?" we heard a woman's voice.

"Okay, I suppose."

Our ears perked even more.

"Make a fist, please."

"The better to smack you with," Mr. Lombardi joked.

"Now why would you ever want to hurt me?" she laughed.

"Because you're about to hurt me!"

Joey heard the laughter of another woman, who then began speaking in a low, smoky voice. "That's his wife, Marie," he whispered. "She went in there with him."

"Joey, are you positive?"

"Gail, I'd bet a hundred dollars on it. There have been all sorts of rumors lately that he's sick, but no one knows for sure what it is or how serious it is."

"Well, I hope like hell you'll respect his privacy then, and not go blabbing this to the world."

Joey put his hands up to his chest with mock indignation. "Moi?"

He was so preoccupied with excitement over being near "The Man," that he barely recognized Frankie being pushed down the hall in a wheel chair, twenty pounds lighter, wrapped in a blanket, a baseball cap covering his now bald head, dark half-moons beneath his eyes.

"Stop!" Frankie commanded the orderly.

Joey had been forewarned, but was still dumbstruck and unprepared for the distilled shock he felt at the sight of his beloved cousin.

"Frankie?" Joey finally and painfully whispered. "How are you doing, man?"

Not realizing until that moment how much he'd missed Joey, Frankie's hard-headedness suddenly melted and, for the first time in weeks, he openly cried.

"I'm so sorry," he said. "I didn't want you to see me like this."

Joey laughed.

"You think this is funny?" asked Frankie.

Joey looked vainly at the ceiling to control his emotions, then squarely back at Frankie as tears began streaming down his face, too. "Do you remember these immortal words? *'Just remember, I'm not cutting you any breaks. You're gonna learn to walk a straight line on those crutches and then get into fighting shape if you want to play on my team.'*"

Frankie nodded his head, a slight grin encasing his face.

"Do you remember that? 'Cause I sure do. I hated you for kicking my ass that night. But you know what? You were right. And I wouldn't be where I am today without you. So guess what?" Joey emphatically added. "You're on *my* team now. And I'm not cutting *you* any breaks. You're gonna get back into fighting shape and make it back home and back to Prep. You hear?"

Frankie was about to respond when suddenly his eyes widened and his jaw fell slack. He was now looking past Joey and down the corridor as if just seeing a ghost.

"How long will he be gone?" we heard a woman's voice. Joey and I turned.

"Probably an hour or so, Mrs. Lombardi," said an orderly. "X-Rays usually take a little while."

Frankie shook his head in disbelief. Less than thirty feet away, looking gaunt and likewise dressed in a hospital gown while being transported in a wheelchair, was his idol.

Frankie looked at me, then Joey, then back at the scene unfolding before him.

"Holy cow. It's 'The Man,'" he barely whispered. "I am in the hospital with 'the Man.'"

Chapter 45

*I*t might have been a joyful discovery for those two that Lombardi was practically within the same distance of a first down. But quite sadly, "The Man" had an unpublicized and virulent form of colon cancer. Respecting the Lombardis' privacy, Frankie and Joey kept this fact to themselves. Though they strove in sometimes the most undignified manner to glean information about him from all of the nurses.

It was actually the best thing that could have happened to both boys. Having Vince Lombardi nearby energized Frankie in a way that I hadn't seen in well over a month. Lombardi's mere proximity helped him to focus on what he wanted most out of life – to get well and to work in the NFL. In Joey's mind, this was fate. The inimitable coach would get through his illness, just like Frankie, and then he and Frankie would one day be employed by "The Man," with Joey playing offense and Frankie coaching.

Joey would frequently peek outside Frankie's room and report the comings and goings. A number of times he saw Marie and their two grown children, and even the Redskins' owner, Edward Bennett Williams. There were several people about whom he was clueless, but he would describe them right down to the tips of their shoes or the white tab in their Roman collars. And while all of this curiosity played out in Frankie's hospital room, back home I was facing a curious group myself. Particularly insistent was Patty.

"Gail," she demanded one day. "I want to know why Frankie left me without saying good-bye. That's really mean."

"Well, let's call him," I said, shortly getting him on the phone.

"Hey, Patty. How's my sweet girl?"

"I'm mad at you," she said angrily. "Why did you run away?"

"Patty, I haven't run away. I'm just on a vacation. And I'll be home soon."

"You went on a vacation without me? That's mean."

"Well, where I am children aren't allowed."

"Are you at the Chevy Chase Club?"

Frankie laughed. "I'm not far from it."

"When are you coming home?"

"Soon. I'll be home very soon. And Patty, there's something I need to tell you."

"Yeah?"

"Well, I decided to cut off all of my hair."

"You must look funny."

"Pretty much."

"Is your head cold?"

"Sometimes."

"When are you coming home?" she asked again.

"Like I said, soon. And Patty," he added.

"Yeah?"

"I miss you. And I love you."

"I love you and I miss you, too. Do you want to talk to Baby John?"

"Sure," Frankie chuckled.

"Here," he heard Patty say, obviously handing the receiver over to John. "Say hello," she cooed. John did get in a few legitimate words before banging the receiver on the floor several times.

"That's exactly how I feel sometimes," said Frankie after I picked up again.

We laughed together. And true to his word, Frankie came home.

But not before the unimaginable had happened. One night, later in the week, when I was asleep in a nearby recliner, Frankie became restless. He tried reading but felt distracted and bored. So gathering his robe around himself, he stepped into his slippers then headed out to the hallway to stretch. The rooms were all dim. And, with the exception of monitors beeping, it was very quiet. But the hall was not empty. There, at its end, leaning against a window sill and looking out contemplatively at the night sky was Vince Lombardi. Frankie pretended not to notice who it was but was drawn to him like the Northern Star.

Hearing someone coming from behind, Lombardi slightly turned, then for some reason seeing it was Frankie flashed his trademark grin. "Non est ad astra mollis e terris via."

"Sir?" said Frankie, fairly startled and slightly wondering if the man hadn't lost his mind.

"Non est ad astra mollis e terris via. There is no easy way from the earth to the stars."

Frankie moved closer. "You know, it's really something to behold," Lombardi said, inviting Frankie to join him. It was a clear and brilliant night. Below, they could see Georgetown University's football field where the Redskins now practiced so that Lombardi could oversee their drills from his hospital window. Tonight it was awash in the glow of a full moon. Above, the stars shone bright.

"Do you see that?" Lombardi asked, as if questioning one of his young charges at St. Cecilia High School in Englewood, New Jersey where he'd started his coaching career many years earlier.

"See what, sir?" Frankie nervously asked, looking up.

"The moon. It's really gorgeous tonight. Hard to believe that a man walked up there last summer. Thank God it was an American," he added, then just as nonchalantly started softly singing.

"Fly Me to the Moon," he crooned, then whistled several bars of the popular ballad.

Standing beside the man he most revered, any anxiety Frankie might have felt suddenly dissipated in the off-key, but carefree notes of that tune. He had half-a-mind to sing along with him, but Lombardi turned and started talking to him instead.

"You're awfully young. What brings you here?"

"Leukemia."

"Damn. You doing okay?"

"Much better. I'm told the cancer cells appear to be in remission and that I can finally go home before we start the next round of whatever it is they have in store for me."

"Yeah? I'm going home, too. Tomorrow."

"That's great," Frankie said sincerely.

"Are you in school?" Lombardi asked him.

"No sir. But, I work at a school."

"Which one?"

"Georgetown Prep. I'm..." Frankie started, then hesitated, as his heart was beating fast. "I'm an assistant coach on the JV football team. Offense," he humbly added.

"You don't say?" Lombardi commented with enthusiasm. "The Hoyas, heh? They've had a great couple of seasons."

"You know about them?" Frankie proudly asked.

"Well, of course. They've been IAC champs for two years straight. I know a lot of people with kids there. They've got a great program. And you said you're coaching offense? What do you know, kid, that's how I got my start. How old are you?"

"Nineteen."

"Nineteen, huh? There are days that seems like yesterday to me. I was in college then."

"At Fordham, right?"

"You know that about me?"

"I know who you are, Mr. Lombardi. And I know that you also worked in your Dad's butcher business. I do the same thing."

"Get outta here," Lombardi said, his Brooklyn accent growing thick.

"Well, it's not my Dad's business. But for over two years now I've been 'hoisting heifers.'"

Lombardi grinned. "It bulks you up pretty good, doesn't it?"

"It did. I need to get my strength back."

"You will. Let me ask you something. What do you tell those kids after they lose a game? How do you inspire them?"

Frankie modestly chuckled. "I wouldn't know what to say, sir. Because we've gone undefeated since I started."

Lombardi threw back his head and cracked up laughing. "Wow! You're my kind of man!"

"Thanks. But," Frankie went on more confidently. "A few years ago I was coaching a CYO team, and we suffered our share of losses. And I used to tell those sorry-assed losers..." Frankie said, then caught himself. "Excuse the profanity, sir."

Lombardi was clearly tickled. "Go on, as you 'used to tell those sorry-assed losers?'" he prompted.

"I would tell them that the final step in their last defeat must always be the first step in their next victory."

Lombardi thoughtfully took this in. "I like that, a lot. 'The final step in your last defeat must always be the first step in your next victory,'" he repeated. At last he turned toward the other direction. "I'm going to head back now. But listen," he started, then suddenly hesitated, "What's your name?"

"Frankie. Frankie O'Brien, sir."

"Well, 'Frankie O'Brien, sir,'" he chuckled, "I like you, and it's been a pleasure. I wish you the best of luck with your recovery. And who knows," he added with a twinkle in his eye, "maybe one day you'll come to work for me."

"I would like that very much, Mr. Lombardi," Frankie smiled, then watched as "The Man" shuffled slowly down the hall.

Chapter 46

Frankie was released from the hospital two days after Mr. Lombardi. Just before his arrival home, I pulled Paul, Raymond, Patty, and Timmy aside and told them that while he was away he'd gotten ill, but that he was okay now. I was only game to this charade at Frankie's insistence, as I felt it would be immeasurably easier if everyone just knew the truth. But Frankie had no intention of wallowing in self-pity. He was someone who could get past something if he could just move through it, claiming the sooner the better.

I explained to the children that because Frankie had gotten a little sick that, and at least for now, he needed a lot of rest and the bedroom to himself. Which was true. But I was also trying to keep him from contact with any unnecessary germs. Thankfully it was the summer, and most of the boys were sleeping in the tree house, anyway. Tommy was at Maryland to condition for the football season, and Mary Joyce had remained in Florida. So anyone wanting to sleep inside went into Joey's room.

I disinfected the entire house before Frankie came home. Likewise, I removed John's diaper pail from the bathroom and demanded that every person entering our house become religious about washing their hands. Plus, I insisted they all remove their shoes, as well. I stripped all the bunk beds in Frankie's room, then washed all the linens in piping hot water so that there were fresh sheets on his bed. I dusted, vacuumed and scrubbed every square inch of his room.

And then, very unceremoniously, I picked Frankie up from the hospital and brought him home. All of the children were at the pool, except John, who was being read to by my mother on the porch swing when we arrived back at the house. She smiled at the sight of my car.

"I'm afraid to get out," said Frankie.

"Why?"

"I might scare John."

"Don't be silly. Just put your baseball cap on," I insisted. Which he did, then exited the car. My mother set John down, allowing him to charge for the front gate on his own. Squatting down on the opposite side of it, Frankie immediately engaged in a game of peek-a-boo with his delighted brother. Finally standing up, Frankie was greeted by my unexpectedly composed mother.

"Frankie," she smiled broadly.

Leaning over the fence, Frankie embraced her. Surprisingly neither of them cried. Instead, my mother laughed.

"You're looking just a bit like Uncle Fester, there," she said, referring to the bald-headed, dark-eyed, screwball character from the popular hit show The Adamms Family.

"Better than Lurch! You rang?" he humorously added, mimicking the creepy and gangly butler in the Addams household.

My mother and I laughed.

"How-are-ya-feeling?" she asked more seriously, running her words together as if it didn't matter whether he felt good or bad, as all that truly counted was that he was home.

"I'm feeling okay, thanks."

"The children are all up at the pool. Do you want me to go fetch them?"

"No, thanks. Actually, what I'd really like is a nap."

"Then a nap it is. And I'll bust the first one over the head that wakes you up. 'Cept if it's John. I haven't quite figured out where the off switch is, if you know what I mean."

There was palpable relief on either side of that fence. Frankie, because my mother was sober, my mother, because Frankie was alive. She picked up John, then opened the gate.

"For the love of God," she said, "Welcome home."

As my mother transported John, I carried Frankie's suitcase with his meager belongings up to his room.

"Wow!" he exclaimed. "I barely recognize the place it's so clean."

"Yeah, well, get used to it," I said. "I've threatened bodily injury if any one of those goofs fouls it up."

"Gail," Frankie said, settling down on the bed. "Thank you so much. I don't know what I would have done without you."

"I suspect," I replied with great sincerity, "that you would have managed just fine."

"No," he replied adamantly, "I mean it. Thank you and I love you."

I choked hard. "You're welcome," I said. "And I love you, too. Besides, I know you would have done the exact same for me."

Before long, he was peaceably sleeping, and one-by-one as the children came marching home I made them leave their shoes outside. I wasn't taking any chances. Frankie's immune system had tanked out. And though presumably the cancer was in remission, any kind of bug could set him back. We wondered if it was wise to even bring him home. But home is where he wanted to be.

That night at dinner we all gathered around the table for a dinner prepared by Patty and Paul, while Joey volunteered to lead us in prayer.

"Bless us, O Lord, and these your gifts, which we are about to receive from your bounty. Through Christ our Lord."

Though an amen chorus followed, Joey wasn't finished. His head still bowed, his hands still folded, he added: "And Lord, we deeply thank you for the healing mercy you've provided your humble servant, Francis O'Brien. Amen."

"Amen," we echoed.

"See, I knew you'd be back," my father smiled proudly while digging into his mashed potatoes.

"Why?" said Patty, "Did you think he'd run away for good, too?"

"No, Patty," my father replied warmly. "There was never a doubt in my mind that Frankie would be back home."

Chapter 47

I could see that something was wrong before he even mentioned it. For the first couple of weeks he was back, Frankie was seemingly on the mend. His color was returning to normal. The dark circles beneath his eyes were fading. And he was gaining weight for a change.

But suddenly it wasn't the frequency of his naps that bothered me. It was their length. Presumably his energy level should have been picking up. Instead, one day he came downstairs, turned on his color television then promptly went to sleep on the sofa. He remained there throughout the day and in spite of our noisy comings and goings.

After dinner, and also after barely eating, he excused himself to go to bed. I decided not to say anything, until the next day when I didn't see him.

"Frankie," I said, going to his room about 10:00 a.m. "Are you okay?"

"I'm just sleepy," he drowsily replied, slowly rolling over. As he did, every cell in my body pulsed in fear. I shrieked, then covered my mouth while swallowing hard and taking a huge step back.

"What is it?" he said, his eyes popping wide.

"Your face," I said breathlessly. "It's covered with blood."

Frankie put his hand up to his nose, where indeed fresh blood was trickling out. Quickly I grabbed some tissues and a towel. "Stay down," I said. "And hold your head back."

He did precisely as I instructed. "I'll be right back," I cried.

Leaving his room, I didn't even bother with the telephone. Instead, I ran out the door and straight down the street in search of Doc Warren. He was just finishing up his rounds.

"Doctor Warren," I breathlessly stated. "It's Frankie."

"What's going on?"

"Please come. Now!"

"Right now? I'm wrapping up rounds."

"Oh, Doctor Warren," I pleaded. "He just woke up and his face and his pillowcase are covered with blood. It's just trickling out of his nose like something I've never seen before."

"Jesus, Gail. I'll be right there," he said, grabbing his medical bag then telling one of the nurses he was making an emergency house call. Within minutes we were upstairs in Frankie's room. Only Frankie was passed out cold.

"What's going on?" I begged.

"Gail, call an ambulance," he spoke with calm authority while checking Frankie's vital signs.

"What's happening to him?"

"It's not good," was all he would say while feeling his pulse. He looked up at me.

"I'm worried that his heart might arrest, but we can't give him what he needs most in our little hospital. I've got to get him back to Georgetown as soon as possible. I'll ride with him in the ambulance. Please, call the rescue squad now, then go back and tell the nurses what's going on."

"I'm not leaving him," I cried.

"This is urgent. Do it! Now!"

I nodded, then quickly complied. Upon returning to the house, Doc Warren and Frankie were gone. My anxious mother and all the younger kids were huddled in the living room having just witnessed Frankie's departure on a gurney, out the front gate and into a waiting ambulance that took off with sirens blaring.

"What's going on?" Patty demanded.

I looked at her, then at all the stricken faces. My mother was holding John as if to save her own life. "Uhm, you guys," I said, openly crying and working desperately to find the right words. "Your brother is very sick."

"You act like we're stupid, or something," said an angry Raymond. "Like we can't see that. Just tell us what it is. We can handle it."

"*We can handle it. We can handle it,*" his words echoed in my head. *But I can't,* I thought. *He's dying. Don't you see it? Your mother is dead. Your father's imprisoned. And your beloved brother just passed through the garden gate for probably the very last time. Can you handle it? Can you handle it? Because I can't!* I wanted to scream.

Instead, and with exceptional grace and strength, my mother composed herself and rose to the occasion. Setting John down and holding his diminutive hand, she spoke softly but firmly. "Everybody, gather 'round," she quietly ordered, forming us into one circle. "And please take one another's hand." We did as instructed.

"First, no matter what, I want all of you to promise not to break the circle until I say so. Agreed?"

Everyone nodded.

"Very good. And I would like it if no one would say anything until I'm finished. Promise?"

Again, everyone nodded.

"Very good. Now Raymond, you are exactly right," she said with uncommon stoicism. "Not a single one of you are stupid." She took a deep breath. "Your brother," she started, then stopped. "And remember, don't break the circle until I say so."

Her Irish lilt seemingly softened words that would blow hard. "Your brother is quite sick. He has a form of cancer, called leukemia. And there is a good chance that he will die from it.

"Do not," she quickly implored, looking around at all the horrified faces, "break this circle."

Still clasping to Patty and Raymond, Paul buckled to the floor, his shoulders shaking hard in rhythm with his sobbing. Still, the circle remained intact. My mother continued.

"I want you to know something very important," she said. "That each and every one of you are deeply loved and that Joe and I are always here for you. And just as we are holding ourselves together right now, this is how I hope you will be for the rest of your lives. That you will always be there for one another. And *your* children. Do you understand?"

Heads nodded.

"And now," she said, "Please let go and bow your heads in prayer."

All sobbing, we lowered our heads and crossed our souls.

"In the name of the Father, Son and Holy Spirt. Heavenly Father, in your infinite wisdom and mercy, let your will be done. If you are calling your son Francis O'Brien home, then we pray for his safe journey. If you are willing to allow him to continue sharing his gifts of love on this earth with us, then we give you thanks. Either way, we thank you for the precious gift of his life that you have shared with all of us. Amen."

I watched as my mother wrapped her arms around Patty and held her close. She then managed to embrace each of us – particularly an inconsolable Paul – while offering reassurances of love, but not of Frankie's life.

Chapter 48

*O*n July 29th, Frankie was readmitted to Georgetown University Hospital. Both his red and white blood cell counts were haywire. And though he managed to survive that day, for days thereafter he slipped in and out of consciousness, barely capable of acknowledging any of his visitors.

Even though school and now varsity football were both starting soon, Joey rarely left Frankie's side. Not even after I remarked to him that I'd learned Vince Lombardi had once more been readmitted down the hall — also with grim prospects for survival.

There was a never-ending stream of visitors to Lombardi's room. I would look out and see the Redskins' quarterback coming to pay final respects one minute, followed by a priest, then a politician, a celebrity, then another football player, and on and on.

Even Frankie had his share of priests and football players as visitors. Linebackers from Prep who might have been forged from steel melted like babies while praying at the foot of his bed. His fellow coaches came by, and even some members of his former CYO teams. One by one the members of our family stopped by to see him, including Mary Joyce who traveled up from Florida.

And then, looking like the great white hope in his crisp Naval uniform, in stepped John O'Neill. With somber respect he removed his hat and bowed his head, then while hugging me tenderly kissed my forehead. There wasn't much to say. He could ask how I was; the answer was predictable. He could ask about my family; no one was holding up particularly well. He could ask about Frankie, who was now in a coma. We were praying for a miracle.

"Can I talk to you?" he asked, then led me outside where he gently cupped my face in his hands. "Is there anything I can do for *you*? What do *you* need?"

His words were salve for my soul. Unless he knew how to save Frankie's life, there was really nothing he could do. Still, just knowing that someone was there, that someone had my back and loved me like he did gave me energy to draw another breath.

"I'm exhausted," I said.

"I can see that. What about school?"

It was September the second. Classes at Georgetown University had started. "Not much I can do about it."

John drew me in for another hug and held me tight. Oh, how I loved him, somehow feeling at the moment like I had the entire Navy there to protect me. Retreating back into Frankie's room, John took hold of his beloved friend's hand, shared a fond remembrance, said a prayer, then kissed his forehead good-bye. Hugging Joey, then me once more, he disappeared a short while later leaving me alone with Joey and Frankie for the rest of the night.

As there wasn't another patient in the room at the time, Joey crashed on the other hospital bed. I, however, stole snatches of sleep while sitting in a recliner, and had fallen into a strange dream state when suddenly I jolted awake. The dawn of a new day was breaking. Joey was snoring and Frankie was still tethered to a myriad of machines. Suddenly though, instead of a rhythmic beep, one machine sounded a steady alarm.

"Frankie. Frankie!" I jumped up. His head was limply hanging sideways.

Joey startled awake just in time to see me bolt out the door to the nurse's station.

But no one was there.

"Help," I cried. "Is anybody here?"

One of the nurses emerged from Mr. Lombardi's room. "What's the matter?"

"I don't know," I said. Though I did. "Something's wrong."

She hurried down the hall with me to Frankie's room, where we found Joey beside the bed sobbing while holding Frankie's hand to his face.

"He's gone," he whispered.

And indeed he was. As the nurse checked his vitals and then the machines, she confirmed what we both suspected. She glanced at her watch to note his time of death, then tenderly stroked Frankie's sweet forehead before picking up his chart. "So sad," she quietly added, "Mr. Lombardi just died, too."

Chapter 49

On Labor Day Monday, September 7th, 1970, while the bells of St. Patrick's Cathedral in New York tolled for the soul of Vincent T. Lombardi, just a few blocks from our home the bells of St. Mary of the Mills pealed for Frankie.

Likewise, Frankie's was a service befitting a hero. My father, along with Joey, Tommy, Paul, Raymond, and even John O'Neill, all served as pall bearers. The church was packed with our neighbors and fellow parishioners, as well as Frankie's friends from Laurel High School and even customers from the Laurel Meat Market. There were people from his old neighborhood where he'd cut lawns as a kid. And nearly every football player and coach from Georgetown Prep gathered to bid him farewell, along with numerous young men like Bobby Bickle whose successful football futures had initially been forged on Frankie's CYO teams.

Nadette and my friends from St. Vincent Pallotti were there. And all the priests, along with most of the Pallottine nuns in their full habits, were in attendance. Sister Perpetua sat beside my parents, intermittently holding Patty's hand while John sat on her lap. The other children all sat between me and my parents. My mother held up with amazing strength. My father, like me, was a weepy mess.

How do you eulogize a young man whose life is so unexpectedly cut short? How do you thank God, as my mother suggested, for "the precious gift of his life that you have shared with all of us?"

Frankie had been more than a cousin. He had been a brother and a best friend. And not just to me. I looked around the church and saw countless faces representing countless moments of love and selflessness on his part.

The Mass was just about to begin when Patty, who'd been carrying a grocery bag with her from the Laurel Meat Market, stood up and scooted out to the aisle. Reaching inside she pulled out her toilet-paper pom-pons and placed them atop his casket. Then she pulled out Frankie's miniature blackboard still covered in X's and O's, on which she'd written at the bottom: *Love, Patty.* After placing it against a floral arrangement for the whole congregation to share, she returned to our pew.

Only Patty could have summarized his life as thus. It was all about X's and O's. Not offense. Or defense. Just hugs and kisses.

We buried Frankie beside his mother on the hill behind the church. Then the congregation marched down the street to our house where grills were fired up and, compliments of the Laurel Meat Market, we feasted on chicken, ribs and burgers in his honor; the smoke from that grill doing as much for my soul as the incense in the church.

It was exactly as Frankie would have wished – taking advantage of a perfectly gorgeous summer day to throw a raucous neighborhood barbecue. I could see him barking orders to Paul or Joey to get some more sauce or another plate. I could hear him hollering for the kids to hurry up and wash their hands before he ate all of their ribs. I could see him. I could feel him. I could hear him.

I was devastated.

After the last guest had left and the employees of the Laurel Meat Market were cleaning up, I quietly slipped out and made my way to his grave. Though the air was warm, there was a coolness emanating from the newly-turned dirt. Softly crying, I fell to my knees.

"Frankie, hey, it's me," I whispered, which is what I'd said so frequently after he'd slipped into a coma. So accustomed was I to holding his hand and wiping his brow while praying for a miracle, that grabbing a pile of dirt I clutched it as if molding his hand into mine.

What was I to make of his death? The lost joy of his fellowship? My pain? Everyone's sorrow? It was an interruption of love as I'd never known before.

I adored Frankie O'Brien. Throughout his entire illness he'd maintained a quiet dignity. Which wasn't surprising as the alchemy forged by his mother's love and father's madness seemed to have created a deep wisdom and invincible hardiness of spirit. From a young age he'd learned how to stand-up, stand-down or stand-off depending on the demands of the moment. In his heart he always knew what was right and how to make a difference for the better. I know Sister Perpetua credited me with keeping Frankie and his siblings from an "unfathomable wilderness." Truthfully, Frankie was the shepherd. His resilience carried us all to a place of healing and love. He demonstrated that personal responsibility and hard work were keys to success, and that a healthy, bonded family life truly mattered.

While still clutching the soil, I suddenly recalled Sister Perpetua's exchange with Patty when they'd first met inside the nearby church.

"I imagine that your mother was a very special person, because God wanted her to come to Heaven sooner than anyone expected. And do you know what? I believe your mother is talking with God right now. In fact, she is asking Him to protect you. And God is listening, perhaps needing me to tell you that you are deeply loved and protected by both Him and your mother."

"If God is listening, then tell him to send her back."

My body now heaving with uncontrollable sobs, I looked up at the clear, blue sky and while punching the air with my clenched fist angrily decried, "So God, are you listening? If you are, then send him BACK!"

My words rang into an empty hollow, and soon the air saturated with a stark silence which forced me to soak in my insolence. Finally, exhausted and dejected, I rose. Standing now between Frankie and Aunt Cate's graves, I reluctantly opened my hand to release the dirt. And as I did, a soft, silky breeze unexpectedly picked up, the gentle rippling sound through some nearby trees bidding my attention. I felt a sense of imminence, and so closing my watery eyes I folded my hand around the last bit of dirt and stood perfectly still while the warm, peaceful current touched my skin and seemed to caress my wounded heart. As such, my mind wandered back to a night in the hospital when the rhythmic beeping of the machines to which Frankie was tethered sounded like a metronome of death.

"Why is God doing this to you?" I'd blurted.

"Why are you blaming God?"

"Because I don't want to lose you and, honestly, right now I don't know where God is and my only prayer is for you to live forever and ever." I could barely breathe I was crying so hard. He took my hand and held it over his heart.

"It sounds to me like you're the one who's lost."

"I don't understand. Aren't you mad at God?"

"Never."

"Why?"

"First of all," he chuckled as he squeezed my hand. *"I'm still here, so I believe your prayers have been answered. And then,"* he intoned more seriously, *"Don't you understand that you're dying, too? The only difference is that you're dying in inches and I'm dying in yards. No matter, I believe the end zone is Heaven if we die with a grateful heart for whatever time we've been given. You must give thanks to God for all your blessings along the way, which you can hardly do with a bitter heart. At least for my sake, please remember to mind your spiritual manners,"* he winked while tenderly kissing my hand.

As the breeze slightly waned, I caught the scent of the many freshly-cut flowers and arrangements covering his grave. Blinking my eyes open, I took sight of a single monarch butterfly alighting on a ribbon-bound bouquet of zinnias I'd placed there earlier in the day. I'd cut the lush, orange and pink flowers myself from an overflowing garden at the convent tended to by Patty and Sister Marguerite. I watched intently as the butterfly took flight, then circled around a few times before landing on the tombstone of Caitlin Alana Cavanaugh O'Brien, then returned to dancing on the zinnias. A perfect creature alighting on perfect abundance. Like Frankie's uplifting soul, it also seemed possessed by a happy spiritedness; a joy from absorbing the good and simple things that mattered most. Inwardly I smiled, as the presence of this stunning butterfly forged a badly needed and heartwarming impression upon me.

It made me wonder about Frankie's legacy. How would he really be remembered? As a grunt at the Laurel Meat Market and a part-time football coach? As an unfortunate victim?

There was no one I admired more. I knew I would always remember him as a remarkable hero. The only thing my parents offered him to start was a roof over his head, for which he was incredibly grateful. After suffering so many miserable years of uncertainty and abuse, he strove to make our house a home and deeply appreciated the rich rewards of our blended family life. He was the first to truly join us all together with hearty home-cooked meals that nourished both body and soul. He lived by the virtues of discipline, sacrifice and giving. Frankie O'Brien played hard and taught many of us how to dream big. He demonstrated love, and he thanked God every day for every ounce of good and every second chance that he'd been given on this journey.

I used to feel superior to him – to all my cousins – pre-judging them as pathetic lowlifes simply for living on the wrong side of the track. Frankie changed that, unwittingly teaching me the value of patience. He inspired us all to be better people, to be there for each other, and to try our best no matter what.

As the breeze gently faded and the butterfly flitted away, I let go of the last clump of dirt while quietly promising myself that I would carry his legacy forward. I wasn't sure how. I just knew that one day I would.

Chapter 50

*L*ater that evening, as I was watching John joyfully splash around in the bathtub, I glanced outside and saw Joey lying alone on the tree house bridge. With one arm resting behind his head and the other across his chest, he lay perfectly still while staring at the unfolding night sky. After a spell he came inside, but only to collect his sleeping bag and pillow before retreating out there for the night. His dark mood made it clear he wanted to be left alone.

The following day I returned to Georgetown University, while my parents took Joey back to Georgetown Prep. Returning to school helped to restore some sense of normalcy to my life. It was a different story for Joey. For the next two weeks he languished, unable to concentrate, eat, or play football. For so long he'd been primed to play varsity. And though the coach was willing to cut him a certain amount of slack, his patience was growing thin.

Nothing was the same for Joey. None of it. Neither football, his school-work or even the campus appealed to him anymore. There was an echo of Frankie everywhere and in every thing an expectation of him. Frankie's boosterism had been so influential and omnipresent in his life, that without it Joey's drive to succeed seemed to die with his beloved cousin. And so, without any notice to my parents or the Jesuits, Joey went AWOL.

It took a day for anyone to notice that he was truly missing. Assuming that Joey had gotten some special permission to leave for the evening, his roommate didn't realize there was a problem until the following night at dinner when the resident manager asked him where he was. A search of the premises was conducted, but no Joey. My parents were promptly called. They hadn't seen him either. They called me, and I came directly home. It was nearly midnight when Joey walked in the door.

"Oh, thank God," my mother cried and hugged him. He stood stiff as a tree trunk. "We've been worried sick about you. Where have you been?"

"Hitchhiking."

"Where to?" my father asked.

"No where in particular. I'm okay," he lied. He was quite solemn, once more retreating to the tree house. In spite of my parents' ardent pleas that he return to school, for a week thereafter he either napped, took random bike rides, and at night slept only outside. He was unkempt, hardly eating and barely talking.

The following Saturday afternoon I came home for the weekend and found my parents in the kitchen. "I don't know what to do," my father anguished. "The headmaster at Prep just called and said if Joey doesn't return by Monday, he may face expulsion."

"Well, it's not the end of the world if he finishes up at Pallotti," my mother rejoined.

"That's not the problem, Mary Claire. He doesn't want to go back to school at all."

"For crying out loud, Joe, what would he do with himself? He can't just drop out of high school."

"What do you expect? It's not like I can just drag him off to school then expect him to want to do well. He's in obvious pain."

"Aren't we all?" she said, leaving it at that.

Patty, who'd been quietly despondent herself, overheard the entire conversation from the living room. She possessed her own thoughts on the subject and believed she knew what to do. Unaware of her motive, we all nodded okay when she announced she was heading to the convent — her home away from home.

Early that evening she returned, but not empty handed. Very gingerly she carried Sister Marguerite's soup tureen, as well as a wicker basket hanging from the crook of her arm with a fresh loaf of bread and a brilliant bouquet of late-blooming dahlias from the convent garden. Bedecked in her long, white apron with Rosary Beads suspended from her waist, she did not bring the bounty inside. Instead, she set our weathered picnic table to her liking, then went in search of Joey. He was asleep in his room when she woke him up.

"Joey, please come with me."

He startled, then looked up at her. "Not now Patty! I'm sleeping," he snapped.

"No, you're not."

"Well, I was. Can't this wait?"

"No. I need you to come outside."

Joey resentfully tossed his pillow to the floor. Then following eleven-year-old Patty, found in the final, cooling blush of day that dinner was ready for two.

"Please sit down," she told him. Joey ungraciously obliged.

"What is this all about?"

"I made dinner for you."

"I can see that. But you woke me up for this? I'm not hungry."

"That's rude."

"What? I'm telling you the truth. I'm not hungry."

Ignoring him, Patty opened the tureen and ladled out several hearty portions of her old favorite, then after folding her hands and closing her eyes said grace. Joey cynically watched.

"Please eat," she said, finally looking up.

He reluctantly obeyed, at first only consuming a few mouthfuls of bouillabaisse. After releasing a heavy sigh, he tore off a large piece of homemade bread, which he quietly consumed along with the entire contents of his bowl.

"There, are you happy?" he said, at last setting down his spoon.

"No."

"Then please tell me what this is all about."

"We're both really sad about Frankie."

Joey shrugged his shoulders. "Yeah, so?"

"So, remember when you called me a retard?" Patty asked point blank.

"I never called you a retard."

"Uh-huh. When I first came here, you called me a retard all the time."

"But that was then, Patty. You're not...well, I'm sorry, okay?"

"You also called me dumb."

"Well, then I'm really sorry. Because you're not dumb. At all."

"I know," she said. "But you are."

"Excuse me?"

"Remember when you said I couldn't cook because I was dumb? Well, I can cook. So I'm not dumb. But you know what I can't do? I can't go to your school because I'm retarded."

"You can't go there because it's a school for boys only."

"Do any retarded boys go there?"

Joey restrained himself from being flip. "So how does that make *me* dumb?"

"Because you're really smart."

"So how does being 'really smart' make me 'dumb'?"

"Because there was a time you said I was too dumb to cook. But now I can. Frankie thought I was a good cook and he taught me a lot. My cooking made him happy. And you never thought you could go to that school. But Frankie did. And before Frankie died you were happy. So you have to go back there because it would make Frankie happy. Just like my cooking made him happy."

Joey's voice cracked. "Nothing is the same without him."

"I know."

"That's it? '*I know*.' He was my best friend," he cried, "and I don't know how to manage without him." Propping his elbows on the table, he then held his head in his hands and sobbed, allowing large, salty tears to splash inside his empty soup bowl.

"I know," Patty repeated again with motherly tenderness. "It's *really* sad that he died, and I really miss him, too. But I know God and my mother are taking good care of him. And Frankie wouldn't want me to stop cooking because he died. And you were really happy at that school, so you're really dumb if you don't go back, because that's not what Frankie would want."

"Are you finished?" Joey looked up, his face glistening.

"No, there's more soup. Do you want some?" she said reaching for the ladle.

Her response gripped Joey in the most unexpected way, as he found her simplicity to be a far more nourishing delicacy. In silence and communion with one another, he helped Patty to finish off her bouillabaisse, a healing potion for two truly wounded souls.

Patty then removed everything, including the table cloth and flowers, leaving Joey alone outside and now in the dark to contemplate his stupidity.

The following day he informed my parents that he was ready to go back to Prep.

Chapter 51

Joey made it through that school year and then the next, actually graduating with high honors and receiving a full scholarship to play football at Notre Dame. That year was remarkable for another reason, too, as John O'Neill was prepared to graduate from the Naval Academy. Just before the graduation ceremony in Annapolis, he asked me to help pin his new shoulder boards onto his crisp, white uniform.

"Perfect," I said. "You look so handsome," I smiled broadly.

Truthfully, I was as proud and hopeful as I was full of dread for him. A few months earlier he'd been given a choice on how to spend the balance of his Naval career: on land, at sea, under the sea, or in the air. He'd chosen the latter and would shortly be shipped off to Pensacola, Florida, for flight training.

It was hard to contemplate life without him near. Even harder to consider that he was not only graduating in a time of escalating warfare, but that American fighter jets were highly-desired targets in enemy territory. There seemed to be no shortage of stories concerning pilots who, if they were lucky to survive such an assault, were then captured and tortured. Presently we were alone, but shortly would be leaving for the grand ceremony at the heart of the campus.

"Thanks," he said, glancing in a nearby mirror at his new embellishments. With his black hair and sun-kissed skin from recent sailing excursions around the Academy, he'd truly never appeared more handsome to me. Modestly, he smiled, his dimples making him look boyish. Then he took a deep breath.

"Thanks," he replied again somewhat nervously. "And thanks for always being there for me."

I chuckled. "I think that honor goes to you!"

I could have rapidly ticked off at least a dozen times when he'd done something extraordinary for me. Like helping to buy my car. Or being Patty's good friend. Or saving our lives by fighting off Uncle Francis. Plus, there were no airs about this man. And he loved me exactly the way I was.

"Are you ready?" I chirped.

He turned and nodded, and I saw his expression grow serious.

"Just about," he said, then reached into his pocket. "There's something else that needs to be worn, and I need your help putting it on."

"Sure, what's that?"

"This," he replied.

The size and shimmer of the platinum-set diamond ring he beheld were breathtaking. I started trembling. "Are you officially asking me to marry you?"

Yes, he nodded and slightly grinned, his boyish dimples back on display. Then getting down on one knee and taking my hand, he spoke deeply and sincerely. "Gail Marie, I love you more than you can ever imagine. And nothing I have done before, or ever again, will matter as much as asking you to be my wife. Will you marry me?"

Outside it was seventy-eight degrees and sunny with a cloudless sky. There could not have been a more perfect man nor a more perfect moment – the one I'd dreamt of for so long. It might have been the perfect time to say yes.

But it wasn't. How could I tell the love of my life the answer was no. How could I make him understand the dread I felt over his next five years. That I didn't want him to go to Vietnam. And just as important, how could I tell him that accompaniment on his journey surely meant I would be abandoning mine? How could I tell him that marriage was not going to work with the true murmurs I felt of a far different calling?

"John," I braced myself, taking hold of his hands but not the ring. "I love you, more than any other man on the face of this earth. But.. I really... cannot... marry you."

Epilogue

"**D**r. Gail," the six-year-old repeated, "what color is my cure?"

I stopped hooking up her chemo drip long enough to carefully consider my response. Finally, I spoke.

"Let me show you," I said warmly. "May I have a piece of paper?"

"Yes," she said, blithely handing one over.

"And may I borrow your crayons?"

"Yes," she answered, likewise passing to me the box with its waxy, construction paper smell. I looked inside and finding a dark blue crayon, I drew an arc on the paper.

"What color is this?"

"Blue."

"Exactly. Which is the color of your disease. It makes your body sad and sometimes makes you feel blue." I fished around for another crayon, next drawing a green arc directly beneath the blue one. "What color is this?"

"Green."

"Very good. And that's the color of your medicine. It's also the color of healing, and it will make the blue go away, like new green grass growing in the spring."

I proceeded with yet another crayon. "And this is yellow. And yellow is sunshine. It comes from love and laughter. Which makes the grass grow. And makes the healing happen faster. And then," I said, reaching for the purple, "This is the color of your courage. Whenever you feel scared or blue, then think of yourself as wearing a royal purple robe. It will protect you and make you stronger. Finally," I said, adding the color red, "This is the color of your happy heart because you'll be all better."

"Hey," she grinned. "That's a rainbow!"

"Precisely. The color of your cure is just like a rainbow. There are lots of colors that go into it. And do you know where they all lead?"

"To a pot of gold!" she said excitedly.

"Well, perhaps. But I like to think that a rainbow is like a butterfly's tail. And when you are done with all of your medicine, you will be like a beautiful new butterfly who can fly wherever she wants."

I glanced over at her parents, who I knew were in as much shock and pain as their daughter was in lighthearted innocence. Her mother weakly smiled.

"Look, Mommy," she said. "Dr. Gail drew me a rainbow."

"Thanks, Dr. Gail," her mother said softly and appreciatively, though fear gripped her eyes.

"Now, can we get started?" I asked.

"Yes," my young patient agreed, still smiling. "I want to be a butterfly."

It had been twelve years since I had awakened one summer morning to find Baby John in my bureau drawer. Twelve years since I'd watched him fight for his life. And nearly ten since I had seen Frankie lose the battle for his.

Following the completion of my chemistry degree from Georgetown University, and after graduating with honors from Columbia University's College of Physicians and Surgeons, I was now in the throes of my medical residency, specializing in pediatric hematology and oncology in the Lombardi Cancer Center at Georgetown University Hospital. Gratefully, my patient today stood a far better chance of survival than Frankie had. I felt hopeful that her form of leukemia had been caught early enough to successfully enable her metamorphosis into that beautiful butterfly. I was determined to see that she did.

My pager went off — which was not an uncommon distraction. But this time it was wholly welcomed. After presently finishing up, I told one of the nurses at the station that I was slipping out to the maternity ward and would be back as soon as possible. Scurrying through the hallways and into the ward, I quickly scrubbed and changed into surgical garb before entering the delivery room.

"Where in the hell have you been?" Nadette screamed at me. "I've been holding this kid in for ten extra minutes waiting to see your happy 'f'in' face!"

"Good work," I beamed, then shot a glance at her husband, who looked at me imploringly while squeezing her hand.

"Hey, sis," said Tommy. "We were worried you wouldn't make it."

"I wouldn't have missed this for the world."

"Push!" one of the nurses demanded.

"Push harder," I said, "I can see the crown of the baby's head."

"I am pushing, you moron. Look, don't you think this is just a tiny bit weird," Nadette, said, "I mean, I know we're best friends but, but..." she cut herself off, then let out an agonizing scream.

"You asked me to be here, you big cry-baby. I'll leave if you want me to."

"No, no, don't go," she suddenly begged. "JUST-GET-THIS-KID-OUT-OF-ME!"

"Okay, then. Keep pushing."

Tommy looked ready to pass out.

"Oh, my god, here it comes," she warned us all. And indeed "it" – an eight-pound, thirteen-ounce baby girl – made her debut, announcing her arrival with a glorious cry that pierced the room and then my heart.

"It's a girl. You have a beautiful baby girl," I joyfully cried.

Like Baby John so many years before, she had a shocking amount of black hair. Quickly, the obstetrician severed the umbilical cord, then handed the infant over to me to check her vitals. Everything – absolutely everything about her – was perfect. After weighing her in and wiping her clean, I diapered and swaddled her in a blanket then handed her over to Tommy. He might have been adept at receiving a football, but he handled this bundle like it was a tray full of Waterford Crystal.

"So," I said, picking up her chart and filling in the details of her birth. "What's her name?"

Tommy handed the baby over to Nadette, whose demeanor was now far less demonic.

"Caitlin. Caitlin Cavanaugh Kenealy," said an exhausted, but beaming Nadette.

"Wow," was all I could manage to say. Over the months I'd heard dozens of names for both boys and girls, but never once had Aunt Cate's been mentioned.

In fact, it had been a while since I'd even thought of her, the memory of her sweet face now coming into sharp focus in my mind's eye. Also coming into focus were my mother's words that fateful day Cate's son, my beloved Frankie, had been hauled off to this hospital for the very last time.

"And just as we are holding ourselves together in this circle right now, this is how I hope you will be for the rest of your lives. That you will always be there for one another. And your children. Do you understand?"

Yes, I fully understood, smiling at little Caitlin Cavanaugh Kenealy and then at her mother, realizing how much larger and stronger my circle had grown. I hugged Tommy, who was utterly incapable of controlling his tears. "Congratulations, bro'," I said.

"Thanks," he grinned. "I'm so glad you're here."

I looked at my watch. "Me, too. And I hate to do this, but I've got to get back to my real job," I chuckled. "I'll check in on you soon."

After briefly kissing all three of them, I returned to the Pediatric Oncology Ward. Finally, after wrapping it up for the day, I rejoined them and my entire family as they began crowding into Nadette's room to welcome its newest member. There was my long-sober mother and gray-haired father, proud grandparents for the third time, along with Nadette's overjoyed parents. Of course there was Nadette, holding Caitlin, and Tommy, a budding attorney. Mary Joyce and her husband, who had fortunately relocated from Florida with their two young children, were present, too. MJ was now a stay-at-home mom while her husband taught high school math. They'd been happily married for seven years now.

I smiled at Paul, so tall and handsome, who'd brought his fiancé, a darling young woman whom he'd met at the restaurant he owned and operated on Laurel's Main Street: "Frankie O'Brien's House of Ribs." Years ago it would have been hard to imagine Paul's success, or that Frankie had accumulated so much cash during his short life that it would be possible to seed that venture. But through his hard work – plus earnings from lucky football bets – Frankie had left nearly $50,000 in savings to his siblings, all of whom kicked in to open the restaurant in his honor. After graduating from high school, Paul had combined the inheritance with his own savings and had started the business, which had quickly grown in reputation as one of "The best ribs joints in Maryland."

It was a family-run restaurant, as both my parents worked there part-time, my father helping with electrical or handy work and my mother as a part-time hostess. Timmy and Raymond, respectively a freshman and senior at the University of Maryland, both waited tables there on the weekends. Inspired by Tommy, Raymond was headed to law school in the fall.

Baby John – now "Johnny" and one of Sister Perpetua's shining students at St. Mary of the Mills and standing shoulder-height beside me – also pitched in doing odd jobs as needed, but mostly worked in the kitchen with Patty, who was clearly the mother superior there. Patty, now a happy and well-adjusted young adult, soon arrived with an ever-wise and spry Sister Perpetua along with Joey, who I might have thought would be the real entrepreneur among us. Which he was, but of a different sort as he was now in the business of redeeming souls as a young seminarian at Catholic University. Standing near Joey in his black shirt with Roman collar, I shared his joy as he led the family in a prayer of thanksgiving. After tenderly crossing Caitlin's forehead, he handed her back to Nadette then spiritedly high-fived Tommy.

Quietly, at my behest, Johnny stepped forward. "This is from Gail," he said offering Nadette a small gift-wrapped box, surprisingly adding, "Can I hold her?"

It might have been an odd request coming from any other boy his age. But Nadette warmly nodded approval at her godson, and then carefully they exchanged parcels.

"She's beautiful, Aunt Nadette," he glowed, cradling his mother's namesake.

I watched in silence as Nadette – my sarcastic, goofy, loving, loyal, sister-in-law and lifelong best-friend – opened the box then fell uncharacteristically quiet herself. I had fully expected her to laugh. Instead, she tearfully looked up at me as she clearly understood and respected the gift's deeper meaning. It was a bottle of Jean Naté, the same cologne she'd used to baptize him.

Yes, she nodded while smiling, the look in her eyes conveying great warmth. *Yes, you will be her godmother.*

I knowingly smiled back. But presently if another word was spoken I barely heard it. Instead, I was consumed with watching "Baby John" lovingly handle his newborn cousin, as it was with far more tenderness than how I'd treated him at the same age.

"Caitlin," he cooed. "Did you know you're named after my mother?"

I gasped. Happy-go-lucky by nature, and feeling truly loved in our midst, this child rarely mentioned his real mother and never his "rat-bastard-good-for-nothing-drunk-son-of-a-bitch" father, now long dead from liver damage. It was horrifying to think how he'd experienced his father's manic rage before even taking his first breath. Now as a physician I knew all too well the hell his mother had truly endured to see that he'd survived, and how sorely all of us had underestimated his early needs. Contemplating this, I witnessed a hug between my father and Sister Perpetua, which made me realize another thing about our family circle. Not only had it grown, but within it a debilitating cycle of violence and abuse had been broken.

"Well, it's no mystery how grateful I am for all that you are doing. Besides," my father had said, *"I get the feeling that God is doing his level best to keep this family together, and thankfully found strength in you to help get the job done."*

Their wisdom had been hard to grasp. Preaching to me about God's mysteries only seemed another way of saying, "I really don't know the answers, so just suck it up."

"All God asks is that we love Him and one another with mutual respect," Sister Perpetua's words rang clear. *"Without even thinking about it, you've been following the old Golden Rule: Do unto others whatever you would have them do to you, which has reduced an enormous amount of suffering in your family."*

I began to cry.

"What's the matter?" Patty quickly piped up. "Is it your turn to hold the baby? Well then, Johnny," she carried on without my response. "Give her to Gail."

I choked up even more. With his black mop of hair, bright blue eyes and shy smile, he looked strikingly like Frankie, whom I still missed with all my heart. As he tried handing Caitlin over I recalled how fragile he'd been at exactly the same age, and how he'd nearly died when left in my negligent hands. Instead of taking just her, I embraced them both, then took the baby.

"Do you think it's any different for your cousins?" Sister's faith rang clear. *"They did not create today's troubles. Nor did God. But even in your presently frustrated manner, you've been demonstrating exactly what God and our Savior would wish from you: compassion. You don't know what has to happen somewhere else in order for you to get your way, or to receive God's grace. But God does. His higher priority may have been addressing the needs and prayers of your cousins to give them the chance to stay together as a family."*

I felt someone tap my back and turned to see my mother, her head tilted slightly, her lips parted in a sweet smile. She held out her arms, but not to take the baby. Instead, she held me; she held us, a multi-generational symphony of love. Whereas once a bitter, conscripted teenage soldier in her battles against demons of depression and self-destruction, I was now an educated and self-reliant woman helping to heal and lead others through some of the darkest moments in their lives with genuine skill and encouragement. I loved my mother more than ever, and felt more grateful than ever that *she'd* stayed the course.

"Death leaves a heartache no one can heal. Love leaves a memory no one can steal," was an old Irish proverb she'd shared with me in our darkest moments when dealing with the loss of Frankie. I lived by those words every day. As I kissed her teary face, she suddenly caught sight of another family member entering the room.

"Well, young lady, I think the sun, the moon and stars just appeared," she broadly grinned as my husband, John Aloysius-you're-incredibly-delicious-O'Neill, joined us. Looking more handsome than ever he smiled warmly at me, then kissed and hugged my mother and Patty before tousling Johnny's hair. Still the love of my life, we'd married after I'd finished medical school and he'd finished his official tour of duty. Now an instructor in aeronautical engineering at the Naval Academy, he also – and very proudly – helped to bring home the esteemed Commander-in-Chief Trophy last year while likewise serving as the offensive coordinator on Navy's football team.

He smiled mischievously while locking his eyes with mine, then hugged and kissed me.

I teasingly smiled back. Not wanting to steal the limelight, we'd kept to ourselves that we were now expecting a child of our own. The sun, the moon and a star. Our own happy universe.

Life. It's all about X's and O's. Not offense. Or defense. Just hugs and kisses.

And...thanking God.

Acknowledgments

I'd like to thank the following people for helping me to keep my creative Cuisinart spinning: Dr. Kathy Alley, Maria Amentas, Lynda Bush, Christine Cox-Hill, Stephanie Cooperstein, Alyssa Stalsberg Canelli, Chris Dowd, Mary Harper, Tim Harper, Dena Hirsh, Winnie Holbrooke, Susan Johnson, Sue Kiernan, Shelley Kramm, Pat Lonardo, Denise McGloon, Eileen McNally, Edie Mossberg, Yvonne O'Neill, Dr. Terri Remy, Vanessa Sauter, Caroline Thompson, Andrea Volen, Lisa Walker and Barbara Woodall.

I deeply appreciate the time each of you spent reading early drafts of the manuscript and offering your sound advice and ongoing encouragement. Particularly to my dear friend and lawyer, Lauren Menkes, who read one of the earliest drafts and gave me astounding encouragement (plus good advice).

Also, I am deeply grateful to Michele DeFilippo and her amazing team at 1106 Design for their incredible talent, guidance, and professionalism with the interior layout (electronic and print) as well as website design. Thank you!

Finally, I'd like to thank the late, "Sr. Perpetua Moellering," a Pallottine nun who dedicated her life to serving Christ in the most inspiring ways. It's rare to meet the kind of person who truly embodies the depth of goodness and pure faith that she exuded. While the accounts and likeness of "Sister Perpetua" in the book are fictionalized (with her permission), I have tried to honor her in my story through the messages of love and hope that I sought to convey. A longtime nun at the Pallottine Convent in Laurel, Maryland, after retiring from teaching at St. Mary of the Mills she proceeded to deliver communion and love to the sick in the Laurel community. In a nod to her, when it came time to choose the font for this book I was left with limited choices, but chose the one that immediately stood out: "Perpetua."

Thank you, Sister "P."

About the Author

Stacey Sauter is a Maryland native with a liberal arts degree from the University of Maryland and a Master's Degree in Journalism from Columbia University. She is an award-winning writer and author of multiple books. She presently resides in Maryland where she's at work on her next writing project. She can be contacted at stacey@thorntoncreek-press.com.

2 1982 02941 1844

CPSIA information can be obtained
at www.ICGtesting.com
Printed in the USA
LVHW11s1732041018
592410LV00004B/834/P

9 781732 357402